WRITING AND READING WAR

Society of Biblical Literature

Symposium Series

Victor H. Matthews,
Series Editor

Number 42

WRITING AND READING WAR
RHETORIC, GENDER, AND ETHICS IN
BIBLICAL AND MODERN CONTEXTS

WRITING AND READING WAR

RHETORIC, GENDER, AND ETHICS IN BIBLICAL AND MODERN CONTEXTS

Edited by

Brad E. Kelle

and

Frank Ritchel Ames

Foreword by Susan Niditch

Society of Biblical Literature
Atlanta

WRITING AND READING WAR
RHETORIC, GENDER, AND ETHICS IN BIBLICAL AND MODERN CONTEXTS

Copyright © 2008 by the Society of Biblical Literature

All rights reserved. No part of this work may be reproduced or transmitted in any form or by any means, electronic or mechanical, including photocopying and recording, or by means of any information storage or retrieval system, except as may be expressly permitted by the 1976 Copyright Act or in writing from the publisher. Requests for permission should be addressed in writing to the Rights and Permissions Office, Society of Biblical Literature, 825 Houston Mill Road, Atlanta, GA 30329 USA.

Library of Congress Cataloging-in-Publication Data

Writing and reading war : rhetoric, gender, and ethics in biblical and modern contexts / edited by Brad E. Kelle and Frank Ritchel Ames.
    p. cm. — (Society of Biblical Literature symposium series ; no. 42)
    Includes bibliographical references and indexes.
    ISBN: 978-1-58983-354-8 (paper binding : alk. paper) — ISBN 978-1-58983-398-2 (electronic library copy)
    1. War—Religious aspects—Judaism. 2. War—Biblical teaching. 3. Bible. O.T.—Criticism, interpretation, etc. 4. Rhetoric—Religious aspects—Judaism. 5. Sex role—Biblical teaching. 6. Jewish ethics. I. Kelle, Brad E., 1973- II. Ames, Frank Ritchel.
    BS1199.W2W75 2008
    221.8'35502—dc22   2007015209

16 15 14 13 12 11 10 09 08   5 4 3 2 1
Printed in the United States of America on acid-free, recycled paper
conforming to ANSI/NISO Z39.48-1992 (R1997) and ISO 9706:1994
standards for paper permanence.

Contents

Abbreviations vii

Foreword
   Susan Niditch xi

Introduction
   Victor H. Matthews 1

Part 1: Writing and Reading the Rhetoric of War

The Meaning of War: Definitions for the Study of War in
Ancient Israelite Literature
   Frank Ritchel Ames 19

Military Valor and Kingship: A Book-Oriented Approach to the Study
of a Major War Theme
   Jacob L. Wright 33

Fighting in Writing: Warfare in Histories of Ancient Israel
   Megan Bishop Moore 57

Assyrian Military Practices and Deuteronomy's Laws of Warfare
   Michael G. Hasel 67

Assyrian Siege Warfare Imagery and the Background of a Biblical Curse
   Jeremy D. Smoak 83

Part 2: Writing and Reading the Gender of War

Wartime Rhetoric: Prophetic Metaphorization of Cities as Female
   Brad E. Kelle 95

Family Metaphors and Social Conflict in Hosea
   Alice A. Keefe 113

"We Have Seen the Enemy, and He Is Only a 'She'": The Portrayal
of Warriors as Women
   Claudia D. Bergmann 129

PART 3: WRITING AND READING THE ETHICS OF WAR

Conquest Reconfigured: Recasting Warfare in the Redaction of Joshua
L. Daniel Hawk 145

"Go Back by the Way You Came": An Internal Textual Critique of Elijah's Violence in 1 Kings 18–19
Frances Flannery 161

Shifts in Israelite War Ethics and Early Jewish Historiography of Plundering
Brian Kvasnica 175

Gideon at Thermopylae? On the Militarization of Miracle in Biblical Narrative and "Battle Maps"
Daniel L. Smith-Christopher 197

Bibliography 213

Contributors 241

Index of Ancient Sources 243

Index of Modern Authors 257

Abbreviations

AB	Anchor Bible
ABD	*The Anchor Bible Dictionary.* Edited by David Noel Freedman. 6 vols. New York: Doubleday, 1992.
AfO	*Archiv für Orientforschung*
Ag. Ap.	Josephus, *Against Apion*
AJA	*American Journal of Archaeology*
ANEP	*The Ancient Near East in Pictures Relating to the Old Testament.* Edited by James B. Pritchard. Princeton: Princeton University Press, 1954.
ANET	*Ancient Near Eastern Texts Relating to the Old Testament.* Edited by James B. Pritchard. 3rd ed. Princeton: Princeton University Press, 1969.
AO	*Der Alte Orient*
AOAT	Alter Orient und Altes Testament
ARAB	Daniel David Luckenbill, *Ancient Records of Assyria and Babylonia.* 2 vols. Chicago: University of Chicago Press, 1926–1927.
ASOR	American Schools of Oriental Research
ATANT	Abhandlungen zur Theologie des Alten und Neuen Testaments
ATSHB	*Ancient Texts for the Study of the Hebrew Bible: A Guide to Background Literature.* Edited by Kenton L. Sparks. Peabody, Mass.: Hendrickson, 2005.
BA	*Biblical Archaeologist*
BAR	*Biblical Archaeology Review*
BBB	Bonner biblische Beiträge
BBR	*Bulletin of Biblical Research*
BETL	Bibliotheca ephemeridum theologicarum lovaniensium
BHS	*Biblia Hebraica Stuttgartensia.* Edited by K Elliger and W. Rudolph. Stuttgart: Deutsche Bibelgesellschaft, 1983.
Bib	*Biblica*
BibInt	*Biblical Interpretation* (journal)
BibInt	Biblical Interpretation (series)
BibOr	Biblica et orientalia
BJRL	*Bulletin of the John Rylands University Library of Manchester*

BJS	Brown Judaic Studies
BM	British Museum
BN	*Biblische Notizen*
BNTC	Black's New Testament Commentaries
BR	*Biblical Research*
BZ	*Biblische Zeitschrift*
BZAW	Beihefte zur Zeitschrift für die alttestamentliche Wissenschaft
CBQ	*Catholic Biblical Quarterly*
CBQMS	Catholic Biblical Quarterly Monograph Series
CC	Continental Commentary
Cher.	Philo, *De cherubim*
COS	*The Context of Scripture*. Edited by W. W. Hallo. 3 vols. Leiden: Brill, 1997–2002
CQ	*Classical Quarterly*
CRINT	Compendia rerum iudaicarum ad Novum Testamentum
CSCO	Corpus scriptorum christianorum orientalium
CSHJ	Chicago Studies in the History of Judaism
CTM	*Concordia Theological Monthly*
D	Deuteronomist
Decalogue	Philo, *On the Decalogue*
Dtr	Deuteronomistic
DtrH	Deuteronomistic History
EBib	Études bibliques
EdF	Erträge der Forschung
EHAT	Exegetisches Handbuch zum Alten Testament
ER	*The Encyclopedia of Religion*. Edited by Mircea Eliade. 16 vols. New York: Macmillan, 1987.
ETL	Ephemerides theologicae lovanienses
EvT	*Evangelische Theologie*
FAT	Forschungen zum Alten Testament
FCB	Feminist Companion to the Bible
FOTL	Forms of the Old Testament Literature
GCT	Gender, Culture, Theory
HALOT	L. Koehler, W. Baumgartner, and J. J. Stamm, *The Hebrew and Aramaic Lexicon of the Old Testament*. Translated and edited under the supervision of M. E. J. Richardson. 4 vols. Leiden: Brill, 1994-1999.
HAT	Handbuch zum Alten Testament
HDR	Harvard Dissertations in Religion
HSM	Harvard Semitic Monographs
HTR	*Harvard Theological Review*
HTS	Harvard Theological Studies
HUCA	*Hebrew Union College Annual*
ICC	International Critical Commentary

IDB	*The Interpreter's Dictionary of the Bible*. Edited by G. A. Buttrick. 4 vols. Nashville: Abingdon, 1962.
IEJ	Israel Exploration Journal
Il.	Homer, *Illiad*
Int	Interpretation
IOS	Israel Oriental Society
JAOS	Journal of the American Oriental Society
JBL	Journal of Biblical Literature
JCS	Journal of Cuneiform Studies
JFA	Journal of Field Archaeology
JFSR	Journal of Feminist Studies in Religion
JJS	Journal of Jewish Studies
JNES	Journal of Near Eastern Studies
JPS	Jewish Publication Society
JSOT	*Journal for the Study of the Old Testament*
JSOTSup	Journal for the Study of the Old Testament Supplement Series
KBo	Keilschrifttexte aus Boghazköi. WVDOG 30, 36, 68–70, 72–73, 77–80, 82–86, 89–90. Leipzig: Hinrichs, 1916–.
KUB	Keilschrifturkunden aus Boghazköi
LdÄ	Lexicon der Ägyptologie. Edited by W. Helck, E. Otto, and W. Westendorf. Wiesbaden: Harrassowitz, 1972.
LCL	Loeb Classical Library
LHB/OTS	Library of Hebrew Bible/Old Testament Studies
MDAI	Mitteilungen des Deutschen archäologischen Instituts
MDOG	Mitteilungen der Deutschen Orient-Gesellschaft
Mor.	Plutarch, *Moralia*
Moses	Philo, *On the Life of Moses*
MT	Masoretic Text
NCB	New Century Bible
NEA	Near Eastern Archaeology
NEAEHL	*The New Encyclopedia of Archaeological Excavations in the Holy Land*. Edited by E. Stern. 4 vols. Jerusalem: Carta, 1993.
NEchtB	Neue Echter Bibel
NICOT	New International Commentary on the Old Testament
NIGTC	New International Greek Testament Commentary
Numen	Numen: International Review for the History of Religions
OBO	Orbis biblicus et orientalis
ÖBS	Österreichische biblische Studien
Off.	Cicero, *De Officiis*
OIP	Oriental Institute Publications
OTL	Old Testament Library
OTP	*Old Testament Pseudepigrapha*. Edited by James H. Charlesworth. 2 vols. Garden City. N.Y.: Doubleday, 1983–1985.

OTS	Old Testament Studies
OtSt	Oudtestamentische Studiën
PEQ	*Palestine Exploration Quarterly*
RB	*Revue biblique*
RIDA	*Revue internationale des droits de l'antiquité*
RIMA	The Royal Inscriptions of Mesopotamia, Assyrian Periods
RIMB	The Royal Inscriptions of Mesopotamia, Babylonian Periods
RQ	*Römische Quartalschrift für christliche Altertumskunde und Kirchengeschichte*
SAA	State Archives of Assyria
SBB	Stuttgarter biblische Beiträge
SBLABS	Society of Biblical Literature Archaeology and Biblical Studies
SBLAcBib	Society of Biblical Literature Academia Biblica
SBLDS	Society of Biblical Literature Dissertation Series
SBLSBL	Society of Biblical Literature Studies in Biblical Literature
SBLSCS	Society of Biblical Literature Septuagint and Cognate Studies
SBLSP	Society of Biblical Literature Seminar Papers
SBLSymS	Society of Biblical Literature Symposium Series
SBTS	Sources for Biblical and Theological Study
SemeiaSt	Semeia Studies
SubBi	Subsidia biblica
SVTP	Studia in Veteris Testamenti pseudepigraphica
TA	*Tel Aviv*
TBAT	Theologische Bücherei, Altes Testament
Thucydides	Thucydides, *History of the Peloponnesian War*
TLZ	*Theologische Literaturzeitung*
TOTC	Tyndale Old Testament Commentaries
TUAT	*Texte aus der Umwelt des Alten Testaments*. Edited by Otto Kaiser. Gütersloh: Mohn, 1984–.
UF	*Ugarit-Forschungen*
Verr.	Cicero, *In Verrem*
VT	*Vetus Testamentum*
VTSup	Supplements to Vetus Testamentum
WMANT	Wissenschaftliche Monographien zum Alten und Neuen Testament
WUNT	Wissenschaftliche Untersuchungen zum Neuen Testament
ZA	*Zeitschrift für Assyriologie*
ZABR	*Zeitschrift für altorientalische und biblische Rechtsgeschichte*
ZAW	*Zeitschrift für die alttestamentliche Wissenschaft*
ZNW	*Zeitschrift für die neutestamentliche Wissenschaft und die Kunde der älteren Kirche*

Foreword

Susan Niditch

It has been a pleasure to participate in the Consultation on Warfare in Ancient Israel held at the Society of Biblical Literature's Annual Meeting since 2004, and it is an honor to provide a brief foreword to the collection of essays drawn from those sessions.

I myself was first motivated to write on war and ancient Israel by my students' frank discomfort with biblical passages that portray or expound upon war. While students could deal with material that seemed to partake of heroic and epic encounters, perhaps because of previous familiarity with Homer's work, the cold description of rules for the ban and its application, especially in the "conquest accounts" of Joshua, seemed to challenge all they expected to find in the "Good Book." How could a just God demand that everything that breathes be devoted to destruction: men, women, children, and infants?

The war literature of the Hebrew Bible is, in fact, so exciting to study and teach precisely because it challenges culturally and normatively based assumptions about our own traditions and about the nature of all human intercourse. On the one hand, we explore important and revealing threads in Israelite culture, in its variety and its larger ancient Near Eastern context. There are many biblical war views developed in response to a variety of historical, ideological, political, ecological, and technological realities. There is no one biblical view of war any more than there is a simple unilinear Israelite religion. The ban is one war ideology among many. Hence, a number of the essays in this volume discuss a range of war portrayals and their various ethical implications, their significance for understanding the redaction history of biblical texts, and the cultural synergy between ancient Israel and its neighbors. Another set of essays explores the rhetoric of war as biblically presented, language that serves as a mirror of culture. A special interest of several of these papers is in the gendered implications of biblical passages dealing with war.

The war texts of the Hebrew Bible, however, not only provide us our entry into the complexities of Israelite culture—for contemporary Westerners, a long-ago world that arose in a far-away place—but also serve to show us something about ourselves. Sigmund Freud described what he regarded as universal impulses in all human beings, the forces of *thanatos* or "death" and *eros* or "love." We are capable, depending upon many factors, of relating to one another in terms of a competition to the death that assures survival and in terms of the brotherhood, cooperation, and understanding that resolves conflict, assuring survival on different terms. These two impulses are at play in the Hebrew Bible as in the geo-political realities of our own times. As I was working on my book, *War in the Hebrew Bible*,[1] I heard an interview on National Public Radio with American servicemen during the first Gulf War concerning their attitudes to the fighting. To my surprise, American fliers and soldiers expressed a range of views about their enemies and their martial activities that tallied surprisingly well with several of the war ideologies I had been exploring among the Israelite writers of the Bible: the enemy was the "other"; war is hell and "collateral damage" inevitable; our cause is just and God is on our side; war is contest and described in the metaphor of sport. Similarly, in his brilliant works, *Achilles in Vietnam* and *Odysseus in America*, psychotherapist and classicist Jonathan Shay describes the parallels to be drawn between the psychic traumas suffered by ancient and modern warriors.[2] He discusses the difficult passages between war and peace that need to be negotiated when the hero returns from the terrible, circumscribed, death-filled theater to the workaday world of family and home. Shay explores the ways in which human beings, ancient and modern, experience and respond to war.

Biblical texts, of course, bear a special burden as they are and have been used to justify action in the present, to frame contemporary political undertakings within the realm of the sacred and the divinely ordained. It is thus with special self-awareness, thoughtfulness, and caution that we approach war in the Hebrew Bible attuned both to the specificity and time-bound nature of ancient Near Eastern views of war, but also to the influence they have upon us and what they, in universal ways, reveal about our own capacity for *eros* and *thanatos*.

---

1. Susan Niditch, *War in the Hebrew Bible: A Study in the Ethics of Violence* (New York: Oxford, 1993).

2. Jonathan Shay, *Achilles in Vietnam: Combat Trauma and the Undoing of Character* (New York: Atheneum, 1994); idem, *Odysseus in America: Combat Trauma and the Trials of Homecoming* (New York: Scribner, 2002).

Introduction

Victor H. Matthews

The SBL Warfare in Ancient Israel Consultation has established an ambitious agenda for itself, to discuss "*all* aspects of ancient Israel's multifarious war traditions." Given such a broad field of study, the participants have great latitude in the topics they choose to explore. As a result, the papers presented in any given year may touch on narrowly focused themes or on a much fuller range of possible or imagined topics without any danger of exhausting the overall subject. This current volume, collecting a sample of those that have been presented during the recent sessions of this consultation, distinguishes itself with its variety and its attention to ideology, literary traditions, and the physical horrors of war. In the course of my discussion below, I will intersperse summaries of the collected articles with my own examination of some of the theoretical and real aspects of warfare in the ancient Near East.

But in exploring such a rich topic, it is also necessary to recognize the many paths that may lead to better understanding of how warfare has marked human cultures. It has its seasons (spring in 2 Sam 11:1), its rhetoric, its unusual heroes (Ehud in Judg 3), its strategies, its motives, its weapons, and its multifaceted examples of human courage, fear, and pain—all of which contribute to the mosaic we call war. For ancient Israel, war was a constant companion, always nearby or just over the horizon. But its absence would not be regretted by those like Isaiah (2:4) and Micah (4:3), who had intimate experience of war as their land was ravaged by the Assyrian invaders and who dreamed of a time when the people would no longer need to "learn war any more." While warfare has its purpose in the ideology of the origin of the nation and its acquisition of the Promised Land (see Hawk's article in this collection), it also has its dark side, playing on the conscience of the people in later periods of their history and requiring a reassessment of how it has contributed to the shaping of their identity as a people.

As Megan Bishop Moore's article, "Fighting in Writing: Warfare in Histories of Ancient Israel," observes, "war is everywhere in the evidence for ancient Israel," and deserves close attention by those who wish to write histories of ancient Israel. War as an event has political implications, but, as she notes, the "implications of war for society, societal structures, individuals, and daily life have not been studied in much detail." Recognizing that there is still a great deal of work to be done on this subject, Moore suggests that scholars should consider such questions as: "Was war *the* story of ancient Israel? Should war usurp religion as the prevailing social reality or condition that defines life and community, both the big events and daily existence, in histories of ancient Israel? Is war in fact the common thread of Israelite unity, religious or political, the man behind the curtain so to speak that is pulling the strings of ancient Israel from top to bottom?"

Perspectives on Warfare

To provide a sense of the scope of possible avenues of research on ancient Near Eastern warfare, I would suggest the following nondefinitive list of areas of study as a starting point.

Methods of warfare would include predatory and defensive strategies, tactics, logistics,[1] and rules of engagement, as well as weapons, technology,[2] training and the building of the social identities of warriors and their commanders, information gathering (Josh 2:1),[3] and the architectural designs that are described in ancient texts, depicted in ancient art forms, and discovered and analyzed by archaeologists.[4] It should be understood that there often is a clear disconnect

---

1. There is a huge body of literature that treats modern logistical analysis as it applies to the theory of war. One recent example that assesses this literature is Domício Proença Jr. and E. E. Duarte, "The Concept of Logistics Derived from Clausewitz: All That Is Required So That the Fighting Force Can be Taken as a Given," *The Journal of Strategic Studies* 28 (2005): 645–77.

2. See the discussion of the advancements in the technology of war during the Assyrian period in Stephanie Dalley, "Ancient Mesopotamian Military Organization," in *Civilizations of the Ancient Near East* (ed. Jack M. Sasson; Peabody, Mass.: Hendrickson, 1995), 417–19.

3. For the role and importance of intelligence gathering, see Christian E. Hauer, "Foreign Intelligence and Internal Security in Davidic Israel," *Concordia Journal* 7 (1981): 96–99; and Victor H. Matthews, "Messengers and the Transmission of Information in the Mari Kingdom," in *Go To The Land I Will Show You: Studies in Honor of Dwight W. Young* (ed. V. H. Matthews and J. Coleson; Winona Lake, Ind.: Eisenbrauns, 1996), 267–74. A modern examination of its abiding importance in terms of overall military operations is found in William M. Darley, "Clausewitz's Theory of War and Information Operations," *Joint Force Quarterly* 40 (2006): 73–79.

4. One of the first attempts at providing a comprehensive resource demonstrating how archaeologists attempt to re-create aspects of ancient warfare is Yigael Yadin's *The Art of Warfare in Biblical Lands in the Light of Archaeological Discoveries* (London: Widenfeld & Nicolson, 1963). More recent examples include Israel Eph'al, *Siege Warfare and Its Ancient Near Eastern Manifestations* [Hebrew] (Jerusalem: Magnes, 1996); Philip J. King and Lawrence E. Stager, *Life in Biblical Israel* (Louisville: Westminster John Knox, 2001), 223–58; and Ze'ev Herzog, "Settlement and Fortification Planning in the Iron Age," in *The Architecture of Ancient Israel* (ed. A. Kempinski and R. Reich; Jerusalem: Israel Exploration Society, 1992), 231–74.

between the physical remains uncovered in excavations and the description of events in ancient representations of events.[5]

Rhetoric of warfare would include the real-time rhetorical displays of leaders raising martial spirit (2 Sam 20:1), the recounting of the exploits of heroes (2 Sam 23:8–39), self-justifying statements by scribes employed to express national ideology and theological underpinning for military campaigns (Judg 2:11–23), artistic representations of warfare,[6] ritual performances designed to raise martial spirit or invoke divine aid,[7] taunting by individual soldiers (2 Sam 5:6), their commanders (2 Sam 10:3–4), and political or clerical representatives (2 Kgs 18:19–35), cries for victory, help, or retribution (Pss 12; 20; 137), and expressions of longing for a cessation of conflict and a peaceful world (Isa 65:17–25).

Physical aspects of warfare includes depictions in art, song (Exod 15:1–18), and writing of the carnage of war, as well as the use of mutilation of humans (Judg 1:6–7) or animals (2 Sam 8:4),[8] mass executions (2 Sam 8:2), and public displays of ferocity toward both combatants and civilians (2 Kgs 8:12).

Ideological aspects of warfare includes concepts of identity and victimization as they apply to gender,[9] the development and perpetuation of national ideologies, the sense of entitlement that applies to a "great" people in their exercise of military campaigns, and the use of "holy war" as a justification for genocide.[10]

Object of warfare includes the expressed desire for territorial gain, preemptive attacks to forestall real or imagined aggression by others, expulsion of occupying forces,[11] the acquisition of control over populations and natural resources, the

---

5. See the discussion of history and historiography in Victor H. Matthews, *Studying the Ancient Israelites: A Guide to Sources and Methods* (Grand Rapids: Baker, 2007), 159–97.

6. See in particular the depictions of Assyrian military campaigns and the brutal treatment of captives in Erica Bleibtreu, "Grisly Assyrian Record of Torture and Death," *BAR* 17.1 (1991): 53–61, 75.

7. See the discussion of cylinder seals from the Middle and Late Bronze Age depicting rows of dancers with their hands on one another's shoulders that may be a form of prebattle ritual in Amihai Mazar, "Ritual Dancing in the Iron Age," *NEA* 66 (2003): 126–32. Prebattle invocations are also described in Richard H. Beal, "Hittite Military Rituals," in *Ancient Magic and Ritual Power* (ed. M. W. Meyer and P. A. Mirecki; Leiden: Brill, 1995), 63–76.

8. Tracy Lemos, 'Shame and Mutilation of Enemies in the Hebrew Bible," *JBL* 125 (2006): 225–41.

9. See, e.g., Susan Niditch "War, Women, and Defilement in Numbers 31," *Semeia* 61 (1993): 39–57.

10. See Yair Hoffman, "The Deuteronomistic Concept of the *Herem*," *ZAW* 111 (1999): 196–210.

11. Again it is necessary to caution that ancient inscriptions often are drafted as propaganda designed to glorify particular rulers and to justify aggressive actions. On this see John A. Emerton, "The Value of the Moabite Stone as an Historical Source," *VT* 52 (2002): 483–92; and V. Philips Long, "How Reliable Are Biblical Reports? Repeating Lester Grabbe's Comparative Experiment," *VT* 52 (2002): 367–84.

creation of fear/awe and the submission of enemies, and the demonstration of divine pleasure with a distinct population.

Results of warfare includes psychological effects on conquered peoples and on the populace of the "winning" nation or group, acquisition of territory and resources, environmental changes, heightened levels of authority, and the need to continue a policy of perpetual warfare to justify political positions or to maintain a facade of martial character as part of an established national ideology. Treaty formats and legal statutes are also created to deal with issues related to marshalling of troops, loss of property, care of and legal statements concerning prisoners of war,[12] extradition, settling of boundaries, and determination of tribute payments.[13]

Theoretical Aspects of Warfare

The difficulties of providing an all-encompassing or even adequate definition for warfare are aptly demonstrated in Frank Ames's contribution to this volume, "The Meaning of War: Definitions for the Study of War in Ancient Israelite Literature." In his examination of various definitions, Ames comes to the conclusion that war, in its complexity, resists definition. As a result, "War is a construct of the academic imagination"; it is what we see and what we say it is. Scholars therefore strive to map out its intricacies as a phenomenon, relating or "mediating" the data collected from a variety of sources to human history and behavior. He makes the telling point that war to a scribe in ancient Israel may not mean the same thing to a modern scholar of strategic theory. Our etic limitations allow only a measure of understanding of ancient thought or social practice.

Still, to provide an introduction to the subject of this volume, I will turn briefly to some of the theoretical underpinnings of warfare in modern scholarship. For those who consider warfare to be a "functional system," what matters is how something works rather than why it occurs.[14] Warfare simply is and therefore can be studied as a cultural phenomenon. Such an approach assumes that societies are definable and that it is the natural function of societies to compete

---

12. See Victor H. Matthews, "Legal Aspects of Military Service in Ancient Mesopotamia," *Military Law Review* 94 (1981): 135–51.

13. Ogden Goelet Jr. and Baruch A. Levine, "Making Peace in Heaven and on Earth: Religious and Legal Aspects of the Treaty between Ramesses II and Hattusili III," in *Boundaries of the Ancient Near Eastern World: A Tribute to Cyrus H. Gordon* (ed. M. Lubetski, C. Gottlieb, and S. Keller; JSOTSup 273; Sheffield: Sheffield Academic Press, 1998), 252–99; and George Mendenhall, "The Suzerainty Treaty Structure: Thirty Years Later," in *Religion and Law: Biblical-Judaic and Islamic Perspectives* (ed. E. B. Firmage, B. G. Weiss, and J. W. Welch; Winona Lake, Ind.: Eisenbrauns, 1990), 85–100.

14. Andrew P. Vayda, foreword to *Pigs for the Ancestors*, by Roy A. Rappaport (New Haven: Yale University Press, 1968), x.

with one another as well as with and for the natural environment. In such a situation, warfare is considered to be endemic to human culture and a factor in the political and economic development and evolution of society. This persistent struggle, often brought on by the tensions caused by overpopulation or strains on natural resources, in turn requires continuous adaptation to both the natural and human environment.[15] Chronic warfare would therefore be considered an element in cultural survival as well as a system that could be advantageous in terms of maintaining political sovereignty and group identity.[16] In effect, a society can be caught up in a vicious cycle of endless warfare based on the assumed need to expand or defend territory, to maintain or enlarge economic resources,[17] and to uphold a reputation for ferocity and/or ruthlessness.[18] Taken to its extreme, then, warfare becomes the "cultural equivalent of natural selection," with "the less well adapted falling by the wayside."[19]

It seems, however, that this approach sometimes can error by overgeneralizing, assuming that warfare influences or creates a competitive spirit between groups or nations in exactly the same way or even that it is possible to define effectively the needs or desires of the competing groups.[20] Warfare is simply too complex an activity to be categorized in such a narrow or rigid manner. It should not be like a literary "type scene" that can be plugged into a narrative at the appropriate place. Social conflict at any level is not simply a way to manifest and ease pent-up anger or to express superior status. It is more likely to be seen as one means of resolving disputes so that there can be a restoration of social

---

15. See the discussion of these assumptions and a critique of their validity in Christopher R. Hallpike, "Functionalist Interpretations of Primitive Warfare," *Man* 8 (1973): 451–70. A more recent treatment of the subject is found in Jonathan Haas, "Warfare and the Evolution of Tribal Polities in the Prehistoric Southwest," in *The Anthropology of War* (ed. J. Haas; Cambridge: Cambridge University Press, 1990), 171–89.

16. Napoleon A. Chagnon, "Yanomamö Social Organization and Warfare," in *War: The Anthropology of Armed Conflict and Aggression* (ed. M. Fried, M. Harris, and R. Murphy; New York: Natural History Press, 1968), 112.

17. William W. Newcomb ("A Re-examination of the Causes of Plains Warfare," *American Anthropologist* 63 [1950]: 317–18) defines war as "a type of armed conflict between societies, meeting in competition for anything which is valued by the groups involved ... and is motivated by economic need, and the biological competition of societies, real or imagined, basic or otherwise."

18. An argument could be made that the apparently endless wars of the Assyrian kings were the result of these factors. Certainly the political rhetoric of the Assyrian Annals suggests that a king's stature as a ruler was based on his ability to conduct successful military campaigns every year. See Bustenay Oded, *War, Peace and Empire: Justifications for War in Assyrian Royal Inscriptions* (Wiesbaden: Reichert, 1992).

19. Robert L. Carneiro, foreword to *The Evolution of War*, edited by Keith F. Otterbein (Cambridge, Mass.: HRAF Press, 1970), xii.

20. Hallpike, "Primitive Warfare," 466.

cohesion.[21] Furthermore, the extinction or the survival of a group or nation is not totally dependent upon a single factor. Warfare and the political and social aftermath perpetuated by the "winners," particularly when the aim is genocide or "ethnic cleansing," may result in mass killings and the transfer of populations. However, that does not in every case insure the total extinction of a group or the impossibility of its future revival.[22]

At its heart, therefore, a functionalist view of warfare sees it as an aggressive form of human behavior that centers on the desire for power or the need to defend oneself from perceived and real dangers. It often feeds on the short-term necessities created by political policies, which may include creating an atmosphere of fear and apprehension and upon greed.[23] Predatory nations or groups go to war to extend their authority over others, to add or recapture territory (1 Kgs 22:3), to obtain wealth or greater access to natural resources, and to demonstrate in a very physical and iconic way the mastery of an intricate art form.[24] Studies have also shown that organizational complexity is a factor in the intensity and frequency of warfare. It can also serve as the impetus for the rise of individual leaders or the foundation for the establishment of more complex political systems such as the shift from chiefdom to monarchy in ancient Israel.[25]

Jacob L. Wright's article in this collection, "Military Valor and Kingship: A Book-Oriented Approach to the Study of a Major War Theme," provides a comparison of war narratives in the books of Judges and Samuel, and touches on the ideological character of the military with respect to a central idea of war: the nexus between military leadership and monarchic rule. His aim is to show how these books differ in their treatment of this nexus. The first section offers a general overview of the widespread political logic in ancient Western Asia according to which valor on the battlefield predestines one to assume the throne. He then turns to four

---

21. See the expression of this theory of social conflict in Max Gluckman, *Custom and Conflict in Africa* (Oxford: Blackwell, 1963), 4.

22. See the discussion of the post–World War II displacement of the German population from east central Europe in Robert M. Hayden, "Schindler's Fate: Genocide, Ethnic Cleansing, and Population Transfers," *Slavic Review* 55 (1996), 727–48, in particular the definition of genocide on 729–30.

23. See Stephen H. Lekson, "War in the Southwest, War in the World," *American Antiquity* 67 (2002): 607–24, especially 618.

24. See the short study of the wars of Hazael in Gershon Galil, "War, Peace, Stones and Memory," *PEQ* 139 (2007): 79–84, which characterizes the turbulent period described in 2 Kings as well as the tactics employed by the short-lived regional empire of the Arameans.

25. See the discussion of this political development in Victor H. Matthews and Don C. Benjamin, *Social World of Ancient Israel, 1250–587 BCE* (Peabody, Mass.: Hendrickson, 1993), 96–109. For a cross-cultural approach to this subject, I recommend Anne P. Underhill, "Warfare and the Development of States in China," in *The Archaeology of Warfare: Prehistories of Raiding and Conquest* (ed. Elizabeth N. Arkush and Mark W. Allen; Gainesville: University Press of Florida, 2006), 253–85.

texts in the books of Judges and Samuel that grapple with this nexus. In the end he offers some general conclusions related to the reasons for the varying approaches toward this nexus in Judges and Samuel and then considers their implications for the study of war in the Hebrew Bible as a whole. In summary, his aim is to show that the popular strategy of legitimizing a king's rule by recourse to military valor and leadership became in Judges and Samuel the subject of an extended discourse on not simply individual kings but the institution of kingship as a whole.

The development of professional military cadres and the invention of more advanced weaponry generally correspond to the establishment of centralized governments and their access to the resources to support these groups and foster new technologies.[26] The glorification of the warrior, of battle, and even of death in battle then takes on a psychological aura similar to other physically gratifying pleasures and becomes the source of honor for participants and of envy for those who cannot or did not participate. Warfare provides a license for the lawful killing of other men and the plundering of the enemy's property, thereby proving one's superiority over another person and demonstrating an ability to deprive that enemy of his life, property, and pride.[27] It also provides opportunities to taunt the enemy, and this form of speech is a cultural window into concepts of honor and shame, social identity, and gender roles.

Several papers in this collection address cultural expressions of or attitudes toward warfare and the way that the enemy is to be addressed or treated. For instance, two papers deal with the use of taunting speech and in particular the use of gender-specific language in reference to the enemy and their cities. Claudia D. Bergmann, in "We Have Seen the Enemy, and He Is Only a 'She': The Portrayal of Warriors as Women," notes how warfare is able to fine-tune taunting as a strategy to demean an enemy. She points out that the metaphorical comparisons include both the sense of pain and terror found in battle and in child birth, and the shrieking of warriors and women in fear of death or shrinking from their responsibility. In her feminist reading of biblical and ancient Near Eastern texts, Bergmann notes that warriors are not compared to stereotypically weak and subjugated women but to women experiencing the life-threatening crisis of giving birth who are on the crossroads between life and death. Women struggling to give birth were, in fact, held in the highest regard and compared to warriors who fought and maybe died as heroes of their people. This is a very apt metaphor in the sense that the warriors are not necessarily displaying cowardice but are distracted by what is about to happen to them and become excessively concerned with self instead of with the team effort of battle. This article suggests that readers and interpreters alike need to distinguish between texts that compare warriors

---

26. Ross Hassig, *War and Society in Ancient Mesoamerica* (Berkeley and Los Angeles: University of California Press, 1992), 15–17.

27. Hallpike, "Primitive Warfare," 459.

with women giving birth and texts that compare warriors with women in general. Both metaphors are possible, but they do not convey the same message, just as the terminology used for them is not the same.

Employing a similar line of analysis, Brad E. Kelle, in "Wartime Rhetoric: Prophetic Metaphorization of Cities as Female," complements Bergmann's article and plays on the use of feminine labels during warfare. Kelle examines the prophetic texts that personify cities as females and how they function rhetorically within the prophet's discourse. His conclusion is that the prophetic metaphorization of cities as female is rhetoric crafted for times of warfare: it is a specific way of drawing upon a well-established metaphorical tradition to critique the centers of power, especially the males who occupy those centers, and to alter the audience's perspective on both the powerful and the deity. Thus, when these texts describe the destruction of the city, they frequently employ the metaphorical language of physical and sexual violence against a woman. For instance, the open gate or the despoiled virgin fit these metaphorical images. Certainly there is a language of war that employs marshal statements, assertions of supremacy, taunts, and threats. This posturing, while contained in written form in the biblical narrative, probably reflects spoken statements during prebattle exchanges or even during negotiations. However, since prophets seldom go to battle or would present taunting statements to an enemy force face to face, it may be assumed that they are employing rhetorical phrases or methods in common use by kings, ambassadors (the Rabshakeh in Isa 36), or by common soldiers. Of course, if what the prophet speaks is designed to raise the martial spirit of the Israelite kings and commanders, then there is a specific audience in play. Yet, as Kelle notes, the fact that the prophets personify cities as female exclusively in contexts of destruction and employ language of physical and sexual violence *in those contexts* suggests that these texts do not have established practices against real women in view. It is possible that shaming punishments were more threat than reality, but since we do not have eye-witnesses to judicial procedure, that is only speculation. In warfare, however, atrocities do occur, and these statements may be designed to shock a city's population into realizing that it could happen to them and their city. Rhetorically, then, the imagery exploits cultural stereotypes in order to shame its male audience by playing upon male fears of the woman as "other."

Ultimately, however, just because a system, like warfare, exists, does not mean it is universally or even minimally essential to maintaining a social system or serves as a defining characteristic of a particular society.[28] It is not "an endemic condition of human existence, but an episodic feature of human history."[29] War is

---

28. See the range of discussion on this topic in Keith Otterbein, "A History of Research on Warfare in Anthropology," *American Anthropologist* 101 (1999): 794–805.

29. Raymond C. Kelly, *Warless Societies and the Origin of War* (Ann Arbor: University of Michigan Press, 2000), 75.

not necessary to effect change, determine national or tribal boundaries, provide a test of national fidelity to a god, or give "successive generations" a means of learning the martial skills (despite the statement in Judg 3:2). Warfare is simply one of many possible alternative solutions to social conflict that may just as effectively be dealt with through economic reform, diplomacy, or technological advances. Furthermore, warfare may be a contributor to national ideology and identity and to social change, but its contributions are not so dominant that attitudes toward war cannot change.

Brian Kvasnica, in his article on the transformation of attitudes toward unrestricted plundering during times of war in the Second Temple period, entitled, "Shifts in Israelite War Ethics and Early Jewish Historiography of Plundering," points to the development of "heightened sensitivities to ethical questions" involved with this traditional practice by armies. It is his assertion that cultures can differentiate themselves by setting aside "normal" behaviors and by promoting a shift in ideology. In this way, the exegetes of the Hellenistic period promoted a prohibition against plundering, drawing authority from an "amplified understanding of the Decalogue," the application of which was then "expanded to apply to enemies as well as neighbors, to situations of war as well as peace."

To be sure, warfare has definite patterns, its affect on human cultures deserves close study, and this study may be advanced by archaeological research. It serves a variety of causes and purposes, places strains on the resources of the participants, and may well disrupt the normal flow of activity of groups and nations to such an extent that they evolve into newly changed entities. War, in fact, is a social stressor that tests the flexibility, endurance, and viability of populations within contested areas, but it is certainly not the only one.

Frances Flannery's article, "'Go Back by the Way You Came': An Internal Textual Critique of Elijah's Violence in 1 Kings 18–19," speaks to these social stresses and to the re-evaluation of earlier struggles in the light of revised social and political situations. In her examination of the contest between Elijah and the prophets of Baal on Mount Carmel, she analyzes two chiastic structures in 1 Kgs 18–19 that she believes are an indication of a "heavy" reworking of original traditions, "an early Ephraimite kernel that is pre-Dtr." Around this earlier core of material she posits a postexilic Dtr author or redactor (Cross's Dtr[2]) who has crafted a "tightly woven critique of Eliahu's warlike behavior," with an emphasis that is "consonant with much literary activity in the postexilic era, with many having concluded that the violent reforms of Josiah and Jehu had not saved Judah from defeat." What stands out, then, is a critique of Elijah's bloody solution, the massacre of the Baal prophets, and a defense of Obadiah's "nonretributive, pacifistic defense of Yahwism" as "an alternate vision for triumphing over an unjust regime." Pacifism is, of course, an alternative to active engagement in conflict, but it can result in the extermination of a resistance movement if it is not handled carefully and given wide publicity.

Depictions and Aspects of Warfare

While warfare generally requires planning and elaborate staging, the ferocity of the moment in individual engagements, sometimes captured in ancient depictions of battle found in Egypt and Mesopotamia, transcends battle plans or the grand strategies of generals. And, as Jan Breemer has noted, "all wars are not created equal," nor can they all be analyzed according to a set pattern or method.[30] In the ancient world, as in today's conventional conflicts, war and the way in which it is later depicted in story, song, and art,[31] often depend upon the courage, skill, fidelity, and luck of individual warriors, who collectively and in one-on-one struggles, using spear and sword, manage to survive while killing or at least pushing back the enemy upon the field of battle.

Although ancient armies or segments of armies move across the terrain, taking on the aspect of huge, cancerous organizations or swarms of locust (Joel 1:4) destroying or maiming all in their path, by modern standards they were quite small. However, the magnitude of the event and its significance tend to grow when the winners tell of their victory or depict it, as monumental art forms do, so that pharaohs and kings stand forth (usually in larger than life-size aspect) as the dominant force in the battle. In this way, war has both a real and an ideal character. Of course, chance has no place in the ideal depiction or recounting of a battle, but it often is the deciding factor in the real world.[32]

For example, many extrabiblical accounts, such as the Assyrian Annals, provide descriptions of military campaigns.[33] The same series of military engagements are also depicted in wall reliefs in the royal palace at Nineveh, providing graphic representations that may not exactly match the written accounts but raise additional questions for researchers. Since they are standardized renditions, Assyrian scribal accounts contain lists of rebellious cities or rulers, campaigns organized and carried out against defaulting allies or vassals (generally at the

---

30. Jan S. Breemer, "Statistics, Real Estate, and the Principles of War: Why There Is No Unified Theory of War," *Military Review* 86 (2006): 84–89.

31. Consider the cosmological implications of the "Song of the Sea" (Exod 15:1–18), with its depiction of the manipulation of creative elements in the destruction of an Egyptian army, and the comical account of the Israelites' victory over the Amalekites in the Sinai trek, in which the deciding factor is whether Moses can hold up his arms throughout the battle (Exod 17:8–16—especially the charge to Moses to write down an account of the event as a future reminder of the enmity between Israel and the Amalekites in vv. 14–16).

32. Carl Von Clausewitz, *On War* (ed. M. Howard; trans. P. Paret; Princeton: Princeton University Press, 1976), 75–89.

33. For example, see the discussion of the Annals of Sennacherib in Walter Mayer (translated by Julia Assante), "Sennacherib's Campaign of 701 BCE: The Assyrian View," in *'Like a Bird in a Cage': The Invasion of Sennacherib in 701 BCE* (ed. L. L. Grabbe; JSOTSup 363; London: Sheffield Academic Press, 2003), 168–200; and Antti Laato, "Assyrian Propaganda and the Falsification of History in the Royal Inscriptions of Sennacherib," *VT* 45 (1995): 198–226.

instigation of divine command), and tactical details about the use of siege engines and other methods to capture rebel cities.[34]

Their rhetorical style also includes the proviso that military operations begin at the command of the gods, thereby making this a "just war" that has been declared against the enemy, who is always described as having brought this disaster upon themselves. The offending states and their rulers have sinned against the god Ashur and have carelessly committed a string of standard "misdeeds."[35] Furthermore, they have failed to show proper obeisance by bowing at the feet of their Assyrian overlord or have foolishly resisted being absorbed into the empire or the hegemonic control of Assyria (= "did not submit to my yoke"). Assyrian records also stipulate that their rulers are justified in their aggressive actions because they are men "who love righteousness" and who act to preserve justice and end treachery, giving "aid to the destitute" and redressing wrongs.[36] In the end, the degree of potency with which the Assyrian kings exercised their divinely mandated, retaliatory missions is a demonstration that the king is being fortified and assisted by the gods of Assyria, who function as "the great judge of heaven and earth" through a trial by combat.[37]

The recounting of miraculous victories in the face of overwhelming odds or through the direct intervention of a god or gods becomes a literary genre of its own within these collections of battle accounts. As Daniel L. Smith-Christopher argues in his article, 'Gideon at Thermopylae? On the Militarization of Miracle in Biblical Narrative and 'Battle Maps,'" it has become for some scholars a tendency to overlook the character of this genre and instead interpret "the 'miraculous' elements in these narratives as 'solid military strategy,' and thus praise the military wisdom of the biblical 'heroes' who are presented as quite rational strategists." Instead, he advocates analyzing battle reports as rhetorical statements that are reflections of the "language of anguish." Thus to re-create battle maps based on the accounts in Joshua or elsewhere in the text may be

---

34. K. Lawson Younger Jr., *Ancient Conquests Accounts: A Study in Ancient Near Eastern and Biblical History Writing* (JSOTSup 98; Sheffield: JSOT Press, 1990), 68.

35. Oded, *War, Peace and Empire*, 43.

36. Ibid., 32–33.

37. Ibid., 38–39. This martial tone, mixed with pious expressions of obedience and devotion to the patron gods of Assyria, are quite common in the Annals. For example, Tiglath-pileser I (1114–1076 B.C.E.) boasts that "with the help of Ashur and Shamash ... I ... am conqueror of the regions from the Great Sea which is in the country Amurru as far as the Great Sea which is in the Nairi country" (*ANET*, 275). During a campaign, Ashurnasirpal II (883–859 B.C.E.) claims that kings of "all the surrounding countries came to me, embraced my feet" (*ANET*, 275–76). Similarly, Shalmaneser III (858–824 B.C.E.), during a campaign to quash a rebellion by a coalition of kings, characterized himself as being assisted by the god Nergal, slaying "their warriors with the sword, descending upon them like Adad when he makes a rainstorm to pour down" (*ANET*, 277).

doing damage to both the historicity of the accounts and to the character of their style of composition.

The ancient Near Eastern national ideologies also take into account the concept of patron gods who actively fight for their chosen state, people, or city.[38] For instance, when the biblical narrative includes the fantastic scenario of the battle with the Amalekites (Exod 17:8–16) and the capture of the besieged city of Jericho (Josh 6:1–25), an effort is made by the authors to characterize these actions as the work of the divine warrior. There is no disguising the text by offering alternative solutions or including realistic preparations for battle. Instead, what is called for is complete obedience to instructions that have no military value and simply serve as a showcase for God's intervention and a demonstration of the rewards garnered by the faithful.

The nature of divinely ordained or inspired conflicts, including those in the name of territorial expansion and acquisition, is explored in the essay by L. Daniel Hawk, "Conquest Reconfigured: Recasting Warfare in the Redaction of Joshua." Hawk examines Josh 2–12 and its so-called "holy war theology" in the light of the different version of Israel's origins in the land found in the story of Rahab (Josh 2) and the story of the Gibeonite deception (Josh 9–11). He concludes that these accounts represent "a comprehensive redactional program that defuses the ethnic antagonism of the conquest traditions by redefining the 'enemy' in political rather than ethnic terms and by dissolving the internal boundaries that separate Israelites and Canaanites." In this reshaping of the conquest traditions, the kings of the land become the true enemy, while the people, represented by the nonmilitaristic Rahab and the Gibeonites, become much less threatening. What results, in his opinion, is a "theological resource for other nations and peoples who care to rethink and reflect on traditions of violent origins and the ethnic residue of such traditions in their corporate consciousness." In that sense, Hawk's reading of this narrative coincides with the view expressed by John Stoessinger that leaders and their personalities play a pivotal role in "pushing nations over the threshold into war."[39]

Complementing the story told in the Assyrian Annals are the reliefs that decorate the royal palaces in their capital cities. These artistic representations of events are part of a conscious scheme to impress visitors. They were intentionally and strategically placed on the walls leading from the entrance way to the throne room, and they clearly were designed to intimidate visitors or foreign ambassadors as they approached the king's audience chamber. The message they convey,

---

38. See the discussion in Bustenay Oded, "'The Command of the God' as a Reason for Going to War in the Assyrian Royal Inscriptions," in *Ah, Assyria … Studies in Assyrian History and Ancient Near Eastern Historiography Presented to Hayim Tadmor* (ed. Mordecai Cogan; Jerusalem: Magnes, 1991), 223–30.

39. John E. Stoessinger, *Why Nations Go to War* (7th ed.; New York: St. Martin's, 1998), xi.

presented in a linear sequence of scenes, provides a version of "reality" and events that appeals to the national ideology of Assyria and, in this at times idealized view of the world, has more to do with that ideology than reality.[40] In addition, their intention is to convey the fact that the king of Assyria is all-powerful and that his armed forces are always invincible.[41]

Unfortunately, we lack clear information on the training of royal artists or on the infusing of the royal ideology that contributed to the creation of this visual form of political rhetoric. However, since this is a record that provides useful information on the Assyrian view of their activities, it is appropriate that the article by Michael G. Hasel, "Assyrian Military Practices and Deuteronomy's Laws of Warfare," examines the visual data in terms of biblical and Assyrian accounts. His use of multiple sources of information on the exact time sequence associated with the punitive destruction of fruit trees around Israelite cities during the Assyrian campaign in Judah allows him to come to the conclusion that "the destruction of trees and orchards occurs after a city is abandoned, defeated, destroyed, and/or burned to the ground." His analysis also concludes that "the use of fruit-bearing trees for the construction of siege works, battering rams, and other major siege machines cannot be supported by the currently known textual and iconographic sources describing and depicting ancient Assyrian warfare."

Costs and Effects of War

Warfare places a strain on all parties and its effects are material and psychological. For those engaged in offensive operations, an initial expense is required to marshal the resources (men and material) necessary to sustain field operations. While an army may in part live off the land that is conquered, this is only a partial solution, and lines of communication and supply must be maintained. This is why in antiquity it was difficult to keep an army in the field year round and why campaigns were focused on smaller segments of real estate. For those who found themselves on the defensive, the cost of building and maintaining walls, towers, gates, and other installations was also a drain on time and resources. Of course, their motivation of survival provides a balance to the costs.

The aesthetic talent associated with war is associated with the intricate visualization of the "ground" upon which the armies will fight. Every hill and valley, stream or lake will become a factor in the game. When warfare moves to siege operations, the outcome is then determined by the practical and physical aspects

---

40. See the very helpful analysis of Assyrian reliefs and their relation to the written Annals in Irene Winter, "Royal Rhetoric and Development of the Historical Narrative in Neo-Assyrian Reliefs," *Studies in Visual Communication* 7 (1981): 2–38.

41. Ruth Jacoby, "The Representations and Identification of Cities on Assyrian Reliefs," *IEJ* 41 (1991): 112–13.

of engineering feats, such as the development of siege engines and more efficient weapons. Finally, when the dust has settled and it is time to tell the story of the battle and its outcome, the aesthetic dimension comes into play, with art and literature serving as the king's and general's tools. In this arena of the mind and the eye, propaganda and psychological representation of how the war was fought and won become products of the imagination and means of advancing national ideology, the glorification of rulers, and the vilification of the enemy. Warfare in this way moves off the battlefield, while holding on to its bloody results as the basis for the creation and maintenance of national ideologies.

One example of how national identity is threatened during a time of chronic warfare is found in Alice A. Keefe's article, "Family Metaphors and Social Conflict in Hosea." She examines Hosea's imagery of the female figure and female fidelity as social symbols of Israelite society during the tumultuous eighth century B.C.E. Her essay considers not only the "marriage" metaphor of Hos 1–3 but also several other metaphors involving women's bodies and acts of sexual transgression that are scattered throughout the rest of the book of Hosea. These graphic metaphors include the slashing open of pregnant mothers (13:16; 14:1), breached birth and female sterility (9:11–14), the death of children with their mothers (10:14b), and the fathering of alien (illegitimate) children (5:7). In this way, the social symbolism carried by images of female sexuality and reproduction in biblical literature is emblematic in the prophet's commentary of the condition and fate of the nation of Israel in a time of intensifying societal disruption, political strife, and the imminent threat of Assyrian invasion.

While warfare has immediate costs and effects on the participants, there is an interesting tendency in the literature of the ancient Near East to find ways to fend off or reverse the devastating aspects of conflict. In this way the scars are smoothed over, the destroyed buildings and fields are restored, and the psychological trauma is soothed or forgotten. One way of illustrating this is by examining the common practice of cursing the enemy, calling on the gods not only to assist armies in the systematic destruction of property and peoples but to deprive the enemy of the normal fruits of their labors. The Assyrians often boasted in their propagandistic accounts that they would besiege enemy cities, deport their citizens, and "cut down their fruit trees and orchards." This language is then translated into the more familiar biblical curse, "You will build a house but not dwell in it; you will plant a vineyard but not drink its wine," variations of which are found in Amos 5:11 and Isa 5:8–17 and serve there as a theodicy justifying Yhwh's willingness to allow Israel to suffer at the hands of the Assyrians. Interestingly, however, in Jeremy D. Smoak's survey of postexilic biblical texts in "Siege Warfare Imagery and the Background of a Biblical Curse," he demonstrates that "the reversal of this curse [using the curse's original association with Assyrian warfare tactics, such as siege, deportation, and exile] functioned as a powerful slogan for the restoration community following the exile (Jer 31:4–6; Isa 65:21–22; Ezek 28:26)."

Final Thoughts

While the intention of this essay is to serve as a general introduction to the academic study of warfare and to the papers presented in this volume, I trust that it may also serve as a spark for future research. As archaeologists produce and analyze additional physical evidence from the ancient Near East, as art historians continue to delve into the ideologies of ancient representational propaganda, and as historians and literary critics throw new light on interpreting biblical narratives and extrabiblical textual remains, it is to be expected that this volume will be only one of many future treatments of the subject of warfare. Clearly, there is much work yet to be done on this topic and on the larger effort to examine, analyze, and reconstruct the world of ancient Israel.

Part 1
Writing and Reading the Rhetoric of War

The Meaning of War: Definitions for the Study of War in Ancient Israelite Literature

Frank Ritchel Ames

Question

War is a reality bound by the human imagination, a defined reality, and its definition has become increasingly problematic. Terrorist activities by international networks and search-and-destroy missions by bordered nations are forcing the surrender of the notion that war is a "difference arising between two states and leading to the intervention of armed forces," an understanding of war articulated in the 1949 Geneva Conventions.[1] Given such a definition, when armed conflict is not between nations, it is not a war, and it is not war, if the opponents are not uniformed armies.[2] To quote Julie Hirschfeld Davis reflecting on the assault of 11 September 2001 and the formal but unofficial declarations of war made before the U.S. Congress on 20 September: "If this means war, what does 'war' mean?"[3]

The question, which has immediate relevance to national policy and international diplomacy, can also be raised in the study of ancient Israel and the Hebrew Bible, and it should be raised. It is a question that begs an answer. Susan Niditch recognized the importance of a working definition of war in her 1993 *Semeia* article on women and war. Niditch wrote,

> I have implicitly referred to Deuteronomy 20 and Judges 19–21 as war texts, but political scientists and anthropologists have long debated what constitutes and properly defines war.... Is a disagreement between in-marrying groups that leads to violent aggression, killing, and counter attack to be considered war or something else called "fighting" or "feud"? Some scholars would say the latter....

---

1. Article 2, Convention (I) for the Amelioration of the Condition of the Wounded and Sick in Armed Forces in the Field. Geneva, 12 August 1949.

2. Gary D. Solis, "Are We Really at War?" *United States Naval Institute. Proceedings* 127/12 (2001): 34–39.

3. Julie Hirschfeld Davis, "If This Means War, What Does 'War' Mean?" *CQ Weekly* 59/35 (2001): 2110.

> Others would draw a sharp distinction between war as an organized, constructive activity involving a "systematic pursuit of political objectives" and "fighting" of a "more exotic type" including raids for purposes of head-hunting or to obtain victims for human sacrifice or to steal wives.... If one begins to define war as requiring a centralized state apparatus, standing armies, generals, and strategy, then much primitive warfare becomes something other than war. One begins to wonder whether the activity described in Judges 19–21 or the less than fully organized melées of Joshua are wars.[4]

Definition is a prerequisite to classifying historical events, identifying relevant texts, formulating and testing hypotheses, and comparing findings. In biblical scholarship as well as in other academic disciplines, a definition of war must be articulated, not assumed. Definition is not the end that war scholars seek, but it is a necessary first step.

What is war? Or better, how might those who study the Hebrew Bible and ancient Israel define war? A single, all-purpose definition is neither possible nor desirable in war research.[5] What can be achieved, however, and what is vital is clarity and precision: an explicit recognition and articulation of what one is investigating at a particular moment. Those who study ancient Israelite war, like others who pursue the academic study of religion, "must," to borrow a phrase from Jonathan Z. Smith, "be relentlessly self-conscious."[6] Admittedly, scholars obsess over definition, but rightly so, for words shape the worlds that scholars and their readers inhabit, including worlds at war. So here I will indulge a common academic obsession and will take up the modest but necessary task of evaluating types of definitions and their applicability to studies of ancient Israelite warfare and its representations in the Hebrew Bible, inviting reflection, drawing conclusions, and suggesting directions. Because much has been written about war outside the field of biblical studies, the treatment will be interdisciplinary and will, so to speak, plunder the Egyptians on behalf of those who study biblical texts and their social

---

4. Susan Niditch, "War, Women, and Defilement in Numbers 31," *Semeia* 61 (1993): 43.

5. William J. Hamblin offers a similar assessment: "Different definitions of warfare are often related to the fact that anthropologists, archaeologists, historians, and other scholars, although all dealing with the same phenomenon, each approach the issue by asking different types of questions and attempting to answer those questions with different types of evidence and methodologies. Our concern then should not be defining 'what is war?', but rather 'what type of model or definition for warfare is most helpful in understanding the issues and questions related to the strengths and limitations of a given discipline, methodology or body of evidence?' A universally useful definition of war is not only unattainable, but undesirable. Rather, such definitions should be viewed as more or less useful models for answering a specific range of questions with certain types of methodology" (*Warfare in the Ancient Near East to 1600 BC: Holy Warriors at the Dawn of History* [Warfare and History; London: Routledge, 2006], 11).

6. Jonathan Z. Smith, *Imagining Religion: From Babylon to Jonestown* (CSJH; Chicago: University of Chicago Press, 1982), xi.

contexts. The discussion will also reflect my own concern to explore, from vantage points within the humanities and social sciences, not only what it meant to be an ancient Israelite but what it means to be human in a world at war. The definitions presented will be classified as descriptive, moral, or theoretical—categories that are neither exclusive nor exhaustive—but broad and heuristic. Examples in each category follow, beginning with the descriptive. The survey is representative, not comprehensive, and underscores problems and directions in defining war.

Descriptive Definition

In the widely used reference work *The Encyclopedia of Religion*, Bruce Lincoln defines war as *violence between rival groups*, a simple definition that neither evaluates nor legislates; it neither explains nor theorizes; rather, it names, categorizes, and differentiates—an essential albeit circumscribed task. Lincoln describes and does so with detail and nuance. To quote Lincoln's definition in full, war is "organized and coherent violence conducted between established and internally cohesive rival groups. In contrast to numerous other modes of violence, it is neither individual, spontaneous, random, nor irrational, however much—like all varieties of violence—it involves destructive action, even on a massive scale."[7] The essence of war, in this definition, is *organized violence*. War is distinguished from other violent activities in that it is prosecuted not by an individual but by a social group, and not with wild abandon but with purpose and resolve. It is a communal activity, and it remains so regardless of popular support or widespread dissent. It is also a rational activity in spite of the general madness of it all. Here *The Encyclopedia of Religion* does not drift from its anthropological moorings, for Lincoln's definition of war is not unlike Malinowski's: "armed conflict between two independent political units, by means of organized military force, in the pursuit of a tribal or national policy."[8] In Malinowski's definition, if the conflict involves identifiable social groups of any type, whether tribes *or* nations, then it is war. In contrast, the definition set forth by Jacek Kugler in *The Oxford Companion to the Politics of the World* reflects the interests of the political scientist, not the anthropologist. Kugler references Malinowski but then writes, "The more restricted definition used here conceptualizes war as events that produce substantial militarized arms conflict between organized military forces of independent nations."[9] In Kugler's definition, only international conflict—that is,

---

7. Bruce Lincoln, "War and Warriors: An Overview," *ER* 15:339.
8. Bronislaw Malinowski, "An Anthropological Analysis of War," in *War: Studies from Psychology, Sociology, Anthropology* (rev. ed.; ed. L. Bramson and G. W. Goethals; New York: Basic Books, 1968), 28.
9. Jacek Kugler, "War," in *The Oxford Companion to the Politics of the World* (2nd ed.; ed. J. Krieger; New York: Oxford University Press, 2001), 894.

armed conflict between sovereign states—qualifies as war. Given such a definition, civil war, regardless of scope or duration, is not war.

The definitions applied in biblical studies tend to be anthropological rather than political in orientation, reflecting the discipline's close relationship with religious studies and a need to span the range of violent conflicts portrayed in the Bible. William Klassen, writing for the *Anchor Bible Dictionary* and as a member of the biblical studies guild, defines war as "a state of armed conflict between two groups of people in which lethal violence is used to coerce one to do the other's will."[10] Klassen's definition applies equally to the Syro-Ephraimite war, a conflict between the sovereign states of Damascus and Israel (2 Kgs 15–16; 2 Chr 27–28; Isa 7), and the revenge of the rape of Dinah, a vendetta carried out by Dinah's brothers, Simeon and Levi, against Hamor's son and the other men of Shechem (Gen 37). War, given this type of broad anthropological description, can be family feud or clash of nations. The definition is, in a word, inclusive.

Roland de Vaux's extended treatment of war in the dated-but-classic work *Ancient Israel: Its Life and Institutions*, does not include a definition; rather, the treatment serves as a definition. De Vaux defines war by offering a thick description that entails an interpretation of cultural discourse, or what Clifford Geertz calls a "sorting out the structures of signification."[11] War is one of several complex institutions described by de Vaux, and a reader may infer from the details that war amounts to a holy siege carried out by armed warriors from or against fortified cities.[12] More recent surveys of ancient Israelite culture, such as Victor H. Matthews and Don C. Benjamin's *Social World of Ancient Israel: 1250–587 BCE*, Philip J. King and Lawrence E. Stager's *Life in Biblical Israel*, and Oded Borowski's *Daily Life in Biblical Times*, offer much the same: no formal definition per se but a useful, multiple-page description of war personnel, equipment, strategies, ideologies, and historic battles.[13] Brad E. Kelle's focused treatment, *Ancient Israel at War 853–586 BC*, follows suit.[14] These works do not succinctly define; they define through extended description and interpretation. For these biblical scholars, if war is hell, then the devil is in the details, and so is the def-

---

10. William Klassen, "War in the NT," *ABD* 6:867.

11. Clifford Geertz, *The Interpretation of Cultures* (New York: Basic Books, 1973), 9.

12. Roland de Vaux, *Ancient Israel: Its Life and Institutions* (trans. J. McHugh; Biblical Resource Series; Grand Rapids: Eerdmans, 1997; repr., London: Darton, Longman & Todd, 1961), 211–67.

13. Victor H. Matthews and Don C. Benjamin, *Social World of Ancient Israel: 1250–587 BCE* (Peabody, Mass.: Hendrickson, 1993), 96–109; Philip J. King and Lawrence E. Stager, *Life in Biblical Israel* (Library of Ancient Israel; Louisville: Westminster John Knox, 2001), 223–58; Oded Borowski, *Daily Life in Biblical Times* (SBLABS 5; Atlanta: Society of Biblical Literature, 2003), 35–42.

14. Brad E. Kelle, *Ancient Israel at War 853–586 BC* (Essential Histories 67; Oxford: Osprey, 2007).

inition. Interpretation is integral to thick description,[15] and the description of holy war given by Matthews and Benjamin illustrates the case, for they explicate social rationale or cultural motive: "the prisoners and plunder were executed or burned, not as a sadistic act of revenge but to transfer them to the divine assembly."[16] Their description explores the outer and inner contours of war: what the ancient warriors did and why.

A definition of war, of course, need not be thick with details to be useful; it need only be clear and specific. How specific? The degree depends on the nature of the research. Useful studies of the metrics of war require precise operational definitions. Economists Paul Collier and Anke Hoeffler, for example, define civil war as "an internal conflict with at least 1,000 combat-related deaths per year," and they distinguish civil war from massacres by stipulating that "both government forces and an identifiable rebel organization must suffer at least 5% of these fatalities."[17] Unambiguous definitions do facilitate research and are essential in empirical studies. In scholarship as well as in battle, someone must estimate the cost, number the brave, and count the fallen, although tallies and percentages disturb not only by what they reveal about the realities of warfare but by what they might reveal about the detachment of those who study war. The calculus of war achieves power and unsettles through its matter-of-fact simplicity.

Moral Definition

War, however, is never simple; it is not bloodless; it has a human face.[18] For this reason, there are moral questions to be considered in warfare and in defining war. The justness and humanity of war are subject to ethical and legal scrutiny, and a definition can be formulated in such a way that it not only describes but judges. It can be patently or subtly laden with values, either assuming or expressing an ethical perspective. Chris Hedges proffers a value-laden definition of war in the title of his critically acclaimed work, *War Is a Force That Gives Us Meaning*.[19] He writes, "Most of us willingly accept war as long as we can fold it into a belief system that paints the ensuing suffering as necessary for a higher good, for human beings seek not only happiness but also meaning. And tragically war

---

15. Geertz, *Interpretation of Cultures*, 20.
16. Matthews and Benjamin, *Social World of Ancient Israel*, 95.
17. Paul Collier and Anke Hoeffler, "Greed and Grievance in Civil War," *Oxford Economic Papers* 56 (2004): 565.
18. See, e.g., John Keegan's detailed accounts of historic battles at Agincourt, Waterloo, and Somme in *The Face of Battle* (New York: Penguin, 1974); and Paul Bentley Kern's descriptions in *Ancient Siege Warfare* (Bloomington: Indiana University Press, 1999).
19. Chris Hedges, *War Is a Force That Gives Us Meaning* (New York: Anchor Books, 2003), 17.

is sometimes the most powerful way in human society to achieve meaning."[20] This definition, which is interesting from a theoretical perspective, reinforces a moral agenda. In the book's introduction, Hedges explains, "I wrote this book not to dissuade us from war but to understand it. It is especially important that we, who wield such massive force across the globe, see within ourselves the seeds of our own obliteration. We must guard against the myth of war and the drug of war that can, together, render us as blind and callous as some of those we battle."[21] For Hedges, understanding propels action. He defines war as a force that reveals and shapes human identity and purpose; he then cautions readers against embracing "the myth of war" that blinds and hardens those who fight. War, Hedges asserts, is a poison that transforms humans into sightless, rabid beasts who turn and devour one another without compassion and who, like the animals in Jonah's Nineveh, must repent in sackcloth and ashes (see Jonah 3:7–9). Drawing from the prophetic traditions of the Bible, he characterizes his book as a "call for repentance."[22] His explanation of war is not merely an academic pursuit; rather, it is a journalistic call for action, an admixture of reporting and opinion, recent history and ethical perspective. By defining war as an experience that dehumanizes yet confers meaning, Hedges seeks to expose and condemn war and war's excesses, although he does not call for an end to war. His definition, subtle in its rhetoric, is a prelude to a heart-wrenching morality tale based on firsthand experiences of war in Central America, Gaza, and the Balkans.[23]

The face that a moral definition of war can unmask is that of a brute beast, not unlike biblical images of warriors as lions and casualties as prey (see Ezek 19). Warriors, it seems, must become and envision something less than human to overcome the terror and remorse of slaughter, to engage in killing that under usual circumstances would be prohibited by law and conscience.[24] War, after all, is a state in which the killing of other human beings is rendered legal, necessary, honorable, and, as Lincoln points out, "even glorious, by virtue of the fact that they belong to a rival group to whom ethical norms do not extend, the enemy having been effectively defined as subhuman or even nonhuman."[25]

From a philosophical perspective, every definition of war, from simple description to complex theory, has a normative dimension with practical conse-

---

20. Ibid., 10.
21. Ibid., 17.
22. Ibid.
23. As Niditch has observed, "Portrayals of war reveal a culture's fundamental values" ("War, Women, and Defilement," 43).
24. See Sam Keen, *Faces of the Enemy: Reflections on the Hostile Imagination* (enlarged ed.; New York: Harper & Row, 2004).
25. Lincoln, "War and Warriors," 342.

quences.[26] One's definition of war differentiates casualty and victim, warrior and murderer, soldier and terrorist. Such words sanction and condemn, and for this reason independent groups that attack bordered nations call themselves armies, not terrorists, and refer to their deeds as military actions, not terrorist acts. In the rhetoric of armed conflict, terrorism tends to be what *they* do to *us*, not what *we* do to *them*. War rhetoric is never disinterested, and definitions serve political ends regardless of intention.[27]

Even a definition seemingly unburdened by values can be construed as value-laden within a particular context. Here is a definition that appears not to be value-laden: war is the use of armed force against other human beings. To the pacifist, however, the use of armed force in and of itself is immoral. War is considered immoral within Mennonite and Amish communities by definition and, ethnographic controversies aside, within social groups such as the West Malaysian Semai.[28] One Semai leader explained, "Other people kill us, we don't kill other people. We never get so angry that we go to war."[29] Pacifistic sensibilities can be embedded in the social conscience of small or large groups and even in a nation's foundational documents. Article 9 of the constitution of Japan, for example, "renounce[s] war as a sovereign right of the nation and the threat or use of force as a means of settling international disputes," and since its post–World War II enactment, the article has constrained military activities and shaped the conscience of the nation—although I would not aver that any social group, either primitive or modern, is innately or uniformly pacifistic.[30] Japan does not have an *offensive* army or navy but does maintain formidable *self-defense* forces with one of the larger defense budgets in the world.[31] More recent legislation suggests that

---

26. Uwe Steinhoff made this point in a talk entitled "What Is War?" See Thomas Hippler, "Uwe Steinhoff: What Is War?" (The Oxford Leverhulme Programme on the Changing Character of War Lunchtime Discussion Series, Week 4, 2 November 2004), 1; online: http://ccw.politics.ox.ac.uk/events/archives/mt04_steinhoff.pdf.

27. Joseph S. Tuman, *Communicating Terror: The Rhetorical Dimensions of Terrorism* (London: Sage, 2003), 9–10.

28. Clayton Robarchek and Robert Knox Dentan, "Blood Drunkenness and the Bloodthirsty Semai: Unmaking Another Anthropological Myth," *American Anthropologist* 89 (1987): 356–65.

29. Robert Knox Dentan, "Spotted Doves at War: The *Praak Sangkill*," *Asian Folklore Studies* 58 (1999): 420.

30. Chuma Kiyofuku, "The Choice Is Clear: Diplomacy over Force," *Japan Quarterly* 38/2 (1991): 142. See also the qualifications regarding categorization and oversimplification expressed about the Semai in Robert Knox Dentan, "Hawks, Doves, and Birds in the Bush: A Response to Keith Otterbein, Neil Whitehead, and Leslie Sponsel," *American Anthropologist* 104 (2002): 278.

31. Japan's defense budget, according to the CIA, trails only the United States, China, and France ("Active Duty: Cautiously, Japan Returns to Combat, In Southern Iraq," *The Wall Street Journal* [January 2, 2004]: A1).

"Japan is drifting away from pacifism."[32] Ambivalence toward war is common in the contemporary world and is evident in the contours of ancient biblical traditions. The author of Ps 120 expresses a hawkish desire that adversaries feel the sting of fire-sharpened arrows (120:1–4a) but in the psalm's complaint and expression of innocence asserts a desire for peace:

> Woe to me, for I sojourned Meschech;
> I lived with the tents of Kedar.
> Too long I lived my life
> with a despiser of peace!
> I seek peace, and I speak truth;
> they want only war. (120:4b–7)[33]

I am neither advocating nor objecting to value-laden definitions, nor am I sanctioning or condemning the use of armed force; I am underscoring the fact that definitions of war, even seemingly disinterested definitions formulated for the study of ancient Israel and the Hebrew Bible, are inextricably tangled up with values and assume or assert a moral outlook. Legal definitions, of course, are intrinsically ethical, for they are prescriptive in nature and function in the adjudication of court cases. Military definitions are ethical, for terms of engagement accompany doctrines of war. Academic definitions, likewise, are ethical, for they seek to describe human realities that carry flesh-and-blood implications. If the verdicts of the courts are *de jure,* then the findings of the academy are *de facto,* and, at the end of the day, it often proves easier to overturn the judgment of the courts than a well-founded consensus of scholars.

---

32. Wu Xinbo, "The End of the Silver Lining: A Chinese View of the U.S.–Japanese Alliance," *The Washington Quarterly* 29, no. 1 (Winter 2005/2006): 125.

33. The lines in 120:7, אני שלום וכי אדבר המה למלחמה, are problematic in their simplicity. The first and last clauses are verbless, and the translator may supply the verb "is" in both: "I am for peace," and "they are for war." Or the translator may offer the equivalent in a more paraphrastic rendering: "I seek peace," and "they want war." A translator could use personification, reflecting the psalmist's style in v. 3: "I am peace," and "they are war." The ל in v. 7 may function as a preposition, direct object, or particle of emphasis. Understanding the ל to show emphasis, Dahood translates, "but they, [want] only war" (Mitchell Dahood, *Psalms 101–150: Introduction, Translation, and Notes* [AB 17A; Garden City, N.Y.: Doubleday, 1965], 194). Following Kraus, I emend כי to כן, "truth" (Hans-Joachim Kraus, *Psalms 60–150* [trans. H. C. Oswald; CC; Minneapolis: Augsburg, 1989], 423). Similarity between the two Hebrew terms, a likely contrast between truthful advocacy of peace in v. 7 and violent lying in vv. 2–3 in the design of the psalm, and the difficulty of the expression as it stands support the emendation (cf. *BHS* and Exod 10:29).

Theory-Laden Definition

Definitions may be descriptive or moral, but they may also assume or advance a theory. Hubert C. Johnson defines warfare as "permissible and controlled violence," a concise definition shaped by centuries of debate regarding a state's right to employ force to protect its people and interests.[34] Those who study the origin and evolution of war, who seek to understand the conditions that attend the onset, outcome, and abatement of war, tend to formulate working definitions that reflect or support a particular model or theory. This is appropriate and necessary. T. Clifton Morgan observes, "Most of us would agree that we know a war when we see one. Therefore, the necessity to devise a precise definition only arose when we began to seek a scientific understanding of the causes of war."[35] Definition, Morgan recognizes, is the first step in an argument.[36] Different definitions of war, therefore, may be required to argue effectively for different theories. Those who regard war as a product of human genetics and propose a sociobiological explanation of necessity will define war differently than those who regard it as a product of social diffusion or cultural evolution.[37] A definition often epitomizes a theory.

This is true of the most celebrated and debated definition of war in modern military history: Carl von Clausewitz's "war is merely the continuation of policy [*Politik*] by other means," a definition found in his thorny, posthumous volume, *On War*.[38] The definition has its ambiguities but may well be a double entendre, for the German word *Politik* can refer to politics as well as policy, and his volume argues that the prosecution of war entails an often-surprising interaction of human intentions and unpredictable realities.[39] Violence, chance, and politics collide in warfare, and people, commanders, and politicians must reckon with ends and means, although the exigencies of war ultimately make it impossible to control either.[40] The prosecution of war, Clausewitz argued, has limits and is part

---

34. Hubert C. Johnson, "Warfare, Strategies and Tactics of," in *Encyclopedia of Violence, Peace, and Conflict* (ed. L. Kurtz; 3 vols.; New York: Academic Press, 1999), 3:759–60.

35. T. Clifton Morgan, "The Concept of War: Its Impact on Research and Policy," *Peace & Change* 15/4 (1990): 416.

36. Ibid.

37. Keith F. Otterbein, "A History of Research on Warfare in Anthropology," *American Anthropologist* 101 (1999): 794–805; James Chowning Davies, "Human Nature, Views of," in Kurtz, *Encyclopedia of Violence, Peace, and Conflict*, 2:153.

38. Carl von Clausewitz, *On War* (ed. and trans. M. Howard and P. Paret; Princeton: Princeton University Press, 1976), 87.

39. Christopher Bassford, "Interpreting the Legacy of Clausewitz," *Joint Force Quarterly* 35 (2004): 19. See also Hugh Smith, *On Clausewitz: A Study of Military and Political Ideas* (New York: Palgrave Macmillan, 2005).

40. Clausewitz, *On War*, 579.

of a political continuum.[41] He does not define war as organized violence, although there is organization and the means are violent. He does not identify the participants, although his definition assumes that they are armies and states. He does not define war as either moral or immoral. Rather, war is defined as a form of political process, a process used to implement policy objectives and resolve conflicts of interests. Morgan, refining the concept, treats war as a means of conflict resolution and places it on a continuum with other means, showing how conflicts are resolved by voting, adjudication, bargaining, or force.[42] Similarly, William T. R. Fox relates these means to the number and role of participants: the resolution of a conflict by the affected, a third party, the principals, or the strongest party.[43] Clausewitz's definition captures a grand theory of war as *Realpolitik*.

The expression of theory is patent in Gerhard von Rad's definition in *Holy War in Ancient Israel*. In the book's first chapter, entitled, "The Theory of Holy War," von Rad writes, "The highpoint and the conclusion of the holy war is formed by the *ḥērem*, the consecration of the booty to Yhwh. As is the case for the entire holy war, this too is a cultic phenomenon: human beings and animals are slaughtered, gold and silver and the like go as קֹדֶשׁ into Yhwh's treasury (Josh. 6:18–19)."[44] Von Rad defines holy war as "a cultic phenomenon" and elsewhere as "an eminently cultic undertaking—that is, prescribed and sanctioned by fixed, traditional, sacred rites and observances."[45] Building on the insights of Julius Wellhausen and Friedrich Schwally, von Rad argued that war, for the ancient Israelites, was religious in nature.[46] Schwally, whose legacy includes the introduction of the label "holy war" into the vocabulary of biblical studies, concluded that ancient Israelites regarded war to be a large-scale sacrifice.[47] Israel's neighbors, Hamblin observes, embraced similar notions:

> For the ancients, *war was the means by which the gods restored cosmic order through organized violence undertaken in their names by their divinely ordained kings*. Or to put it in Clauswitzian [sic] terms, "war is the continuation of *divine* policy by other means." Whatever other modern models we might wish to apply

---

41. Steven J. Lepper, "On (the Law of) War: What Clausewitz *Meant* to Say," *Airpower Journal* 13/2 (1999): 105.

42. Morgan, "Concept of War," 420.

43. William T. R. Fox, "World Politics as Conflict Resolution," in *International Conflict and Conflict Management* (ed. R. O. Matthews; Scarborough: Prentice-Hall, 1984), 7–14.

44. Gerhard von Rad, *Holy War in Ancient Israel* (trans. and ed. M. J. Dawn; Grand Rapids: Eerdmans, 1991), 49.

45. Ibid., 51.

46. Ben C. Ollenburger, "Gerhard von Rad's Theory of Holy War," in von Rad, *Holy War in Ancient Israel*, 3–6, 12.

47. Ibid., 5.

to our study of ancient Near Eastern warfare to help illuminate certain questions, this definition must never be far from our mind.[48]

In addition, those who read and write about war must be mindful of the distinction between emic and etic definitions. Von Rad theorized about the beliefs and practices of ancient Israelites, not about war as a human phenomenon. He did not seek to understand war per se, but Israel's understanding of war in an evolving tradition.

Conclusions

What, then, is war? First and foremost, war is a *construct* of the academic imagination. Every aspect of war research entails projection as well as appreciation. War is what we see it as and what we say it is. As Mark J. Fretz notes, "What distinguishes a butcher knife from a soldier's dagger is the context in which the implement is used."[49] Is the stake in Jael's hand a tent peg or a sword? The answer depends on where the stake is driven. Is Jael a soldier or a civilian? It depends on what we imagine. Is Jael a champion or a murderer? The evaluation depends on the allegiances of the author and the reader.

Second, war is a *phenomenon* that scholars attempt to identify, evaluate, and explain. War is a construct subject to our descriptive abilities, moral sensibilities, and theories, and every definition is laden in some way, but part of the scholar's responsibility is formulating definitions that are not overburdened. Admittedly, no phenomenon is self-defining, and all definitions remains subject to revision, but there is a phenomenon to be studied. War, in short, is real, and the scholar must attend to its realities. Useful definitions describe, and their formulations attend closely to *genera* (what war has in common with other phenomena) and *differentia* (what distinguishes it from other phenomena). Useful definitions will be shaped by observable phenomena.

Third, war is *mediated*. Those who study ancient Israelite war and its representations in the Hebrew Bible do so indirectly; they study artifacts and texts that come from other times and places. Texts and artifacts are our partners in a reconstruction of past events and ancient imaginations. The voices that speak through ancient texts assert ideas about war, ideas that the scholar wants to understand, explain, and evaluate. Indeed the biblical scholar must attend to the voices that echo in ancient texts, but the scholar must not feel bound to an ancient vocabulary. Scholarly definitions of ancient phenomena must be etic, not emic. The definition of war applied by the modern scholar need not be the definition assumed by the ancient scribe. To advance the field, definitions must be imposed, not adopted,

---

48. Hamblin, *Warfare in the Ancient Near East*, 12.
49. Mark J. Fretz, "Weapons and Implements of Warfare," *ABD* 6:893.

even when the scholar is attempting to comprehend ancient understandings of war. War is begging for fresh definition, and it may be time to rethink some of the discipline's most revered constructs. Schwally concluded that "war is a continuous, highly expanded sacrifice."[50] He described an ancient understanding of war, not necessarily a current understanding of war. Familiar rubrics and definitions have served the field well, and much has been accomplished by defining ancient Israelite war as holy war, but even this is a construct subject to revision, and it is an emic, not etic, understanding of war. Neither can it serve as an encompassing understanding for ancient Israel, for "not all Israelite war," as Victor Matthews rightly observes, "is holy war." Israelite war was at times predatory, territorial, opportunistic, and not necessarily waged for divine honor.[51]

Fourth, war is all too *human*, and a scholar makes a significant contribution by thinking about ancient Israelite war as a human as well as an Israelite phenomenon. We study the events and traditions of antiquity because they have present value. Here I am not thinking about biblical texts as guides to faith, although I am a person of faith, but as expressions of what it means to be human. In studying war and peace, the scholar benefits from the realization that nothing human can be foreign—a perspective that gives significance to the study of the past but in no way negates the need for criticism or admiration of the past. I study ancient peoples because I want to know who I am and what made me this way, as well as to understand what nobility entails. In the study of ancient Israelite war and war in the ancient Near East, biblical scholars have an opportunity to think about war as a human phenomenon and to move from specific examples to general theories.

War historian John Keegan concluded that "war is collective killing for some collective purpose," then added, with a measure of resignation, "that is as far as I would go in attempting to describe it."[52] He likens war to a virus that has the capacity to mutate and thus to resist eradication. War, likewise, will always resist definition, for armed conflict is a complex and evolving phenomenon.[53] The complexity may tempt the biblical scholar to imitate Brien Hallett, author of *The Lost Art of Declaring War*, who attends to the functions of war declarations more than broader war definitions, for there is "an ambiguity inherent in the word *war*."[54] This, to me, seems unsatisfactory and unnecessary. Every definition discriminates

---

50. Quoted in Ollenburger, "Gerhard von Rad's Theory of Holy War," 5.
51. Victor Matthews, personal communication, 10 September 2007.
52. John Keegan, *War and Our World: The Keith Lectures* (New York: Vintage, 1998), 72. See also the review of Keegan's book by Ian McAllister in *Peacekeeping & International Relations* 29/3–4 (2000): 24.
53. Jyri Raitasalo and Joonas Siplila, "Reconstructing War after the Cold War," *Comparative Strategy* 23 (2004): 256.
54. Brien Hallett, *The Lost Art of Declaring War* (Champaign: University of Illinois Press, 1998), 74. It is useful to distinguish "the enmity of war" or the social, economic, and legal conditions, and "the violence of combat" or military engagement (ibid., 107). Groups need not be

but leaves a remainder; something is brought in, and something is left out. This is why the scholar not only defines but redefines. War is a construct of the academic imagination. Although "map is not territory," to borrow another phrase from Jonathan Z. Smith, those who would understand more about the world of war in ancient Israel and a world still at war must have a map or, like true explorers, must create one.[55]

---

engaging in combat to be at war. See also Ryan C. Hendrickson, review of Brien Hallett, *The Lost Art of Declaring War*, *The American Political Science Review* 93 (1999): 754.

55. Jonathan Z. Smith, *Map Is Not Territory: Studies in the History of Religions* (Chicago: University of Chicago Press, 1993), 289–310.

Military Valor and Kingship: A Book-Oriented Approach to the Study of a Major War Theme

Jacob L. Wright

"My argument is that War makes rattling good history; but Peace is poor reading."[1]

That the Hebrew Bible continues to exert a fascination on readers is arguably related in no small measure to its abundance of war stories, and especially to its diversity of depictions and notions of war. Unfortunately, much of biblical scholarship has focused on only one of these ideas, namely "holy war" or "Yhwh-war." This narrow research trajectory has a long history,[2] but it gained great momentum with the publication of Gerhard von Rad's *Der heiliger Krieg im alten Israel*.[3] Although scholars have long criticized von Rad's thesis and the amphictyony theory upon which it is based, most studies of war in ancient Israel have carried on the tradition of scholarship he established.[4]

---

1. Spirit Sinister in Thomas Hardy's *The Dynasts* (London: Macmillan, 1904–8), part 1, act 2, scene 5.
2. See, e.g., Friedrich Schwally, *Der heilige Krieg im alten Israel* (Leipzig: Dietrich, 1901); Otto Weber, *Ancient Judaism* (trans. and ed. H. H. Gerth and D. Martindale; Glencoe, Ill.: Free Press, 1952; orig. 1917–19), 118–46; Henning Fredriksson, *Jahwe als Krieger: Studien zum alttestamentlichen Gottesbild* (Lund: Gleerup, 1945); Roland de Vaux, *Ancient Israel* (New York: McGraw-Hill, 1965), 1:213–66
3. (ATANT 20; Zurich: Zwingli Verlag, 1951); Eng., *Holy War in Ancient Israel* (trans. and ed. Marva J. Dawn; intro. Ben C. Ollenburger; biblio. Judith E. Sanderson; Grand Rapids: Eerdmans, 1991).
4. Here is a selective bibliography of monographs: Rudolf Smend, *Yahweh War and Tribal Confederation: Reflections upon Israel's Earliest History* (trans. M. G. Rogers; Nashville: Abingdon, 1970; orig. 1966); Albert E. Glock, *Warfare in Mari and Early Israel* (Missoula, Mont.: Scholars Press, 1973); Fritz Stolz, *Jahwes und Israels Krieg: Kriegstheorien und Kriegserfahrungen im Glaube des alten Israels* (ATANT 69; Zurich: Theologischer Verlag, 1972); Patrick D. Miller Jr., *The Divine Warrior in Early Israel* (HSM 5; Cambridge: Harvard University Press, 1973; repr., Atlanta: Society of Biblical Literature, 2006); Duane L. Christensen, *Transformations of the War Oracle in Old Testament Prophecy: Studies in the Oracles against the Nations* (HDR 3; Missoula,

In her 1993 work *War in the Hebrew Bible*, Susan Niditch presents an alternative to von Rad's approach. Whereas von Rad had sought to discover and repristinate *the* idea of war that underlies the biblical accounts, Niditch demonstrates that these accounts reflect perspectives and ideologies that are often at odds with each other and that should not be facilely subsumed under a single rubric. Similarly, von Rad had sifted through texts and created a catalogue of the basic features of the institution of holy war.[5] In contrast, Niditch offers exemplary and

---

Mont.: Scholars Press, 1975); Peter C. Craigie, *The Problem of War in the Old Testament* (Grand Rapids: Eerdmans, 1978); Millard C. Lind, *Yahweh Is a Warrior* (Scottsdale, Pa.: Herald, 1980); Moshe Weinfeld, "Divine Intervention in War in Ancient Israel and in the Ancient Near East," in *History, Historiography and Interpretation: Studies in Biblical and Cuneiform Literature* (ed. Hayim Tadmor and Moshe Weinfeld; Jerusalem: Magnes, 1983), 121–47; Edgar W. Conrad, *Fear Not Warrior: A Study of 'al tira' Pericopes in the Hebrew Scriptures* (BJS 75; Chico, Calif.: Scholars Press, 1985); T. Raymond Hobbs, *A Time for War: A Study of Warfare in the Old Testament* (OTS 3; Wilmington, Del.: Glazier, 1989); Sa-Moon Kang, *Divine War in the Old Testament and in the Ancient Near East* (BZAW 177; Berlin: de Gruyter, 1989); Andreas Ruffing, *Jahwekrieg als Weltmetapher: Studien zu Jahwekriegstexten des chronistischen Sondergutes* (SBB 24; Stuttgart: Verlag Katholisches Bibelwerk, 1993); Tremper Longman III and Daniel G. Reid, *God Is a Warrior* (Grand Rapids: Zondervan, 1995); and Eckart Otto, *Krieg und Frieden in der hebräischen Bibel und im alten Orient: Aspekte für eine Friedensordnung in der Moderne* (Theologie und Frieden 18; Stuttgart: Kohlhammer, 1999). Several important articles are also worth mentioning: Manfred Weippert, "'Heiliger Krieg' in Israel und Assyrien: Kritische Anmerkungen zu Gerhard von Rads Konzept des 'Heiligen Krieges im alten Israel,'" *ZAW* 84 (1972): 460–93; Gary N. Knoppers, "'Battling against Yahweh': Israel's War against Judah in 2 Chr. 13:2–20," *RB* 100 (1993): 511–32; idem, "Jerusalem at War in Chronicles," in *Zion, City of Our God* (ed. Richard S. Hess and Gordon J. Wenham; Grand Rapids: Eerdmans, 1999), 55–76. The most incisive critique of von Rad is presented by Knoppers: "In many respects the interpretive option advanced by von Rad presents a false dichotomy. Every holy war is by its very nature spiritual, ritual, and cultic.... Yet in so far as a holy war involves groups of people, weapons, conflict, injury and death, it is also political, social, and martial" ("Jerusalem at War," 74–75).

5. Significantly, he could not isolate one text that includes all of these features; therefore, he simply presented an accumulative list: (1) the sounding of the trumpet as the announcement of the holy war (Judg 3:27; 6:34–35; 1 Sam 13:3); (2) the designation "people of Yhwh" for the army (Judg 5:11, 13; 20:2); (3) the sanctification of the warriors (Josh 3:5; 1 Sam 14:24; 21:6; 2 Sam 1:21; 11:11–12; Num 21:2; Judg 11:36; Deut 23:10–15); (4) sacrifices and/or the consultation of Yhwh (Judg 20:23, 26, 27; 1 Sam 7:9; 13:9–10, 12; 11:4; 14:8–9; 30:4; 2 Sam 5:19, 23); (5) the announcement by Yhwh, "I have given ... into your hand" or similar phraseology (Josh 2:24; 6:2, 16; 8:1, 18; 10:8, 19; Judg 3:28; 4:7, 14; 7:9, 15; 18:10; 20:28; 1 Sam 14:12; 17:46; 23:4; 24:5; 26:8; 1 Kgs 20:28); (6) the announcement that Yhwh goes out before the army (Judg 4:14; Deut 20:4; 2 Sam 5:24; Josh 3:11); (7) the designation of the war as "Yhwh's war" and the enemy as "Yhwh's enemy" (Exod 14:4, 14, 18; Deut 1:30; Josh 10:14, 42; 11:6; 23:10; Judg 20:35; 1 Sam 14:23); (8) the command not to fear (Exod 14:13; Deut 20:3; Josh 8:1; 10:8, 25; 11:6; Judg 7:3; 1 Sam 23:16; 30:6; 2 Sam 10:12); (9) the fear of Yhwh among enemy troops (Exod 15:14–16; 23:27–28; Lev 26:36; Deut 2:25; 11:25; Josh 2:9, 24; 5:1; 7:5; 10:2; 11:20; 24:12; 1 Sam 4:7f–8; 17:11; 28:5); (10) the war-shout (Judg 7:20; Josh 6:5; 1 Sam 17:20, 52); (11) the "ban" (Exod 23:27; Deut 7:23; Josh 10:10, 11; 24:7; Judg 4:15; 7:22; 1 Sam 5:11; 7:10; 14:15, 20); (12) the

sensitive close readings of key war texts that reflect the plurality of the Bible's representations of war. As a testimony to the positive impact of Niditch's approach, the Warfare in Ancient Israel Consultation held at the SBL Annual Meeting has set for itself the goal of fostering the discussion of *all* aspects of ancient Israel's multifarious war traditions.

In this essay I will tread the path paved by Niditch—a path that leads to the central ideas of war in the Bible—by following the varied topography of the biblical texts, rather than flattening their contours into conformity with a one-dimensional map. The topography that I will chart is, however, not just individual accounts attesting the central biblical ideas of war but also the biblical *books* in which these accounts have received their transmitted shape.

Past research has shown little interest in the ideologies of war espoused by individual biblical books.[6] This neglect is surprising, given the fundamentally different notions found, for example, already in Genesis and Exodus. In the former, Israel is born in the land, treaties are made between neighbors (21:22–34; 26:26–33; 31:43–54), disputes over land and water sources (a popular *casus belli*) are resolved by means of physical separation (13:1–18; 26:20–34; 34:1–35:5), and a war is fought for the sake of—not against—one's neighbors (Gen 14).[7] In the latter, Israel has its origins outside the land,[8] wars are fought in the name of or by Israel's God (Exod 14–15; 17), all covenants with the indigenous inhabitants of the land are proscribed (23:32), and the inhabitants themselves are to be wiped

---

dismissal of the troops with the cry, "To your tents, O Israel" (2 Sam 20:1; 1 Kgs 12:16; 22:36). See von Rad, *Der heilige Krieg im alten Israel*, 6–14. The influence of Max Weber's "ideal type" thinking is evident here. That von Rad was directly influenced by Weber's study of holy war in ancient Israel cannot be doubted, given the book's occasional references to *Das antike Judentum*.

     6. Although scholars often compare the conquest ideologies of Joshua and Judges, they rarely study the different ideologies of war in these books. An exception is the book of Chronicles, whose ideas of war have been examined in a number of important studies. See Ingeborg Gabriel, *Friede über Israel: Eine Untersuchung zur Friedenstheologie im Chronik I 10–II 36* (ÖBS 10; Klosternueberg: Österreichisches Katholisches Bibelwerk, 1990); Ruffing, *Jahwekrieg als Weltmetapher*; Knoppers, "Battling against Yahweh;" idem, "Jerusalem at War in Chronicles;" and Philip R. Davies, "Defining the Boundaries of Israel in the Second Temple Period: 2 Chronicles 20 and the 'Salvation Army,'" in *Priests, Prophets, and Scribes: Essays on the Formation and Heritage of Second Temple Judaism in Honour of Joseph Blenkinsopp* (ed. E. Ulrich et al.; JSOTSup 149; Sheffield: JSOT Press, 1992), 43–54.

     7. For important observations on survival strategies in Genesis, see David L. Petersen, "Genesis and Family Values," *JBL* 124 (2005): 5–23.

     8. That Genesis and Exodus have been brought together at a very late stage is argued now by a number of scholars; see most recently, Thomas B. Dozeman and Konrad Schmid, eds., *A Farewell to the Yahwist? The Composition of the Pentateuch in Recent European Interpretation* (SBLSymS 34; Atlanta: Society of Biblical Literature, 2006). Without the redactional concatenation, the books represent different accounts of Israel's origins, one autochthonous and the other allochthonous.

out in battle (23:23–33). Although most books are not as radically different as Genesis and Exodus, they do seem to have their own ideology of war. However, the tendency hitherto has been to lump these ideologies together under book-transcending rubrics, such as "Deuteronomistic" or "Priestly."

Given the desideratum of book-oriented study, this essay undertakes a test-case comparison of two books with respect to a central idea of war. Specifically, it looks at how the books of Judges and Samuel treat the nexus between military leadership and monarchic rule, or the political logic that valor on the battlefield predestines one to assume the throne. In the first section of the essay, I present a general overview of this nexus in ancient Western Asia. I then turn to examine four texts in the books of Judges and Samuel that grapple with the nexus, each in its own way. Finally, I investigate some of the possible reasons for the varying approaches toward this nexus in Judges and Samuel and then consider their implications for the study of war in the Hebrew Bible as a whole.

War and the Military in Ancient Royal Ideology

Rulers in ancient Israel shared with their neighbors throughout the Fertile Crescent a number of strategies with which they legitimated their monopoly of force. One can perhaps distinguish here the medium from the message, although the two are, of course, mutually dependent. Media included various genres of inscriptions and iconographic representations, monumental building projects, personal regalia, retinue and court, processions and rituals, and even day-to-day behavior.[9] The messages communicated via these media were countless and all interconnected. In the ancient Near East, these include varying emphases upon the masculine ruler's divine election or creation in the image of a god, his marriage to a female deity, his indispensable place in the cosmic order, his role in rituals that maintain this order, his responsibility to represent his people vis-à-vis the divine world, his piety, his commitment to social welfare and justice, his wealth, his wisdom, his energy to undertake ambitious building projects, his physical stature and appearance, or simply the continuity between his reign and that of a predecessor.[10] But

---

9. On quotidian behavior, see Erving Goffman, *The Presentation of Self in Everyday Life* (New York: Doubleday, 1959), whose ideas apply even more to the personalities cultivated by rulers. See also the comments of Rodney Barker in *Legitimating Identities: The Self-Presentation of Rulers and Subjects* (Cambridge: Cambridge University Press, 2001), 31.

10. On the topic in general, see the summary given by Gebhard J. Selz, "Über Mesopotamische Herrschaftskonzepte: Zu den Ursprüngen mesopotamischer Herrscherideologie im 3. Jahrtausend," in *Dubsar anta-men: Studien zur Altorientalistik: Festschrift für Willem H. Ph. Römer* (ed. M. Dietrich and O. Loretz; AOAT 253; Münster: Ugarit-Verlag, 1998), 281–344, esp. 322–23; and Ursula Magen, *Assyrische Königsdarstellungen: Aspekte der Herrschaft* (Baghdader Forschungen 9; Mainz: von Zabern, 1986). I refer throughout this paper to the ruler with masculine pronouns, since human kingship in ancient Israel was typically gendered as a male role.

the message the ancient royal courts most often highlighted, and thus apparently regarded as primary, was the king's valor on the battlefield and his special relationship with his deity when fighting his enemies. Thanks to the military might of this divinely appointed "shepherd,"[11] the land enjoyed peace and prosperity during the length of his reign.[12]

The pronounced martial emphasis is witnessed already in the iconography of the earliest civilizations. Thus, the Narmer Palette, one of the world's oldest historical documents (thirty-first century B.C.E.), presents the pharaoh wielding a mace over a kneeling prisoner.[13] Similarly, the Victory Stela of Naram-Sîn, ruler of (one of) Mesopotamia's first empire(s) (twenty-third century B.C.E.), depicts the king flaunting his weapons and standing over his much smaller enemies. Both the Palette and the Stela assign the gods a prominent role.[14]

---

11. On the topos of shepherd, see John W. Waters, "The Political Development and Significance of the Shepherd-King Symbol in the Ancient Near East and in the Old Testament" (Ph.D. diss., Boston University, 1970). In the mid-third millennium, the idea of the king as the shepherd of his people, warding off enemies and tending his flock on pastures, is most beautifully enshrined in an inscription of Lugal-zagesi of Uruk: "From East to West the god Enlil would not have him an opponent. Under his (Lugal-zagesi's) rule, all the lands lie on green pastures—the land Sumer plays before him merrily" (text and translation by Horst Steible, *Die altsumerischen Bau- und Weihinschriften* [2 vols.; Freiburger Altorientalische Studien 5/2; Wiesbaden: Steiner, 1982], 317, no. "Uruk: Luzag. 1"; col II: 12–20).

12. It is important to remember that these messages were addressed to a relatively small circle. For example, in the case of the Neo-Assyrian palace reliefs, it is debatable whether even foreign delegations and official visitors would have had the opportunity to view, and be influenced by, what we consider to be the most important exemplars. This fact may be compared to low levels of literacy, which would have severely limited the effectiveness of royal inscriptions in mass propaganda. With regard to premodern strategies of legitimation, one should avoid dualistic structures of the king versus the subjects. The most important audience of royal self-representations was the intermediary group of the court and officials directly responsible to the king. As Bruno Jobert and Pierre Müller emphasize, rulers legitimate their power first to themselves and their immediate staffs (their "referential hinterland"), and only secondarily to the masses whom they regard as their subjects (*L'État en action: Politiques publiques et corporatismes* [Paris: Presses Universitaires de France, 1987]).

13. For precursors to this motif, see, e.g., Sylvia Schoske, "Das Erschlagen der Feinde: Ikonographie und Stilistik der Feindvernichtung im alten Ägypten," (Ph.D. diss., University of Heidelberg, 1982); and the brief overview by Dietrich Wildung, "Erschlagen der Feinde," *LdÄ* 2:14–17.

14. Moreover, Naram-Sîn was the first king to arrogate to himself a divine status, and on the stela he is portrayed wearing the horned headdress denoting divinity. He referred to himself as "the husband/warrior of Ishtar," the goddess of love and war, and he emphasized the warlike aspect of this deity (*'ashtar annunitum*). On the stela, see Irene Winter, "Sex, Rhetoric, and the Public Monument: The Alluring Body of Naram-Sîn of Agade," in *Sexuality in Ancient Art: Near East, Egypt, Greece, and Italy* (ed. N. B. Kampen; Cambridge: Cambridge University Press, 1996), 11–26. This quality of the divine body of the king is rather close to the idea of the two bodies of the king in mediaeval Europe: Ernst Kantorowicz, *The King's Two Bodies: A Study in*

These ancient images of warriors may be compared to many biblical representations of leaders such as Joshua and David, who display both military valor and a special status vis-à-vis the divine. The closest parallels to the royal ideologies in Mesopotamia and Egypt are, however, found in texts such as Ps 2. Like the Egyptian king, this "son of god" will smash his enemies with an iron mace and "dash them in pieces like a potter's vessel" (2:7–9).[15] More common than this idea of sonship is what we may call the "simultaneity" of the god and the king on the battlefield. This way of thinking is mirrored in Ps 18, which adeptly interweaves poetic threads that describe the fighting god and the fighting king: Yhwh both saves the king from his enemy and equips him to fight for himself.[16]

One of the reasons why ancient kings were so fond of depicting themselves as great warriors is that their power-bases commonly viewed victories on the battlefield as divine confirmation of the king's rule.[17] Enemy attacks, along with famine, plagues, and other catastrophes, were accordingly dangerous for a ruler

---

Mediaeval Political Theology (2nd ed., Princeton: Princeton University Press, 1966). The deification of Naram-Sîn of Akkade can be pinned down to a historical event: when "the Four Corners of the World" rose in rebellion against him and his city Akkade, he victoriously fought "nine campaigns in one year" and saved Akkade from destruction. Gratefully, the city fathers of Akkade asked the gods for permission to worship Naram-Sîn as "god of their city." Thereafter his name was written with a divine determinative and a temple was built for him in Akkade. See the summary given Walther Sallaberger and Aage Westenholz, *Mesopotamien: Akkade-Zeit und Ur III-Zeit* (ed. P. Attinger and M. Wäfler; OBO 160; Göttingen: Vandenhoeck & Ruprecht, 1999), 51–54. The idea of the divine nature of the king can be traced back to the middle of the third millennium. In the "Stela of the Vultures," Eannatum, prince of Lagash, is portrayed as engendered by the city god Nin-Girsu himself, adopted by Inanna-Ishtar, the goddess of war, and nursed by the mother-goddess Nin-Hursag. That is why he grows into a giant warrior of five cubits tall, able and ready to subdue the enemy country to his lord Nin-Girsu (text and translation in Steible, *Die altsumerischen Bau- und Weihinschriften*, 120ff., no. "Ean. 1"; esp. col. IV: 9–V:17).

15. On the ruler's divine sonship in biblical literature (e.g., Ps 89:27; 2 Sam 7:14; Isa 9:6), see the seminal article by Gerhard von Rad, "Das judäische Königsritual," *TLZ* 72 (1947): 211–15; as well as Hellmut Brunner, *Die Geburt des Gottkönigs: Studien zur Überlieferung eines altägyptischen Mythos* (Wiesbaden: Harrossowitz, 1986); Eckart Otto, "Ps 2 in neuassyrischer Zeit: Assyrische Motive in der judäischen Königsideologie," in *Textarbeit: Studien zu Texten und ihrer Rezeption aus dem Alten Testament und der Umwelt Israels: Festschrift für Peter Weimar* (ed. K. Kiesow and T. Meurer; AOAT 294; Münster: Ugarit-Verlag, 2003), 335–49; and Markus Saur, *Die Königspsalmen: Studien zur Entstehung und Theologie* (BZAW 340; Berlin: de Gruyter, 2004), 25–46. For the Neo-Assyrian parallels to the phrase "dash in pieces," see Bob Becking, "'Wie Töpfe Sollst Du Sie Zerschmeissen': Mesopotamische Parallelen zu Psalm 2,9b," *ZAW* 102 (1990): 56–79, here 63–78. For the dating of the iron mace to the eighth century b.c.e. and later, see Andre Lemaire, "'Avec un Sceptre De Fer' : Ps. II,9 et l'archéologie," *BN* 32 (1986): 25–30.

16. See Klaus-Peter Adam, *Der königliche Held: Die Entsprechung von kämpfendem Gott und kämpfendem König im Psalm 18* (WMANT 19; Neukirchen-Vluyn: Neukirchener, 2001).

17. See Mario Liverani, *Prestige and Interest: International Relations in the Near East ca. 1600–1100 B.C.* (History of the Ancient Near East 1; Padova: Sargon, 1990), 150–71.

insofar as these same power-bases could interpret them as punishment for the king's failure to comport himself in keeping with the expectations of a deity or deities. An ancient monarch thus had a vested interest in presenting an image of a leader who witnessed success on his campaigns.

Such "theological" motivations for the emphasis on military prowess must be balanced by a consideration of other factors that are more sociopolitical in nature. The power-base of a ruler was usually already convinced that secure borders and access to resources abroad constituted the preconditions for domestic prosperity. By emphasizing military prowess, the court hoped to demonstrate that the king was indeed capable of securing the borders and ensuring a free flow of resources (both human and material).

Whereas past treatments of kingship in Israel and Judah discuss at length the mythological and cultic aspects, they often give short shrift to these more pragmatic, political factors. Yet one should not lose sight of the evidence witnessing to the sociopolitical importance of the military in Israelite and Judean society. For example, the books of Samuel and Kings, in passages that likely stem from annals and source material, refer to a number of instances of usurpation. Of these, most may be described as military putsches. They are set in scenes of military engagement (battles, sieges, or the camp), and the usurpers are supported by the armed forces or identified as high-ranking officers. With so many Israelite kings owing their office to the military, one would expect royal ideology to be bellic in character.

Putsches in Israel

Name	Text	Location	Office/Title
1. Absalom b. David	2 Sam 15–19	Hebron	none
2. Sheba b. Bichri	2 Sam 20	Abel of Beth-Maacah	none
3. Adonijah b. Haggith	1 Kgs 1–2	none	none
4. Baasha b. Ahijah of the house of Issachar	1 Kgs 15:25–32	during the siege of Gibbethon of the Philistines	none
5. Zimri	16:8–14	the palace at Tirzah	the king's "servant, commander of half of the chariotry"
6. Omri	16:15–20	while encamped at Gibbethon of the Philistines	"the army commander"

7. Tibni b. Ginath	16:21–22	none	none
8. Jehu b. Jehoshaphat b. Nimshi	2 Kgs 9:1–10:17	Ramoth-gilead	an "army commander" (status not clear)
9. Shallum b. Jabesh	15:8–13	either "in public" or "at Keblaam/Ibleam"	none
10. Menahem b. Gadi	15:14–16	Samaria	none
11. Pekah b. Remaliah	15:23–29	Samaria	the king's šališ
12. Hoshea b. Elah	15:30–31	none	none

This is not the only evidence indicating that the military played a central role in Israelite society as a whole. The Kurkh Monolith inscription of Shalmaneser III ascribes two thousand chariots to the Omride armies. Even if the author of the inscription has exaggerated the size of the chariot units, as often suggested, the human and natural resources necessary for the support of even five hundred chariots would have been considerable.[18] Indeed, the chariot-equine industry would have represented one of the most substantial sectors of the economy. Not only do horses create exorbitant costs in water, feed, stables, training grounds, and trainers, but also the manufacture of chariots required expensive materials and technological know-how.[19] Given their central place in Israelite society, we can appreciate why the biblical authors identify one of the usurpers of the throne as "the commander of half of the chariotry" (1 Kgs 16:8).

Chariots also represented prestige objects and powerful aspects of the monarch's self-image. This point is illustrated by 2 Sam 15:1 and 1 Kgs 1:5. In their bids for the throne, the first thing that Absalom and Adonijah do is to acquire a chariot as well as horses and fifty runners. Furthermore, the biblical passages that polemicize against (foreign) kings often refer to chariots (see Exod 14; Josh 11; Judg 4–5). One should also not forget that both the "law of the king" in 1 Sam 8 and the circumscription of royal prerogatives in Deut 17 link kingship first and foremost to the costs invested in chariots and horses.

Adding to the textual evidence, Rüdiger Schmitt has helpfully collected various representations of royal power in the iconographic materials from Iron Age

---

18. See, however, Deborah O. Cantrell (chs. 36 and 37) in *Megiddo IV: The 1998–2002 Seasons* (ed. I. Finkelstein et al.; Emery and Claire Yass Publications in Archaeology; Monograph Series of the Institute of Archaeology 24; Tel Aviv: Tel Aviv University, 2006).

19. See the evidence collected by Anja Herold, *Streitwagentechnologie in der Ramses-Stadt: Bronze an Pferd und Wagen* (Forschungen in der Ramses-Stadt; Die Grabungen des Pelizaeus-Museums Hildesheim in Qantir–Pi–Ramesse 2; Maniz: von Zabern, 1999).

II Israel and Judah.[20] Among the seals and seal impressions, several from IA IIB Hazor, Tel Dan, and Gezer depict chariots,[21] while a handful from Judah portray a galloping horse.[22] These images may be compared to other martial motifs, such as what seems to be the king or a royal official striking a bound captive found on some seals.[23] Also noteworthy are the two *sr hʿyr* impressions from IA IIC Judah showing the king with bow and arrows standing adjacent to an official with a raised right hand.[24]

THE NEXUS OF MILITARY LEADER AND KING IN FOUR BIBLICAL NARRATIVES

Having briefly examined some of the historical evidence for the place of war and the military in the societies and monarchic ideologies of the ancient Near East, we may now focus our attention on the biblical material and observe how it consistently presents a collective body—either a territory, Israel as a whole, or the militia—appointing its war leader to be its ruler in peacetime. Here we will confine the discussion to four accounts, two from Judges and two from Samuel.

The first—and perhaps best—example of a military hero becoming king is the story of David's rise to power. After David fells Goliath, the women of Israel come out to greet the returning troops. Their song, "Saul has slain his thousands, and David his myriads,"[25] causes great concern for the reigning king, who remarks: "All that remains for [David] is the kingdom!" (1 Sam 18:6–9). The cynical statement proves prophetic as the narrative unfolds, and in 2 Sam 5 all the tribes of Israel come to Hebron in order to anoint David. When explaining their

---

20. Rüdiger Schmitt, *Bildhafte Herrschaftsrepräsentation im eisenzeitlichen Israel* (AOAT 283; Münster: Ugarit-Verlag, 2001).

21. See the discussion in ibid., 114–16.

22. Ibid, 127–30. Chariots and horses, as well as warriors, are especially popular motifs in the iconography of the Aramean or Neo-Hittite states; see Paul Dion, *Les Araméens à l'âge du fer: Histoire politique et structures sociales* (EBib NS 34; Paris: Gabalda, 1997), images 1–21.

23. Schmitt, *Bildhafte*, 28, 110–13

24. Ibid, 166–68 The weapons are here attributes of royal power, which have been interpreted as being presented to the official in an investiture or delegation rite. However, the raised hand of the official represents more likely an expression of loyalty. In contrast to the official, the king displays his weapons as a sign of his ultimate authority.

25. When isolated from its context and Saul's interpretation, it is not clear that the song attributes greater military success to David. רבבות ("myriads") may simply represent an attempt to find a parallel to אלפים ("thousands"). Nevertheless, the fact that the women sing David's praises along with those of Saul would have sufficed to cause consternation for the latter. By portraying the song as both instilling fear in Saul and being heard beyond Israel's borders (1 Sam 21:11; 29:5), the authors of Samuel affirm the political and social power of the collective memory of war inscribed in these songs composed and performed by women. See Exod 15:21 and Judg 11:34, as well as the article by Carol Meyers, "Of Drums and Damsels: Women's Performance in Ancient Israel," *BA* 54 (1991): 16–27.

decision, they refer to his past military exploits: "Long before now, when Saul was king over us, you were the one who led Israel to war and brought it back" (5:2).[26] Even though Saul was formally the incumbent on the throne, David was de facto Israel's king because he behaved as such by leading the nation into battle.[27] The Israelite tribes significantly do not present David's divine election as the first and primary motivation for their decision to anoint him. Rather, they begin by affirming their common kinship (5:1),[28] then recall David's proven record on the battlefield (5:2a), and only thereafter refer to divine approbation: "And Yhwh said to you: 'You shall shepherd my people Israel; you shall be ruler [נגיד] of Israel'" (5:2b).

The second example of a war leader assuming the throne is 1 Sam 11. This account portrays how Saul, by means of a graphic threat, galvanizes Israel into a unified force that succeeds in vanquishing the Ammonites.[29] Thereafter, the entire force goes to Gilgal and declares their hero king (v. 15). When read as the continuation of chapter 10, the narrative evinces the structure of a ring composition of A-B-X-B'-A'.[30]

---

26. When first expressing their desire for a king in 1 Sam 8, the people assign a military function ("go out before us [ויצא לפנינו]; cf. והמוציא והמביא את ישראל] and fight our battles," v. 20) to the two primary tasks of a monarch. In 2 Sam 5:2, David is not just "the one who led Israel to war" (המוציא) but also "the one who brought it back" (המביא), which means that he was successful. Going to war is one thing; coming home is another.

27. Performance is central to royal legitimation strategies. The king must not just claim to be wise but must also demonstrate wisdom in action, as Solomon does in 1 Kgs 3. The same goes for performance in rituals, sacrifices, and even succession: being the legitimate successor does not suffice; the ruler must also behave as one's predecessor. When one conducts himself as a king, one runs the risk of arousing suspicion of monarchic aspirations (see, e.g., 2 Sam 15:1–6; Neh 6:1–9).

28. Compare the criterion of kinship for the appointment of a king in Deut 17:15.

29. The parity between Saul's curse and its effect does not escape the reader's attention: The cattle of the one who does not "go out to battle" will be cut up into multiple pieces. In the end, all the people "go out to battle as one man." Instead of the one becoming many, the many become one. Furthermore, it is possible that the team (צמד) of cattle (v. 7) in Saul's symbolic act stands for Israel and Judah, who are numbered in the following verse (300,000 Israelites and 30,000 Judeans). An older version of the chapter seems, however, to have referred only to Israel (see vv. 3, 7, 13, 15). Indeed, it is possible that the whole or most of vv. 6–8 has been added by a later hand in order to emphasize the pan-Israelite involvement in the battle. Without this scene, Saul (see "he said" in v. 9 LXX) promises deliverance to the messengers and later leads either his own troops (העם) or those of Jabesh-gilead (11:11). For similar proposals, see Reinhard G. Kratz, *Die Komposition der erzählenden Bücher des Alten Testaments* (Götttingen: Vandehhoeck & Ruprecht, 2000), 176, n. 80.

30. For a somewhat different structural analysis, see Joshua Berman, *Narrative Analogy in the Hebrew Bible: Battle Stories and Their Equivalent Non-battle Narratives* (VTSup 103; Leiden: Brill, 2004), 102–14.

A. Saul is anointed and proclaimed king at Mizpah (10:1–26)

    B. Certain scoundrels scorn Saul and ask, "Can this guy save us?" (10:27)

        X. The battle of Jabesh-Gilead (11:1–11)

    B'. The people desire to kill those who had formerly scorned Saul, and Saul attributes the "salvation" to YHWH (11:12–13)

A'. At Gilgal "the kingship" is "renewed" (11:14–15)

This structure seems to have emerged gradually in the composition of 1 Sam 9–11 and to have taken its point of departure from an older narrative in 11:1–11, 15*. Accordingly, the statement in verse 14 represents an attempt by a later author of the chapter to explain why the people crown Saul again after they had just proclaimed, "Long live the king!" (10:24). In order to resolve the tension and to explain Samuel's absence in the activities of 11:15–16, the redactor presents the prophet as taking the initiative to "renew" or "inaugurate" (חדש, piel) the monarchy (11:14).[31] The following line reads, "And all the people ... made Saul king there before YHWH." After 11:14, however, we would expect to read instead that they followed Samuel's advice and "renewed the monarchy."[32] The paragraph in 11:12–13, which continues the thought begun in 10:27, appears to be a further attempt to harmonize chapters 10 and 11. Everything in the account has been shaped with 11:15–16 in view. Because Saul demonstrates military leadership and rescues the inhabitants of Jabesh-Gilead, he is rewarded with a royal title. The insertion of 11:12–13, along with chapters 9–10 upon which the paragraph depends, robs the account of this climax by already referring to Saul as king.[33] Nevertheless, it permits this figure to respond to the people's thinking and to affirm that he does not deserve the royal title because of his prowess on the battlefield: "For today YHWH has brought salvation [תשועה] to Israel" (11:13b).[34]

---

31. For an alternative explanation, see Diana Vikander Edelman, *King Saul in the Historiography of Judah* (JSOTSup 121; Sheffield: JSOT Press, 1991), 65, and the older literature cited there.

32. The LXX offers a more unified edition of verses 14–15, in which Samuel is the subject of the final three clauses, yet it still does not report that the kingdom was renewed in Gilgal. Instead, it reads: "And all the people went to Galgala, and Samuel anointed [ἔχρισεν] Saul there to be king before the Lord in Galgala...."

33. Already Julius Wellhausen pointed out the tensions between chapters 10 and 11: (1) the soldiers who joined Saul in 10:26 seem no longer to be at his disposal in ch. 11; (2) the messengers do not come to Gibeah because of Saul, which is surprising if he had already been proclaimed king of Israel; (3) he is plowing in the field, a task usually left to servants (of kings); (4) when he comes home, no one behaves as if the news was meant more for him than anyone else, and he must inquire about the cause for the mourning. See *Die Composition des Hexateuchs und der historischen Bücher des Alten Testaments* (3rd ed.; Berlin: Reimer, 1899), 241.

34. The verse both responds to the question in 10:27 ("Can this guy save us? [מה ישענו זה])

As for the two cases in the book of Judges, both Gideon and Jephthah are not described as kings. However, their status is comparable to that of Saul and David insofar as a collective body or its representatives give power and authority to them as a reward for military leadership. Jephthah is unique among the four insofar as the body that makes him their ruler is Gilead rather than Israel as a whole.³⁵ A further distinction is that the elders of Gilead already make a pact to make Jephthah chieftain (ראש) before he goes to battle.

Spurned by the Gileadites, Jephthah had pursued an existence on the periphery of society by forming a band and marauding in the land of Tob. Now faced with Ammonite aggression, the elders of Gilead recognize their need for Jephthah's martial skills and plead with him to be their leader: "Come be our commander [קצין], so that we can fight the Ammonites" (11:6). The text recounts at length the protracted negotiations, and it seems quite possible that here an older story line has been amplified to create a pendant to the negotiations between Israel and Yhwh in 10:10–16. The parallelism between to the two chapters is difficult to mistake: just as the Gileadites had no need for Jephthah until the outbreak of military conflict, so the Israelites had abandoned Yhwh as long as they did not require Yhwh "to save" (להושיע) them. As illustrated below, the two sides of the accounts are bound together by the promise made by the Gileadite officers: "The man who is the first to fight the Ammonites will be chieftain over all the inhabitants of Gilead" (10:18).³⁶

    A. Negotiations with Yhwh (10:10–16)

        B. War with the Ammonites (10:17)

            X. Introduction to Jephthah (10:18–11:3)

        B'. War with Ammonites (11:4)

    A'. Negotiations with Jephthah (11:5–10)

---

and defines the author of the "salvation" (תשועה) in 11:9. See also 9:16 and 10:1, where the primary responsibility of King Saul is to "save" Israel from the hand from its enemies.

35. 1 Sam 11 may also have originally presented Saul as being proclaimed king solely by the army; see n. 29 above.

36. See the similar prebattle agreement in Judg 1:12. The beginning of the fight against the Ammonites may be compared to a similar expression in 13:5 with respect to the Philistines. The wars against the Ammonites and Philistines play particularly important roles in the solidification of the reigns of Saul and David, and it is likely that the authors of these passages had the book of Samuel in view. Although Reinhard Müller makes this point, he interprets it as evidence for a promonarchic stance of the book of Judges: what the judges just begin is finished during the monarchy (see *Königtum und Gottesherrschaft: Untersuchungen zur alttestamentlichen Monarchiekritik* [FAT 2/3; Tübingen: Mohr Siebeck, 2004], 64–68). This may, however, be an overinterpretation of the evidence, since one can easily read it the other way around.

In contrast to this neat ring-compositional structure, the narrative surroundings are much messier. It is true that, prior to the negotiations with Yhwh in 10:10–16, the Israelites suffer defeat in war, whereas after the negotiations with Jephthah, the Gileadites vanquish their enemies. However, the situation is not *in statu quo res erant ante bellum*, to use an old peace-treaty expression. The victory is severely mitigated, both by Jephthah's oath (11:30–40) and intertribal jealousy that breaks out into internecine war between Gilead and Ephraim (12:1–6).

Although the Gideon story resembles the Jephthah story by casting a dark shadow upon the feat of the war hero,[37] it also differs significantly from it with respect to the nexus between military leadership and monarchic rule. Immediately after Gideon consummates his war against the Midianites by slaying two of their kings (8:21), the men of Israel petition him: "Rule over us—you, your son, and your grandson as well, for you have saved us [הושעתנו] from the Midianites" (8:22). Whereas Saul had attributed "salvation" (תשועה) to Yhwh yet nevertheless reigned as king, Gideon does not deny that he "saved" Israel yet attributes sole sovereignty to Yhwh.[38] Moreover, the men of Israel are willing to grant authority and power to their war hero as well as his sons and grandsons. The reward is nothing less than Israel's self-commitment to submit to a dynasty of rulers as payment for Gideon's subjugation of their perennial (see 6:1–6) enemies. The Israelites' commitment to dynastic rule is rather surprising, since this narrative and those examined above emphasize performance as the precondition for the occupation of the throne.

Although the term "king" (מלך) does not occur in the account, the monarchic principle is undeniable. In response to the Israelites' petition, Gideon states, "I will not rule over you, nor shall my son rule over you. For it is Yhwh who rules over you." The use of "rule" (משל) has most likely been influenced by the use of the term in the story of Abimelech (9:2), whom the book of Judges presents as Gideon's/Jerubbaal's son. Although Gideon rejects the offer to rule over Israel and claims that Yhwh alone rules, he offers an alternative that serves *ad maiorem gloriam Gedeonis*: the representation of the divine ruler, which Gideon makes with

---

37. Cf. also the transition of the larger framework to the Gideon story proper (6:11 with 11:1), as well as the Ephraimite episodes (8:1–3 with 12:1–6).

38. Much of this irony can be explained as the product of a redaction in 1 Sam 11, since the older narrative already presented Saul becoming king and later authors attempted to reorient the narrative by having Saul attribute the "salvation" to Yhwh. An additional explanation for the irony is found in extensive theological reflection in the introduction to the Gideon account. Yhwh begins by commanding, "Go in this strength of yours and save Israel from the hand of the Midianites…" (6:14). Although Gideon is here a "valiant warrior" (see 6:12), his response presents a different image: "Please, my lord, how can I save Israel? Why, my clan is the humblest in Manasseh, and I am the youngest in my father's household" (6:15). The reason for Gideon's success is then spelled out: "Yhwh replied, 'Because I will be with you and you will strike the Midianites, every one of them!'" (6:16). See also Judg 5:36–37.

the earrings taken as booty as well as the royal robes and jewelry of the Midianite kings, rests in "his city" (בעירו) of Ophrah. The account manifests several parallels to the story of the golden calf in Exod 32. In both, the main protagonist (either Aaron or Gideon) beckons the Israelites to give them their earrings (cf. the wording of Exod 32:2 with Judg 8:24), and from these they "make" a symbol of divinity.[39] In Judg 8, the divine symbol becomes a "snare" (מוקש) especially for Gideon and his "house," a term with associations to the kind of ruler dynasties that had just been rejected.

To summarize our findings thus far, each of the four accounts presents an individual who had demonstrated military leadership and prowess assuming the position of preeminent ruler. For the collective groups from which these rulers emerge, war is such an overriding concern that they pay an extremely high political price to one who promises to guarantee victory and peace. In 2 Sam 5:1–3 the Israelite elders are willing to give Saul's throne to his former political opponent, while in the three remaining accounts the price involves nothing less than a transformation of the political and social order: decentralized, pluralistic political bodies transfer authority and decision-making prerogatives to a single individual. A military leader's newly achieved authority is institutionalized by popular choice. In the case of Gideon, the Israelites even obligate themselves to a dynasty in return for a warrior's subjugation of their enemies. What is striking about our accounts is that the groups pay the price so readily and willingly. The authors seem to presuppose—or are making the claim—that definitive conquest in wartime and supreme rule in peacetime belong in a politically logical sequence.[40]

---

39. For the connections to Exod 32, see Uwe Becker, *Richterzeit und Königtum: Redaktionsgeschichtliche Studien zum Richterbuch* (BZAW 192; Berlin: de Gruyter, 1990), 181.

40. To be distinguished from these accounts are the notices of military putsches, which are discussed above. The differences between the two literary representations are instructive. In the former, a collective political entity, such as the elders of Israel, crowns a military hero (2 Sam 5:1–3). In the latter, a military leader assumes the throne by means of force and coercion. Whereas the first type of accounts serves the interests of the ruler because it emphasizes the consent of the ruled, an account of a coup d'état most often stems from a source critical of the ruler. From the perspective of the military coup itself, however, the same principle of recognition for achievement or valor can be at work on a smaller scale. Within the confined group of the army, the one who distinguishes himself in battle, or at least succeeds in presenting himself as a worthy military leader, rises to the top. In a society in which the military exerts great influence, this figure often assumes control of the civil government or throne. The putsch presupposes the existence of a (powerful) professional military. In the biblical representations of early Israel, this social group is not yet formed. Instead, all able-bodied men are expected to participate in the national militia. Based upon the "democratic" principle that all who fight have a right of *suffragium* in the assembly (for Greece, see Pierre Vidal-Naquet, *The Black Hunter: Forms of Thought and Forms of Society in the Ancient World* [trans. A. Szegedy-Maszak; Baltimore: Johns Hopkins University Press, 1986], 85–105), several biblical texts present the army as the body politic that determines who rules in peacetime. Thus, 1 Sam 11

Divine Rule and Its Relationship to War in Judges and Samuel

As noted above, many biblical and extrabiblical texts reflect the notion that in times of war the king enjoyed a special relationship with his god, which can be described as the simultaneity between the fighting god and the fighting king. We also observed that many of the accounts of warriors becoming rulers employ the term "to save" (ישע, hiphil). These passages may be compared to a number of texts that describe a deity "saving" the king as the representative of his people.[41] In turning now to an examination of how the books of Judges and Samuel treat the nexus between martial valor and kingship, we begin by observing the reservations expressed in the Tanakh with respect to the simultaneity of the fighting king and god as well as human kingship as a whole.

In the depiction of the formative period in the books of Genesis to Judges, most kings are foreign rulers who threaten Israel's existence. The point is perhaps most salient in the book of Joshua. It uses the word "king" no less than seventy times, and in each case it refers to foreign rulers whom the Israelites vanquish under the leadership of a nonmonarchic war leader. The only pentateuchal book that refers to Israel's own king is Deuteronomy, and it significantly assigns no military role to his office (17:14–20).

In delineating the rules of engagement, Deut 20 describes the army in terms that mirror the book's unique ideal of Israelite society.[42] It refers to a national militia (rather than a standing army, 20:2–3) and temporally appointed generals (20:9), yet never even mentions the king, the most important figure in the armies of ancient Western Asia. With respect to the chariots of foreign armies (20:1), the priests are commanded to address the fears these armies arouse among the Israelite forces by proclaiming before battle that "it is YHWH your God who marches with you to fight against your enemy for you, to save [להושיע] you" (20:4). In contrast to many psalms and extrabiblical texts, YHWH accompanies Israel in battle and saves the people as a whole rather than just the king. And instead of saving Israel through the person of the king, YHWH fights alone.

---

links העם (11:11–12) as the troops to כל העם (11:15) who crown Saul king (see כל העם for the armed forces who proclaim Omri king in the war-camp in 1 Kgs 16:16–17). Similarly, the Gideon story links איש ישראל who show up to fight (before the reduction to 300 men; 7:8) to the same איש ישראל who petition Gideon to rule over them (8:22). To this, one may compare accounts of military putsches originating on the battlefield (see the table above and especially example 2). Hence, the two types of accounts are after all quite similar.

41. For example the Mesha Stela line 4 reads: כי השעני מכל המלכן, "For he [Kemosh] saved me from all kings" (adapted from William F. Albright, "Palestinian Inscriptions," *ANET*, 320–22). Among the older references in the Psalms, see 18:4 and 21:2.

42. The development of a standing army and expensive weaponry like chariots was one of the main catalysts for social stratification in ancient societies; see my *War and the Formation of Society in Ancient Israel* (New York: Oxford University Press, forthcoming).

As often in the Bible, the rules of engagement ground their trust in Yhwh on the experience of the exodus (Deut 20:1). The account of this first and most important war in Israel's collective memory concludes: "Thus Yhwh saved [ויושע] Israel that day from the Egyptians" (Exod 14:30). In affirming Yhwh as Israel's primordial and eternal king, the biblical authors depict this deity as the divine warrior who, beginning with the first national war at the Sea of Reeds, "saves" Israel from its enemies. While many texts, especially those found in the book of Psalms, draw a correlation between the divine and human warriors, others drive a schism between the two, rendering thereby Israel's human warrior-king dispensable. As expected, the Song of the Sea, which ascribes "salvation" (ישועה) to the divine warrior (Exod 15:2; see also 14:13), ends by proclaiming the deity's kingship: "Yhwh will reign [ימלך] for ever and ever!" (15:18). In this pivotal account, a human pendant to the Egyptian king is absent among the Israelite armies.

The four stories in Judges and Samuel considered above evince a similar structure: a hero "saves" a collective body from their enemies, and the collective body in turn makes (or attempts to make) him their ruler in peacetime. Yet we also notice two fundamental differences between these two books. The first has to do with the attitude toward kingship itself. With respect to the monarchy, the book of Samuel is highly ambivalent. For the most part, the book embraces the office and the various ideologies of monarchic rule supporting it. Although 1 Sam 8 and 12 are critical of Israel's desire for a human king, presenting it as a rejection of Yhwh's kingship, these texts do not completely reject the monarchy as a political option.[43] In contrast to Samuel's presentation of military heroes becoming kings, the book of Judges portrays Yhwh as commissioning temporary saviors and judges who rescue Israel from its enemies.[44] To a greater measure than the book of Samuel, the authors of Judges cast dark shadows on any attempt by a military hero to acclaim too much honor (= political capital) for himself. Thus, when Deborah agrees to accompany Barak into battle, she warns him that "there will be no glory for you in the course you are taking, for Yhwh will deliver Sisera into the hands of a woman" (4:9). As already pointed out, the conclusion to the Gideon story links an episode of apostasy to Israel's decision to establish a dynastic line of rulers proceeding from Gideon (8:22–27). The accounts of Abimelech

---

43. For a diachronic analysis of the attitude of the book of Samuel to the monarchy, see the classic works by Timo Veijola, *Die ewige Dynastie: David und die Entstehung seiner Dynastie nach der deuteronomistischen Darstellung* (Suomalainen Tiedeakatemia Toimituksia 193; Helsinki: Suomalainen Tiedeakatemia, 1975); and idem, *Das Königtum in der Beurteilung der deuteronomistischen Historiographie: Eine redaktionsgeschichtliche Untersuchung* (Suomalainen Tiedeakatemia Toimituksia 198; Helsinki: Suomalainen Tiedeakatemia, 1977); and the recent critique of these studies in Müller, *Königtum*, 1–11.

44. Insightful studies of the formation of Judges have been undertaken, inter alia, by Yairah Amit, *The Book of Judges: The Art of Editing* (trans. J. Chipman; BibInt 38; Leiden: Brill, 1998); and Becker, *Richterzeit und Königtum*.

and Jephthah are even more critical of this drive for power. Either the authors of the book had stories at their disposal that perfectly suited their purposes, or they have reworked older sagas to present the male protagonists (in stark contrast to the female protagonists) attempting to arrogate supreme rule to themselves and thereafter meeting tragic ends.[45]

The second fundamental difference between Judges and Samuel relates to the reason for war. In Judges, Israel's sin constantly forms the ultimate *casus belli*. As spelled out in the prooemium to the book (2:11–23), the people turn from Yhwh and worship the gods of their neighbors; in turn, Yhwh punishes them with war. In keeping with this overarching principle, the book never presents war as a natural political phenomenon. It is rather always directly related to Israel's prior transgressions. In stark contrast to Judges, the book of Samuel never ascribes a punitive function to war but presents it as an unavoidable evil, a constant of the human condition. In the first account of war, the narrator simply states that Israel "went out to meet the Philistines in battle" (1 Sam 4:1). The Philistines do not attack the Israelites, as they and others do in Judges.[46] Nor is the appearance of the enemy linked to "the evil in the sight of Yhwh," as it is in Judg 13:1. Similarly, the Ammonite aggression is not elicited by Israel's sin. Nahash simply goes up and besieges Jabesh Gilead (1 Sam 11:1).[47] Nowhere are we told, as in Judges (see 10:7; cf. 3:12–13), that the Ammonites are sent to execute retribution for offenses against Yhwh. Most other battles in Samuel are initiated by Saul and David in the process of consolidating their reigns. The only times war is presented as punishment is in Samuel's speech recalling the period of the Judges (1 Sam 12:9–11).

These two aspects of the narratives in Judges and Samuel are intimately connected. As pointed out above, valor on the battlefield is the most popular way of legitimating monarchic rule in both biblical and extrabiblical evidence from the ancient Near East. The book of Samuel links war directly to the origins and chief responsibility of Israel's kings. After the people voice their desire for a king, Samuel describes the role of the king with reference to many military functions (1 Sam 8:11–18). Thereafter, the people affirm that a king would make them like all the nations insofar as he would both judge them and fight their battles (8:20). Similarly, as observed above, the Israelite men defend their decision to anoint

---

45. The final section of the book may represent an attempt to harmonize this tenor of the book with the narrative of Samuel inasmuch as it describes the chaos that characterized an era without a king (17:6; 18:1; 19:1; 21:25). This promonarchic section, however, never portrays wars with Israel's external enemies. Like 1 Sam 8:1–5, it links (the lack of) human kingship to rising internal social abuses and in this way implicitly assigns the monarchy the task of establishing justice within society. However one interprets this section, it throws in sharp relief the stance vis-à-vis the monarchy in the first sixteen chapters.

46. See, however, 1 Sam 13:5; 29:1–11; 31:1; 2 Sam 5:17–18, 22.

47. Also, the longer reading provided by the Cave 4 text from Qumran does not mention any transgression on the part of Israel.

David as king by referring not least to his military leadership (2 Sam 5:1–3). Further examples are not wanting. Indeed, the book of Samuel depicts all the actions of Saul and David in the contexts of various battles and wars. These figures consolidate their reigns in wartime. Inasmuch as war provides the *raison d'être* for kingship in this book, war must be presented as essential rather than accidental to Israel's historical experience (to use Aristotelian language).

In contrast to Samuel, the book of Judges assigns a punitive function to war. Because sin constitutes the *causa sine qua non* of war, there is no need for a king. Israel simply needs to desist from its unfaithfulness. Gideon's rejection of the offer to establish a dynastic rule over Israel therefore does not represent a peripheral idea but instead an elaboration of the book's central message. Similarly, the judges and saviors do not represent kings on a smaller scale but rather reconfigurations of the monarchic institution.[48] They are appointed for a period of time to perform the task of rescuing Israel from its enemies. According to the book, they do not organize professional armies, nor do they radically change the face of Israelite society. Because the land had already been conquered during the days of Joshua, they do not need to expand national territory. Instead, they must simply guard the divinely achieved—and, because of sin, temporarily forfeited—status quo.[49] Thus, after Othniel subjugates Cushan-rishathaim, the land has rest (שקט, qal; 3:11; see also 3:30; 5:31; 8:28). Moreover, the book reports repeatedly that the judges "save" Israel without referring to their subsequent enthronement. In this way, the book breaks the natural nexus between military valor and monarchic rule. Even Yhwh, who is celebrated as Israel's warrior in Judg 4–5, is not proclaimed king, which contrasts starkly with the very similar account of Exod 14–15.[50] In the story of

---

48. Just as much as Israel's early kings in the book of Samuel, the judges are almost completely consumed with military tasks (the chief exception is Deborah in 4:5). Yet in contrast to Samuel, the book of Judges does not present Israel's military heroes becoming kings and in this way disassociates the role of military deliverer from dynastic ruler.

49. This point applies, of course, to an earlier edition of the book, before the addition of 1:1–2:5 reporting the failure to drive out the inhabitants of the land. The older introduction begins in 2:6–9 with a *Wiederaufnahme* of the conclusion to the book of Joshua and identifies Israel's enemies with its neighbors round about (2:14), not with the former inhabitants in its midst, as in 1:1–2:5. Although the redactional framework of each story can be divided according to this criterion, the stories themselves often cannot insofar as they constitute to a large extent older, pre-edited material. For literary analyses of the end of Joshua and the beginning of Judges, see Erhard Blum, "Der kompositionelle Knoten am Übergang von Josua zu Richter: Ein Entflechtungsvorschlag," in *Deuteronomy and Deuteronomic Literature: Festschrift C. H. W. Brekelmans* (ed. M. Vervenne and J. Lust; BETL 133; Leuven: Leuven University Press, 1997), 181–212. The protection of the status quo also characterizes Samuel's work in 1 Sam 7 (esp. v. 14, which describes the return of the towns and territory taken by the Philistines), which is heavily influenced by the book of Judges.

50. For a comparison of these two accounts, see Alan Jon Hauser, "Two Songs of Victory: A Comparison of Exodus 15 and Judges 5," in *Directions in Biblical Hebrew Poetry* (ed. E. R.

Gideon, the book of Judges treats the problem explicitly by portraying the military hero rejecting the offer to establish a dynastic rule (8:22–23). In addition to the explicitly antimonarchic account of Abimelech (Judg 9), the story of Jephthah, in treating the case of a warrior who becomes the head of society, describes the high price paid for this position: a tragic vow as well as internecine jealousy and warfare (11:29–12:6).

The chief differences between Judges and Samuel can be isolated to an extra redaction in the book of Judges. This redaction, which holds the book of Judges together, indicates that the book likely originated after the first versions of Samuel (and Kings) had already been composed. By creating an intermediate era initiated by a generation "who did not know YHWH" (2:10),[51] it explains how the hegemony established by Joshua had been largely forfeited by the time of Samuel. Moreover, the statement "he did evil in the sight of YHWH," recurring throughout Kings, is applied in Judges not to the kings of Israel and Judah but rather to the people as a whole. The responsibility of the rulers who represent their peoples is democratized so that the nation itself anticipates the later behavior of its kings. Similarly, the many explicit literary connections in Samuel to Judges all seem to have been added at a later point.[52] Due to these observations, one must consider more seriously suggestions like those of Ernst Würthwein, according to which the earliest Deuteronomistic redaction of the Former Prophets encompassed solely the books of Samuel and Kings.[53] The book of Judges accordingly may have been composed as a literary bridge that joins this account of Israel's kings (Samuel–Kings) to the narrative of Israel's conquest of the land in Genesis/Exodus–Joshua.[54]

The Exodus–Joshua account dispenses with this equation of military valor and monarchic rule by portraying YHWH as fighting the pharaoh alone at the Sea of Reeds and Israel's early (military) leaders as nonkings. Yet the early versions of this Exodus account probably do not so much oppose the monarchy itself as attempt to reconceptualize Israel's identity. In order to affirm that the peoples of the kingdoms of Israel and Judah share common roots, they write a history that treats the period prior to political divisions. In contrast to Samuel and Kings, which make a similar point by focusing on the relationship of the respective royal houses, the Genesis/Exodus–Joshua account constructs a collective memory of the people and deliberately begins the story long before the emergence of Isra-

---

Follis; JSOTSup 40; Sheffield: JSOT Press, 1987), 265–84.
    51. Cf. "who did not know Joseph" (Exod 1:8) in the redactional bridge between Genesis and Exodus–Joshua.
    52. See Kratz, *Komposition*, 174–77, 219–25; Müller, *Königtum*.
    53. Ernst Würthwein, "Erwägungen zum sog. deuteronomistischen Geschichtswerk: Eine Skizze," in *Studien zum Deuteronomistischen Geschichtswerk* (ed. E. Würthwein; BZAW 227; Berlin: de Gruyter, 1994), 1–11.
    54. See Kratz, *Komposition*. 193–219.

el's monarchies. Although a royal court probably would not have welcomed the account insofar as it lacks a symbol (other than the national God Yhwh) with which a king could identify himself, one should probably not assign a conscious antimonarchic stance to its authors.[55]

As a later work than Genesis/Exodus–Joshua and Samuel–Kings, the book of Judges is more consistently critical of the monarchy and the royal ideology that equates the warring king with the warring god. By drawing on stories of war heroes that are quite similar to those in the book of Samuel, the authors of Judges obliquely criticize the Israelites' impulse to install their military leaders as kings. As already observed, they do this in two ways. First, the book presents a set of parallels with which the reader can compare similar episodes in the book of Samuel. After reading the book of Judges, one will view the book of Samuel in a different light. Second, the book of Judges renders the monarchy "accidental" by attributing war to sin rather than a natural condition, as in Samuel. If Israel would remain faithful to Yhwh, it would not need a judge or a king to rescue it. The last four chapters of Judges, which may well constitute a secondary addendum to the book, emphasize the need for a king in Israel (17:6; 18:1; 19:1; 21:25), but they do so by depicting *internal* chaos rather than wars with external enemies. The king's role is thus presented in relation to social order, as in 1 Sam 8:1–5.

Although Judges is probably a later composition than Samuel, its message has made an unmistakable impact on the final shape of the latter. Thus, in the last battle before the inauguration of the monarchy, Israel petitions Samuel, who is identified as a judge, not to cease from crying to Yhwh so that Yhwh would "save" the nation from the hands of the Philistines (1 Sam 7:8). In response to Samuel's burnt offerings, Yhwh then thunders from heaven and throws the Philistines into confusion so that they could be routed before Israel (7:10). The act of throwing Israel's enemies into confusion (המם) is reported in the accounts of those great battles in which Yhwh fights directly for Israel (Exod 14:24; Josh 10:10; Judg 4:15), and it is not surprising that the same divine action is portrayed at this momentous occasion as well. Samuel commemorates the event by placing a stone between Mizpah and Shen, which he names Eben-ezer: "For thus far [עד הנה] Yhwh has helped us" (1 Sam 7:12). This stone marks a *lieu de mémoire*, to borrow a concept of Pierre Nora.[56] It exists not only on a geographical map imagined for us by the author but also on the narrative map of Israel's history.

---

55. Expansions, such as those emphasizing the slaughter of kings in Joshua, are, however, difficult to distinguish from explicitly antimonarchic texts elsewhere in the Bible and may already presuppose the latter.

56. "A *lieu de mémoire* is any significant entity, whether material or non-material in nature, which by dint of human will or the work of time has become a symbolic element of the memorial heritage of any community" (Pierre Nora, "From *lieux de mémoire* to Realms of Memory," in *Conflicts and Divisions* [vol. 1 of *Realms of Memory: Rethinking the French Past*; ed. P. Nora and L. D. Kritzman; New York: Columbia University Press, 1996], xv–xxiv, here xvii).

From this point, everything changes. In the immediately following chapter, the people voice their desire for a king and Samuel describes the radical changes that Israelite society will undergo as it moves from the ideal time of the judges to the period of the monarchy (1 Sam 8:11–18).

In contrast to Judges, the book of Samuel does not present war—and therewith the need for judges and kings—as a consequence of sin. Nevertheless, several key passages cast aspersions on the institution of the monarchy by identifying Israel's desire for a king of its own—who "will go out at our head and fight our battles" (1 Sam 8:20)—as apostasy. In response to Samuel's remonstrations, YHWH states: "They have not rejected you; it is me they have rejected as their king" (8:7). Later, after Saul is enthroned, Samuel delivers a speech in which he reflects upon Israel's desire for a king in relation to its history of war (1 Sam 12). In each case YHWH "sent" someone who delivered their ancestors from their oppressors (12:8–11) without assuming the throne. In this way, Samuel can make the point that it was YHWH who ultimately delivered Israel from its enemies. The nexus between salvation in wartime and rule in peacetime is expressed in the promise made by an earlier generation: "Deliver us from the hands of our enemies and we will serve you" (12:10). This promise was inexplicably broken when the present generation saw Nahash the king of the Ammonites coming against them. Samuel recalls, "You said to me, 'No, but a king shall reign over us,' although YHWH your God is your king" (12:12).

In the end, however, the final form of Samuel accepts the emergence of the monarchy reported in older versions of the book and reconciles it in various ways with the kingship of YHWH. As already seen, the account in 1 Sam 11 presents Saul emphasizing that it is YHWH who "brought salvation to Israel" (11:9).[57] Similarly, in 2 Sam 3:18 Abner strives to persuade the Israelites to accept David as king by appealing not to David's performance but rather to YHWH's promise to "save" Israel from its enemies through David. Salvation as the prerequisite for kingship is thus ascribed in the final analysis to Israel's divine king. The most important evidence indicating that the book follows Judges in rethinking the nexus between martial valor and human kingship is found in the larger compositional ordering of the narratives: 1 Sam 9–10 and 16 present Samuel anointing, respectively, Saul and David as king. We are not told why specifically they are chosen,[58] yet

---

57. The addition of 1 Sam 11:6a ascribes Saul's victory to "the divine spirit" that seizes Saul before his first action of consolidating an army. It is not a coincidence that the addition is comparable to similar statements in Judges; see 3:10; 11:29; 13:25; 14:6, 19; 15:14. For a discussion of more recent literature on this subject, see Eckart Otto, "Tora und Charisma: Legitimation und Delegitimation des Königtums in 1 Samuel 8–2 Samuel 1 im Spiegel neuerer Literatur," *ZABR* 12 (2006): 225–44.

58. Physical appearance is implicitly one of the primary criteria. Both are said to be beautiful in appearance (9:2; 16:12; 17:42). Saul is not only the best-looking man in Israel but also a head taller than everyone else (9:2). Later, however, YHWH tells Samuel when anointing a new

one thing is clear: the anointing accounts directly precede the pivotal reports of Saul's and David's first battles in 1 Sam 11 and 17. Accordingly, the reader should understand that the divine choice of these figures as Israel's kings has nothing to do with their prior martial feats.[59] Rather, their success on the battlefield is the product of their prior anointing, which Samuel undertakes in accordance with the divine, inscrutable will.[60] Nevertheless, the commission and function of these kings is still to "save" Israel from its enemies, and in this way the book of Samuel in its final form succeeds in reversing the age-old nexus between martial valor and monarchic rule.[61]

Summary and Conclusions

In this essay I have endeavored to set forth an approach to the study of war in the Hebrew Bible that, in keeping with the work of Niditch, appreciates its diversity of ideas yet that also pays attention to their shaping in individual biblical books. In order to illustrate this approach, I have focused on one idea and two books.

---

king, "Do not view his appearance or the height of his stature. ... Mortals look with [?] the eyes, but Yhwh looks with [?] the heart" (16:7).

59. Within the book of Samuel, one can observe a discourse on the relationship between popular and divine choice unfolding in passages such as 1 Sam 8:18; 10:24; 12:13; 16:8–13; 2 Sam 6:21; and 16:18.

60. For a different interpretation of the arrangement of these narratives, see Baruch Halpern, *The Constitution of the Monarchy in Israel* (HSM 25; Chico, Calif.: Scholars Press, 1981), 13–19; and Edelman, *King Saul*, 31–33. All this raises further doubts on Albrecht Alt's distinction between a charismatic ideal in Israel and a dynastic ideal in Judah. According to the former, a king is first divinely chosen then later physically installed. See Albrecht Alt, "Das Königtum in den Reichen Israel und Juda," *VT* 1 (1951): 3–22 (repr. in *Kleine Schriften zur Geschichte des Volkes Israel* [2 vols.; Munich: Beck, 1953], 2:116–34; trans. by R. A. Wilson as "The Monarchy in the Kingdoms of Israel and Judah," in Alt, *Essays on Old Testament History and Religion* [Garden City, N.Y.: Doubleday, 1968], 311–35).

61. Of course, the idea that a king was already divinely chosen before proving himself on the battlefield is an old one and would have coexisted with martial valor as the primary justification for rule. It is comparable to the early modern conceptions of *Dei gratia* as the legitimization of monarchic authority. This obtains all the more once a dynasty is established and the choice of king becomes a matter of succession. Nevertheless, for our study it is important to recognize that the book of Samuel depicts the divine selection of Saul and David after an earlier edition of the work had already portrayed these two figures assuming political office after demonstrating military leadership, as in the story of Jephthah. That David seems to have been introduced for the first time in 1 Sam 17:12–15 has been recognized by many scholars since Julius Wellhausen. With respect to Saul, the account of the anointing in 1 Sam 9–10 appears to be quite old. Nevertheless, the story of him becoming king after vanquishing the Ammonites in chapter 11 creates tension with the foregoing narrative, so that it is likely chapter 11 either antedates chs. 9–10 (9:1–2 can be read as continuing in 11:1ff.) or that the two accounts were composed independently of each other and arranged in their present order at a later stage.

My aim has been to show that the popular strategy of legitimizing a king's rule by recourse to military valor and leadership became in Judges and Samuel the subject of an extended discourse not simply on individual kings but on the institution of kingship as a whole.

The natural progression from a hero "saving" his people to ruling as king is treated variously in the two books we studied, yet both are united in their attempt to rethink this nexus. The book of Judges presents a punitive conception of war. Insofar as Israel remains faithful to its God, it can avoid war altogether. However, because Israel is prone to sin, it requires periodic local judges and saviors—not dynastic rulers—who reestablish national sovereignty and the ideal of territorial, tribal diversity instituted in the ideal age of Joshua. According to Judges, Israel's unity is found not in its monarchy but in its common devotion to one God.

The book of Samuel, in portraying national unification and consolidation under centralized political rule, argues for a different conception of war. Rather than punishment, war is an unavoidable condition of Israel's premonarchic existence, and Israel requires the hand of a powerful warrior to gain lasting supremacy over its enemies. Insofar as the older editions of the book present Saul and David rising to power and consolidating various territories into one kingdom primarily by martial means, war is firmly embedded in the book's ideology of kingship. Nevertheless, the final redactions of the work struggle with this ideology and attempt to bring it into consonance with the recurring biblical theme of divine kingship, namely, that YHWH saved Israel in the defining moment of its history and thus deserves recognition as its primordial and eternal king. Judges severs the natural nexus between military valor and dynastic rule by presenting heroes saving their peoples yet not assuming the throne. In contrast, the book of Samuel still embraces the nexus yet ultimately reverses it. This work not only attributes "salvation" ultimately to YHWH, as in Judges, but also and above all narrates the divine appointment of Saul and David as kings *before* they ever fight their first battles. Hence, their success on the battlefield is the confirmation, not the prerequisite, for their reigns.

To conclude, the question poses itself as to why these two books reflect at such length on war and the institution of the monarchy. The question is, of course, quite complex and deserves a protracted treatment. Briefly, however, war, for a nation, constitutes the threat par excellence. Floods, famine, and other natural catastrophes afflict regions defined according to natural geographical boundaries. In contrast, war by definition is directed against a collective political body. The subject of the Bible is the people of Israel and its land. Therefore war, as a force that threatens to break an established bond between a people and a land, became a central theme in many biblical books. From the evidence of the prophets, this literary project seems to have attained new dimensions in the eighth century, as one recognized in the Assyrian Empire a much greater military opponent than heretofore. The political challenge prompted in some circles a project of reconceptualizing Israel's identity, and this effort continued in the following centuries, which witnessed the demise and transformation of Israel's and Judah's political institutions. As part of this effort, the book of Judges provides a new hermeneutical framework for the reading of Samuel (and Kings) by imagining Israel's history without a monarchy at its center. According to the final editions of both Judges and Samuel, it was not Israel's royal houses but its God who must be acknowledged as the unifying and sustaining factor in its history.

Fighting in Writing:
Warfare in Histories of Ancient Israel

Megan Bishop Moore

Anyone familiar with the recent study of Israel's past knows that scholars will debate the merits of almost every proposed historical scenario, presupposition, and method. The availability and use of evidence for ancient Israel is at the core of this debate. In general, historians consider the Bible's value as evidence for premonarchic times to be low, but opinions about its reliability as a source of information about the later first millennium B.C.E. vary.[1] The paucity of written records from central Palestine in the Iron Age contributes to the problem of evaluating and using the Bible as historical evidence, and thus additional historical information about Israel and Judah must be garnered from records of the great ancient powers such as Egypt, Assyria, and Babylon. Such extrabiblical texts may provide information and details about ancient Israel and Judah—even information that appears to correlate with the biblical story—and iconography from these same cultures can provide some additional insight but a history of Iron Age central Palestine written using only ancient records would be skimpy indeed.[2] The value of archaeology for writing Israel's history is also debated. Sometimes archaeological findings can contribute to the understanding of a historical event, but archaeology's pursuit of cultural change and traditional history's focus on events are not the same endeavor.[3] These debates over how to use the Bible, extrabiblical texts, and archaeology as evidence have led to the current situation, where

---

1. I have discussed these topics at length in Megan Bishop Moore, *Philosophy and Practice in Writing a History of Ancient Israel* (LHB/OTS 435; New York: T&T Clark, 2006).

2. See, e.g., J. Maxwell Miller, "Is It Possible to Write a History of Israel without Relying on the Hebrew Bible?" in *The Fabric of History: Text, Artifact and Israel's Past* (ed. D. Edelman; JSOTSup 127; Sheffield: JSOT Press, 1991), 93–102.

3. As noted by the eminent archaeologist Lewis R. Binford, "an accurate and meaningful history is more than a generalized narrative of the changes in composition of the archeological record through time" ("Archaeological Perspectives," in *New Perspectives in Archaeology* [ed. S. R. Binford and L. R. Binford; Chicago: Aldine, 1968], 11). Cf. Diana Vikander Edelman, "Doing History in Biblical Studies," in Edelman, *Fabric of History*, 13–25.

historians' attention has turned to even broader methodological questions such as: What can we know about Israel's past? How do we come to know it?

War in Historical Evidence

War is one topic that does not necessarily need to get bogged down in the evidence/methodology quagmire. There are plenty of mentions of war in the Bible. While scholars do not consider some of these stories about war to be factual (e.g., the conquest stories in Joshua), the Bible does envision greater Israel as a nation born into military conflict and embroiled in it or its possibility throughout its existence. War, according to the Bible, brought the scattered tribes together (Judges), prompted Israel to entreat Yhwh for a king (1 Sam 8:20), and brought on the great catastrophes of Israel's and Judah's history, namely, the destructions of the kingdom of Israel (2 Kgs 17) and Jerusalem (2 Kgs 24:13–25:21). Israel's God, Yhwh, is a war-god who fights alongside his people (e.g., Josh 3:10), or against them, if necessary (e.g., Jer 21:3–6). War, however abstract, is also the New Testament's apocalyptic future, when the ultimate battle will vanquish darkness and set up God as king above all forever without enemies (e.g., Rev 18–21).

War and its effects can also be seen on a smaller scale in the Hebrew Bible. Specific battles are the setting for miracles by Yhwh, such as the plague he puts on the Philistines in 1 Sam 5 and the lifting of the Assyrians' siege of Jerusalem in 2 Kgs 19. War pervades the prophetic books, inspiring the oracles against the nations and numerous predictions about Israel's and Judah's fate.[4] Warfare and battles provide the prophets, psalmists, and the authors of wisdom literature with metaphors that they use to express an array of emotions, including pain and triumph.[5] On a more mundane level, reports of the conduct of battle can be found throughout the Pentateuch and historical books (e.g., 2 Sam 11). In short, war is prominent in the Bible.

War is also prominent in ancient epigraphical evidence from and about Israel. The first correlations between the Hebrew Bible and ancient historical records come from other nations' records of wars: Omri appears in the Mesha inscription,[6] Ahab in Shalmaneser III's monolith inscription,[7] and Jehu "son of Omri" in Shalmaneser's Black Obelisk inscription.[8] Merneptah's mention of his destruction

---

4. See John H. Hayes, "The Usage of Oracles against Foreign Nations in Ancient Israel," *JBL* 87 (1968): 81–92.

5. Brad E. Kelle, "Warfare (Imagery)," in *Dictionary of the Old Testament: Wisdom, Poetry, and Writings* (ed. T. Longman III and P. Enns; Downers Grove, Ill.: Intervarsity Press, forthcoming).

6. *COS* 2.23:137–38.

7. *COS* 2.113A:263.

8. *COS* 2.113F:268.

of Israel should perhaps also be included here.[9] In any case, it is fair to say that the majority of ancient epigraphical information about Israel and Judah is related to conquests, battles, and wars.[10]

War is the context for many of the epigraphic remains from Iron Age Palestine, as well. The Lachish ostraca are one example.[11] They date from the early sixth century B.C.E. and apparently allude to the fall of Judean towns to the Babylonians at this time.[12] In fact, at Lachish we have an amazing confluence of evidence relating to war. Lachish is the subject of the most excellent iconographical representation of any place or event in Iron Age Palestine: the wall reliefs depicting the Assyrian siege of the city, found in Sennacherib's palace at Nineveh.[13] The siege ramp shown on the reliefs has been found at Tell ed-Duweir, the site of ancient Lachish, and the tell also yielded hundreds of arrowheads, as well as slingstones, scale armor, and mass graves, generally understood as repositories for the bodies of civilians killed in the Assyrian attack.[14] The Bible also alludes to the conflicts at Lachish, although the severity of the Assyrian siege is not evident in 2 Kgs 18 (cf. 2 Chr 32), and only Jeremiah mentions the Babylonian siege there (Jer 34:7). In any case, war contextualizes and unifies the material and textual remains relating to Lachish, and war is Lachish's most evident story, whether told archaeologically or historically.

Although not as spectacular as Lachish, the archaeological records of most other sites in Iron Age Palestine show signs of destruction likely attributable to war. In fact, the destruction (often by conflagration), abandonment, and rebuilding of a site leave important breaks in the archaeological record that allow researchers to differentiate that site's occupational levels. In other words, we often have archaeological strata and thus the ability to date occupations and

---

9. *COS* 2.6:41.

10. Including also the annals of Tiglath-pileser (e.g., *COS* 2.117A:286; 2.117C:288) and Sargon II (e.g., *COS* 2.118A:293; 2.118D:295–96); Sennacherib's account of the siege of Jerusalem (*COS* 2.119B:302–3); and the Babylonian Chronicle (*COS* 1.137:467–68).

11. Six of these appear in *COS* 3.42:78–81. Their translator, Dennis Pardee, notes that "they provide glimpses of the workings of the royal administration, primarily military" (78). Other epigraphic remains from Iron Age Palestine can be tied by extension to war. The Samaria ostraca (*ANET*, 321) and Arad ostraca (*COS* 3.43:81–93) are apparent evidence of taxes paid in kind and goods redistributed. It is likely that the need for taxes was directly related to the need to support military bureaucracies in Israel and Judah. The Siloam water tunnel and its inscription (*COS* 2.28:145–46) can be reasonably assumed to relate to war, as the tunnel was probably part of Hezekiah's preparations for revolt against Assyria and/or a necessary improvement in the water system brought on by the influx of refugees to Jerusalem after the Assyrian destruction of Samaria and the kingdom of Israel.

12. See also *ATSHB*, 460–61.

13. Accompanied by a short inscription (*COS* 2.119C:304).

14. David Ussishkin, *The Conquest of Lachish by Sennacherib* (Tel Aviv: Tel Aviv University Institute of Archaeology, 1982), 54–57.

destructions within a relatively short time frame, thanks to military conflict. It is fair to say, then, that war is prominent in the archaeological record.

To sum up so far: war is prominent in all types of evidence scholars use to reconstruct ancient Israel. While much about ancient Israel, both general and specific, is debated, the claims that war happened in Iron Age Palestine, that we know some things about who was fighting, why they were fighting, and what the wars' outcomes were are claims that, in general, are not debated.

War in Modern Histories of Israel

The prominence of war in evidence for ancient Israel might lead one to assume that modern histories of Israel are dominated by war. This is not the case. War and battles rarely command special attention; rather, warfare typically is mentioned in service of a larger question.[15] This can be demonstrated by a survey of appearances of the battle of Qarqar in recent histories. In 853 B.C.E. at Qarqar, the Assyrian king Shalmaneser III met a coalition of states opposing his advance into the eastern Mediterranean seaboard. Recalling the event in his monolith inscription, Shalmaneser claims to have won,[16] but "such claims cannot necessarily be taken at face value. Even if victorious ... the Assyrians apparently did not return to the region until 849 and when they did return they once again had to fight."[17]

In general, Qarqar appears in histories of ancient Israel because Shalmaneser III's account of it mentions the Israelite king Ahab. These mentions typically lead to the discussion of two specific historical issues. The first is chronology. Since Ahab appears in the inscription and the date of the battle is known to have been 853 B.C.E., the inscription provides an absolute marker on which to hang biblical chronology.[18] The second issue that histories tend to highlight is the inscription's

---

15. One notable exception is Brad E. Kelle, *Ancient Israel at War 853–586 BC* (Essential Histories 67; Oxford: Osprey, 2007).

16. Specifically, Shalmaneser boasts that he filled the plain and blocked the Orontes River with the corpses of the enemy and left with their "chariots, cavalry, (and) teams of horses" (*COS* 2.113A:263–64).

17. Iain Provan, V. Philips Long, and Tremper Longman III, *A Biblical History of Israel* (Louisville: Westminster John Knox, 2003), 370 n. 32.

18. E.g., J. Maxwell Miller and John H. Hayes, *A History of Ancient Israel and Judah* (2nd ed.; Louisville: Westminster John Knox, 2006), 292, 299; Gösta W. Ahlström, *The History of Ancient Palestine* (Minneapolis: Fortress, 1993), 562, 577; Provan, Long, and Longman, *Biblical History of Israel*, 199. The monolith's mention of other kings at Qarqar allows us to know about and date some Transjordanian rulers, as well (Ahlström, *History of Ancient Palestine*, 641, 644 n. 4). On the other hand, Shalmaneser names Hadadezer as the Aramean king at the battle, complicating the already difficult task of deciding who ruled the Arameans at the time of Ahab. For discussion of the apparent contradictions of the Assyrian and biblical evidence with each other and within themselves, see Edward F. Campbell Jr., "A Land Divided: Judah and Israel from the Death of Solomon to the Fall of Samaria," in *The Oxford History of the Biblical World* (ed.

report that Ahab commanded ten thousand soldiers, two thousand chariots, and seven hundred cavalry, "the largest chariot force in the coalition and one that was equal to that of Assyria at the height of its power in the following decade."[19] Some scholars believe that this number indicates Ahab was an important figure in the anti-Assyrian coalition, perhaps himself the chief of a large group that included Judah and others, [20] and/or a wealthy king who himself had a large supply of horses.[21]

Besides offering specific information about Ahab and chronology, the battle of Qarqar is sometimes portrayed as having wider political implications. For one, it is a clear example of resistance to the Assyrians in the Levant,[22] and the question of how to deal with the Assyrians dominates the political and prophetic discourse of Israel and Judah that is recorded in the Bible for almost two centuries (although histories rarely extend the significance of Qarqar to note this fact). Historians also have observed that knowledge of events at Qarqar might shed light on Israel's conflicts closer to home. For instance, did Israel's alliance with its sometime enemy Aram prevent the resumption of hostilities between the two for a time after Qarqar?[23] Also, did the Moabite king Mesha, author of another of our war-related epigraphic remains from the Iron Age, take some of Israel's land while Ahab was occupied at Qarqar?[24] Do these events point to a weaken-

---

M. D. Coogan; Oxford: Oxford University Press, 2001), 223–25. A related question is whether the biblical accounts of Ahab's reign in 1 Kings and conflicts between the "king of Israel" and the "king of Damascus" reported during that time are accurate. For a review of the issues and a discussion of the help Shalmaneser's account of Qarqar can give in answering this question, see Hershel Shanks, *Ancient Israel: From Abraham to the Roman Destruction of the Temple* (rev. ed.; Washington, D.C.: Biblical Archaeology Society, 1999), 320 n. 22.

19. Kelle, *Ancient Israel at War*, 35.

20. E.g., ibid., 36; see also Victor H. Matthews, *A Brief History of Ancient Israel* (Louisville: Westminster John Knox, 2002), 65; and Campbell, "Land Divided," 219. For skepticism of the claim that Ahab was a prominent member of the coalition, see Provan, Long, and Longman, *Biblical History of Israel*, 370 n. 31; and Ahlström, *History of Ancient Palestine*, 578 n. 2, who argues that the absence of Ahab's name in a shorter account of the battle at Qarqar found on Shalmaneser's throne base indicates that Ahab was not a significant leader at the battle.

21. Amihai Mazar, *Archaeology of the Land of the Bible 10,000–586 b.c.e.* (New York: Doubleday, 1990), 477, uses the number of Ahab's chariots listed by Shalmaneser to argue that certain pillared buildings at Megiddo were stables for the many horses that he would have needed.

22. E.g., Miller and Hayes, *History of Ancient Israel and Judah*, 308-10; Ahlström, *History of Ancient Palestine*, 577, 601-2; Matthews, *Brief History of Ancient Israel*, 65–66; Campbell, "Land Divided," 220.

23. Ahlström (*History of Ancient Palestine*, 579) argues that it is unlikely that Aram and Israel, allies at Qarqar, resumed their hostilities shortly afterward. On the other hand, Provan, Long, and Longman (*Biblical History of Israel*, 264) assert that the Israel-Aram alliance waned quickly.

24. E.g., Ahlström, *History of Ancient Palestine*, 581; and Matthews, *Brief History of Ancient*

ing Omride dynasty and a prime opportunity for a usurper such as Jehu?[25] Gösta Ahlström even uses the example of Qarqar to suggest that the Israelites might have had more success against the Assyrians in the late eighth century if they had not forgotten "the model of Qarqar" and the anti-Assyrian coalition that fought there.[26] It should be noted, however, that Qarqar and its consequences do not always merit extended discussion in histories of Israel.[27] One might speculate that Qarqar's lack of importance to these histories could be related to the fact that the Hebrew Bible does not mention the battle.

It is clear that histories of ancient Israel recognize war as an important historical event and that historians have analyzed some of the consequences of war and battles. On the other hand, the preceding discussion of a very important and relatively well-known battle from Israel's past demonstrates that the discussion of war in histories of Israel is rather narrow. Histories rarely offer a detailed discussion of war itself, and historians' analyses of the ramifications of war tend to elucidate other political questions or events. However, an expansion of the discussion of both the details of war and the consequences of war in many spheres, including social, cultural, religious, and economic, would lead to a more complete and more accurate portrait of Israel's past.

In order to use evidence about war to its fullest potential, historians of ancient Israel will have to explore aspects of war that are of little or no interest to ancient recorders or the biblical writers. For instance, the Deuteronomistic History does not mention Qarqar, and it interprets the reasons for and consequences of war in religious terms. Elsewhere in the Bible we find an occasional snapshot of the personal and immediate consequences of war—a king sacrificing a child (2 Kgs 16:3); a haughty Assyrian general prancing around the walls, shouting intimidating remarks in the presence of the besieged populace (2 Kgs 18:28–35)—but we have very few of these stories. The lover of the Song of Songs does not march off to battle and die, we do not hear the voices of women who are left to tend the

---

Israel, 66 (citing M. Elat, "The Campaigns of Shalmaneser III against Aram and Israel," *IEJ* 25 [1975]: 25–35).

25. E.g., Kurt L. Noll, *Canaan and Israel in Antiquity: An Introduction* (London: Sheffield Academic Press, 2001), 222.

26. Ahlström, *History of Ancient Palestine*, 715.

27. E.g., Philip R. Davies and John Rogerson, *The Old Testament World* (2nd ed.; Louisville: Westminster John Knox, 2005), 77, where Qarqar simply is noted as evidence of the Omrides' many "Internal and External Conflicts." See also Mario Liverani, *Israel's History and the History of Israel* (London: Equinox, 2005), 143, who calls Qarqar "famous" but whose discussion of the battle is limited to repeating the troop numbers attributed to Ahab (112). Siegfried Herrmann, *A History of Israel in Old Testament Times* (rev. ed.; Philadelphia: Fortress, 1981); and J. Alberto Soggin, *An Introduction to the History of Israel and Judah* (3rd ed.; London: SCM, 1999 [1984]) do not mention Qarqar at all.

homestead without men, and children do not witness the rape and murder of their parents before being taken into slavery.

On the other hand, historians attempting to develop the understanding and discussion of war in their histories will not have to start from scratch. Several publications about Israel's past include information on war and battles and interpretations of their significance. For instance, the colorful and accessible *Life in Biblical Israel* by Philip J. King and Lawrence E. Stager includes a section called "Warfare, Armies, and Weapons," which has a nice discussion of weaponry, fortifications, armies, strategy, and Assyrian and Babylonian tactics of warfare.[28] King and Stager draw on biblical, epigraphic, iconographic, and archaeological evidence to paint a detailed picture of war itself and the political and social processes that supported it. Similar discussions can be found in Benedikt S. J. Isserlin's *The Israelites*[29] and, in an older work, Roland de Vaux's *Ancient Israel: Its Life and Institutions*.[30] Brad E. Kelle's *Ancient Israel at War 853–586 B.C.* is a stand-alone discussion of the same topics.[31] It is worth noting, however, that none of these works is a traditional event-oriented, chronological history of Israel.

Also, some historians have recognized that war's effects ripple from the political realm into many others. For instance, Martin Noth observed in his *History of Israel* that the organization of warriors was directly tied to tribal and even family organization.[32] Recently, the revised edition of *A History of Ancient Israel and Judah* by J. Maxwell Miller and John H. Hayes has delved into war in more depth than most other histories. In their reconstruction, the repercussions of war are seen in economics and daily life.[33] In addition, Miller and Hayes allude to the actual process of calling up men who leave their families and thus alter the economy, and they spend some time on the outcome of war, such as when property gets redistributed in the aftermath of destruction (Jer 39:10; 2 Kgs 25:12).[34] War is, for them, not simply an event that explains a power shift, but an event that has some consequences in everyday life. William F. Albright made an even more daring assessment of war's importance in ancient Israel in his *From the Stone*

---

28. Philip J. King and Lawrence E. Stager, *Life in Biblical Israel* (Library of Ancient Israel; Louisville: Westminster John Knox, 2001), 223–58.

29. Benedikt S. J. Isserlin, *The Israelites* (Minneapolis: Fortress, 2001 [1998]), 192–203.

30. Roland de Vaux, *Ancient Israel: Its Life and Institutions* (Biblical Resource Series; Grand Rapids: Eerdmans, 2001 [1958–60]), 213–67.

31. Kelle, *Ancient Israel at War*.

32. Martin Noth, *The History of Israel* (2nd ed.; New York: Harper & Row, 1960 [1950]), 107. This, however, is the only page referenced to the topic "war" in the index.

33. E.g., "When a city dared to resist the Syrians and fell under siege, inflation and exorbitant prices prevailed (2 Kgs 6:24–25). One story tells of a widow about to lose her children to slavery because of debts (4:1–7). We read of cannibalism even in Samaria, parents eating their children (6:24–31)" (Miller and Hayes, *History of Ancient Israel and Judah*, 358).

34. Ibid., 485.

Age to Christianity. Albright offers war, particularly the Babylonian invasions of Judah, as the reason for "growing insecurity, when the very foundations of life were trembling." This state of affairs, he argues, prompted the effort to reclaim the Mosaic traditions and begin the inquiry into the past that led to proper history writing and the Deuteronomistic History.[35] The examples of Miller and Hayes's and Albright's use and understanding of war are exceptional, but they demonstrate that war profoundly affects the economy, religion, and other aspects of society and individual life and that histories are richer for their inclusion.

By asserting that histories of ancient Israel should include more of these types of details of war and battles as well as a broader look at the effects of war, I am, on the one hand, asserting that the genre of Israel's history should be broadened. History, traditionally understood, is a chronological narrative of events, and most current histories of Israel follow this model.[36] On the other hand, history in the twentieth century has broadened its subject to include day-to-day experience, or the life experiences of the so-called "common person," as well as the social structures people create.[37] Nonnarrative portraits of Israel's' past, such as those by King and Stager, Isserlin, and de Vaux, fall into this category. Israel's history should provide a chronological narrative of events that played out on the grand stage, such as the battle of Qarqar, while at the same time pulling back the curtain and peeking behind it to show how war was conducted and how war affected society and individuals. This approach is well-rounded, uses many kinds of available evidence, and potentially helps make the past more real for the reader. The abundant coverage of ancient Israelite archaeology in the popular press and the frequent use of reenactments in television documentaries on biblical history indicate to me that people crave pictures to go along with the story of ancient Israel. More detailed attention in histories of ancient Israel to war and battles themselves, as well as their consequences, could provide some of those pictures.

---

35. William F. Albright, *From the Stone Age to Christianity: Monotheism and the Historical Process* (2nd ed.; Garden City, N.Y.: Doubleday, 1957), 315.

36. With the exception of Soggin (*Introduction to the History*), which puts the discussion of the "Foundation of the State" (David's and Solomon's reigns) before "The Traditions about the Origins of the People" (patriarchs, exodus, settlement, and judges).

37. In the discipline of history, a focus on the so-called "common people" and also everyday life has been called "History from Below." For a discussion of the development of and difficulties of history from below, see Jim Sharpe, "History from Below," in *New Perspectives on Historical Writing* (ed. P. Burke; University Park: Pennsylvania State University Press, 1992), 24–41. Histories that have social structures or non-self-referential entities as their subject were given a philosophical defense by Michel Foucault in *The Archaeology of Knowledge* (World of Man; New York: Pantheon, 1972 [1969]). For further discussion and analysis, see Peter Burke, "Overture: The New History, Its Past and Its Future," in Burke, *New Perspectives on Historical Writing*, 1–23.

Histories of ancient Israel do combine the discussion of events in Israel's past with attention to at least one comprehensive topic: religion. Historians not only pull back the curtain to show religion's influence on events; they often place it on the main stage. Historians understand Israelite religion as closely tied to a number of past realities, including government and dynastic succession, economics (such as the temple economy), and even daily life. However, religion seems to be the only nonevent about which there is the widespread perception that increased knowledge of it, both detailed and general, helps us understand events in ancient Israel and the community of ancient Israel itself.

The prevalence of religion in histories of ancient Israel actually strengthens the argument that war should be better understood and discussed. Israelite religion, specifically Yahwism, cannot be understood outside of war, neither at its genesis, somewhere in the murky beginnings of the Israelite tribes, nor at its end, when Yhwh raises up Cyrus and returns in glory across the desert to Jerusalem. The close association of religion and war continues into the Hellenistic and Roman periods in the form of Jewish zealotry (e.g., the Maccabees) and, as noted previously, the imagery of war defines apocalypticism, which flourished in Roman Palestine in both Jewish and Christian circles.

To sum up my argument: I have observed that war is everywhere in the evidence for ancient Israel and thus potentially everywhere yet often nowhere in histories of ancient Israel. I have shown that historians recognize war as an event that has political implications but that the implications of war for society, societal structures, individuals, and daily life have not been studied in much detail. I have asserted that histories written with more attention to war would better reflect the context of our written sources for Israel's past, especially extrabiblical sources. I have also suggested that details about war, battles, and their consequences can find a place in histories and that these details would provide valuable pictures that would help people better relate to and understand Israel's past.

In conclusion, attention to war and its many implications would paint a picture of ancient Israel where not only did kings go to battle, dynasties shift, and tributes get paid, but where the chief god Yhwh sat in his house ready to go to battle with his enemies; kings such as Ahaz and Manasseh and even everyday people offered up their sons and daughters as sacrifices to keep this warrior-god on their side; a society where, for about 250 years, someone from almost every generation experienced a siege, or at least lost family members to the army; a land where territory shifted, economies collapsed, refugees fled, and people witnessed unspeakable horrors. Further attention to war in Israel's past will necessitate consideration of other questions, such as: Was war *the* story of ancient Israel? Should war usurp religion as the prevailing social reality or condition that defines life and community, both the big events and daily existence, in histories of ancient Israel? Is war, in fact, the common thread of Israelite unity, religious or political, the man behind the curtain, so to speak, that is pulling the strings of ancient Israel from top to bottom? Perhaps further research can explore these questions. In any case,

I believe that the evidence points to the conclusion that war played a larger part in Israelite life at all levels than is apparent in current histories of Israel.

Assyrian Military Practices and Deuteronomy's Laws of Warfare

Michael G. Hasel

In the authoritative *Anchor Bible Dictionary*, Moshe Weinfeld wrote, "Deuteronomy has become the touchstone for dating the sources in the Pentateuch and the historical books of the Old Testament."[1] Following the work of W. M. L. de Wette in 1805, the temporal provenience or *Sitz im Leben* for Deuteronomy proposed by historical-critical scholarship generally reflected the Hezekianic-Josianic reforms of the seventh century B.C.E., and the book was considered the work of the Deuteronomist (D).[2] Today the single-author theory has been refined and revised by an increasingly complex number of hypothetical authors and/or redactors, including: (1) a Deuteronomistic (Dtr) school of traditionalists; (2) multiple exilic and postexilic redactions; (3) a double redaction that includes Dtr¹ (Josianic) and Dtr² (exilic), and other variations.[3]

The vigorous discussion over sources has caused some, such as Rolf Rendtorff, virtually to abandon the "documentary hypothesis,"[4] and there exists today a

---

1. Moshe Weinfeld, "Deuteronomy, Book of," *ABD* 2:174.
2. W. M. L. de Wette, "Dissertatio critico-exegetica qua Deuteronomium a propribus pentateuchi libris diversum, alius cuiusdam recentioris auctoris opus esse monstratur" (doctoral diss., Jena, 1805).
3. For an overview of these positions and other proponents see the surveys of Horst D. Preuß, *Deuteronomium* (EdF 164; Darmstadt: Wissenschaftliche Buchgesellschaft, 1982), 1–74; Thomas C. Römer, "The Book of Deuteronomy," in *The History of Israel's Traditions: The Heritage of Martin Noth* (ed. S. L. McKenzie and M. P. Graham; JSOTSup 182; Sheffield: JSOT Press, 1994), 178–212; Erik Eynikel, *The Reform of King Josiah and the Composition of the Deuteronomistic Historian* (OtSt 33; Leiden: Brill, 1996), 7–31; Thomas C. Römer and Albert de Pury, "Deuteronomistic Historiography (DH): History of Research and Debated Issues," in *Israel Constructs Its History: Deuteronomistic History in Recent Research* (ed. A. de Pury, T. C. Römer, and J.-D. Macchi; JSOTSup 306; Sheffield: JSOT Press, 2000), 24–141.
4. Rolf Rendtorff, *The Problem of the Process of Transmission in the Pentateuch* (JSOTSup 89; Sheffield: JSOT Press, 1990); idem, "Between Historical Criticism and Holistic Interpretation: New Trends in Old Testament Exegesis," *Congress Volume: Jerusalem, 1986* (ed. J. A. Emerton; VTSup 40; Leiden: Brill, 1988), 298–303; idem, "The Paradigm Is Changing: Hopes

trend to deny the existence of a Deuteronomistic History (DtrH) altogether[5] (not including revisionist proposals redating its composition to the third and second centuries B.C.E.[6]). Yet despite the intense debate, these dynamic hypotheses of the nineteenth century, designated by Römer and Brettler as "constructions of modern scholarship," continue to have strong adherents even now in the twenty-first century.[7]

One impetus for Deuteronomy's date, among others, revolves around the laws of warfare in Deuteronomy. According to Gerhard von Rad, the laws of warfare in Deuteronomy "presuppose conditions regarding politics and strategy such as are inconceivable before the period of the monarchy."[8] A. D. H. Mayes cogently suggested that the siege prohibitions in Deut 20 were written as a polemic or protest against those practices.[9] If this law was written as a polemic, the question that follows is: What particular country or culture destroyed fruit trees for the purposes of building siege works? Could this protest or polemic provide a possible

---

and Fears," *BibInt* 1 (1993): 34–53; Erhard Blum, *Studien zur Komposition des Pentateuch* (BZAW 189; Berlin: de Gruyter, 1990); David M. Carr, *Reading the Fractures of Genesis: Historical and Literary Approaches* (Louisville: Westminster John Knox, 1996); on recent challenges to the existence of OK?J, see Jan Christian Gertz, Konrad Schmid, and Markus Witte, eds., *Abschied vom Jahwisten: Die Komposition des Hexateuch in der jüngsten Diskussion* (BZAW 315; Berlin: de Gruyter, 2002).

5. Ernst Würthwein, *Studien zum deuteronomistischen Geschichtswerk* (BZAW 227; Berlin: de Gruyter, 1994): 1–11; Claus Westermann, *Die Geschichtsbücher des Alten Testaments: Gab es ein deuteronomistisches Geschichtswerk?* (TBAT 87; Gütersloh: Mohn, 1994); A. Graeme Auld, *Joshua Retold: Synoptic Perspectives* (Edinburgh: T&T Clark, 1998), 120–26; James Richard Linville, *Israel in the Book of Kings: The Past as a Project of Social Identity* (JSOTSup 272; Sheffield: JSOT Press, 1998), 46–73; Ernst Axel Knauf, "Does the 'Deuteronomistic Historiography' (DtrH) Exist?" in de Pury, Römer, and Macchi, *Israel Constructs Its History*, 388–98.

6. Philip R. Davies writes: "I doubt whether the term 'Deuteronomistic History' should continue to be used by scholars as if it were a fact instead of a theory" (*In Search of "Ancient Israel"* [JSOTSup 148; Sheffield: JSOT Press, 1992], 131); cf. Niels-Peter Lemche, "The Old Testament—A Hellenistic Book?" *SJOT* 7 (1993): 163–93.

7. For a recent example of combining two traditionally variant views, of having both a Hexateuch and the DtrH, see Thomas C. Römer and Marc Z. Brettler, "Deuteronomy and the Case for a Persian Hexateuch," *JBL* 119 (2000): 401–19; see also de Pury, Römer, and Macchi, *Israel Constructs Its History*, and the discussion by Raymond F. Person Jr. (*The Deuteronomic School: History, Social Setting, and Literature* [SBLSBL 2; Atlanta: Society of Biblical Literature, 2002], 1–16) for current state-of-the-art appraisals of D and the DtrH.

8. Gerhard von Rad, *Deuteronomy: A Commentary* (Philadelphia: Westminster, 1966), 132–33; see also idem, *Der Heilige Krieg im Alten Israel* (4th ed.; Göttingen: Vandenhoeck & Ruprecht, 1965), 70.

9. A. D. H. Mayes states, "Israel shared with many others the common practice of destroying the natural resources of life in the country invaded by her armies. The prohibition here [in Deut 20:19] is a deuteronomic protest against a practice considered unnecessarily destructive" (*Deuteronomy* [NCB; Grand Rapids: Eerdmans, 1979], 296).

means for finding a provenience for this law? Already in 1886 August Dillmann proposed that these laws reflected Assyrian military practices based on earlier source-critical analysis.[10] Later commentators assumed that the laws of warfare reflected either Assyrian[11] or Babylonian[12] siege tactics reflecting the sociopolitical milieu of the seventh–fifth centuries B.C.E. Despite the fact that Peter Craigie, Jeffrey Tigay, and most recently James K. Hoffmeier have recognized that the types of siege warfare described in Deuteronomy are common to several periods of history, including contexts in the second millennium,[13] others, including Van Seters, Frankena, and Weinfeld, have focused solely on first-millennium comparative studies to the exclusion of second-millennium sources, assuming an Assyrian *Vorlage* to the treaties[14] and military practices[15] outlined in Deuteronomy through Judges. Because of this preconceived provenience, the comparative sources are often limited within the Assyrian corpus of literature.[16]

---

10. August Dillmann, *Die Bücher Numeri, Deuteronomium und Josua* (Leipzig: Hinrichs, 1886).

11. S. R. Driver, *A Critical and Exegetical Commentary on Deuteronomy* (ICC 5; New York: Scribner's, 1916), 240; George Adam Smith, *The Book of Deuteronomy in the Revised Version: With Introduction and Notes* (Cambridge Bible for Schools and Colleges; Cambridge: Cambridge University Press, 1918), 249; Götz Schmitt, *Du sollst keinen Frieden schließen mit den Bewohnern des Landes Die Weisungen gegen die Kanaanäer in Israels Geschichte und Geschichtsschreibung* (BWANT 91; Stuttgart: Kohlhammer, 1970), 138; Walter J. Harrelson, "Law in the OT," *IDB* 4:85; Weinfeld, *Deuteronomy and the Deuteronomic School*, 50–51.

12. Norbert Lohfink, *Theology of the Pentateuch: Themes of the Priestly Narrative and Deuteronomy* (Minneapolis: Fortress; 1994), 55–75; A. D. H. Mayes, "Deuteronomy 4 and the Literary Criticism of Deuteronomy," *JBL* 100 (1981): 23–51; Georg Braulik, *The Theology of Deuteronomy: Collected Essays* (BIBAL Collected Essays 2; Richland Hills, Tex: BIBAL, 1994), 151–64; Ronald E. Clements, "The Deuteronomic Law of Centralization and the Catastrophe of 587 BC," in *After the Exile: Essays in Honour of Rex Mason* (ed. J. Barton and D. J. Reimer; Macon, Ga.: Mercer University Press, 1996), 5–25; Frank Crüsemann, *The Torah: Theology and Social History of Old Testament Law* (Minneapolis: Fortress, 1996), 204–12.

13. J. A. Thompson, *Deuteronomy: An Introduction and Commentary* (TOTC; Downer's Grove, Ill.: InterVarsity Press, 1974) 224; Peter C. Craigie, *The Book of Deuteronomy* (NICOT; Grand Rapids: Eerdmans, 1976), 276–77; Jeffrey H. Tigay, *Deuteronomy* (JPS Torah Commentary; Philadelphia: Jewish Publication Society, 1996) 190–91; James K. Hoffmeier, trans., "The Annals of Thutmose III (2.2A)" *COS* 2.2A:12 n. 61.

14. R. Frankena. "Vassal-Treaties of Essarhaddon and the Dating of Deuteronomy," in *Oudtestamentlich Werkgezelschap in Nederland* (ed. P. A. H. de Boer; OtSt 14; Leiden: Brill, 1965), 122–54; Moshe Weinfeld, "Traces of Assyrian Treaty Formulae in Deuteronomy," *Bib* 46 (1965): 417–27; idem, "Deuteronomy: The Present State of Inquiry," *JBL* 87 (1967): 254.

15. Von Rad, *Deuteronomy*, 132–33; see also idem, *Der Heilige Krieg*, 70; Weinfeld, *Deuteronomy and the Deuteronomic School*; John Van Seters, "Joshua's Campaign and Near Eastern Historiography," *SJOT* 2 (1990): 12.

16. Both Weinfeld and Van Seters restricted their study to first-millennium examples. Van Seters only surveyed three Assyrian texts from Sargon II, Esharhaddon, and Ashurbanipal ("Joshua's Campaign," 6–12); see the critique by James K. Hoffmeier, "The Structure of Joshua

Most assuredly the Assyrians are known for their sophisticated military tactics, their use of extensive siege equipment, and their psychological warfare in their efforts to expand and maintain their empire.[17] Life-support sources were always essential for the survival of both a besieged city and for the attacking armies. But what relationship did these have to the construction of siege works as outlined in Deut 20:19–20? Were fruit trees ever destroyed? What was the motivation for such destruction? Was it as reprisal for an uncooperative enemy? Was it part of a general "scorched earth" policy? Were these fruits and produce used for the feeding of enemy troops? If such destruction of life-support systems took place, it would be significant in this line of questioning to establish when the destruction began. Was it before, during, or after the siege? If the destruction occurred before or during the siege, one may assume that some of the wood from felled trees may have been used for the building of siege works. If these activities took place after a siege, there would no longer be a need for siege works.

The law concerning siege works was recently reinvestigated in order to develop an understanding of what the laws of warfare in Deuteronomy expressed to Israel and to compare the laws against the contextual framework of ancient Near Eastern military activity.[18] This cross-cultural, comparative approach is essential in order to elucidate the historical and cultural background of the text on the basis of contrasts and parallels.[19]

Assyrian Textual Sources

The written records of the Assyrians describe in vivid detail their confiscation and destruction of trees, fruit trees, grain, and other life-support subsistence

---

1–11 and the Annals of Thutmose III," in *Faith, Tradition, and History: Old Testament Historiography in Its Near Eastern Context* (ed. A. R. Millard, J. K. Hoffmeier, and D. W. Baker; Winona Lake, Ind.: Eisenbrauns, 1994), 166; idem, *Israel in Egypt* (New York: Oxford University Press, 1997), 40–42; the exception is Edward Noort ("Das Kapitulationsangebot im Kriegsgesetz Dtn 20:10ff. und in den Kriegserzählungen," in *Studies in Deuteronomy in Honour of C. J. Labuschagne on the Occasion of His 65th Birthday* [ed. F. García Martínez, A. Hilhorst, J. T. A. M. G. van Ruiten, and A. S. van der Woude; VTSup 53; Leiden: Brill, 1994], 199–207), who investigates Egyptian sources but restricts his analysis to the reign of Ramses III.

17. On the Assyrian practice of psychological warfare, see H. W. F. Saggs, *The Might That Was Assyria* (London: Sidgwick & Jackson, 1984), 248–50; Erika Bleibtreu, "Grisly Assyrian Record of Torture and Death," *BAR* 17/1 (1991): 52–61, 75.

18. Michael G. Hasel, *Military Practice and Polemic: Israel's Laws of Warfare in Near Eastern Perspective* (Berrien Springs, Mich.: Andrews University Press, 2005); idem, "The Destruction of Trees in the Moabite Campaign of 2 Kgs 3:4–27: A Study in the Laws of Warfare," *AUSS* 40 (2002): 197–206.

19. For a detailed exegesis of Deut 20, see Hasel, *Military Practice and Polemic*, 21–49.

strategies of the enemy.[20] The first military reference to cutting down orchards comes from the Middle Assyrian ruler Tiglath-pileser I. In his campaign against Suhi he claims, "Their orchards I cut down."[21] Later it is purported, "How many of their lofty cities he smashes! (From) their [fi]elds of sustenance he rips out the grain. He cuts down their fruit; the orchard he destroys. [O]ver their mountains he makes the Deluge pass."[22] Tukulti-Ninurta II (890–884 B.C.E.), in his attack against the land of Mushki, claims to burn their cities with fire and "the crops of their fields (orchards)...."[23] Unfortunately, the text is incomplete. However, the context suggests confiscation or destruction.

Ashurnasirpal II destroys the cities of Lakê and Suhi and says, "I reaped their harvest."[24] Later he asserts, "I reaped the barley and straw of the land of Luḫutu (and) stored (it) inside."[25] At the city of Amedu he boasts, "I fought my way inside his gate (and) cut down his orchards."[26] On the Kurkh monolith (BM 125) Ashurnasirpal says, "I reaped the harvest of the land(s) Nairi (and) stored (it) for the sustenance of my land in the cities of Tušḫa, Damdammusa, Sinabu, (and) Tidu."[27]

This same claim is repeated on the Nimrud monolith.[28] Shalmaneser III (858–824 B.C.E.) states in Year 3, "Ahuni, son of Adini, I shut up in his city, carried off the grain (*lit.* crops) of his (fields), cut down his orchards."[29] In his eighth year in battles against the rebels in Babylonia, he claims to have defeated the king

---

20. Erika Bleibtreu, "Zerstörung der Umwelt durch Bäumefällen und Dezimierung des Löwenbestandes in Mesopotamien," in *Der orientalische Mensch und seine Beziehungen zur Umwelt, Beiträge zum 2. Grazer morgenländischen Symposion (2.–5. März 1989)* (ed. B. Scholz; Grazer morgenländische Studien 2; Graz: GrazKult, 1989), 219–33; Steven W. Cole, "The Destruction of Orchards in Assyrian Warfare," in *Assyria 1995: Proceedings of the 10th Anniversary Symposium of the Neo-Assyrian Text Corpus Project, Helsinki. September 7–11, 1995* (ed. S. Parpola and R. M. Whiting; Helsinki: Neo-Assyrian Text Corpus Project, 1997), 29–40. Hammurabi's Code, no. 59, states that it is forbidden to cut down trees without consent (Theophile J. Meek, trans., "The Code of Hammurabi," *ANET*, 169; see also Thompson, *Deuteronomy*, 224). Evidently this was not enforced for military campaigns.

21. *ARAB* 1:99 §310.

22. LKA 63 r. 14–18; see Victor Hurowitz and Joan Goodnick Westenholz, "LKA 63: A Heroic Poem in Celebration of Tiglath-pileser I's Musru and Qumana Campaign," *JCS* 42 (1990): 14–18.

23. *ARAB* 1:132 §413.

24. *RIMA* 2:214, iii 32; *ARAB* 1:161 §472.

25. *RIMA* 2:218, iii 82.

26. *RIMA* 2:220, iii 109; *ARAB* 1:168 §480.

27. *RIMA* 2:261–262, iii 96–97; *ARAB* 1:182 §502. This appears to be the first direct reference that the grain is being used as food for the military; see Barbara Cifola, "Ashurnasirpal II's 9th Campaign: Seizing the Grain Bowl of the Phoenician Cities," *AfO* 44/45 (1997/1998): 156–58.

28. *RIMA* 2:251, iv 107–108.

29. *ARAB* 1:229 §620.

Marduk-bêl-usâte. "I shut him up in his city, I carried off the grain of his fields, I cut down his orchards, I turned aside (*lit.* dammed) his river."[30] In year 18 Shalmaneser marches against Hazael of Aram and likewise shuts him up in his city. "His orchards I cut down."[31] In the so-called Suḫu Annals the leaders of certain Aramaic tribes plot to make war against the land of Suḫu. They state, "We will go and attack the houses of the land of Suḫu; we will seize his cities of the steppe; and we will cut down their fruit trees."[32] This inscription clearly indicates that the destruction of orchards was intended after the cities themselves were conquered. The land of Suḫu is depicted on Shalmaneser III's Black Obelisk (Register IV), where five date palms serve as a background to the scene.[33] In his fourth campaign, Shamshi-Adad V (823–811 B.C.E.), the son and successor of Shalmaneser III, states of the cities Datêbir and Izduia, "Their plantations I cut down. Their cities I destroyed, I devastated, I burned with fire."[34]

Already during this earlier period, references appear for the cutting of cedars and cypress timbers for tribute and export to Assyria. Tiglath-pileser I makes several references to the cutting of cedars.[35] Shalmaneser III likewise refers to this practice during year 1 when he advances to the Mediterranean,[36] in years 17 and 18 when he goes up to Mount Amanus,[37] and in year 26 during a campaign against the Cicilian cities.[38]

This brief survey indicates that the destruction of orchards and the confiscation of grain had already begun in Assyria as early as the twelfth century B.C.E. (Tiglath-pileser I) and was predominant by the ninth century. In these texts there is rarely any explicit purpose stated for cutting down orchards. Several possible reasons may be suggested: (1) the overt destruction of the life-subsistence system of the inhabitants as either a part of siege tactics or a punishment for rebelling against Assyria; (2) the feeding of the Assyrian armies; (3) a reprisal for an unconquered city; or (4) the building of siege equipment.[39]

---

30. Ibid., 1:230 §622.
31. Ibid., 1:243 §672. This is confirmed by the Berlin statue from Ashur, which states of the same campaign against Hazael, "His orchards [I cut down]..." (1:246 §681).
32. I am grateful to Professor K. Lawson Younger for pointing out this reference. See his translation, "Ninurta-Kudurrī-Uṣur—Suḫu," *COS* 2.115B:279. He states further, "Clearly, the intent of these Arameans was the destruction of the fruit trees after their conquest of the cities" (personal communication with K. Lawson Younger, 14 June 2004).
33. *ANEP*, 122.
34. *ARAB* 1:258 §724.
35. Ibid., 1:96 §297, 1:98 §306, 1:99 §306.
36. Ibid., 1:201 §558, 1:216 §600, 1:234 §633.
37. Ibid., 1:205 §574, 576.
38. Ibid., 1:208 §583.
39. On these possibilities, see Cole, "Destruction of Orchards," 34.

The contextual setting of the statements makes the last suggestion unlikely. In all the texts surveyed, the cutting down of orchards occurs after the claim that the city is captured, destroyed, defeated, and the booty carried away. In many cases the destruction of fruit trees occurs when "describing incomplete sieges."[40] As Hayim Tadmor observes, the cutting down of trees may have served as a "face-saving device employed in a report about an uncompleted siege."[41] In other words, because of frustrated efforts to defeat a city, the army is forced to move on but first destroys the fruit trees in reprisal. Since these orchards "would have been a potential source of tax revenue for state treasuries,"[42] the attitude of the Assyrians may have been one of open hostility. Since they could not use trees for their benefit, certainly they would ensure that their enemy could not use them for their own.

Significantly, the grain in only two texts is used for the feeding of the Assyrian army, and there is no indication in the texts of the ninth century and earlier that the orchards were cut down for food. Indeed, why cut down the trees when all that is required to feed the army is the fruit?[43] The texts point to a blatant destruction of the life-support system, not as part of siege tactics but as recompense for a rebellious enemy—one that was either defeated or that could not be defeated. This conclusion is supported by the texts of the eighth and seventh centuries.

In the eighth century B.C.E., the major military tactic of confiscating and destroying the life-subsistence economies continues. The annals of Tiglath-pileser III (744–727 B.C.E.)[44] record an attack against the land of Mukania. "His gardens ...... plantations, which were without number, I cut down, not one escaped."[45] Likewise concerning Kîn-zêr, son of Amukkâni, "I shut up in Sapie.... The mulberry (?) groves which were (planted) along his (city) walls, I cut down; not one was left (*lit.* escaped). The date palms within the confines of his land I destroyed."[46]

Sargon II boasts in annals at Dur-Sharrukin, year 12, "I let my army eat (the fruit) of their orchards; the date palms, their mainstay, the orchards, the wealth

---

40. Ibid.
41. Hayim Tadmor, *The Inscriptions of Tiglath-pileser III, King of Assyria: Critical Edition with Introductions, Translations, and Commentary* (Jerusalem: Israel Academy of Sciences and Humanities, 1994), 79.
42. Ibid.
43. Ibid., 79, on the time required to grow date palms and other fruit trees.
44. The most recent work on these inscriptions is found in Tadmor, *Tiglath-pileser III*; see also Bustenay Oded, "The Inscriptions of Tiglath-pileser III: Review Article," *IEJ* 47 (1997): 104–10.
45. *ARAB* 1:279 §776.
46. Ibid., 1:285 §792.

of their province, I cut down."⁴⁷ In year 13 he states, "the palms I cut down...."⁴⁸ The letter to Ashur recounting the events of the eighth campaign states, "their crops (and) their stubble I burned, their filled up granaries I opened and let my army devour the unmeasured grain. Like swarming locusts I turned the beasts of my camps into its meadows, and they tore up the vegetation on which it (the city) depended, they devastated its plain."⁴⁹ In the same text, Sargon states, "Their bounteous crops I burned up, [their filled up granaries I opened] and let my army devour the unmeasured grain."⁵⁰ This theme is repeated again in more detail.⁵¹

This is quite a vivid and extensive description with its emphasis on the totality of the destruction of gardens, orchards, and forests. However, it must be pointed out that Sargon does not make use of the timber of these trees for siege works. Instead, this description appears after Sargon says of the city wall, "with iron axes and iron hoes I smashed like a pot and leveled it to the ground."⁵² This indicates that Sargon had already gained entrance into "Ulhu, the store city of Ursâ."⁵³ After entrance has been made and his soldiers eat from the granaries, they level the city and gather the trees into a pile and burn them. It is the final act ensuring total destruction. Here we have the wanton destruction of the life-support system, which is completely wasted. Such treatment of fruit-bearing trees is repeated several times in this important inscription; each time cut trees are piled together, followed by a massive conflagration of orchards and forests.⁵⁴ The conclusion again is that this Assyrian tactic was a part of the punishment for rebellion.

Like Sargon, the campaigns by Sennacherib also testify to similar campaign tactics.⁵⁵ During his first campaign against Babylonia, recorded on a text now located in the British Museum,⁵⁶ Sennacherib boasts, "A total of 88 strong, walled cities of Chaldea, with 820 hamlets within their borders, I besieged, I conquered, I carried away their spoil. The grain and dates which were in their plantations,

---

47. Ibid., 2:16 §32.
48. Ibid., 2:20 §39.
49. Ibid., 2:85 §158.
50. Ibid., 2:86 §159.
51. Ibid., 2:87 §161, 2:88–89 §161.
52. Ibid., 2:87 §161.
53. Ibid. On the location of these polities, see Oscar White Muscarella, "The Location of Ulhu and Urse in Sargon II's Eighth Campaign, 714 B.C.," *JFA* 13 (1986): 466–75.
54. *ARAB* 2:90 §164, 91 §165.
55. Daniel David Luckenbill, *The Annals of Sennacherib* (OIP 2; Chicago: University of Chicago Press, 1924).
56. BM 113203; first published by S. Smith, *The First Campaign of Sennacherib, King of Assyria, B.C. 705–681* (London: Luzac, 1921).

their harvest of the plain, I had my army devour."[57] In the same text he states, "The Arabs, Aramaeans, Chaldeans, who were in Uruk, Nippur, Kish, Harsagkalamma, together with the citizens, the rebels (sinners), I brought forth and counted as spoil. The grain and dates which were in their plantations, the planting of their garden-beds, the harvest of their plain and highlands (?) I had my troops devour."[58] On the Bellino Cylinder his attack against the land of Elippi resulted in first the destruction of cities and then the cutting down of orchards: "over their fertile (?) fields I poured out misery."[59]

These records testify that the fruit-bearing trees and grain were confiscated to feed the Assyrian army. Again the context implies that the confiscation of grain and dates occurred *after* the besieged cities were conquered or destroyed and the spoil carried away. There is no record that vegetation or orchards were used for the construction of siege works, nor is there any *written* record of trees being cut down for such a purpose.

Iconographic Sources

The iconography of Assyrian military tactics affirms that fruit trees remained standing during the siege and were cut down only subsequent to the defeat of the enemy city. In order to recognize this pattern, it should be pointed out that the Assyrians portrayed their military activity against cities in two ways: (1) by depicting the siege and battle in progress; and (2) by showing the city after it had been conquered and while the spoils and captives were being carried away.[60] Some of the reliefs depict a narrative progression from one scene to another. In most cases, the reliefs depict the battle as it is taking place. The king or army is in action against the city.

As already noted, battering rams, tunneling, sapping, and scaling ladders are all tactics used against the enemy cities. In the midst of these scenes, which show the Assyrians at war, the artisans provide details of the surrounding countryside. These depictions often include fruit trees, vines bearing grapes, and other vegetation.[61] At the northwest palace of Nimrud, Ashurnasirpal II is shown leading with fire of arrows the assault of a city. As a battering ram attacks the walls,

---

57. Luckenbill, *Annals of Sennacherib*, 54:51.
58. Ibid., 54:53.
59. Ibid., 59:29.
60. In some reliefs these stages of warfare are conflated and show a progression of the results of war. Such reliefs are the most instructive because they depict what happened before and after the battle. An example is the campaign by Sennacherib against the city of Lachish.
61. On the general depiction of vegetation in Assyrian art, see Pauline Albenda, "Landscape Bas-Reliefs in the Bīt Ḥilāni of Ashurbanipal," *BASOR* 224 (1976): 49–72; 225 (1977): 29–48; on the specific depiction of the destruction of orchards, see Bleibtreu, "Zerstörung der Umwelt," 220–21; and Cole, "Destruction of Orchards," 29–40.

fugitives flee for their lives, swimming on skin floats to another city while pursued by archers. In the background, trees, including a standing date palm with fruit, are depicted intact.[62] Also in the throne room at Nimrud, Ashurnasirpal is shown leading a chariot charge against a city. Above his chariot the enemies lie beheaded and strewn on the battlefield. Around them numerous shrubs and bushes remain standing.[63] Below the attacked city several fruit-bearing trees and a shrub are found standing. An enemy soldier is being killed behind one of the trees.[64]

At the central palace of Tiglath-pileser III in Nimrud, a city is shown empty after the siege is complete. Two battering rams stand abandoned at either side of the gate. Women and children captives are being carted off. Inside the city, a single date palm stands full of fruit.[65] In another scene, a fortified city is being stormed by battering rams while it is defended by archers. A date palm full of fruit is shown immediately outside the walls on the *tel*.[66] Above the battering ram another date palm with hanging fruit is standing.[67] Two more fruited date palms are depicted on either side of the archers and above a second battering ram (fig. 1).[68]

In Sennacherib's palace in Nineveh, the iconography associated with the siege of Lachish indicates that fruit and other trees remained standing during and after the city's siege and attack. This campaign against Judah is described in

---

62. BM 124536; BM 124539; Richard D. Barnett and Werner Forman, *Assyrian Palace Reliefs and Their Influence on the Sculptures of Babylonia and Assyria* (London: Batchworth, 1960), 22–23; John Malcolm Russell, "The Program of the Palace of Assurnasirpal II at Nimrud: Issues in the Research and Presentation of Assyrian Art," *AJA* 102 (1998): pl. IV, Room B, slabs 17–18. The upper portion of the slabs show the attack in progress, while the lower portion depicts the tribute presented to the king.

63. BM 124556; Barnett and Forman, *Assyrian Palace Reliefs*, 24; Russell, "Program of the Palace," pl. IV, Room B, slab 4.

64. BM 124555; Barnett and Forman, *Assyrian Palace Reliefs*, 25; Russell, "Program of the Palace," pl. IV, Room B, slab 3.

65. BM 118882; Barnett and Forman, *Assyrian Palace Reliefs*, 35–36; C. J. Gadd, *The Stones of Assyria* (London: Chatto & Windus, 1936), pl. 11.

66. BM 118903; Barnett and Forman, *Assyrian Palace Reliefs*, 38; Gadd, *Stones of Assyria*, 12.

67. The date palm is depicted at a strange angle and might appear to be falling. However, the enemy archer who has fallen with his head against it while an Assyrian is stabbing him with a spear from behind appears to be the reason for this angle. The context does not favor the interpretation that the date palm is being or has been cut down. No axes or other equipment are seen for this interpretation to be warranted.

68. Richard D. Barnett and Margarete Falkner, *The Sculptures of Aššur-nasir-pali II (883–859 B.C.), Tiglath-pileser III (745–727 B.C.), Esarhaddon (681–669 B.C.) from the Central and South-West Palaces at Nimrud* (London: British Museum Press, 1962), 81, pl. XXXII; Gadd, *Stones of Assyria*, 12.

Figure 1. Nimrud. Tiglath-pileser III attacks a Babylonian city.
C. J. Gadd, *The Stones of Assyria* (London: Chatto & Windus, 1936), 12.

biblical accounts and Sennacherib's annals[69] and is pictured on twelve slabs in a ceremonial room at Nineveh.[70] Finally, the reconstruction of this event is augmented by the archaeological record at the site itself.[71]

---

69. On the biblical description of these events and their correlation with historical records and archaeological evidence, see Siegfried H. Horn, "Did Sennacherib Campaign Once or Twice Against Hezekiah?" *AUSS* 4 (1966): 1–28; William H. Shea, "Sennacherib's Second Palestinian Campaign," *JBL* 104 (1985): 401–18; idem, "The New Tirhakah Text and Sennacherib's Second Palestinian Campaign," *AUSS* 35 (1997): 181–87; idem, "Jerusalem under Siege: Did Sennacherib Attack Twice?" *BAR* 25/6 (1999): 36–44, 64; and the responses by Mordecai Cogan, "Sennacherib's Siege of Jerusalem," *BAR* 27/1 (2001): 40–45, 69. For an overview, see Brevard S. Childs, *Isaiah and the Assyrian Crisis* (SBT 2/3; London: SCM, 1967). For Sennacherib's annals, see Luckenbill, *Annals of Sennacherib*, 29–35.

70. David Ussishkin, "The 'Lachish Reliefs' and the City of Lachish," *IEJ* 30 (1980): 174–95; idem, *The Conquest of Lachish by Sennacherib* (Tel Aviv: Tel Aviv University, Institute of Archaeology, 1982).

71. David Ussishkin, "Lachish: Renewed Archaeological Excavations," *Expedition* 20/4 (1978): 18–28; idem, "Excavations at Tel Lachish 1978–1983: Second Preliminary Report," *TA*

On slab 1 at Nineveh, three rows of infantry are shown attacking the city with arrows, spears, and sling stones. Above them are vines filled with grapes and other fruits. Trees remain standing even among the top row of archers.[72] After the siege and attack, the captives and spoil are carried by hand and by wagon to Sennacherib, who is seated in the royal tent on his throne (slabs 4–8). The countryside is depicted with standing trees, grape-bearing vines, and fruit-bearing trees (see also slabs 9–12). It appears that during the attack the fruit trees were preserved even with at least seven battering rams engaged, the largest number shown on any Assyrian relief. Even the use of logs in the construction of the siege ramp does not give a clear indication that these were fruit trees that were destroyed.[73] In another scene dating to Sennacherib, his infantry is shown advancing to the siege of a city. Between the two registers of advancing troops, alternating trees and fruit trees are depicted.[74] Sennacherib receives captives from the town of Sakhrina. In the background one sees a row of palms laden with dates.[75]

In the palace of Ashurbanipal in Nineveh,[76] a different scene shows the Elamite town Khamanu abandoned and in flames as its walls are systematically destroyed by Assyrian soldiers. In the foreground the Assyrians are carrying off the spoils from the city gate. Six trees stand behind them.[77] Another scene in the north palace of Kuyunjik depicts the triumph of Ashurbanipal over the allies of the king of Babylon. The uppermost register records the city under attack, its gatehouses on fire. The trees, however, remain standing on all sides (fig. 2).[78]

In the preceding survey of Assyrian military iconography, the focus has been on the depiction of standing fruit trees before, during, and after campaigns against cities. There are occasions, however rare, when trees are being cut down. Here again it is the sequence of events that is significant. The relief in Ashurnasirpal's northwest palace at Nimrud is not sufficiently clear in establishing a sequence.[79] However, the bronze reliefs of Shalmaneser III preserve a scene of the

---

10 (1983): 97–175; idem, "Lachish," *NEAEHL* 3:897–911.

    72. Ussishkin, *Conquest of Lachish*; Barnett and Forman, *Assyrian Palace Reliefs*, 44–47, 49.

    73. Ussishkin, *Conquest of Lachish*, 100, 105.

    74. Gadd, *Stones of Assyria*, pl. 16.

    75. Ibid., pl. 19.

    76. On the depictions of grapevines in the iconography of Ashurbanipal, see Pauline Albenda, "Gravevines in Ashurbanipal's Garden," *BASOR* 215 (1974): 5–17.

    77. BM 124919, 134386; Richard D. Barnett, *Sculptures from the North Palace of Ashurbanipal at Nineveh (668–627 B.C.)* (London: British Museum Press, 1976), pl. LXVI; Gadd, *Stones of Assyria*, pl. 43; Barnett and Forman, *Assyrian Palace Reliefs*, 132.

    78. BM 124945, 124946; Gadd, *Stones of Assyria*, pl. 26; see also Barnett, *Sculptures from the North Palace*, pl. D.

    79. In this poorly preserved scene, only the legs of soldiers cutting trees down with axes can still be made out. It is not clear what the context of this scene is nor whether these are fruit or another type of tree; see Barnett and Falkner, *The Sculptures of Aššur-nasir-pal*, pl. CXIV; see also Bleibtreu, "Zerstörung der Umwelt," 230, fig. 1.

Figure 2. Kuyunyik Assurbanipal attacks while trees stand.
C. J. Gadd, *The Stones of Assyria* (London: Chatto & Windus, 1936), pl. 26.

city of Urartu.[80] It is apparent that the city is defeated. Its walls are abandoned by defenders and consumed by flames. It is in this precise moment of annihilation that the city's orchards are being systematically cut down by soldiers wielding axes.[81]

The same pattern is found in other Assyrian reliefs depicting the cutting down of trees. During Sennacherib's campaign against Illubru, the city is shown next to a wide river, guarded by long, low walls and protected by equidistant towers. The city is surrounded by trees.[82] Several factors indicate that the city has been conquered and the siege is over. First, a long line of Assyrian soldiers can be seen exiting the city gate carrying the spoils and treasures of the city. Second, the walls are aflame. Third, the defenders of the city are not depicted, an indication that the fighting has ceased. In this state, after the defeat of the city, a single Assyrian soldier can be seen to the right of the city along the banks of the river, wielding an axe against a tree. This is not a fruit tree. Four other trees

---

80. Leonard W. King and E. A. Wallis Budge, *Bronze Reliefs from the Gates of Shalmaneser, King of Assyria, B.C. 860–825* (London: British Museum Press, 1915), pl. VIII, band II/2, upper register.

81. The destruction is consistently by means of various types of axes, never by the saw, which was introduced for felling trees in Europe during the eighteenth century (Bleibtreu, "Zerstörung der Umwelt," 226 n. 10).

82. A. T. Olmstead, *History of Assyria* (New York: Scribner's, 1923), fig. 128; Russell *Sennacherib's Palace without Rival at Nineveh* (Chicago: University of Chicago Press, 1991), 70–71, fig. 39. There is no textual verification of this destructive action in the annals; see Luckenbill, *Annals of Sennacherib*, 61–62.

are also depicted as fallen immediately below the line of soldiers carrying the booty. In the lower left corner of the relief, a fruit-bearing vine remains standing. This relief demonstrates again that the destruction of trees occurred only after a city was defeated, not before.[83] In another scene found at Sennacherib's northwest palace, the Assyrians have apparently taken one of the principle cities of Babylonia,[84] and Assyrian soldiers are depicted cutting down palm trees laden with fruit outside and inside the walls of the city. The city has been defeated, as the Assyrians are within the city walls cutting down trees. The defeated enemy comes to greet them as men beat on drums and women proceed behind them clapping their hands.

The city of Dilbat is not mentioned in Sennacherib's annals, but its vivid depiction in Room III of Sennacherib's southwest palace is a graphic example of the destruction of fruit trees.[85] In this scene there is clear evidence once again that the city has been defeated. A line of soldiers in the lowest register carries off the spoils. Assyrians are shown in the towers of the city. Two Assyrians in the lower right are playing lyres in celebration of the defeat. Behind the city and in the upper register the Assyrians are shown cutting down the date palms. They work in pairs. One tree has been sufficiently cut, and two Assyrians are pushing it over. The next two trees are depicted with one Assyrian soldier harvesting the dates while his partner strikes the tree trunk with his axe. Once again, this occurs after the city has been defeated.

In summary, the analysis of the textual and iconographic evidence allows for several significant conclusions. First, trees are depicted standing during the onslaught and battle against the city. There is no evidence of trees being cut down during this stage of battle. Second, in many scenes, even after a city has been captured, both fruit-bearing date palms, vines, and other trees are illustrated intact, surrounding a captured city that is being destroyed by flames. Finally, in only a few instances are trees shown to be cut down. This consistently occurs only *after* the city has been conquered and the enemy is vanquished. These depictions confirm the annals and other historical records, which indicate that the destruction of trees and orchards occurs after a city is abandoned, defeated, destroyed, and/or burned to the ground. This sequence of events further supports the conclusion

---

83. Olmstead states that "the Assyrians cut down the trees to construct the 'great flies of the wall' which were to force the capture of the city. It was fired [set aflame] and the long line of warriors carried off the arms" (*History of Assyria*, 311). However, there is no evidence of this from the text or from the reliefs themselves (see n. 161). Luckenbill posits that the "great wall flies" were "some siege engine" (*Annals of Sennacherib*, 62).

84. This probably represented Sennacherib's first Babylonian campaign; see Richard D. Barnett, Erika Bleibtreu, and Geoffrey Turner, *Sculptures from the Southwest Palace of Sennacherib at Nineveh* (2 vols.; London: British Museum Press, 1998), 1:130–31, 2: pls. 460–61.

85. Russell, *Sennacherib's Palace*, 153, 154, fig. 78; Barnett, Bleibtreu, and Turner, *Sculptures*, pl. 49.

that the use of fruit-bearing trees for the construction of siege works, battering rams, and other major siege machines cannot be supported by the currently known textual and iconographic sources describing and depicting ancient Assyrian warfare. Parallels for this practice must be sought elsewhere.[86]

---

86. For an extended discussion of further first and second millennium sources, see Hasel, *Military Practice and Polemic*, 95–123.

Assyrian Siege Warfare Imagery and the Background of a Biblical Curse

Jeremy D. Smoak

A number of studies over the past century have shown that there are numerous points of contact between Assyrian military propaganda and the biblical texts.[1] In general, these studies have pointed to the vast influence that both Assyrian textual and iconographic propaganda had upon the cultural discourse of Assyria's neighbors, particularly ancient Israelite and Judean societies.[2] One particularly notable, yet somewhat neglected, imprint of Assyrian military propaganda is a well-known biblical curse that threatens Israel with the following: "You will build a house but not dwell in it; you will plant a vineyard but not drink its wine." A review of biblical literature reveals that this particular curse held an especially prominent place in ancient Israel's discourse over warfare and its consequences. Over a dozen biblical texts cite the curse or allude to its imagery. Many of the references to the curse in the biblical texts associate it with siege warfare imagery or Assyrian military tactics. For instance, both Amos and Isaiah allude to the curse alongside descriptions of siege and exile (Amos 5:11; Isa 5:8–17). Zephaniah and

---

1. See most recently Cynthia R. Chapman, *The Gendered Language of Warfare in the Israelite-Assyrian Encounter* (HSM 62; Winona Lake, Ind.: Eisenbrauns, 2004); see also Peter Machinist, "Assyria and Its Image in First Isaiah," *JAOS* 103 (1983): 719–37; Chayim Cohen, "Neo-Assyrian Elements in the First Speech of the Biblical Rab-Šaqe," *IOS* 9 (1979): 32–48; Shemaryahu Talmon, "Polemics and Apology in Biblical Historiography: 2 Kings 17:24–41," in *The Creation of Sacred Literature* (ed. R. E. Friedman; Berkeley and Los Angeles: University of California Press, 1981), 57–75; Shalom M. Paul, "Sargon's Administrative Diction in II Kings 17:27," *JBL* 88 (1969): 73–74; Hayim Tadmor and Mordechai Cogan, "Ahaz and Tiglath-pileser in the Book of Kings: Historiographic Considerations," *Bib* 60 (1979): 491–508; William Moran, "The Ancient Near Eastern Background of the Love of God in Deuteronomy," *CBQ* 25 (1963): 77–87; Moshe Weinfeld, "The Loyalty Oath in the Ancient Near East," *UF* 8 (1977): 379–414.

2. On Assyrian iconography and its place in Assyrian military propaganda, see Irene Winter, "Royal Rhetoric and the Development of Historical Narrative in Neo-Assyrian Reliefs," *Studies in Visual Communication* 7 (1981): 2–38.

Deuteronomy also refer to the curse within the context of horrors associated with siege (Zeph 1:13; Deut 28:30).

Scholars have long noted that the threat of war forms the background of this curse.[3] Nevertheless, there has been little discussion of its exact trajectory within biblical warfare rhetoric. An examination of Assyrian sources points to certain aspects of Assyrian military propaganda as the background of the curse within early biblical discourse. For instance, Assyrian sources frequently pair descriptions of the destruction of houses with descriptions of the destruction of vegetation such as vineyards or orchards. Several iconographic sources also depict the deportation of people from cities or homes together with the destruction of vegetation. An examination of these sources clarifies the curse's trajectory and significance within the biblical literature.

THE DESTRUCTION OF AGRICULTURE IN ASSYRIAN TEXTS AND ICONOGRAPHY

One of the more significance shifts that accompanied the increasing Assyrian presence in the Levant during the eighth century was the shift from open-field battle to siege warfare.[4] Both the Assyrian and biblical sources, for instance, indicate that during this period siege warfare gradually displaced battle in open fields. This trend is especially noticeable in Assyrian iconographic sources, which increasingly depict Assyrian kings laying siege to well-fortified cities as opposed to meeting their enemies in open-field battle.

Naturally, the increased dependence upon siege warfare during this time brought with it new battle tactics and techniques, many of which are alluded to in Assyrian and biblical sources. Assyrian sources indicate that one of the most devastating tactics that the Assyrian army employed during or following a siege was

---

3. For previous discussion of the curse and the motif of building and planting, see Robert Bach, "Bauen und Pflanzen," in *Studien zur Theologie der atltestamentlichen Überlieferungen* (ed. R. Rendtorff and K. Koch; Neukirchen-Vluyn: Neukirchener, 1961), 22; Daniel L. Smith, *The Religion of the Landless: The Social Context of the Babylonian Exile* (Bloomington, Ind.: Meyer Stone, 1989), 130–34; Carey Ellen Walsh, *The Fruit of the Vine: Viticulture in Ancient Israel* (Harvard Semitic Museum Publications; Winona Lake, Ind.: Eisenbrauns, 2000), 63–67.

4. See Israel Eph'al, *Siege and Its Ancient Near Eastern Manifestations* (Jerusalem: Magnes, 1996); idem, "Ways and Means to Conquer a City, Based on Assyrian Queries to the Sungod," in *Assyria 1995: Proceedings of the 10th Anniversary Symposium of the Neo-Assyrian Text Corpus Project, Helsinki, September 7–11, 1995* (ed. S. Parpola and R. M. Whiting; Helsinki: Neo-Assyrian Text Corpus Project, 1997), 49–54; idem, "On Warfare and Military Control in the Ancient Near Eastern Empires: A Research Outline," in *History, Historiography and Interpretation: Studies in Biblical and Cuneiform Literatures* (ed. H. Tadmor and M. Weinfeld; Jerusalem: Magnes, 1983), 88–106; Alfred C. Mierzejewski, "La technique de siège assyrienne aux IX–VII siècles avant notre ère," *Etudes et Travaux* 7 (Varsovie): 11–20; see also A. Leo Oppenheim, "Siege-Documents from Nippur," *Iraq* 17 (1955): 69–89.

the destruction of agricultural support systems.[5] This practice is vividly portrayed in numerous Assyrian iconographic sources from the first millennium. Assyrian textual sources are also littered with descriptions of the Assyrians chopping down trees, orchards, vineyards, and other agricultural produce of their enemies. For instance, in the Suḫu Annals of Shalmaneser III, the king boasts, "We will go and attack the houses of the land of Suhu; we will seize his cities of the steppe; and we will cut down their fruit trees."[6] In the Nimrud Monolith, Shalmaneser boasts, "Ahuni, son of Adini ... I shut up in his city, carried off the crops of his (fields), cut down his orchards."[7] A review of other Assyrian inscriptions reveals that descriptions of the destruction of vegetation formed a regular motif associated with siege during this period.

Scholars have long sought to understand the exact purpose behind the Assyrian destruction of agriculture. Past studies claimed that the destruction of trees and other vegetation enabled the Assyrians to build siege equipment during a prolonged siege or feed the Assyrian army.[8] More recent studies provide two alternative explanations for this practice. Some studies have argued that the destruction of agriculture was used to punish a rebellious vassal of the empire. Other studies have argued, however, that the description of destruction of agriculture in the campaign narratives is a face-saving device. In other words, the descriptions attempt to conceal the fact that the Assyrians were unsuccessful in taking a city.[9] Steven Cole, for example, notes that many of the descriptions of the destruction of orchards occur when the Assyrians did not take the city.[10] This is particularly true of the annals of Tiglath-pileser III and Sargon II. More often

---

5. On this military tactic, see Erika Bleibtreu, "Zerstörung der Umwelt durch Bäumefällen und Dezimierung des Löwenbestandes in Mesopotamien," in *Der orientalische Mensch und seine Beziehungen zur Umwelt, Beiträge zum 2. Grazer morgenländischen Symposion (2.-5. März 1989)* (ed. B. Scholz; Grazer morgenländische Studien 2; Graz: GrazKult, 1989), 219–33; Steven W. Cole, "The Destruction of Orchards in Assyrian Warfare," in Parpola and Whiting, *Assyria 1995*, 29–40; Bustenay Oded, "Cutting Down the Gardens in the Descriptions of the Assyrian Kings—A Chapter in Assyrian Historiography," in *Michael: Historical, Epigraphical and Biblical Studies in Honor of Prof. Michael Heltzer* (ed. Y. Avishur and R. Deutsch; Tel Aviv: Archaeological Center Publications, 1999), 27*–36*. See also Michael G. Hasel's essay in this volume ("Assyrian Military Practices and Deuteronomy's Laws of Warfare") and idem, *Military Practice and Polemic: Israel's Laws of Warfare in Near Eastern Perspective* (Berrien Springs, Mich.: Andrews University Press, 2005).

6. Grant Frame, *Rulers of Babylonia: From the Second Dynasty of Isin to the End of Assyrian Domination (1157–612 BC)* (RIMB 2; Toronto: University of Toronto Press, 1995), 295.

7. *ARAB* 1:229 §620.

8. See Cole, "Destruction of Orchards," 34.

9. Hayim Tadmor, *The Inscriptions of Tiglath-pileser III, King of Assyria* (Jerusalem: Israel Academy of Sciences and Humanities, 1994), 79; Hasel, *Military Practice and Polemic*; Cole, "Destruction of Orchards," 34.

10. Cole, "Destruction of Orchards," 34.

than not, the descriptions of the cutting down of orchards in their annals occurs in places where it appears that the kings failed to capture a city or its leader.[11] A close reading of these inscriptions suggests that the destruction of vegetation was directed toward rural populations who had fled to the cities for protection. In these cases, the descriptions of the destruction of vegetation partially served to conceal the ultimate failure of the Assyrians to take the city.

A closer examination of the relationship between the campaign narratives and the iconography brings further clarity to this problem. First, the iconographic sources often juxtapose the destruction of agriculture with the destruction and looting of the city, which culminated in the deportation of the city's elite. The iconography at Sennacherib's southwest palace is particularly instructive in this regard. In a scene depicting the siege of the city of Dilbat, Assyrian soldiers cut down date palms while other soldiers remove spoil from the conquered city.[12] The scene places the destruction of vegetation alongside the burning of city buildings and the removal of its population. It is also during this stage of the siege in many Assyrian sources that the local inhabitants are removed from their homes and depicted as being deported from the city.

A similar picture emerges from the other iconography of Sennacherib's palace at Nineveh. In a scene depicting Sennacherib's capture of Illubru, Assyrian soldiers are depicted carrying away the spoils of the city and leading the inhabitants out of the city into captivity.[13] In the same scene, an Assyrian soldier is presented hacking down a tree while all of these events transpire. A bronze relief of Shalmaneser III also depicts Assyrian soldiers chopping down trees during the final stages of the destruction of a city in Urartu.[14] Again, the order of events in the relief connects the destruction of the city's vegetation with the final stages of the city's destruction after the Assyrians had taken the city.

The order of events described in the Assyrian textual sources largely parallels that of the iconographic sources. The Assyrian inscriptions nearly always situate descriptions of the destruction of vegetation *after* descriptions of the capture and looting of cities. For example, the annals of Sargon II closely connect the decimation of vegetation with the destruction of a city:

> Into Ulhu, the store-city of Ursa I entered triumphantly; to the palace, his royal abode, I marched victoriously. The mighty wall, which was made of stone from

---

11. Tadmor, *Tiglath-pileser III*, 78:1'–12' (Ann. 23); see also ibid., 162:23–24; and Henry W. F. Saggs, *Iraq* 17 (1955): pl. V (after p. 50) r. 11'–15' (NL 2).

12. John M. Russell, *Sennacherib's Palace without Rival at Nineveh* (Chicago: University of Chicago Press, 1991), 154, fig. 78.

13. Ibid., 70–71, fig. 39.

14. Leonard W. King and E. A. Wallis Budge, *Bronze Reliefs from the Gates of Shalmaneser, King of Assyria, B.C. 860–825* (London: British Museum Press, 1915), pl. VIII, band II/2, upper register.

the lofty mountain, with iron axes and iron hoes I smashed like a pot and leveled it to the ground.... Into his pleasant gardens, the adornments of his city which were overflowing with fruit and wine ... came tumbling down.... His great trees, the adornment of his palace, I cut down like millet (?), and destroyed the city of his glory, and his province I brought to shame. The trunks of all those trees, which I had cut down, I gathered together, heaped them in a pile and burned them with fire. Their abundant crops, which (in) garden and marsh were immeasurable, I tore up by the root and did not leave an ear to remember the destruction.[15]

Again, the sequence of events described in the annals is important. The description of the destruction of vegetation follows the description of the breach of the city walls and the final capture of the city. The narration of the conquest of other cities follows the same order of events. For instance, the description of Sargon II's conquest of the land of Aiadi states:

I sent up large numbers of troops against their cities and they carried off large quantities of their property, their goods. Their strong walls, together with 87 cities of their neighborhood, I destroyed, I leveled to the ground. *I set fire to the houses with them*, and made the beams of their roofs like flame. Their heaped-up granaries I opened and let my army devour unmeasured quantities of barley. *Their orchards I cut down*, their forests I felled; all their tree trunks I gathered together and set them on fire.[16]

An examination of several other Assyrian sources reveals that there was a purposeful attempt to portray the destruction of vegetation after the destruction of a city.

A number of Assyrian textual sources specify vineyards or wine as an object that was singled out by the Assyrians following a successful siege. For instance, in his description of the looting of Ulhu, Sargon boasts, "Its guarded wine cellars I entered, and the widespreading hosts of Assur drew the good wine from the bottles like river water."[17] Later in the description of Sargon's conquest of the lands of the Manneans and Nairi, the king brags, "I cut down great quantities of its vines, I made an end to its drinking." Like the iconographic and textual sources described above, these texts may indicate that the Assyrians only destroyed vegetation as punishment against a rebellious or incompliant enemy, since these descriptions of the destruction of viticulture also follow the description of the breach of city walls or the capture of the city in the inscriptions.[18]

---

15. *ARAB* 2:87 §161. On the inscriptions of Sargon II, see also Andreas Fuchs, *Die Inschriften Sargons II aus Khorsabad* (Göttingen: Cuvillier, 1994).
16. *ARAB* 2:91–92 §166.
17. Ibid., 2:87 §161.
18. Hasel, *Military Practice and Polemic*, 62.

A number of Assyrian campaign narratives also contain descriptions of the destruction of houses and other physical structures following descriptions of a successful siege. In fact, several textual sources closely situate descriptions of the destruction of houses with descriptions of the destruction of agriculture. For example, in the description of Sargon's conquest of the land of Aiadi, the king boasts that he "set fire to the houses" and then "cut down their orchards."[19] Several other textual sources also closely situate references to houses and agriculture as objects of destruction. The order of events is similar in Sargon's description of his conquest of the lands of Manneans and Nairi. After describing the successful scaling of the wall of their cities, he brags, "I set fire on their beautiful dwellings, and made the smoke thereof rise and cover the face of heaven like a storm.... I cut down its splendid orchards, I cut down great quantities of its vines, making an end of its drinking."[20] A similar description of a successful siege occurs in Sargon's letter to Ashur recounting the events of his eighth campaign. In the description of his conquest of the city of Ushkaia in Urartu, Sargon claims that he set fire to the dwellings and then left its fields as if destroyed by a flood.[21] Sennacherib's annals also often pair descriptions of the destruction of homes, or the deportation of people from homes, with descriptions of the devastation of vegetation.[22]

Assyrian inscriptions and iconography also closely situate depictions of mass deportation with those of the destruction of cities and agricultural support systems. The pictorial battle scenes prove to be particularly instructive here. As noted above, several scenes juxtapose the deportation of people with the destruction of vegetation and the burning of the city. Hence, Assyrian iconography suggests that the threat in the curse that one will build a house but not dwell in it may reflect this Assyrian practice of deportation. Several Assyrian textual sources also juxtapose descriptions of the destruction of vegetation with descriptions of deportation. For instance, in the campaign narrative of Sennacherib's conquest of the land of Ellipi, he boasts, "Their orchards I cut down, over their fertile fields I poured out misery.... The people, great and small, male and female, horses, mules, asses, cattle and sheep, without number, I carried off and brought them to naught."[23] Thus, it is likely that both the references to deportation and the destruction of houses in the Assyrian sources are implied in the biblical threat against the habitation of houses.

The Assyrian sources described above provide compelling contexts in which to situate the early history of the biblical curse. Specifically, the pairing of ref-

---

19. *ARAB* 2:91 §166.
20. Ibid., 2:90 §164.
21. Ibid., 2:85 §158.
22. Daniel D. Luckenbill, *Annals of Sennacherib* (OIP 2; Chicago: University of Chicago Press, 1924), 58–59:23–32.
23. Ibid., 59:29.

erences to houses and vegetation in the campaign narratives may explain the pairing of these objects in the biblical curse. More importantly, these sources suggest a location for the curse within the context of siege warfare propaganda. The Assyrian sources locate the descriptions of the destruction of houses and agriculture during the final stages of a siege. This location clarifies the exact trajectory of the curse within early biblical discourse. The curse threatened the successful capture of a city, which culminated in deportation, destruction of houses, and the devastation of agriculture. An examination of the curse in representative biblical texts demonstrates this idea. Amos's citation of the curse, for example, occurs alongside threats predicting the destruction of fortresses (5:9), exile (5:5), and wailing in city streets and vineyards (5:17). In a similar fashion, Isaiah's allusion to the curse appears alongside images clearly associated with siege, such as a population held within a city dying from hunger and thirst (5:11–13). The use of the curse in Zephaniah is also set within images reminiscent of warfare (1:12–16). These texts combined with the Assyrian sources suggest that the curse reflected part of Israel's experience with Assyrian siege propaganda and tactics. Within this context, the curse came to threaten the successful capture of a city, which culminated in the removal of people from their houses and the destruction of the city's vegetation.

The Function of the Assyrian and Biblical Imagery

As an example of the issue raised above concerning the function of the Assyrian actions and representations, Michael Hasel's recent study of the siege relief scenes argues that the depiction of the destruction of vegetation during the burning of a city in the iconography suggests that the Assyrians may have only destroyed an enemy's vegetation as a final punishment following a successful siege.[24] In a similar vein, Hasel contends that the presentation of the destruction of vegetation after the description of the taking of the city in the campaign narratives also indicates that the Assyrians only destroyed vegetation following a siege. Although this is an intriguing idea, it may not take seriously enough the overall purpose of the scenes and their relation to Assyrian treaty curses and the biblical curse. It is equally likely that the portrayal of trees and other vegetation in the scenes alongside the image of deported peoples was meant as a visual curse of sorts rather than a realistic sequencing of events. Another way to explain the juxtaposition of events in the battle scenes is to see them as an attempt to illustrate as many of the curses found in the Assyrian treaties as possible. Understood in this way, the imagery in the scenes may be seen primarily as an attempt to depict the materialization of the treaty curses. This explanation of the battle scenes would also explain the parallels between the relief scenes and inscriptions described above.

---

24. Hasel, *Military Practice and Polemic*.

The juxtaposition of events in both the iconographic and textual sources derives from a common effort by the Assyrians to depict the king's campaigns precisely as the materialization of the treaty curses. In fact, the Assyrian annals contain explicit statements describing campaigns as the agents that caused curses to fall upon rebellious peoples. For instance, Ashurbanipal's annals describing his campaign against the Arabian tribes state that, during the king's campaign, "(the gods inflicted upon them) as many curses as are written in their loyalty oaths."[25] In this way, the depiction of the king's actions as a materialization of the curse also portrays the king as the one who is loyal to the treaty.

This interpretation may further clarify the connection between the biblical curse and the imagery in the Assyrian sources. The juxtaposition of the city's trees alongside images of deportees who are being paraded out of the city may be intended to evoke an image of having the fruit of one's labor enjoyed by an enemy. Hence, the picture of Assyrian soldiers chopping down date palms and other vegetation stands alongside that of other soldiers burning the city and taking captives; that is, the battle scenes portray the deportation of the city's inhabitants from their homes while soldiers begin enjoying their agriculture. These battle scenes may thus be understood as a form of visual curse, which reinforced the efficacy of curses found in the treaty oaths.

In this vein, it is noteworthy that houses, orchards, fields, and other vegetation form some of the most significant objects promised in Assyrian land grants and threatened in Assyrian treaties. For instance, one of the curses contained in the treaties of Esarhaddon threatens his vassals in the following words:

> May Adad, the canal inspector of heaven and earth, cut off sea[sonal flooding] from your land and deprive your fields of [grain], may he [submerge] your land with a great flood; may the locust who diminishes the land devour your harvest.[26]

One also sees frequent references to "towns, fields, houses, and orchards" in the Assyrian land-grant texts from the eighth century B.C.E.[27] The repetition of these objects in the campaign narratives, land grants, and treaties may suggest that the biblical curse's connection of houses and vineyards originated in the context of vassal diplomacy. Perhaps Israel's experience with Assyrian propaganda, rather than actual warfare, generated the biblical curse against houses and vineyards.

---

25. Maximilian Streck, *Assurbanipal und die letzten assyrischen Könige bis zum Untergange Ninivehs* (Leipzig: Hinrichs, 1916), 76:60.

26. Simo Parpola and Kazuko Watanabe, *Neo-Assyrian Treaties and Loyalty Oaths* (SAA 2; Helsinki: Helsinki University Press, 1988), §47, 440–43.

27. For examples, see Laura Kataja and Robert Whiting, eds., *Grants, Decrees and Gifts of the Neo-Assyrian Period* (SAA 12; Helsinki: Helsinki University Press, 1995).

Along these lines, several recent studies propose that other elements of Assyrian battle-relief scenes are also visual representations that illustrate curses found in Assyrian and biblical texts. For instance, Irene Winter understands the depiction of enemy bows broken or strewn across battlefields as an illustration of Assyrian curses that threaten the breaking of enemy bows.[28] Similarly, Cynthia Chapman argues that the portrayal of women in some of the Assyrian battle scenes also reflects curses found in several biblical texts.[29]

These studies further the contention raised here about the relationship between the Assyrian siege propaganda and the biblical curse. In general, they highlight how curses formed an important thread in Assyrian propaganda, which held together the various mediums of wartime rhetoric, from iconographic depictions to vassal oaths to campaign narratives. This aspect of Assyrian propaganda explains the background and prominence of the biblical curse on houses and vineyards. Within warfare rhetoric, the curse threatened the consequences of an Assyrian siege, namely, that an enemy would enjoy the fruit of one's labor. As such, the curse embodied the horrors associated with Assyrian military tactics, such as deportation and exile. Given the curse's association with these military tactics, it is no surprise that postexilic biblical literature reformulates the curse into a blessing signifying return and reconstruction. These texts use the reversal of this curse as a powerful slogan for the restoration community following the exile (Isa 65:21–22; Jer 31:4–6; Ezek 28:26)[30] and thus further reinforce the curse's original association with Assyrian warfare tactics and curses, such as siege, deportation, and exile.

---

28. Irene Winter, "Sex, Rhetoric, and the Public Monument: The Alluring Body of the Male Ruler in Mesopotamia," in *Sexuality in Ancient Art: Near East, Egypt, Greece, and Italy* (ed. N. Kampen et al.; Cambridge: Cambridge University Press, 1996), 11–26 (11–13). See further and developed more in idem., "Tree(s) on the Mountain: Landscape and Territory on the Victory Stele of Naram-Sin of Agade," in *Landscapes: Territories, Frontiers and Horizons in the Ancient Near East: Papers Presented to the XLIV Rencontre Assyriologique Internationale Venezia, 7–11 July 1997* (ed. L. Milano et al.; Padova: Sargon, 1999), 66–72. For general discussion, see Chapman, *Gendered Language*.

29. See Chapman, *Gendered Language*.

30. For discussion of the blessing in these texts, see Shalom M. Paul, "Literary and Ideological Echoes of Jeremiah in Deutero-Isaiah," in *World Congress of Jewish Studies 5* (Jerusalem: Magnes, 1971), 102–20.

Part 2
Writing and Reading the Gender of War

Wartime Rhetoric: Prophetic Metaphorization of Cities as Female

Brad E. Kelle

For contemporary readers, prophetic texts that describe the violation of a woman are disturbing, to say the least. "I will direct my passion against you.... they shall cut off your nose and ears.... they shall strip you of your clothing and take away your dazzling jewels" (Ezek 23:25–26 JPS); "I will lift up your skirts over your face and display your nakedness to the nations and your shame to the kingdoms" (Nah 3:5 JPS). In most cases, these are not likely to be the texts that readily come to mind for people when they think of the prophetic books. Contemporary readers are more likely to gravitate to prophetic words that imagine an era where "the wolf shall live with the lamb" (Isa 11:6 NRSV) or declare YHWH's requirements "to do justice, and to love kindness, and to walk humbly with your God" (Mic 6:8 NRSV). Readers from the tradition of Protestant Christianity, for example, will find no appearances of Ezek 23 or Nah 3 in their standard lectionary that guides the church's reading and preaching. Because of the troubling nature of such texts, however, much scholarly discussion has taken place concerning how one might understand their origins, functions, and ramifications. As part of that discussion, scholars often emphasize that texts such as these are personifying ancient *cities* as females and using this violent language to describe *city* destruction.[1]

---

1. For a list of recent works discussing the personification of cities as females, see Peggy L. Day, "The Personification of Cities as Females in the Hebrew Bible: The Thesis of Aloysius Fitzgerald, F.S.C.," in *Social Location and Biblical Interpretation in Global Perspective* (vol. 2 of *Reading from This Place*; ed. F. Segovia and M. Tolbert. Minneapolis: Fortress, 1995), 283 n. 1. See also Brad E. Kelle, *Hosea 2: Metaphor and Rhetoric in Historical Perspective* (SBLAcBib 20; Atlanta: Society of Biblical Literature, 2005), 81–109; Peggy L. Day, "Yahweh's Broken Marriages as Metaphoric Vehicle in the Hebrew Prophets," in *Sacred Marriages in the Biblical World* (ed. M. Nissinen and R. Uro; Winona Lake, Ind.: Eisenbrauns, forthcoming); Gail A. Yee, *Poor Banished Children of Eve: Woman as Evil in the Hebrew Bible* (Minneapolis: Fortress, 2003), 111–34; Mary E. Shields, *Circumscribing the Prostitute: The Rhetorics of Intertextuality, Metaphor, and Gender in Jeremiah 3:1–4:4* (JSOTSup 387; London: T&T Clark, 2004); Chayim Cohen, "The 'Widowed' City," *JANES* 5 (1973): 75–81; John J. Schmitt, "The Gender of Ancient Israel," *JSOT* 26 (1983):

This study examines prophetic texts that personify cities as females.[2] The study of the broad phenomenon of female symbolization in the Hebrew Bible goes beyond this scope and continues to take on new dimensions.[3] The specific task here, however, is to explore the prophetic personifications of cities and how they function rhetorically within the prophet's discourse. Three observations on these texts may provide a perspective on their nature and function in the ancient context as well as on their problems and possibilities for contemporary readers. To anticipate the conclusion: the prophetic metaphorization, or development of the metaphor of the endangered or violated woman to represent the threatened or destroyed city, is rhetoric crafted for times of warfare: it is a specific way of drawing upon a well-established metaphorical tradition to criticize the males who occupy the centers of power and to alter the audience's perspective on both the powerful and the deity.

What and Where? The Metaphorization of Cities in Prophetic Texts

Throughout the Hebrew Bible, both Israelite and non-Israelite cities appear as wives, brides, mothers, and whores.[4] These personifications include at least fourteen different cities that are represented as female in prophetic texts.[5] The history

---

115–25; idem, "The Motherhood of God and Zion as Mother," *RB* 92 (1985): 557–69; Elaine R. Follis, "The Holy City as Daughter," in *Directions in Biblical Hebrew Poetry* (ed. E. Follis; JSOT-Sup 40; Sheffield: JSOT Press, 1987); Odil H. Steck, "Zion als Gelande und Gestalt," *ZTK* 86 (1989): 261–81; Mark E. Biddle, "The Figure of Lady Jerusalem: Identification, Deification, and Personification of Cities in the Ancient Near East," in *The Biblical Canon in Comparative Perspective* (ed. K. L. Younger Jr., W. W. Hallo, and B. Batto; Ancient Near Eastern Texts and Studies 11; Lewiston, N.Y.: Mellen, 1991), 173–94; Fokkelien van Dijk-Hemmes, "The Metaphorization of Woman in Prophetic Speech: An Analysis of Ezekiel XXIII," *VT* 43 (1993): 162–70; Julie Galambush, *Jerusalem in the Book of Ezekiel: The City as Yahweh's Wife* (SBLDS 130; Atlanta: Scholars Press, 1992); Ehud Ben Zvi, "Observations on the Marital Metaphor of YHWH and Israel in Its Ancient Israelite Context: General Considerations and Particular Images in Hosea 1.2," *JSOT* 28 (2004): 363–84.

2. The major representative prophetic texts that personify cities as females include Isa 1:8, 21–31; 16:1; 23:1–18; 40:1–2; 47:1–15; 49:14–26; 50:1–3; 51:3, 17–23; 52:1–2, 7–8; 54:1–7; 60:1–22; 62:1–12; 66:7–12; Jer 2:2, 16–28a, 32–37; [3:1–13?]; 5:7–11; 6:2–8; 13:22–27; 18:13; 46:11; 49:3–6, 23–27; 50:42; Ezek 16:1–63; 23:1–49; 26:1–21; [Hos 2:4b–25?]; Amos 5:2; Mic 1:6–9, 13; 4:8–13; 5:1–2; Nah 3:1–7, 8–17.

3. See, e.g., Yee, *Poor Banished Children*.

4. E.g., Isa 49:14–26; 50:1; 54:6; 62:1–5; Jer 2:2; 3:1, 8; Lam 1–2; Ezek 16; 23; Nah 3. For additional examples, see T. David Andersen, "Renaming and Wedding Imagery in Isaiah 62," *Bib* 67 (1986): 75–80.

5. Alice Laffey (*An Introduction to the Old Testament: A Feminist Perspective* [Philadelphia: Fortress, 1988], 162) identifies the following: Gaza (Amos 1:7), Rabbah (Amos 1:14) and her daughters (Jer 49:3), Samaria (Amos 3:9) and her daughters (Mic 4:8), the daughter of Gallim (Isa 10:30), the daughter of Tarshish (Isa 23:10), Sidon (Isa 23:4) and her daughter (Isa 23:12),

of research on this issue has largely focused on trying to discover the possible mythological backgrounds of the Hebrew Bible's practice of female personification. In 1972, Aloysius Fitzgerald concluded that the Hebrew Bible's practice is not simple personification but draws upon the background of a pattern of West Semitic thought in which cities were seen as goddesses who were married to the patron gods of the cities.[6] Fitzgerald based this conclusion on evidence such as Assyrian personal names in which a city is seen as feminine (e.g., Aššur-šar-rat, "Ashur is queen"), similar titles for capital cities and goddesses (e.g., בת), city names that seem to be derived from the names of male deities, and Phoenician coins of the Hellenistic period that have representations of and inscriptions about a deified city personified as a woman.[7] The proper construal of this evidence, however, has been heavily debated, and a possible mythological background for the female personification of cities remains uncertain. For example, Peggy Day has offered a point-by-point refutation of Fitzgerald's thesis that rejects the idea

---

Tyre (Isa 23:15) and her daughters (Ezek 26:6, 8), Bethlehem Ephrathah (Mic 5:2), and Sodom (Ezek 16:46, 48–49) and her daughters (Ezek 16:53, 55).

There is an ongoing debate over whether peoples/nations are personified as female in prophetic texts. For example, Laffey (ibid., 163) maintains that some prophetic texts do personify countries as females. The majority of the texts that she cites, however, refer to the "daughter(s)" or "virgin" of a particular country from which she extrapolates that the country as a whole is personified as a mother (e.g., Isa 16:2; 47:1; Jer 18:13; 46:11; 50:42; Ezek 16:27, 57; 32:18; Amos 5:2). These constructions are perhaps more rightly understood, however, as designations for a city, particularly a capital city. See Aloysius Fitzgerald, "*BTWLT* and *BT* as Titles for Capital Cities," *CBQ* 37 (1975): 167–83; Frederick W. Dobbs-Allsopp, "The Syntagma of *bat* Followed by a Geographical Name in the Hebrew Bible: A Reconsideration of Its Meaning and Grammar," *CBQ* 57 (1995): 451–70; and John J. Schmitt, "The Virgin of Israel: Referent and the Use of the Phrase in Amos and Jeremiah," *CBQ* 53 (1991): 365–87. Thus, the present study presumes that the syntagma בת + GN or בתולת + GN is a reference to a city. Additionally, this study distinguishes between simple references to cities as feminine objects and full or partial *personifications* of cities as females. The latter are the focus of inquiry here. The simple use of feminine pronouns or verbs with a city name does not necessarily indicate personification (see Frederick W. Dobbs-Allsopp, *Weep, O Daughter of Zion: A Study of the City-Lament Genre in the Hebrew Bible* [BibOr 44; Rome: Pontifical Biblical Institute, 1993], 37 n. 245).

6. Aloysius Fitzgerald, "The Mythological Background for the Presentation of Jerusalem as a Queen and False Worship as Adultery in the Old Testament," *CBQ* 34 (1972): 406–13. Fitzgerald notes that this thesis was already suggested by Julius Lewy, "The Old West Semitic Sun-God Hammu," *HUCA* 18 (1944): 436–43.

7. See also Biddle ("Figure of Lady Jerusalem," 174–75), who argues that a close relationship between cities and goddesses can be found in texts even earlier than those cited by Fitzgerald. In East Semitic texts, cities were closely "identified" with a goddess, who was their patron, but in later West Semitic texts the cities themselves became deified as goddesses. Due to its monotheistic perspective, however, Biddle concludes that the Hebrew Bible evidences only the personification, not deification, of cities as female entities.

of a background of deification of feminine cities.[8] Yet, even while challenging the supposed mythological background, Day readily acknowledges that both the Hebrew Bible and extrabiblical texts frequently represent cities as females.[9] At the very least, then, the metaphorizations of cities as females in the prophetic books seem to rest upon a long-standing and widespread tradition, evidenced throughout the ancient Near East, in which cities were personified as various types of female figures, with or without mythological connections.[10]

Leaving the discussion of potential backgrounds aside, let us focus more closely on the rhetorical arrangement and function of the personification texts themselves. A close analysis of prophetic texts that personify cities as females, such as those cited at the outset of this article, leads to a first observation: when these texts describe the *destruction* of the city, they frequently employ the metaphorical language of physical and sexual violence against a woman.[11] Six texts are primary in this regard: Isa 47:1–5; 52:1–2; Jer 13:22–27; Ezek 16:1–63; 23:1–49; Nah 3:1–7. The two texts quoted at the outset of this article, Ezek 23:25–26 and Nah 3:5, typify this metaphorical practice by referring to imminent destruction as the "stripping" or displaying of "nakedness" of the personified female. Ezekiel 16:37–41 illustrates this practice because it contains language of stripping and

---

8. See Day, "Personification of Cities," 282–302. For full discussion, see Kelle, *Hosea 2*, 86–90.

9. See also Richtsje Abma, *Bonds of Love: Methodic Studies of Prophetic Texts with Marriage Imagery (Isaiah 50:1–3 and 54:1–10, Hosea 1–3, Jeremiah 2–3)* (SSN 40; Assen: Van Gorcum, 1999), 22; Biddle, "Figure of Lady Jerusalem," 186. Galambush (*Jerusalem in the Book of Ezekiel*, 20) suggests that the concept of the city as a goddess married to the patron god may have functioned only as a type of conceptual metaphor that was the unacknowledged source of language about capital cities.

10. One may gain an indication of the antiquity of this practice of thinking of cities as feminine from the Amarna letters. In these texts, even though the Akkadian word for city is masculine, the scribes consistently made it feminine to conform to their metaphorical tradition (see John J. Schmitt, "Yahweh's Divorce in Hosea 2—Who Is That Woman?" *SJOT* 9 [1995]: 123).

11. As Harold C. Washington ("'Lest He Die in the Battle and Another Man Take Her': Violence and the Construction of Gender in the Laws of Deuteronomy 20–22," in *Gender and Law in the Hebrew Bible and the Ancient Near East* [ed. V. H. Matthews, B. M. Levinson, and T. Frymer-Kensky; JSOTSup 262; Sheffield: Sheffield Academic Press, 1998], 198) summarizes: "The Hebrew prophets develop this personification into an elaborate metaphorical picture where the objects of military attack (cities and land) are depicted as feminine, the attack itself is figured as sexual assault, and the soldiers in their military advance (in some cases along with God, the ultimate instigator of the punishing violence) are portrayed as rapists." See also Pamela Gordon and Harold C. Washington ("Rape as a Military Metaphor in the Hebrew Bible," in *A Feminist Companion to the Latter Prophets* [ed. A. Brenner; FCB 8; Sheffield: Sheffield Academic Press, 1995], 308–25), who also note that the image of a conquered city as a raped woman is prevalent in classical Greek and Roman literature.

even dismemberment of a woman yet proceeds in the same breath to describe the destruction of towers, platforms, and houses:

> I will deliver you [f. sg.] into their hands, and they shall throw down your platform and break down your lofty places; they shall strip you of your clothes.... they shall stone you and cut you to pieces with their swords. They shall burn your houses and execute judgments on you in the sight of many women. (16:39–41 NRSV)

The relevant texts seem to indicate that the commonly noticed prophetic imagery of physical and sexual violence against women appears *only in* the context of the destruction of a *city* that is personified as a woman. Although some have suggested that the city may be a metonym for the nation, people, or land,[12] the only "wife" Yhwh is ever said to divorce, violently or nonviolently, in the prophetic texts seems to be a city, and the violent imagery of exposing the genitals occurs only in texts relating to cities and their destruction.[13] Two possible exceptions to this conclusion are the description of "Rebel Israel" and "Faithless Judah" in Jer 3:1–13 and the threatened punishments against the unnamed "wife/mother" in Hos 2:4b–25. The passage in Jer 3 indeed seems to personify something other than a city, but it does not employ the language of physical and sexual violence against the women. Additionally, some scholars have forwarded textual arguments that the references there should be understood as the cities of Samaria and Jerusalem.[14] Likewise, the similarity of the language and imagery in Hos 2 to the other texts that personify cities as females leads some interpreters to conclude that the unspecified woman in the metaphor of Hos 2 should be seen as the city Samaria.[15] Even if one allows for these exceptions, however, the majority of the relevant texts favor the conclusion that the language of physical and sexual violence against women in the prophetic texts is metaphorical and conventional language for describing the destruction of a city.

Although the language of these descriptions is often noted by readers, particularly those attentive to gender concerns, it is not often analyzed within the context of prophetic personifications of cities in general. Considering this context leads to a second, broader observation. Not only do prophetic texts *describe* city destruction with language of physical and sexual violence, but a survey of references to women within the prophetic texts indicates that cities are personified

---

12. So Yee, *Poor Banished Children*, 117; see discussion below.
13. John J. Schmitt, "The Wife of God in Hosea 2," *BR* 34 (1989): 7–11.
14. See Fitzgerald, "*BTWLT* and *BT*," 177; Galambush, *Jerusalem in the Book of Ezekiel*, 20; Schmitt, "Gender of Ancient Israel," 115–25. Cf. Shields, *Circumscribing the Prostitute*, 15.
15. For full argumentation that the wife/mother in Hos 2 should be understood as the city of Samaria, see Kelle, *Hosea 2*, 82–94. See also Schmitt, "Wife of God," 5–18; and Jacques Vermeylen, "Os 1–3 et son histoire littéraire," *ETL* 79 (2003): 28, 43.

as females exclusively in contexts of destruction, even if that destruction takes the form of a threatened action or present state.[16] Jeremiah 49:23–27, for example, personifies Damascus as a mother and includes the statement, "Damascus has grown weak, she has turned around to flee, trembling has seized her, pain and anguish have taken hold of her, like a woman in childbirth" (Jer 49:24 JPS). Micah 1:1–9 applies the personification of whore to Samaria in a similar context of looming destruction: "So I will turn Samaria into a ruin in open country ... and lay her foundations bare ... and all her harlot's wealth be burned, and I will make a waste heap of all her idols" (Mic 1:6–7 JPS). Babylon also receives some of its clearest female personification in Second Isaiah's proclamation of its military destruction: "Come down and sit in the dust, virgin daughter Babylon.... strip off your robe, uncover your legs, pass through the rivers.... I will take vengeance, and I will spare no one" (Isa 47:1–3 NRSV).

Texts outside of the prophetic corpus do occasionally personify cities in other contexts (e.g., Ps 48:12), but within the prophetic corpus, only Isa 16:1, which refers to "the mount of the daughter of Zion," does not seem to fit a context of destruction. The personified Zion is mentioned here, however, only in passing as part of a larger warfare oracle about the destruction of and fugitives from Moab. This shared context of destruction even appears to hold for the several instances, particularly in Second Isaiah, in which Zion is personified as a wife and mother in statements of hope for the future.[17] Isaiah 54:1, for instance, addresses Zion and states, "Shout, O barren one, you who bore no child! Shout aloud for joy ... for the children of the wife forlorn shall outnumber those of the espoused—said the Lord" (JPS). Similarly, Isa 62:4 proclaims, "You [f. sg.] shall no more be termed Forsaken, and your land shall no more be termed Desolate; but you shall be called My Delight Is in Her, and your land Married; for the LORD delights in you, and your land shall be married" (NRSV). Although these personifications of Zion proclaim a future restoration, they imply a *present* state of destruction.

Thus, we have two observations about the prophetic texts that personify cities as females: (1) when they *describe* the destruction of the city, they frequently make use of the metaphorical language of physical and sexual violence against a woman; and (2) even though the majority of these texts do not *describe* the destruction, prophetic texts personify cities as females only when referring to cities that will be or have been destroyed.

---

16. See the list of major representative prophetic texts in n. 2. See also Gordon and Washington, "Rape as a Military Metaphor"; Fitzgerald, "Mythological Background," 416; Schmitt, "Wife of God," 10–11; Galambush, *Jerusalem in the Book of Ezekiel*, 25–26.

17. See, e.g., Isa 40:1–2; 49:14–27; 50:1–3; 51:3, 17–23; 52:1–2; 54:1–17; 60:1–22; 62:1–12; 66:7–12. For a general discussion of the metaphor of "Daughter Zion" in Isaiah, see Mary Donovan Turner, "Daughter Zion: Giving Birth to Redemption," in *Pregnant Passion: Gender, Sex, and Violence in the Bible* (ed. C. A. Kirk-Duggan; SemeiaSt 44; Atlanta: Society of Biblical Literature, 2003), 193–204.

These observations suggest that there is a conventional character to the female personifications and the violent language that goes with them. A helpful way to explore this character and its interpretive implications is to ask why a prophet would employ such language. What would be its rhetorical effect upon an audience?[18] Recent investigations have turned to this question from feminist, materialist, and socioeconomic perspectives.[19] Perhaps we may add one more voice, our third observation, to the discussion about the rhetorical possibilities of this prophetic metaphorization.

How and Why? The Rhetorical Function of the Metaphorization of Cities

Within scholarship on the prophets, interpreters like Michael Fox, John Barton, and Yehoshua Gitay have foregrounded a "rhetorical-critical" approach.[20] Unlike more stylistic-oriented approaches, this rhetorical criticism takes its cue from the study of rhetoric in its classical conception, that is, rhetoric as the study of the ways in which a discourse attempts to persuade a given audience.[21] The interaction among the speaker or author, the speech or text, and the audience or reader dominates the concerns of interpretation. Binding these elements together is the

---

18. As van Dijk-Hemmes ("Metaphorization of Woman," 163) phrases the question for Ezek 23, "What makes it necessary to present a reenactment of Israel's history within this specific metaphorical language?"

19. See especially Alice A. Keefe, *Woman's Body and the Social Body in Hosea* (JSOTSup 338; GCT 10; Sheffield: Sheffield Academic Press, 2001) and Yee, *Poor Banished Children*.

20. Michael Fox, "The Rhetoric of Ezekiel's Vision of the Valley of the Bones," *HUCA* 51 (1980): 1–15; repr. in *The Place Is Too Small for Us: The Israelite Prophets in Recent Scholarship* (ed. R. Gordon; SBTS 5; Winona Lake, Ind.: Eisenbrauns, 1995) 176–90; John Barton, "History and Rhetoric in the Prophets," in *The Bible as Rhetoric: Studies in Biblical Persuasion and Credibility* (ed. M. Warner; Warwick Studies in Philosophy and Literature; London: Routledge, 1990), 51–64; Yehoshua Gitay, *Prophecy as Persuasion: A Study of Isaiah 40–48* (Forum theologiae linguisticae 14; Bonn: Linguistica Biblica, 1981); idem, "Rhetorical Criticism and Prophetic Discourse," in *Persuasive Artistry* (ed. D. F. Watson; Sheffield: Sheffield Academic Press, 1991), 13–24; idem, "Prophetic Criticism—'What Are They Doing?': The Case of Isaiah—A Methodological Assessment," *JSOT* 96 (2001): 101–27. See also Kelle, *Hosea 2*, 21–44; Brad E. Kelle, "Ancient Israelite Prophets and Greek Political Orators: Analogies for the Prophets and Their Implications for Historical Reconstruction," in *Israel's Prophets and Israel's Past: Essays on the Relationship of Prophetic Texts and Israelite History in Honor of John H. Hayes* (ed. B. E. Kelle and M. Bishop Moore; LHB/OTS 446; New York: T&T Clark, 2006), 57–82; Lawrence Boadt, "The Poetry of Prophetic Persuasion: Preserving the Prophet's Persona," *CBQ* 59 (1997): 1–21; Gary V. Smith, *The Prophets as Preachers: An Introduction to the Hebrew Prophets* (Nashville: Broadman & Holman, 1994).

21. In this regard, the prophets may be somewhat analogous to the political orators/rhetoricians from ancient Greece (e.g., Demosthenes in the fourth century B.C.E.). See Kelle, "Ancient Israelite Prophets," 57–82.

so-called "rhetorical situation." The rhetorical situation is not simply the historical context but is a complex entity that includes shared symbolic traditions, perspectives, and beliefs.²²

The rhetorical perspective raises several considerations concerning the conventional character of the metaphorization of cities and its communicative effect, the first of which is somewhat striking. The recognition that the prophets personify cities as female exclusively in contexts of destruction and employ language of physical and sexual violence *in those contexts* suggests that these texts do not have established practices against real women in view. Interpreters have often tried to connect this language with practices regarding women in legalities of marriage and adultery in the ancient world. For example, scholars have generally considered the stripping and exposing of the genitals to be a part of the legal punishment for adulteresses in the ancient Near East.²³ Day has formulated a detailed critique of the evidence for this correspondence and emphasized the figurative language involved.²⁴ Similarly, Robert Carroll has noted that the language in these texts represents neither real violence envisioned against an actual female nor the characteristic attitudes of the prophets themselves toward women.²⁵ The language within the personification of cities represents a shared metaphorical tradition for city destruction in the rhetorical context of the ancient Near East.

Let me be quick to assert, however, that recognizing the ancient metaphorical tradition that gives rise to these violent texts does not remove the dangerous potential of such language.²⁶ Metaphorical language, even that in the service

---

22. Compare Lloyd F. Bitzer, "The Rhetorical Situation," in *Rhetoric: A Tradition in Transition* (ed. W. R. Fisher; Ann Arbor: University of Michigan Press, 1974), 247–60; and Duane F. Watson, "The Contributions and Limitations of Greco-Roman Rhetorical Theory for Constructing the Rhetorical and Historical Situations of a Pauline Epistle," in *The Rhetorical Interpretation of Scripture: Essays from the 1996 Malibu Conference* (ed. S. Porter and D. Stamps; JSOTSup 180; Sheffield: Sheffield Academic Press, 1999), 125–51.

23. E.g., Samuel Greengus, "A Textbook Case of Adultery in Ancient Mesopotamia," *HUCA* 40–41 (1969–70): 33–44. For the general view that this metaphorical language is about personal female subjects, see Gordon and Washington, "Rape as a Military Metaphor," 323–24.

24. Peggy L. Day, "Adulterous Jerusalem's Imagined Demise: Death of a Metaphor in Ezekiel XVI," *VT* 50 (2000): 285–309; idem, "The Bitch Had It Coming to Her: Rhetoric and Interpretation in Ezekiel 16," *BibInt* 8 (2000): 231–54.

25. Robert P. Carroll, "Desire under the Terebinths: On Pornographic Representation in the Prophets—A Response," in Brenner, *Feminist Companion to the Latter Prophets*, 277. See also Barbara R. Rossing, *The Choice between Two Cities: Whore, Bride, and Empire in the Apocalypse* (HTS 48; Harrisburg, Pa.: Trinity Press International, 1999), 88, and the similar stress on the figurative nature of the language in these texts in Day, "Yahweh's Broken Marriages" and "Metaphor and Social Reality: Isaiah 23.17–18, Ezekiel 16.35–37 and Hosea 2.4–5," in *Inspired Speech: Prophecy in the Ancient Near East: Essays in Honor of Herbert B. Huffmon* (ed. J. Kaltner and L. Stulman; New York: T&T Clark, 2004), 63–71.

26. For examples of the wide-ranging feminist critiques of the gender and marriage imag-

of the description of city destruction, can have a surplus of meaning that gives rise to real violence. Such language also certainly reflects the societal perspectives, shared beliefs, and perhaps the male imagination of ancient Israelite culture in which women were thought of as subordinate and vulnerable to a powerful, particularly a conquering, male.[27] As Ehud Ben Zvi observes, this metaphorical imagery was rhetorically effective precisely because it operated within a culture in which gender relations were seen as hierarchical and asymmetrical.[28] Nonetheless, the conventional nature of the texts calls for an explanation of these metaphorizations that contextualizes them within the rhetorical situation that generated the discourse.[29]

From this rhetorical perspective, then, we may make a third and final observation about these prophetic personification texts. Not only do these texts share the context of destruction and the use of language of physical violence, but also they almost always personify a *capital* city. The subjects of choice for

---

ery in such texts, see Brenner, *Feminist Companion to the Latter Prophets*; Renita J. Weems, *Battered Love: Marriage, Sex, and Violence in the Hebrew Prophets* (Minneapolis: Fortress, 1995); Gerlinde Baumann, *Love and Violence: Marriage as Metaphor for the Relationship Between YHWH and Israel in the Prophetic Books* (trans. L. Maloney; Collegeville, Minn: Liturgical Press, 2003); Rut Törnkvist, *The Use and Abuse of Female Sexual Imagery in the Book of Hosea: A Feminist Critical Approach to Hos 1–3* (Women in Religion 7; Uppsala: Acta Universitatis Upsaliensis, 1998); J. Cheryl Exum, *Plotted, Shot and Painted: Cultural Representations of Biblical Women* (JSOTSup 215; GCT 3; Sheffield: Sheffield Academic Press, 1996); Christl Maier, "Jerusalem als Ehebrecherin in Ezechiel 16: Zur Verwendung und Funktion einer biblische Metapher," in *Feministische Hermeneutik und Erstes Testament: Analysen und Interpretationen* (ed. H. Jahnow; Stuttgart: Kohlhammer, 1994), 85–105; idem, "Die Klage der Tochter Zion: Ein Beitrag zur Weiblichkeitsmetaphorik im Jeremiabuch," *BThZ* 15 (1998): 176–89; Linda Day, "Rhetoric and Domestic Violence in Ezekiel 16," *BibInt* 8 (2000): 205–30. But see also the measured concern over the simplistic literalization of violent husband imagery for YHWH in Peggy L. Day, "Yahweh's Broken Marriages" and "A Prostitute Unlike Women: Whoring as a Metaphoric Vehicle for Foreign Alliances," in Kelle and Moore, *Israel's Prophets and Israel's Past*, 167–73.

27. For example, commenting on Hos 1–3, Keefe (*Woman's Body*, 146) explains, "From whatever critical perspective a feminist reader might approach Hosea, the text offers offense. First, as the gender assignments of the metaphor liken maleness to divinity and femaleness to sinful humanity, the hierarchy of male over female is reinforced, and the natural inferiority of femaleness is implied. Second, the very structure of the metaphor rests upon the socio-legal premises that males have exclusive rights over their wives." See also Shields, *Circumscribing the Prostitute*, 68–70. Obviously, this kind of imagery also has the potential to inscribe these very gender relations as the picture of what the relationship between a man and woman is supposed to be (Carol J. Dempsey, "The 'Whore' of Ezekiel 16: The Impact and Ramifications of Gender-Specific Metaphors in Light of Biblical Law and Divine Judgment," in Matthews, Levinson, and Frymer-Kensky, *Gender and Law*, 56).

28. Ben Zvi, "Observations on the Marital Metaphor," 370.

29. Carroll, "Desire under the Terebinths," 299. See also Baumann, *Love and Violence*, 25, 33.

these prophetic metaphorizations are the seats of power themselves: Nineveh, Babylon, Samaria, Jerusalem, and so on.[30] Also noticeable in this regard is that many, but not all, of the texts add the dimension of personifying these cities as women engaged in fornication and/or adultery and so deserving of the punitive destruction.[31] Certainly the violation of women as a metaphor fits the destruction of capital cities, for the stripping, penetration, exposure, and humiliation of the women is analogous to siege warfare, with its breaching of the wall, entrance through the gate, and so forth. Yet the combination of symbolic conventions and capital cities suggests that the prophets are engaged here in an ideological struggle. Even as the females in the texts represent the cities, the cities represent other entities, which are the objects of a prophetic ideological critique, an attempt to persuade someone of something and presumably against something else.

So what is the ideological critique in the prophetic metaphorization of cities, and how does it work? Answers to this question vary among recent works, but an emerging point of agreement in scholarship is that these texts engage in the rhetorical act of feminizing at least a portion of their male audience. That is, a woman, particularly a sexually and physically violating and violated woman, becomes the symbol that represents the behavior and status of at least some males within the community.[32] Rhetorically, the imagery exploits cultural stereotypes

---

30. This observation again presumes that the syntagma בת + GN or בתולת + GN is best understood as a reference to the capital city and not the country as a whole (see Dobbs-Allsopp, "Syntagma"). For a different view, see Turner, "Daughter Zion," 194. For some personifications of cities that are not capitals, see Gallim (Isa 10:30) and Tarshish and Sidon (Isa 23:10, 12). For the connections between capital cities and destruction in wider biblical and extrabiblical traditions, see Dobbs-Allsopp, *Weep, O Daughter of Zion*.

31. E.g., see Ezek 16; 23; Nah 3; but cf. Isa 40:1–2; 49:14–27; 52:1–2. See Kelle, *Hosea 2*, 81–94. Ben Zvi ("Observations on the Marital Metaphor," 369) proposes that such female personifications developed from the need to portray an entity (for him, monarchic Israel) as sinful. Since that entity was depicted as a woman, the imagery demanded that the woman be portrayed as "an extremely 'bad' wife" whose punishment was justified, and the image of the fornicating or adulterous woman served this end.

32. See Yee, *Poor Banished Children*, 98; Keefe, *Woman's Body*; Day, "Yahweh's Broken Marriages"; Carroll, "Desire under the Terebinths"; Ben Zvi, "Observations on the Marital Metaphor"; Harry A. Hoffner, "Symbols for Masculinity and Feminity," *JBL* 85 (1966): 326–34; Mary J. Winn Leith, "Verse and Reverse: The Transformation of the Woman Israel in Hosea 1–3," in *Gender and Difference in Ancient Israel* (ed. P. Day; Minneapolis: Fortress, 1989), 95–108; Phyllis Bird, "'To Play the Harlot': An Enquiry into an Old Testament Metaphor," in Day, *Gender and Difference*, 75–94; Judith Frishman, "Why Would a Man Want to Be Anyone's Wife? A Response to Satlow," in *Families and Family Relations as Represented in Early Judaisms and Early Christianities: Texts and Fictions—Papers Read at a NOSTER Colloquium in Amsterdam, June 9–11, 1998* (ed. J. W. van Henten and A. Brenner; Studies in Theology and Religion 2; Leiden: Deo, 2000), 43–48; Corrine L. Patton, "'Should Our Sister Be Treated Like a Whore?' A Response to Feminist Critiques of Ezekiel 23," in *The Book of Ezekiel: Theological and Anthropological Perspectives* (ed. M. S. Odell and J. T. Strong; SBLSymS 9; Atlanta: Society of Biblical Literature,

in order to shame its male audience by "playing upon male fears of the woman as 'other.'"³³ As Shields observes, "[T]he metaphor itself also introduces opposing characters, placing the (male) audience in opposition to God, this time as promiscuous wives in relation to God the husband."³⁴

As a side note, evidence from biblical and extrabiblical texts and ancient Near Eastern iconography suggests that this particular rhetoric of feminization is likely related to the frequent practice of referring to defeated enemies as women in warfare accounts and political inscriptions and thus gives the language of warfare a gendered character.³⁵ Isaiah 19:16, for example, describes the defeat of the Egyptians by stating, "On that day the Egyptians will be like women, and tremble with fear before the hand that the Lord of hosts raises against them" (NRSV; see also Jer 6:24; 50:24, 37; 51:30; Nah 3:13). Esarhaddon's succession treaty contains a curse that proclaims, "may they make you like a woman before your enemy."³⁶ Additionally, the available evidence points to the conclusion that all such gendered language for warfare is likely related to actual practices of humiliation and perhaps sexual abuse done both to male warriors and female victims in ancient warfare.³⁷ A monument inscription of Esarhaddon, for instance, euphemistically suggests that a wrongdoer's masculinity is transformed into femininity as Ishtar places him bound in front of the feet of his enemy.³⁸

If scholars are in increasing agreement that the female personification of cities serves to feminize at least a portion of the male audience, they diverge over

---

2000), 232; Marie-Theres Wacker, "Frau-Sexus-Macht: Eine feministisch-theologische Relecture des Hoseabuches," in *Der Gott der Männer und die Frauen* (ed. M. Wacker; Düsseldorf: Patmos, 1987), 101–25. For the view that the language is not addressed to males at all, see Gordon and Washington, "Rape as a Military Metaphor."

33. Winn Leith, "Verse and Reverse," 98.

34. Shields, *Circumscribing the Prostitute*, 53.

35. See Cynthia R. Chapman, *The Gendered Language of Warfare in the Israelite-Assyrian Encounter* (HSM 62; Winona Lake, Ind.: Eisenbrauns, 2004); Susan E. Haddox, "(E)Masculinity in Hosea's Political Rhetoric," in Kelle and Moore, *Israel's Prophets and Israel's Past*, 175–200; Claudia D. Bergmann, "We Have Seen the Enemy, and He Is Only a 'She': The Portrayal of Warriors as Women," in this volume.

36. Simo Parpola and Kazuko Watanabe, eds., *Neo-Assyrian Treaties and Loyalty Oaths* (SAA 2; Helsinki: Helsinki University Press, 1988), 56; see also Day, "Yahweh's Broken Marriages."

37. See Daniel L. Smith-Christopher, "Ezekiel in Abu Ghraib: Rereading Ezekiel 16:37–39 in the Context of Imperial Conquest," in *Ezekiel's Hierarchical World: Wrestling with a Tiered Reality* (ed. S. L. Cook and C. L. Patton; SBLSymS 31; Atlanta: Society of Biblical Literature, 2004), 141–57 (149); Day, "Yahweh's Broken Marriages"; Gordon and Washington, "Rape as a Military Metaphor," 308–10; Patton, "Should Our Sister," 233–34; and Exum, *Plotted, Shot and Painted*, 104–5.

38. See Martti Nissinen, *Homoeroticism in the Biblical World: A Historical Perspective* (Minneapolis: Fortress, 1998), 31.

the specific target and purpose of such feminization. It is often suggested that the female cities are *general* metonyms for the nation as a whole.[39] Carroll, for example, identifies the imagery as feminizing males but takes those males as representing the whole society.[40] Some scholars have, however, proposed that the metaphorical females in certain prophetic texts function to feminize the more specific group of the male elite in Israelite or Judean society. Both Gail Yee and Alice Keefe, for instance, read the marriage imagery in Hos 2, which they do not necessarily identify as the personification of a city, as a general attempt to feminize the religious, political, and judicial leaders responsible for unjust changes to Israel's socioeconomic structure.[41] Thus, for example, Hosea employs the metaphor of "Israel's social body as a fornicating female body" in order to depict and critique a "rising market-based economy revolving around interregional trade, land consolidation and cash cropping."[42] The personified females in these metaphors represent the males of the elite political, social, and economic class, whose interests are aligned with those of the royal house.[43] The effort of the metaphorization is to use shame as a means of critiquing the kingdom's male leadership. Yee explains, "The marriage metaphor effectively *feminizes the male ruling hierarchy* by depicting its members collectively in the graphic image of a promiscuous wife … [and] epitomizes a radical loss of status for the elite."[44] Similarly, Ben Zvi suggests that the female imagery in some of the prophetic texts is the language of the elite, seeking to educate members of their own literati by getting them to identify with the subordinate females.[45] Along these lines, Yee changes her focus for the female imagery in Ezek 16 and 23 and sees it as the language of the male, priestly elite that aims to shift their own feelings of defeat, shame, and emasculinization in war to an appropriate female object. Such texts envision the elite's restoration

---

39. See, e.g., Yee, *Poor Banished Children*, 117.

40. Carroll, "Desire under the Terebinths," 288. See also Shields, *Circumscribing the Prostitute*, 66.

41. See Yee, *Poor Banished Children*, 98; Keefe, *Woman's Body*, 199.

42. Keefe, *Woman's Body*, 12.

43. Ibid., 199. See also Yee (*Poor Banished Children*, 83), who relates the critique to Israel's transformation from a native-tributary mode of production to a foreign-tributary mode of production in the eighth century. In this newer mode of production, the ruling elite in particular benefited from the redistribution of wealth from grain, wine, and oil production at the expense of local villagers.

44. Ibid., 98, emphasis original.

45. See Ben Zvi, "Observations on the Marital Metaphor," 363–84. He notes that the female symbols, particularly those texts using the prophetic marriage metaphor, aim to get their audience to identify with the females and thereby to educate them as to how to be subordinate to Yhwh, the "hegemonic partner" of the relationship (see ibid., 372).

as remasculinization and thus strive to gain control over their degrading circumstances.⁴⁶

While seemingly more specific in their interpretation of the female imagery, these views still take the imagery as a whole to be a general characterization and critique of the state of Israelite society and the broad range of political, religious, and social powerbrokers who created it. Yet the three observations we have made about the prophetic texts that personify cities as females suggest that the insights of Yee, Keefe, and others can be further defined and extended in two ways. First, the particular characterization of *capital* cities suggests a closer link for at least the texts discussed in this article with the centers of dynastic *political* power. In this prophetic discourse, these capital cities serve most likely as metonyms specifically for the ruling houses and political elite who sat on their thrones and not simply for an urban, wealthy societal class or local ruling functionaries.⁴⁷ Thus these personifications, which take place in contexts of destruction, offer a war-time critique of political rulers and their actions with an ironic twist. The ruling houses and their powerful elite, who in the ancient rhetorical context of the prophet and his audience would have typically been all male,⁴⁸ are cast as physically threatened and sexually violated females. Although the metaphors may not involve actual women, the fact that the image is a woman is not at all incidental to the rhetoric. The prophetic texts' use of this specific metaphorization of cities suggests that the negative uses of this imagery are critiques of the

---

46. Yee, *Poor Banished Children*, 98, 111–12, 121–22. See also Smith-Christopher ("Ezekiel in Abu Ghraib," 150, 155), who argues that the women in Ezek 16 are symbols of the physical and sexual treatment the Judean exiles themselves received from the Babylonians and are part of the exiles' self-blaming theology designed to take power away from their conquerors by explaining the events as consequences of sin. See further Patton, "Should Our Sister," 237; Jan W. Tarlin, "Utopia and Pornography in Ezekiel: Violence, Hope, and the Shattered Male Subject," in *Reading Bibles, Writing Bodies: Identity and the Book* (ed. T. K. Beal and D. M. Gunn; Biblical Limits; London: Routledge, 1997), 175–83.

47. As Dobbs-Allsopp (*Weep, O Daughter of Zion*, 87) observes, the Hebrew term for city (עיר) "can refer to the actual physical entity of the mortar and brick, roads and houses, or by metonymic extension to the inhabitants of the city." For a broader discussion of this notion, see J. J. M. Roberts ("Bearers of the Polity: Isaiah of Jerusalem's View of Eighth-Century Judean Society," in *Constituting the Community: Studies on the Polity of Ancient Israel in Honor of S. Dean McBride Jr.* [ed. J. T. Strong and S. S. Tuell; Winona Lake, Ind.: Eisenbrauns, 2005], 145–52), who demonstrates that the critique of the royal court as a whole is common throughout the prophetic books, especially in Isaiah.

48. Female rulers, such as Jezebel of Israel, Athaliah of Judah, and Shamshi of Arabia, who are attested in biblical and extrabiblical texts, seem to represent exceptions that highlight the more typical case of male dominance. Interestingly, however, neither biblical nor extrabiblical texts attach negative connotations simply to the fact that these leaders are women. Occupying the authority level just below the king in ancient Israelite polity, the royal house likely included male members of the royal family, as well as "officers" (שׂרים) of various ranks and responsibilities (Roberts, "Bearers of the Polity," 147).

political rulers, urging the community at large to separate from them in some way.[49] As Mary Shields explains concerning Ezek 23, "Gender rhetoric is used to set the reader up to blame the women [i.e., cities representing male political rulers], who, according to the conventional standards, should be grateful that Yhwh took them at all."[50]

That is, the prophets use these female personifications of capital cities in something of a populist discourse that aims to create rhetorical, theological, and political distance between the general population and the rulers whose actions defy, in the prophets' opinions, Yhwh's will for the community. To accomplish this end, the prophetic language attempts to change the audience's perspective on the ruling elite in an ironic way. Within the framework of the shared perspectives of the ancient Israelite community, the most powerful social group—the male, dynastic elite—is cast as the most helpless social group—the sexually violated female.[51] Those who seem to hold unimpeachable power and demand unswerving loyalty, yet whose actions have brought the nation to the present state of war and destruction, are, in fact, vulnerable, shamed, and subordinate. Within the ancient cultural conceptions of honor and shame surrounding women's sexuality, especially unrestrained or defiled sexuality, the very act of personifying the political ruling house as sexually violating and violated females implicitly taps into the audience's culturally approved instinct to disassociate from them as one would from an unfaithful wife.[52] In a society such as ancient Israel's, the sexually violated female takes on a status that dishonors her family. Moreover, biblical, extrabiblical, and iconographic evidence indicates that feminizing language and imagery often appear in relation to foreigners and, specifically, those who are envisioned

---

49. Perhaps the use of personified cities as metonyms for sinful ruling houses also contains an implicit (and perhaps even unintentional) critique of cities and urbanism in general. For considerations of city imagery and city polemic in the Hebrew Bible, see Frank S. Frick, *The City in Ancient Israel* (SBLDS 36; Missoula, Mont.: Scholars Press, 1977); Volkmar Fritz, *The City in Ancient Israel* (Biblical Seminar 29; Sheffield: Sheffield Academic Press, 1995); Lester L. Grabbe and Robert D. Haak, eds., *"Every City Shall Be Forsaken": Urbanism and Prophecy in Ancient Israel and the Near East* (JSOTSup 330; Sheffield: Sheffield Academic Press, 2001); John M. Halligan, *A Critique of the City in the Yahwist Corpus* (Notre Dame: University of Notre Dame Press, 1975); Victor P. Hamilton, *The Book of Genesis Chapters 1–17* (NICOT; Grand Rapids: Eerdmans, 1990), 356–57.

50. Mary E. Shields, "An Abusive God? Identity and Power/Gender and Violence in Ezekiel 23," in *Postmodern Interpretations of the Bible: A Reader* (ed. A. K. M. Adam; St. Louis: Chalice, 2001), 135. Her article offers a feminist critique of this rhetoric and the images of the deity contained therein.

51. So also Yee, *Poor Banished Children*, 82.

52. For example, Haddox ("(E)Masculinity in Hosea's Political Rhetoric," 180) observes, "Becoming like women or being feminized, for example, functions as a metaphor across various cultures to represent loss of social prestige or power. Losing, whether in the area of politics, economics, or class, is equated with feminization."

as already having suffered military defeat.⁵³ Hence, simply by using such feminizing imagery for the ruling houses, the prophets rhetorically cast the political elite of Israel and Judah into the roles of foreigners/outsiders in the midst of the community and depict them as already defeated, even while seemingly at the height of their power. As Inger Skjelsbaek notes, such feminizing tactics, whether physical or rhetorical, have the effect of altering not only the victim's gender but also his or her "ethnic/religious/political identity."⁵⁴ These rhetorical tactics potentially provide even more grounding for the prophets' call to disassociate from those under whose dominion the entire community seems bound to live.

The second way we might extend our observations about the rhetorical effects of the prophetic personification of cities as female is to recognize that this imagery is also a double metaphorization. On the one hand, the discourse serves to change the audience's perspective on the dynastic elite in an ironic way. At the same time, implicitly in most texts but explicitly in some, the discourse functions to alter the audience's perspective on the *deity* by employing irony against the political elite. As noted above, several of the relevant prophetic texts not only personify cities as females but also metaphorize Yhwh as the husband of Samaria and/or Jerusalem. As Gerlinde Baumann has suggested, more attention should be paid to this "God-image" in the Hebrew Bible's metaphors of women.⁵⁵ By metaphorizing Yhwh as the husband of the personified female city, the prophets cast Yhwh as the truly powerful male who holds the fate of the subordinate female in his hands and can punish, shame, and even kill. The power of this double metaphorization is especially poignant in a society such as ancient Israel in which the deity was frequently co-opted by the political elite and portrayed as not only sanctioning their actions but even being inextricably committed to their preservation. In a stunning critique of political power and religious legitimization, the prophetic discourse transforms the audience's imagination by liberating the deity from the male ruling house and casting that very male group into the position of the subordinate female, who may suffer the shame and violence enacted by the powerful, conquering male. The political elite, who had often imposed hegemony over their own people, were now made the subordinate female to Yhwh, an even more powerful male.⁵⁶ Thus, we have in the prophetic metaphorization of cities

---

53. See examples in Chapman, *Gendered Language*.

54. Inger Skjelsbaek, "Sexual Violence and War: Mapping Out a Complex Relationship," *European Journal of International Relations* 7 (2001): 225; cited in Smith-Christopher, "Ezekiel in Abu Ghraib," 149.

55. Baumann, *Love and Violence*, 2.

56. As Haddox ("(E)Masculinity in Hosea's Political Rhetoric," 200) states, "By contrast, the gendered language portrays YHWH as the ultimate masculine figure: the husband to the leaders' wife, the bow-breaker, the one who reveals the leaders' impotency." As a related observation, Patton ("Should Our Sister," 238) notes that such a metaphorization of Yhwh also

as female a doubly ironic critique of power and the powerful in the midst of situations of warfare and destruction, or "wartime rhetoric."

Conclusion

At least two potential implications emerge from this difficult discourse. First, in spite of its power within the ancient rhetorical situation, there can be no doubt that this discourse remains patriarchal in its conventions and assumptions. Although we may want to continue the prophetic critique of political power and religious legitimization, the portrayal of God as the authoritative, violent male is deeply problematic.[57] The established feminist critiques of these texts are well-placed, valid, and important.[58] As Yee concludes, "Feminizing men in a marital relation with a male God reinscribes into the text the ideological and social links among women, subordination, shame, and sin."[59]

Yet, secondly, these violent texts may themselves witness to the instability of patriarchy. For even within the discourse itself, we may witness the ultimate unworkableness of patriarchy. The ruling male elites, the very ones who would use violence to maintain patriarchal power, become the symbolic victims of the same patriarchal structure and violence. Simultaneously, the prophets have to use patriarchal texts and imagery in order to critique unchallenged patriarchal

---

functions to defend the deity from being a "cuckholded husband, i.e., a defeated, powerless, or ineffective god."

57. It should be noted, of course, that this masculine imagery is not the only portrayal of Yhwh in the Hebrew Bible. Several texts, certainly less prevalent but scattered throughout the canon, attribute various female images, such as a mother and a woman in labor, to Yhwh (e.g., Num 11:12; Ps 123:2; Hos 11:1–5; Isa 42:13–14). See Athalya Brenner, "The Hebrew God and His Female Complements," in Beal and Gunn, *Reading Bibles, Writing Bodies*, 56–71.

58. For one, ready example with helpful bibliographic notes, see Shields, "Abusive God," 129–51. See also Robert P. Carroll ("Whorusalamin: A Tale of Three Cities as Three Sisters," in *On Reading Prophetic Texts: Gender-Specific and Related Studies in Memory of Fokkelien van Dijk-Hemmes* [ed. B. Becking and M. Dijkstra; BibInt 18; Leiden: Brill, 1996], 76), who states, "For a violent god breeds violent men—or, better still, violent men produce violent images of gods." For an extended study, see Esther Fuchs, *Sexual Politics in the Biblical Narrative: Reading the Hebrew Bible as a Woman* (JSOTSup 310; Sheffield: Sheffield Academic Press, 2000).

59. Yee, *Poor Banished Children*, 99. See also Fuchs (*Sexual Politics*, 12), who notes that through literary imagery like that discussed here a patriarchal social system becomes "justified, universalized and naturalized." Similar connections between feminine imagery and divine violence also appear in later New Testament books such as Revelation (see Marla J. Selvidge, "Reflections on Violence and Pornography: Misogyny in the Apocalypse and Ancient Hebrew Prophecy," in *A Feminist Companion to the Hebrew Bible in the New Testament* [ed. A. Brenner; FCB 10; Sheffield: Sheffield Academic Press, 1996], 274–86; and Rossing, *Choice between Two Cities*).

authority itself.[60] Implicitly, then, even the males in the prophets' audience, who are urged to break with the ruling house, are confronted with a particular vision of masculinity, a vision that pressures them to avoid being identified as women and to identify with the violent, dominating masculinity of Yhwh.[61] Hence, whether legitimating or critiquing power, the assumptions and conventions of patriarchy ironically permit no escape for *anyone* from the violence of their system.

Perhaps these ancient prophetic attempts to speak into contexts of warfare can inform the contemporary reader's efforts to critique political power and religious legitimization. Or, perhaps we will reject the notion that imagery of male violence can provide a useful critique of power. Perhaps we will seek new images and new metaphors for critique. Or, perhaps we will conclude that some situations are, as Barbara Green says, so "impacted" as to require language and acts of violence.[62] In any case, an awareness of the rhetorical effect and ideological surplus of the prophetic personification of cities should prompt us to examine more closely our own attempts to speak into and out of contexts of war.[63]

---

60. Contrast Gordon and Washington ("Rape as a Military Metaphor," 323), who see these texts as promoting "unchallenged masculine authority."

61. See Shields, "Abusive God," 150; and Washington, "Lest He Die in the Battle," 186. Howard Eilberg-Schwarz (*God's Phallus and Other Problems for Men and Monotheism* [Boston: Beacon, 1994]) further suggests that some applications of such masculine imagery to Yhwh are particularly damaging to men, since they destabilize the concept of masculinity by placing males into the role of the nuptial and/or erotic partner of the male deity.

62. Barbara Green, "Pregnant Passion: Gender, Sex, and Violence in the Bible—A Response to Part 3: Types, Stereotypes, and Archetypes," in Kirk-Duggan, *Fregnant Passion*, 230.

63. I thank the participants in the Warfare in Ancient Israel Consultation of November 2004, the members of the faculties at the Iliff School of Theology and Hartford Seminary, and the students in the Women's Studies Program at Point Loma Nazarene University for their helpful feedback on earlier presentations of this paper. I also thank Dr. Brent A. Strawn for his comments on an earlier draft of the article. Any remaining shortcomings are, of course, solely my own.

Family Metaphors and Social Conflict in Hosea

Alice A. Keefe

Exploration of the symbolic relationships among women, sexuality, and warfare in biblical literature takes us into ancient worlds of meaning that are quite distinct from those familiar to modern readers. If the interpreter is to avoid the pitfall of projecting modern meanings into ancient literature, he or she must consciously identify and bracket the presuppositions about gender and sexuality that have shaped his or her modern worldview and strive to glimpse something of the distinctive sociolinguistic codes informing oral and written discourse in ancient Israel. This paper will illustrate this process by focusing on interpretation of the gendered and sexual metaphors found in the book of Hosea. First, the essay will critique the way that anachronistic projections concerning woman as "the other" have constrained the way modern commentators have read Hosea's imagery. Then it will explore literary and sociological clues that point to an understanding of woman, sexual relations, and patrilineal continuity as symbols for social identity in ancient Israelite literature. In this light, this paper will consider not only the "marriage" metaphor of Hos 1–3 but also several other metaphors involving women's bodies and acts of sexual transgression that are scattered throughout the rest of the book of Hosea. These metaphors include the slashing open of pregnant mothers (13:16; 14:1), breached birth and female sterility (9:11–14), the death of children with their mothers (10:14b), and the fathering of alien (illegitimate) children (5:7). Taking seriously the social symbolism carried by images of female sexuality and reproduction in biblical literature, these violent and disturbing images about women, female sterility, and the death of children will be read as a prophetic commentary upon the condition and fate of the nation Israel in a time of intensifying societal disruption, political strife, and the imminent threat of Assyrian invasion.[1]

---

1. This paper is drawn from the argument set forth in my book, *Woman's Body and the Social Body in Hosea* (JSOTSup 338; GCT 10; Sheffield: Sheffield Academic Press, 2001). For other treatments of Hosea's sexual metaphors in relation to the social and political issues of his time, see Gale A. Yee, "'She Is Not My Wife and I Am Not Her Husband': A Materialist Analysis of Hosea 1–2," *BibInt* 9 (2001): 345–83; idem, *Poor Banished Children of Eve: Woman as*

Constructions of "Woman" in Hosea 1–3

The book of Hosea is best known for its "marriage metaphor" of chapters 1–3, which begins with a divine command to the prophet that he take to himself an אשת זנונים, "woman of promiscuity," and ילדי זנונים, "children of promiscuity" (Hos 1:2).[2] In Hos 2, this woman chases after her lovers, her adultery representing the nation in its unfaithfulness to its divine "husband." In response, Yhwh repudiates both her and her children, although by the end of chapter 2, judgment gives way to an eschatological promise of reconciliation. Most twentieth-century commentators on Hosea have interpreted the figure of this woman of promiscuity and her adulterous activity as pointing to the nation's apostate participation in Canaanite "fertility" religion. This putative fertility religion included polytheistic worship of Canaanite deities, who embodied the sacred powers of fertility and regeneration and, in some reconstructions, sexual rituals, which, by the logic of sympathetic magic, mirrored the sex acts of the gods and thereby furthered the potential fertility of the soil and of wombs.

Although this interpretation has been repeated many times, it rests more upon the projection of anachronistic associations about women and sexuality onto ancient texts than upon our knowledge of the religious situation in ancient Israel. The interpretive move that posits "woman" as a symbol for involvement with apostate fertility religion fits very well with the worldviews regarding women, sexuality, and religion that have dominated Western, and especially Christian, thought for nearly two thousand years. These constructions are indebted to Hellenistic and Christian paradigms of metaphysical dualism in which spirit and matter are placed on opposite poles of a gendered spectrum of value. In this dualistic worldview, those aspects of reality having to do with the body, sexuality, and nature are placed at the lower, material pole of this spectrum of value and are symbolically associated with women and femaleness. Those aspects of reality

---

Evil in the Hebrew Bible (Minneapolis: Fortress, 2003); Marvin L. Chaney, "Accusing Whom of What? Hosea's Rhetoric of Promiscuity," in *Distant Voices Drawing Near* (ed. H. E. Hearon, M. L. Chaney, and A. C. Wire; Collegeville, Minn.: Liturgical Press, 2004), 97–115; Brad E. Kelle, *Hosea 2: Metaphor and Rhetoric in Historical Perspective* (SBLAcBib 20; Atlanta: Society of Biblical Literature, 2003).

2. The expression אשת זנונים which is unique to Hosea, has been translated in many ways, including "wife of whoredoms" (kjv), "wife of whoredom" (nrsv, jps), "wife of fornications" (Douay-Rheims), "adulterous wife" (niv), and "prostitute" (New English Translation). The first term of the phrase (אאשת is clearly the construct form for woman or wife. The second term (זנונים), however, is more difficult to translate. It is a rare form of the root זנה, whose other derivatives concern fornication or prostitution. I prefer to translate this expression as "woman or wife of fornications or promiscuity" in order to avoid the implication that Hosea's wife was a professional prostitute and to stress the repeated, habitual manner of conduct that is implied by the plural intensive (Keefe, *Woman's Body*, 18–21).

having to do with the mind, reason, and divine transcendence are situated at the higher, spiritual pole and are symbolically associated with men and maleness. Woman, sexuality, and nature mark the pole of "otherness" against which the pole of spiritual transcendence is defined. Human and especially female sexuality can therefore have no place within the language of the sacred, except as a point of negation.

The assumption that woman functions as a symbol for that which is "other" or inimical to what is properly Israelite has helped to generate the consensus interpretation of Hosea's sexual language noted above. While nineteenth- and twentieth-century commentators have produced many varied readings of Hosea's marriage metaphor, the common "fertility cult" reading locates the key to interpretation in the deployment of the figure of "woman" as a symbol for sin, temptation, and the lure of the natural.[3] Female fornication in Hos 1–3 is thus usually read as a sign for Israel's involvement with religious ways that are profoundly "other" to transcendent Yahwism, specifically the people's involvement in a syncretistic, nature-worshiping, and eroticized fertility cult. Modern commentators have eagerly speculated about the role of sexual rituals in this fertility cult, and many have suggested that Gomer, Hosea's "wife of promiscuity," served as a sacred prostitute within it. Through such speculations, commentators spice up their writing with racy details about sacred prostitutes and orgiastic rituals, while, at the same time, setting forth a clear opposition between the sexualized, feminine, and morally debased fertility religion of the Canaanites and the transcendent, masculine and morally demanding Yhwh-worship of the Israelites.

A major difficulty with this approach to Hosea's sexual imagery is that the putative fertility cult interpretation no longer accords with scholarship's findings on the character of ancient Israelite religion in the eighth century.[4] Evidence to support the scholarly fantasy of a sex cult in Israel has been found to be lacking.[5] Further, the assumption of a strict opposition between Canaanite fertility religion and Yahwistic transcendence of nature is untenable in light of recent insights into the continuities between Israelite and Canaanite cultures during the Iron Age.[6] Rather than emerging from any solid evidence about the religious situation in eighth-century Israel, scholarly representations of the dichotomy between ancient Canaanite religion and Israelite Yahwism emerge from a commitment to mark

---

3. Ibid., 38–62.

4. Ibid., 50–57; Yee, "She Is Not My Wife," 354–57.

5. E.g., Robert Oden, *The Bible without Theology: The Theological Tradition and Alternatives to It* (San Francisco: Harper & Row, 1987); Joan Goodnick Westenholz, "Tamar, Qedeša, Qadištu, and Sacred Prostitution in Mesopotamia," *HTR* 82 (1989): 245–65.

6. E.g., Michael D. Coogan, "Canaanite Origins and Lineage: Reflections on the Religion of Ancient Israel," in *Ancient Israelite Religion: Essays in Honor of Frank Moore Cross* (ed. P. D. Miller, P. D. Hanson, and S. D. McBride; Philadelphia: Fortress, 1987); Niels Peter Lemche, *Ancient Israel: A New History of Israelite Society* (Sheffield: JSOT Press, 1988).

a clear boundary between "us" (the imagined Israel and its heirs, which include the commentators themselves) and "them" (the imagined pagans and their heirs, which include the commentator's own religious "others").

The reigning "fertility cult" reading of Hos 1–3 leaves the figure of the woman of promiscuity safely contained within familiar symbolic associations of woman with sexual temptation and the dangerous lure of the natural. In this reading, the woman represents the nation only in so far as her adultery allegorically represents its religious involvement in that which is foreign and inimically "other" to proper Israelite Yahwism. This reading also largely ignores other images relating to sexuality and gender found in Hos 4–14, unless they can reinforce this fertility cult thesis.

Some feminist commentators have responded to this interpretive tradition by reversing its theological valuations; rather than being disparaged, the woman's involvement in fertility religion is celebrated as an assertion of a pro-nature, proto-feminist spirituality.[7] Helgard Balz-Cochois, for example, argues that Hosea opposed the popular cults of Asherah, the "Great Mother" who presides over the fertility of fields and wombs, and Astarte, the embodiment of the sacred power of the sexuality and the erotic. Balz-Cochois argues that Israelite women such as Gomer, Hosea's "wife of promiscuity," were attracted to the worship of these Canaanite goddesses because their cults empowered women to serve as priestesses and honored the sacrality of the female body, unlike the patriarchal and androcentric Yahwism promoted by Hosea.[8] This particular feminist reconstruction of Canaanite religion is, however, too indebted to the androcentric tradition of interpretation to provide much liberation from it. Undermining their own desire to resist masculine constructions of religion, feminist scholars who embrace and valorize an ancient goddess-centered fertility religion buy into an imagined construct of ancient religion that is largely the product of the fears and fantasies of modern male interpreters vis-à-vis women, sexuality, and the sacred.[9]

If the woman of promiscuity in Hos 1–2 is not a sign for Israel's involvement with a syncretistic fertility cult, how else might this female symbol be read? The following will set forth an alterative approach to interpreting Hosea's gendered and sexual language that attends to the distinct meanings associated with

---

7. There are several other approaches to Hosea's sexual imagery taken by feminist interpreters. For a summary of these, see Keefe, *Woman's Body*, 146–55.

8. Helgard Balz-Cochois, "Gomer oder die Macht der Astarte: Versuch einer feministischen Interpretation von Hos 1–4," *EvT* 42 (1982): 37–65. See also T. Drorah Setel, "Prophets and Pornography: Female Sexual Imagery in Hosea," in *Feminist Interpretation of the Bible* (ed. L. M. Russell; Philadelphia: Westminster, 1985), 86–95; Fokkelien van Dijk-Hemmes, "The Imagination of Power and the Power of Imagination: An Intertextual Analysis of Two Biblical Love Songs: The Song of Songs and Hosea 2," *JSOT* 44 (1989): 75–88.

9. Jo Ann Hackett, "Can a Sexist Model Liberate Us? Ancient Near Eastern Fertility Goddesses," *JFSR* 5 (1989): 68; Keefe, *Woman's Body*, 62–64.

women and sexuality within the specific social, religious, and discursive contexts within which these prophetic tropes were deployed. The first step in this effort will be to think again about ancient Israelite religion and the religious concerns of Hosea's time without the obscurations imposed by the assumption of a worldview of metaphysical dualism. The second step will be to explore how gendered and sexual language is used as a code for issues of social boundaries and group identity in biblical narratives and then to posit this convention of representation as potentially relevant to the interpretation of Hosea's sexual language.

Women, Sex, and Social Identity in Hosea

As discussed above, the scholarly imagination of Canaanite fertility religion depends upon an understanding of religion in which spirit and matter are neatly separated at opposite ends of the metaphysical spectrum. The spirit/matter dichotomy conditions modern interpreters to think about religion in terms of the human relationship with immaterial, that is, "spiritual" realities. Thus, for most biblical commentators, true religion is defined in terms of relationship with the transcendent and immaterial pole of reality. Israelite or prophetic Yahwism is imagined as such a pure and correct faith, while Canaanite religion, Yahwism's imagined opposite, is seen as a false religion due to its mistaken immersion of the divine in the natural. But if we set aside metaphysical dualism as our template for thinking about religion, we are able to appreciate the ways that the religious imagination is always interdependent with the material conditions of life and the social systems of exchange in any particular time and place. In the religious imagination of ancient Israel, the sacred was manifest not only in beliefs about the transcendent YHWH who dwells "on high." The meaning of the sacred was also embedded within social practices and values revolving around the continuity of the בית אב ("father's house") across the generations, the relationship of these patrilineal families to their patrimonial lands, and the sense of community and identity generated within local networks of exchange and solidarity. Family, land, and communal solidarity were the critical nodes in a matrix of relationships that constituted the prevailing forms of human meaning and identity in this Iron Age agrarian society.

Fertility was certainly an important religious concern within this sacra-social order, given that fertility (of fields, livestock, and humans) was the prerequisite for group survival. Icons of the power of fertility, such as the asherah poles at the public shrines or the female figurines placed on domestic altars, were part of a familiar religious landscape. These icons of fertility are not obviously attacked in Hosea's oracles. His polemics concerning religious practice are clearly directed to Yahwistic practices at the state shrines, where the issue is not the relationship of the deity to nature but the deity's relationship to the power of the state. The monarchies in Israel and throughout the ancient Near East gained their legitimacy through the sponsorship of sacrifices on behalf of the national deity. These points suggest that Hosea's key concern was not fertility religion or nature worship, but the political and economic forces that were undermining the matrix of relationships that defined the sacra-social world as he knew it.

In the ninth and eighth centuries, Israel's socioreligious structure, oriented around the land-holding patrilineal family, was undergoing disruption due to political and economic forces that favored consolidation of subsistence-based family farms into large agricultural estates dedicated to the production of cash crops for trade.[10] The processes of agricultural intensification violated traditional laws regarding the inalienability of patrimonial lands and left many of the most economically vulnerable landless. But these processes were difficult to impede, since they were fueled by larger forces of economic and political transformation in the region. The commercialization of agriculture went hand in hand with a shift toward an economy dependent upon interregional trade, interregional alliances, and concomitant cosmopolitan orientations, all of which were alien to the traditional frontier culture of highland Israel.

Prophetic concern with the issues of land accumulation, circumvention of traditional law, and the oppression of the economically vulnerable is apparent in many stories about and oracles attributed to the ninth- and the eighth-century prophets (e.g., 1 Kgs 21; Isa 5:8; Amos 5:10–12; Mic 2:2). Although Hosea says nothing directly about the issue of patrimonial lands, he is clearly engaged with many of the political and social issues of his time. His oracles about political corruption and regicide, his attacks on the national shrines (which legitimate the authority and power of the monarchy), and his references to recent battles all testify to this engagement. As noted above, however, despite Hosea's obvious concern with political and social issues, many interpreters of Hos 1–3 persistently assume that the sexual metaphors of marriage and adultery must refer to religious issues involving syncretism, polytheism, and the deification of nature, and they ground this assumption in the anachronistic importation of associations of women and human sexuality with the material and profane pole of the matter/spirit dichotomy. Identifying and bracketing the influence of these associations opens anew the question of the indigenous meanings associated with women and human sexuality within Israelite society and biblical literature.

Whereas in the modern world, the meaning of sexuality is linked to the private realm of erotic pleasure and defines the boundary of the nuclear family, in the society of ancient Israel described above, where intergenerational continuity and kinship networks were definitive of the structure and purpose of human

---

10. E.g., John Andrew Dearman, *Property Rights in the Eighth-Century Prophets: The Conflict and Its Background* (SBLDS 106; Atlanta: Scholars Press, 1988); Marvin L. Chaney, "Bitter Bounty: The Dynamics of Political Economy Critiqued by the Eighth-Century Prophets," in *Reformed Faith and Economics* (ed. R. L. Stivers; Lanham, Md.; University Press of America, 1989), 15–30.

existence, human sexuality and sexual acts inevitably evoked much more corporate or public meanings having to do with lineage continuity, community boundaries, and group identity.

Such corporate meanings are visible in those biblical narratives where acts of sexual transgression signal the onset of social violence and disruption.[11] In Judg 19, for example, the rape of an unnamed woman becomes the narrative catalyst for a civil war among the tribes of Israel. The symbolic connection between her raped female body and the social body of Israel is underscored by the gruesome motif in which her body is cut up into twelve pieces and is sent out to the twelve tribes as a call to war. Here the raped and mutilated female body of one woman signifies the condition of the social body of Israel as it dismembers and destroys itself in war. As Susan Niditch has observed, the woman's divided body is a "radical symbolization of Israel's 'body politics,' the divisions in Israel."[12]

A symbolic connection between rape and war can also be seen in 2 Kgs 13, where Amnon's rape of Tamar triggers fratricide and then a civil war between Absalom and the house of his father, David. So also in Gen 34, Shechem's act of sexual transgression, laying with Dinah without her father's permission, becomes the occasion for an attack on the city of Shechem by Jacob's sons. Both of these stories are illuminated in light of the honor/shame system in which the sexual inviolability of female family members signifies the ability of the family or social group to defend its resources and boundaries: the violation of female family members is symbolically an attack upon the family or social group and a demonstration of its weakness, as the brothers of Dinah were well aware.[13] Intersecting dynamics of group identity and sexual transgression also may be seen in the story about David's adultery with Bathsheba (2 Sam 11), which is set against the backdrop of his nation's war with Ammon. As war with a neighboring enemy disturbs the boundaries of the geographical nation, so David's act of sexual violation represents the struggle over issues of identity, that is, who or what Israel is or is not.[14]

It is hardly surprising to discover this convention of representation in biblical literature. In a patriarchal, patrilineal social world such as that of ancient Israel, where the sexual code (particularly as it regulates access to female bodies) is at the foundation of the social structure, defining its internal structure and marking its external boundaries, acts of sexual transgression or violation may offer a primary sign for the disruption of the order of that world. Hence, Claudia Camp

---

11. See Keefe, *Woman's Body*, and Susan Niditch, "The 'Sodomite' Theme in Judges 19–20: Family, Community, and Social Disintegration," *CBQ* 44 (1982): 365–78.

12. Niditch, "The 'Sodomite' Theme," 371.

13. Lyn Brechtel, "What If Dinah Is Not Raped?" *JSOT* 62 (1994): 19–36.

14. Regina Schwartz, "Adultery in the House of David: The Metanarrative of Biblical Scholarship and the Narratives of the Bible," *Semeia* 54 (1991): 45.

concludes that "sexual misconduct both induces and represents social disorder" in biblical literature.[15] In these narratives of sexual violation and social violence, the woman's transgressed-upon sexual body is a sign that represents disrupted social boundaries.[16]

In Hosea, we find another female figure functioning as a symbol of Israelite society (or at least that segment of Israelite society under condemnation by the prophet) and sexual transgression signaling some kind of infraction or sin that aggrieves Yhwh. Following the clue suggested by the narratives of sexual transgression and social violence discussed above leads to the hypothesis that Hosea's female, familial, and/or sexual metaphors may evoke a language of identity about the nation's situation in its present violence and future destruction. Reading these images in relation to the trope of woman's body as the social body, it becomes possible to see that Hosea's disturbing images about women, sexual transgression, female sterility, and the death of children were rhetorically powerful in his time because they evoked a dimension of ancient Israel's language of identity. In this language, fertile womanhood and procreation within the licit context of the patrilineal family was a symbol of the life of the nation, and female fornication, the birth of illegitimate children, the loss of fertility, miscarriages, and the death of mothers with children could therefore symbolize its death.

Reading Hosea's metaphor of Israel as the fornicating wife of God with attention to the social dimensions of sexual symbolism shifts our interpretive perspective in important ways. The dominant reading of Hosea's "marriage" metaphor takes marriage and the theological concept of covenant as the metaphor's proper loci of meaning: as this "woman of promiscuity" betrays her marital obligations by fornicating with her lovers, so Israel betrays its covenant obligations by going after other gods. This focus on the marriage between the woman/nation and the prophet/deity does not, however, adequately account for the role the "children of fornications" play in the complex metaphor. In Hos 1, the parallelism between אשת זנונים and ילדי זנונים, as well as the importance of the children in the extended metaphor that follows in chapter 2, suggest that the children are as much a key to the meaning of the metaphor as the mother.[17] In Hos 1–2, the prophet's commentary about the state of the nation is evoked not only by the

---

15. Claudia Camp, *Wisdom and the Feminine in the Book of Proverbs* (Bible and Literature 11; Sheffield: Almond, 1985), 120.

16. A related metaphor, found in many prophetic oracles, is the personification of cities as female. These texts similarly figure social identity in a female metaphor and liken societal destruction to rape. See the essay by Brad E. Kelle in this volume ("Wartime Rhetoric: Prophetic Metaphorization of Cities as Female") for treatment of this trope. See also Kelle, *Hosea 2*, 81–94; and John J. Schmitt, "The Wife of God in Hosea 2," *BR* 34 (1989): 5–18, who argue that Yhwh's promiscuous wife in Hos 2 is the city of Samaria.

17. Phyllis Bird, "'To Play the Harlot': An Inquiry into an Old Testament Metaphor," in *Gender and Difference in Ancient Israel* (ed. P. L. Day; Minneapolis: Fortress, 1989), 80.

woman of promiscuity, but also by her children of promiscuity, "Jezreel," "Not Pitied," and "Not My People." This point suggests that the trope used in Hosea is not really a *marriage* metaphor but rather a *family* metaphor; it is a parable of a בית אב that has been irrevocably disrupted. If Israelite identity was bound up with the symbolic centrality of the בית אב, then we can read Hosea's family metaphor about a fornicating wife and her illegitimate children as pointing to the disruption or dissolution that identity.

An important clue for the causes of this situation of societal disruption is contained in the name of Gomer's firstborn child of promiscuity. "Jezreel," a name that sounds so much like Israel, was a royal city and so a synecdoche for monarchical power. The prophet's outcry against the "blood of Jezreel," on account of which God will "put an end to the kingdom" (Hos 1:4), evokes memories of the copious blood that the usurper Jehu spilled at Jezreel in his coup against the Omrides. The dynasty Jehu established by the sword lasted through the long reign of Jeroboam II (d. 745 B.C.E.) and ended when Jeroboam's heir, Zechariah, was dispatched by the sword of a new usurper. This regicide was followed by others, leading to a highly unstable political situation. Hosea's naming of his firstborn suggests a critique of the violence that permeated the political climate of his day.

Jezreel is also the name of a geographical location, namely, a fertile valley in the north and an attractive locale for cash-cropping ventures. In this respect, the oracle about the blood of Jezreel brings to mind the story of King Ahab's appropriation of Naboth's patrimonial vineyard by means of false charges and the murder of an innocent man (1 Kgs 21), thus evoking awareness of the violence in the escalating processes of land accumulation in Hosea's time. The name Jezreel is a complex rhetorical tool by which Hosea names the corrupt and blood-soaked royal house as the firstborn "son of promiscuity." In more contemporary language, the prophet is saying that these kings are "bastards."

Further clues about the social or political issues that Hosea evokes through his sexual language are found in Hos 2, which offers an extended riff on the metaphor of the body of the woman of promiscuity as the body of the nation. Here the woman's desire is for her lovers because, as she says, it is they "who give me my bread and my water, my wool and my linen, my oil and my drink" (Hos 2:7b MT). In response, the cuckolded husband YHWH laments that the woman does not remember that it was he who gave her "the grain, the wine, and the oil," which he now threatens to "take back" in their seasons (Hos 2:10b MT). Within the dominant reading that assumes a fertility cult as the referent of this language about fornication, the woman/nation's mistake is theological; she believes that the power of fertility rests with divinities that are imminent in nature and subject to ritual manipulation rather than in the hands of the transcendent YHWH. This standard interpretation, however, overlooks the specific meanings that grain, wine, and oil carried in Hosea's Israel. These were lucrative cash crops in the Iron Age Levant, suitable for export and easy to trade for luxury goods and armaments.[18] Elite strategies of land accumulation aimed at maximizing the production of these crops, even at the cost of displacing families from their patrimonial lands. The metaphor about fornication thus includes commentary on the shift from an economy based on locally controlled subsistence agriculture to an emerging market economy based on cash crops and international trade. The desire of the woman of fornications for the grain, wine, oil, linen, flax, and other commodities reflects critically upon the desire of Israel's powerful elites for the profits and pleasures that this trade produced.

The processes of agricultural intensification were clearly a subject of concern for the eighth-century prophets. Hosea's contemporaries, Amos, Micah, and Isaiah, have much to say about the injustices relating to the elite's circumvention of traditional laws regarding the inalienability of patrimonial lands. Hosea, by contrast, is more focused on issues of corporate identity and its dissolution. This theme, however, can be easily missed unless the interpreter attends to the social dimensions of his sexual and familial language.

Hosea's use of family metaphors is not limited to the book's opening chapters. In Hos 5:7, the prophet offers an alternative play on the motif of illegitimate children:

> They [m. pl.] have acted treacherously against Yhwh;
> for they have fathered alien children [בנים זרים].
> Now the new moon shall devour them with their fields.

This metaphor of fathering alien or illegitimate children, like the metaphor about the "children of promiscuity," may be read as pointing to the threat of social discontinuity, disruption, and the loss of Israelite identity. Illegitimate children fall outside of the boundaries of the structures of meaning and continuity that defined patrilineal Israel. Hence, as a metaphor, the fathering of "alien children" points to deviance from or break-up of the present order. The consequence of this going astray is destruction: "the new moon shall devour them with their fields." As the fields are devoured, so is the nation, as the verses that follow suggest: "Blow the horn in Gibeah, the trumpet in Ramah.... Ephraim shall become a desolation in the day of punishment" (5:8–9a).

It is noteworthy that male fornication also serves in Hosea as a sign of social disruption. In Hos 5:7, discussed above, the blame for the present situation is placed not on women but on the men who metaphorically father alien offspring. Also, male fornication as a trope for political violence appears in Hos 6:10, where deeds of violence are represented as Ephraim's fornication, and in Hos 7:4, where treacherous violence within the royal court is described as men committing

---

18. David Hopkins, "The Dynamics of Agriculture in Monarchical Israel," in *Society of Biblical Literature 1983 Seminar Papers* (SBLSP 22; Chico, Calif.: Scholars Press, 1983), 177–202.

adultery. In Hos 8:9 the prophet critiques the nation's desire to forge alliances with Assyria and other nations through the image of Ephraim "hiring lovers" among the nations. In all of these oracles, the social or political connotations of Hosea's sexual language are obvious.

Oracles about male and female fornication and the begetting of illegitimate children resonate in Hosea with other tropes about identity becoming undone. The theme of inappropriate "mixing," for example, is evoked by a culinary metaphor, in which Hosea complains that Ephraim has "mixed himself with the peoples" (7:8). So mixed, the nation is now like a tasty morsel that other nations may consume, as they are already doing: "aliens have devoured his strength, yet he knows it not" (7 9). Becoming mixed with the nations, the boundaries that define Israel's identity over and against its cultural "others" are compromised; therefore, the prophet warns the people that, fittingly, geopolitical realities will soon swallow them.

In these intersecting images of inappropriate mixing, fornication, and the begetting of alien children, we can see Hosea's persistent concern with the question of Israel's identity as a people. Binding itself in foreign alliances, increasingly dependent upon interregional market economy, and dabbling in cosmopolitan values, Israel has engaged in various forms of interstate "intercourse," which have the effect, says Hosea, of cultural mixing or homogenization. Such intercourse or mixing with the nations leads to the dissolution of Israel's own identity and will soon result, warns Hosea, in literal destruction, ironically at the hands of those very nations with which Israel has become too intimate.

Chapter 2's earlier motif of the woman of promiscuity's pursuit of her lovers, the "baals" (Hos 2:7–9, 15, 19 MT), is also illuminated from the perspective of this concern with Israel's international "affairs." The baals, that is, the lords or deities of the ancient Near East, were no simple fertility deities but gods of the state, signifying specific forms of power and production. In Canaan, Israel's quintessential "other," the deity known specifically as Baal was, according to Coote and Coote, the "patron of commercial agriculture under royal control."[19] From this perspective, the woman's desire for the baals qua lovers may be read as a commentary upon Israel's growing involvement with ideologically foreign modes of production and exchange based upon the commercialization of agriculture and the concentration of power in urban centers.[20] Such involvement necessitates repudiation of values and social structures that were definitive of early Israelite identity.

---

19. Robert B. Coote and Mary P. Coote, *Power, Politics, and the Making of the Bible: An Introduction* (Minneapolis: Fortress, 1990), 43.

20. Keefe, *Woman's Body*, 195–97; Chaney, "Accusing Whom of What," 111–13; Yee, "She Is Not My Wife," 371–81.

In a manner similar to his use of female and familial images, Hosea also addresses the issue of corporate identity in his ominous oracles about a future "return to Egypt" (Hos 7:16; 8:13; 9:3, 6; 11:5). Origin stories or myths are a particularly important ingredient in the identity structures of any human community. Origin stories are not just about the primordial past; they are also about the ideal present, articulating the values and ways definitive of the meaning of a people. Among the ancient Israelites, the story of its origin out of Egypt articulated a common identity for the highland tribes as a people ideologically positioned over against the urban/imperial structures of control and exploitation, aptly symbolized by the emblem of "Egypt." This myth of origins is present in Hosea's oracles. For example, he describes Ephraim as Yhwh's adopted child, called forth out of Egypt (Hos 11:1). Those myths and symbols of identity related to the exodus event, however, are relentlessly reversed in his oracles. The names of Jezreel's younger siblings, "Not Pitied" and "Not My People," negate the covenantal language of the exodus in which Yhwh promises to have pity or compassion on the enslaved Hebrews and binds them to himself as his people at Sinai. More explicit references to the exodus myth are found in Hosea's prophecies about an impeding return to Egypt. In Hos 9:3, the prophet warns that

> They will not dwell in the land of Yhwh;
> but Ephraim will return to Egypt,
> and in Assyria they will eat unclean food.

The same image appears in Hos 11:5:

> He [Ephraim or Israel] will return to the land of Egypt,
> and Assyria will be his king,
> because they have refused to return [to me].

The threat of a return to Egypt in these verses serves as a powerful sign for the meaning of the imminent Assyrian conquest and the ensuing deportation of the propertied class. As the creation of Israel finds mythic expression in a coming forth out of Egypt, so the threat of the nation's uncreation in Assyrian conquest is figured in this specter of a return to Egypt.

For Hosea's ancient Israelite audience, the force of this symbolism was such that the mention of Egypt or the exodus event would have been enough to bring to mind a whole complex of mythic associations that would have resonated deeply in their collective psyche. Such is also the case, I argue, with his disturbing female and familial images. These, too, would have resonated deeply with his audiences as reversals of the language of identity upon which their sense of world was established. Like his rhetoric about Egypt, Hosea's familial metaphors offer powerful and disturbing signs of the negation of Israel's identity.

The adultery metaphor in Hos 1–2, then, works in this way because it is both a marital and maternal metaphor. As such, it participates in and affects a reversal of another important dimension of the symbolism that is constitutive of Israelite identity, namely, Israel as generative mother, symbol of the ongoing life of the people. This function of woman as a symbol of society is easily obscured by the more dominant motif in biblical literature concerning male sexuality as a symbol for corporate identity. It is clear from the ancestor narratives of Genesis, for example, that intergenerational continuity was fundamental to Israel's understanding of its meaning and identity, figuring as a critical locus for the inflow of divine blessings into this people's sacred history. In these narratives, it is male procreative power, lodged in the male genitals, that appears most obviously as the locus of this generative meaning of the people; thus, Israel (the people) is the seed of Israel (Jacob). Such masculine symbolism is at work in Hosea's use of "Ephraim" ("fruitful one") as his preferred name for Israel. Nevertheless, there are hints in Hosea of another dimension to the symbolism of identity that concerns the procreative power of female bodies.

Throughout the book of Hosea, the condition and fate of the nation are figured in graphic images of maternal bereavement, the loss of female fertility, and the death of mothers with their children. The destruction of the nation is figured metonymically in mothers who are "dashed in pieces with their children"; "so," the prophet warns, "it will be done to you Bethel" (10:14b–15a). The same theme is sounded again in Hos 14:1 (MT):

> Samaria has become guilty,
> because she has rebelled against her God.
> They will fall by the sword,
> their little children will be dashed into pieces,
> and their pregnant women will be ripped open.

These graphic images certainly may be read as a reflection of the real consequences of war in which women and children are routinely slaughtered or enslaved. But, as a metonym for the devastation of war, the slaughter of children and mothers and, especially, the slitting open of pregnant women evoke the more far-reaching corporate consequences of Assyrian invasion: the end of Israel. Slaughtered mothers with their children figure the nation as a whole as it is devastated by war.

Another play on maternal symbolism is found in the image of the nation as an unwise fetus: though the "pangs of childbirth come for him..., he does not present himself at the place where children break forth" (Hos 13:13). In this fatal situation of breached birth, both mother and fetus will die, not because of enemy swords, but because the nation's iniquity is "bound up" (13:12). While birth would offer an image of passage and the continuity of social life, the image of a breached birth stands as a symbol of the negation of the future possibilities of this world.

In these images of slaughter and stillbirth, it is not the death of fathers with their sons but of mothers with their children that reverses that symbolism of national identity that is rooted in procreativity and lineal continuity. The most extended metaphor drawing on this theme is found in Hos 9:

> Ephraim: like a bird,
> their glory [כבוד] shall fly away—
> no childbirth, no gestation, no conception.
> Even if they do raise up children,
> I will bereave them—not one will be left.
> Woe to them indeed when I turn away from them! ...
> Give to them, Yhwh—what will you give?
> Give to them a miscarrying womb and dry breasts. (Hos 9:11–12, 14)

Ephraim's כבוד ("glory"), a word often used of the divine presence, is here the nation's children, which Yhwh now threatens to take away. Women's wombs will miscarry and be made barren; breasts will run dry; children will die until none are left. The point is blunt: no children, no people.

The maternal and corporeal elements in such oracles suggest the presence of gynomorphic modes of imagining corporate experience in which a woman's fecund body, generative of the generations, provides a root symbol for the life of this people. Conversely, the barrenness of women and the death of mothers with children are powerful images for the nation's destruction. The nation has become a barren woman, a woman bereaved of her children, a pregnant woman slit open, or one who dies with her infant in a breached birth.

Also at play in Hosea's sexual language is the homology between a woman's body and the fertile land, a religious metaphor with roots in the Neolithic revolution. The sexual transgression of the woman of promiscuity is a figure for the land itself as it "fornicates greatly away from Yhwh" (Hos 1:2), and her punishment—to be stripped naked and made bare like a desert (2:5 MT)—intertwines with other threats in Hosea concerning drought and desolation.[21] The woman of promiscuity is simultaneously the people Israel and the land itself. Land here should not be understood through romantic, modern notions about pristine nature, separate from the human world; rather, the land of which Hosea speaks is inextricably tied up with the identity and life of the people who dwell within it.

Language about women's bodies and sexuality throughout the book of Hosea thus emerges from cultural concerns that include but are not limited to the demand for female fidelity within a patriarchal culture. This language also emerges from cultural concerns with female procreation as definitive of the meaning and identity of this people. Israel is a woman in Hosea's metaphor not simply because women are wives, whose conjugal obligations to their husbands in patriarchal society are analogous to the demands of a jealous god, but because

---

21. Saul M. Olyan, "'In the Sight of Her Lovers': On the Interpretation of *nablūt* in Hosea 2,12," *BZ* 36 (1992): 255–61; Keefe, *Woman's Body*, 213–20.

women are mothers, whose procreativity functions symbolically as a locus of intergenerational and patrilineal continuity, and hence of national identity.

CONCLUSION

In recent years, feminist biblical scholars have given much attention to how women function symbolically within the language of identity found in the biblical texts and have argued for the many ways that images of women and their sexuality often serve to mark the boundaries of Israel's identity or the oppositional pole of "otherness" that threatens that identity.[22] While this analysis has considerably advanced our understanding of the symbolic location of women in biblical texts, it is sometimes applied too monolithically, so that it becomes difficult to discern any other dimensions of female symbolism at work in biblical texts. The above reflections on Hosea's gendered, sexual, and familial language suggest another perspective in which community and continuity in biblical literature can be signified not only by the male body, whose sexual organ serves as the site for the inscription of covenant belonging, but also by the female body, whose womb and breasts are literally a source of the community and figuratively a symbol for its solidarity and continuity.

This perspective on female and familial symbolism leaves us firmly embedded in a patriarchal universe. Hosea's concern with female fidelity presupposes a patriarchal family structure and signals a meaning of a people defined in patrilineal succession. But these reflections suggest a need to adjust our assumptions about the location and function of female symbolism within this patriarchal world. Symbolic language is complex and multilayered, and it may be that within or behind the patriarchal adultery metaphor lies another metaphor, which, once glimpsed, suggests that the identity of Ephraim is not only spoken about using masculine imagery. Rather, maternal images of female fertility and procreation, like the motif of the exodus from Egypt, may also serve as religious language for speaking about the origin, meaning, and identity of this people. And the reversal of that gynomorphic symbolism of identity in Hosea, like his prophecies about a return to Egypt, works rhetorically as a chilling trope of the death of the nation.

---

22. E.g., Howard Eilberg-Schwartz, *The Savage in Judaism: An Anthropology of Israelite Religion and Ancient Judaism* (Bloomington: Indiana University Press, 1990); and Cheryl J. Exum, *Fragmented Women: Feminist (Sub)versions of Biblical Narratives* (Valley Forge, Pa.: Trinity Press International, 1993).

"We Have Seen the Enemy, and He Is Only a 'She'": The Portrayal of Warriors as Women

Claudia D. Bergmann

In the Hebrew Bible and some ancient Near Eastern texts, warriors who are about to lose a war are sometimes metaphorically compared to women and sometimes to women giving birth.[1] In 1954, Delbert R. Hillers called the comparison of men with women a standard curse in antiquity and added that *woman* appears to be a natural simile for *weakness* and *cowardice*.[2] Most recently, Cynthia R. Chapman—although thankfully not subscribing to Hillers's gender biases—still subsumes the very specific comparisons of men with women giving birth into the larger corpus of ancient Near Eastern and biblical texts comparing unsuccessful males to females.[3] Hillers, Holladay, and even Chapman assume that, for an ancient text, a comparison of men with women in general is the same as a comparison of men with women giving birth. But is there really only one metaphor at work, or are there two?

Since Aristotle's classic definition of metaphor as a transfer of the meaning of one word onto an unrelated word, the study of metaphor has blossomed and brought forth different models of what metaphor and simile are and how they relate to each other. In this article, metaphor is understood as an interaction of

---

1. After presenting this paper at the 2005 SBL Annual Meeting, it developed into one of the appendices in my University of Chicago Ph.D. dissertation, a revised version of which was published as *Childbirth as a Metaphor for Crisis: Evidence from the Ancient Near East, the Hebrew Bible, and 1QH XI, 1-18* (Berlin: de Gruyter, 2008). The original version of the article was published in *CBQ* 69 (2007): 651-72 and is reprinted here by permission in a revised version.

2. Delbert R. Hillers, "A Convention in Hebrew Literature: The Reaction to Bad News," *ZAW* 77 (1965): 86-90. Similarly, William L. Holladay, *Jeremiah 2* (Hermeneia; Minneapolis: Fortress, 1989), 167.

3. Cynthia R. Chapman, *The Gendered Language of Warfare in the Israelite-Assyrian Encounter* (HSM 62; Winona Lake, Ind : Eisenbrauns, 2004), 141: "Feminization in both sets of texts [ancient Near East and Hebrew Bible] is used metaphorically to discredit a man on the battlefield, and the associated commonplaces of feminization are broken, missing, or removed weapons, implements of weaving, a bowed posture, labor pains, sexual exposure, and prostitution."

a "target domain" and a "source domain" according to the model of metaphor developed by George Lakoff and Mark Turner.[4] Metaphor provides richer imagery and literary beauty but also deeper meaning and a "redescription" of both domains. It has the power to describe reality in new ways and opens new realms of experiencing the world. Thus, metaphor is not about *deciphering* but *exploring* the expressive potential of a text.

In our specific case(s) of metaphor, ancient Near Eastern and Hebrew Bible texts compare the situations of unsuccessful warriors either to the situation of a woman giving birth or to the situation of a woman in general. In the first scenario, *birth* (Lakoff's "source") functions as the metaphor with which to understand situations of *crisis* (Lakoff's "target"). Birth, and especially difficult birth, can thus be the concept that metaphorically explains the difficult concept of crisis. On the one hand, the birth metaphor highlights the potential for death of the person in crisis but also takes into consideration the potential for a new beginning after the crisis has passed. It also focuses on the images of blood, screaming, and moving back and forth in pain. On the other hand, the birth metaphor downplays potential aspects of a crisis such as depression, suicidal thoughts, or society's ostracizing of the person in crisis.[5]

In the second scenario, however, when men are described as being like women or becoming women, the metaphor is different. Men and women are essentially unlike each other, and it is impossible that a change from one to another can occur naturally. Thus, when it is said that a man becomes a woman, all characteristics commonly associated with the "source" (woman) are now applied to the "target" (man). *Woman* becomes the lens through which to see *man*. Yet, how one understands the entire metaphor depends on one's culturally based definition of *woman*. Hebrew Bible texts that compare warriors to women, for example, often define women as weak and inactive. Ancient Near Eastern texts that make the same comparison tend to associate women with a certain garb and certain tools.

Thus, if Lakoff and Turner's theory of metaphor is applied to the texts in question, one actually finds two different metaphors are at work, namely, (A) *crisis* is (like) *birth*, and (B) *men* are (like) *women*. Although both metaphors use males and females, their meaning and function within a text is different. That is, ancient writers made a fine distinction between these two entirely different types of texts, which differ in both their use of terminology and their use of metaphor.

---

4. George Lakoff and Mark Turner, *More Than Cool Reason* (Chicago: University of Chicago Press, 1989).

5. When the birth metaphor describes crisis in the Hebrew Bible, the "child," i.e., the "result," is not mentioned. Thus, to be precise, it is not the entire process of birth that becomes a metaphor for crisis but the moment of a difficult birth process where mother and child are at the crossroads between life and death.

Each type of text and metaphor aims to achieve different goals and elicits different responses in the reader.

Comparison A: Warriors as Women Giving Birth

Examples for the Use of the Birth Metaphor in the Cultures Surrounding Israel

Ancient Near Eastern texts compare women giving birth and warriors in crisis by linking their defining characteristics and behavior.[6] The Akkadian Sargon Legend AO 6702, for example, portrays two armies ready for battle by utilizing the image of two women experiencing childbirth:

> ^{20}i-h[i-i]l-la ha-h̬i-la-tum ut-ta-am-ma-ka da-ma a-li-ta-an
> The women in labor are giving birth, two women giving birth drenched in blood.[7]

The Lamentation over the Destruction of Ur, a Sumerian lament, describes dead bodies and wounded warriors who line the formerly magnificent streets of the city after the battle. The wounded men are also compared to women giving birth:

> ^{221}i-gi₄-in-zu ki ha-ri-iš-ta ama-ba-ka múd-bi-a mu-un-nú¹-eš
> As if in the place where their mothers had laboured, they lay in their own blood.[8]

An Assyrian royal inscription of Sargon II includes a report about Rusâ, who illegitimately claimed the throne of Urartu. Rusâ's masculinity and subsequently his claim to royalty are discredited by Sargon II in the following way:

> ^{151}ki-ma ^{mí}ha-riš-ti i-na ^{giš}NÁ in-na-di-ma ak-!u ù A.MEŠ i-na pi-i-šu ip-ru-us-ma mu-ru-uṣ la Zi-e e-mid ra-man-šu

---

6. The comparison can, in fact, work both ways: warriors threatened with death can be compared to women during childbirth and vice versa. One example for the latter appears in Ligabue 33–50, a Middle Assyrian medical text. Here a woman has extreme difficulties giving birth. The dangerous situation in which she finds herself is compared to the dangerous situation of a warrior in a battle: "33 The woman in childbirth has pains at delivery, … 37 The mother is enveloped in the dust of death. 38 Like a chariot, she is enveloped in the dust of battle, 39 like a plough, she is enveloped in the dust of the woods, 40 like a warrior in the fray, she is cast down in her blood (see Wilfred G. Lambert, "A Middle Assyrian Medical Text," Iraq 31 [1969]: 28–39).

7. Joan Goodnick Westenholz, Legends of the Kings of Akkade (Mesopotamian Civilizations 7; Winona Lake, Ind.: Eisenbrauns, 1997), 64.

8. For text and translation, see "The Lament for Urim" at http://www-etcsl.orient.ox.ac.uk/.

> Like a woman in labor he was thrown upon the bed, food and water he kept away from his mouth, and a sickness without possibility of healing he put upon himself.[9]

A closer look at the way the birth simile is employed in this text shows that it has more in common with texts that ridicule foreign warriors (see comparison B below) than texts that lift up the severity of a crisis (comparison A), even though this royal inscription, like the Lamentation over the Destruction of Ur, employs the simile *ki-ma* ^{mí}*ha-riš-ti* ("like a woman"). The series of three similes in the larger context of the birth simile (fleeing like a fugitive, hiding in the mountains like a murderer, and retreating to bed like a woman giving birth) suggests that Rusâ's crisis is severe. But Rusâ did not face this crisis bravely, as a male should. His behavior is more like that of a coward who retreats into illness or hides from his responsibilities than that of a woman giving birth. Greek texts written much later also know the comparison of childbirth and war. Euripides, for example, has his heroine Medea measure the dangers of being a warrior and being a pregnant woman:

> λέγουσι δ' ἡμᾶς ὡς ἀκίνδυνον βίον ζῶμεν κατ' οἴκους, οἱ δὲ μάρνανται δορί, κακῶς φρονοῦντες· ὡς τρὶς ἂν παρ' ἀσπίδα στῆναι θέλοιμ' ἂν μᾶλλον ἢ τεκεῖν ἅπαξ.
> They say that we live safe from danger at home while they prove themselves in the war of spears. You fools: I would rather throw myself into the terror of battle three times than give birth just once.[10]

In Sparta, there apparently existed a law that tombstones had to remain without inscription with the exception of tombstones of warriors who had died in battle and of women who had died in labor or after giving birth: πλὴν ἀνδρὸς ἐν πολέμῳ καὶ γυναικὸς τῶν λεχοῦς ἀμοθανόντων.[11] Death on the battlefield and death in the bed of childbirth were thus equated as serving the common good.

The previous examples from cultures surrounding ancient Israel show that warriors in severe crisis were regularly compared to women giving birth. On the psychological level, both groups of people may experience feelings of impending chaos that goes beyond their control. Physically, both can bleed, sweat, cry, and rock back and forth in pain.

---

9. Walter Mayer, "Sargons Feldzug gegen Urartu—714 v. Chr.: Text und Übersetzung," *MDOG* 115 (1983): 65–132, esp. 83; see also Chapman, *Gendered Language*, 35–37.

10. Euripides, *Medea*, 5.248–251, as cited in Ursula Vedder, "Frauentod: Kriegertod im Spiegel der attischen Grabkunst des 4. Jahrhunderts vor Christus," *MDAI* 103 (1988): 161–91, esp. 188.

11. Plutarch, *Lykurg*, 27.3, as cited in Vedder, "Frauentod," 188. For textual emendations, see ibid., n. 134.

The Simile "Like a Woman Giving Birth" in the Hebrew Bible

The Hebrew Bible also uses the image of a woman giving birth as a metaphor for describing different types of crises. These crises may cause fear and anxiety in individuals or groups who face personal oppression, the onslaught of a battle, or the universe-changing events associated with the coming of "that day" or the "Day of the Lord." In some cases, the biblical birth metaphor appears with the simile "like a woman giving birth," ensuring that the reader knows explicitly to whose experience the crisis is likened. This simile seems to be formulaic and appears in various forms: (1) כיולדה, "like a woman giving birth" (Ps 48:7; Isa 13:8; 42:14; Jer 6:24; 30:6; 49:24; 50:43; Mic 4:9, 10; with minor variations in Isa 21:3 and Jer 22:23); (2) כלב אשה מצרה, "like the heart of a woman in צרה-pain" (Jer 48:41; 49:22); (3) כמו הרה תקריב ללדת, "like a woman who is close to giving birth" (Isa 26:17); (4) כחולה, "like one who is sick" (Jer 4:31); (5) כמו אשת לדה, "like a woman giving birth" (Jer 13:21).

In the Hebrew Bible, a semantic field for childbirth language applied to situations of crisis surrounds this simile. Childbirth, as well as the experience of crisis, can cause certain utterances, crying, screaming, or changes in breathing. Both can also change a person's physical appearance, such as the color of one's face or one's posture. Most effects of living through a crisis or through the difficult experience of giving birth, however, are of a psychological nature and influence the mind as well as the body. They can be feelings of fear, terror, distress, and loss of courage. The following texts are two out of many examples where women giving birth and people in crisis are compared explicitly or by means of the true birth metaphor.[12]

The first example concerns individual men experiencing a local crisis and is a showcase for the use of the birth metaphor applied to warriors in crisis. In Jer 30:5–7, the rhetorical question "Can a man give birth?" creates the set-up for the ironic picture that follows. Since men cannot give birth, why do they behave כיולדה? This simile also serves to indicate a physical change in the men experiencing the local crisis. Their faces turn ירקון, "a shade of sickly greenish pale."[13] Terminologically, then, the crisis is qualified as one that can be compared to birth by the simile כיולדה and by the use of the birth metaphor indicator צרה. The additional imagery used is birth-related as well. The warriors no longer hold weapons in their hands but now touch their abdomen as if feeling contractions there. This renders them useless for battle. Because of the terrible crisis of

---

12. While the examples mentioned in this subsection apply the simile "like a woman giving birth," there are many more examples in the Hebrew Bible where the birth metaphor appears without the explaining simile.

13. *HALOT*, 441; Athalya Brenner, *Colour Terms in the Old Testament* (JSOTSup 21; Sheffield: Sheffield Academic Press, 1982), 100–102. Similar changes in one's complexion are also described in the birth metaphor texts Isa 13:8; Nah 2:10; and Joel 2:6, all of which picture terrible crises.

היום ההוא, male behavior now mirrors female behavior. However, the warriors are not compared to stereotypically weak and subjugated women but to women experiencing the life-threatening crisis of giving birth and who are thus at the crossroads between life and death.

The second example comes from a group of texts that picture a threatening crisis as it is about to change the lives of cities and groups at war.[14] Isaiah 13:7–8, which is part of the so-called Babylon pronouncement by the prophet Isaiah, describes fear and terror resulting from the knowledge that the יום יהוה ("day of YHWH") is at hand. It pictures the crisis by means of two memorable images that can be connected to the birth metaphor but are not exclusive to it: the slacking of human hands and the melting of human hearts.[15] The language of verse 8a ensures that the crisis is understood in terms of the birth metaphor. Every term appearing in this half-verse is typical for the application of the birth metaphor (verbs: בהל, אחז, חיל; nouns: ציר, חבל). Hence, the additional simile, "like a woman giving birth," in its most common form (כיולדה) almost seems redundant in light of the plethora of birth terminology surrounding it.

Personal, local, and universal crises caused by oppression, war, and the coming of the Day of the Lord can threaten the lives of individuals and groups in the Hebrew Bible. People in crisis can thus be compared to women giving birth because both stand at the crossroads between life and death. The people affected by crisis know that it cannot be prevented, just as birth cannot be stopped. There is nothing they can do to improve their situation, and the outcome of the crisis is uncertain. As we will see, this is in stark contrast to the situation of warriors who are ridiculed as women. These warriors could survive if they would only not behave like stereotypical women.

Comparison B: Warriors as Women

Feminized Warriors in the Ancient Near East

Peggy Day writes, "[T]he ideal 'man's man' in the ancient Near East was a skilled warrior, whose masculinity was symbolized by the regular accoutrements of war."[16] Aside from owning weapons and using them successfully, owning property and siring offspring were two other elements of gender identification for males. Being or becoming a female was considered utter failure, something that

---

14. These cities and groups can be represented by their kings (Ps 48; Jer 50:43), can include everyone (Isa 13:7), or can concern a city symbolized as a female entity (Jer 6:23; 49:24).

15. The slacking of human hands, often used as a sign for failing courage, also appears in the birth metaphor texts Jer 6:24 and 50:43.

16. Peggy L. Day, "Why Is Anat a Warrior and Hunter?" in *The Bible and the Politics of Exegesis: Essays in Honor of Norman K. Gottwald on His Sixty-Fifth Birthday* (ed. P. L. Day, D. Jobling, and G. T. Sheppard; Cleveland: Pilgrim, 1991), 141–46, esp. 142.

had be avoided at all cost but that could certainly be wished upon one's enemies. Hence, ancient Near Eastern texts, and subsequently texts of the Hebrew Bible, gendered the victor of military actions as male and the defeated enemy as female using such epithets as "woman" or "prostitute."

Two Hittite texts are often quoted as examples of this phenomenon. A prayer to Ištar reads:

> [25]Furthermore, grind away from the men manliness, potency (?) [26](and) health; take away their swords, bows, arrows, [27]daggers, and bring them into the Hatti-land; then put into their hand [28]the distaff and mirror (?) of a woman [29]and clothe them as women....[17]

A soldier's oath, also in the Hittite language, similarly shows that a swearing-in of soldiers could include a curse for those warriors who might break their promises:

> [46]Whoever breaks these oaths..., let these oaths change him from a man into a woman! Let them change his troops into women, [50]let them dress in the fashion of women and cover their heads with a length of cloth! Let them break the bows, arrows (and) clubs in their hands and [iii] [let them put] in their hands distaff and mirror![18]

In these two texts, women and unsuccessful warriors are characterized by their feminine dress and their lack of weapons. As male and female behavior and abilities are stereotyped, so are male and female attire and tools.[19]

This phenomenon is not limited to the Hittite language. A curse contained in an Akkadian treaty between Ashurnirari and Mati'ilu of Arpad found at Nineveh reads:

> [8]If Mati'ilu sins against this treaty of Ashurnirari, king of Assyria, [9]may Mati'ilu become a prostitute and may his warriors become women. [[9]*ih-ti-ti* ᵐKI.MIN *lu* MÍ.*ha-rim-tú* LÚ.ERIM [MEŠ-*šu*] *lu* MÍ.MEŠ...]. [10]Like prostitutes, may they receive their reward in the squares of their city.[20]

---

17. As quoted in Delbert R. Hillers, *Treaty Curses and the Old Testament Prophets* (BibOr 16; Rome: Pontifical Biblical Institute, 1964), 66. Also see Ferdinand Sommer, "Ein hethitisches Gebet," *ZA* 33 (1921): 85–102; and Johannes Friedrich, "Aus dem hethitischen Schrifttum: II. Gebet an die Istar von Ninive, aus fremden Ländern herbeizukommen," *AO* 25 (1925): 20–22.

18. *KBo* VI:34 and its duplicate *KUB* VII:59. See Hillers, *Treaty Curses*, 66–67; Chapman, *Gendered Language*, 53; for an early transcription and translation of the text, see also Johannes Friedrich, "Der hethitische Soldateneid," *ZA* NS 1 (1924): 161–92.

19. Chapman, *Gendered Language*, 54. See also Harry A. Hoffner, "Symbols for Masculinity and Femininity: Their Use in Ancient Near Eastern Sympathetic Magic Rituals," *JBL* 85 (1966): 326–34; Harold Dressler, "Is the Bow of Aqhat a Symbol of Virility?" *UF* 7 (1975): 217–25.

20. Simo Parpola and Kazuko Watanabe, *Neo-Assyrian Treaties and Loyalty Oaths* (SAA 2; Helsinki: Helsinki University Press, 1988), 12. See also Rykle Borger, "Assyrische Staatsver-

The warriors failed to do the work that had previously defined them as soldiers. Now the city gates are open. This fits with the note later in the text that the goddess Ištar may "¹³ take away their [the men's] bow," which makes the soldiers unable to fight and causes them to cry. The curse of Ištar breaking the soldier's bow in the thick of battle can also appear without the comparison of the soldier to a woman. In those cases, the breaking of the bow is followed by the soldier assuming a submissive posture, such as crouching under the feet of his enemy.[21] The severity of the curse in this text is heightened when Mati'ilu is not only described as becoming a woman, a prostitute, but when it is added that he will not have any offspring, that his wives will be old and infertile, and that he will not have any land of his own. Both Mati'ilu and his soldiers thus cease to be men.

A similar curse of feminization is included in Esarhaddon's succession treaty:

> ⁶¹⁶ᶠ·May all the gods who are called by name in this treaty tablet spin you around like a spindle-whorl, may they make you like a woman before your enemy [...*ki-i* MÍ *ina* IGI LÚ.KÚR-*ku-nu le-pa-šu-ku-nu*...].[22]

Although not giving any details about what exactly it means to be like a woman before one's enemies, the curse contains a typical woman's tool, the spindle. This is reminiscent of the above-mentioned Hittite texts where soldiers turn in their weapons and take up tools that characterize them as nonfighting women. Also from this period of the reign of Esarhaddon comes the following inscription on a stela:

> ⁵³ Whoever moves this inscription from its place ... may Ishtar, mistress of war and battle, turn his masculinity ⁵⁶ into femininity [*zik-ru-su sin-niš-a-niš*] and may she force him to sit down bound at the feet of his enemy.[23]

Here the curse does not include much detail about the behavior of the cursed person once he has turned *sin-niš-a-niš*, except for the note that he will be captured, powerless, and inactive when he sits bound at the feet of his enemies. Changes of attire or tools as in the Hittite texts are not mentioned.

A curse contained in the Alalakh tablets also combines the breaking of weapons with the metaphorical switch of a soldier into a woman:

---

träge: Der Vertrag Assurniraris mit Mati'ilu von Arpad," *TUAT* 1:157; Ernst F. Weidner, "Der Staatsvertrag Assurniraris VI von Assyrien mit Mati'ilu von Bit-Agusi," *AfO* 8 (1932–33): 2–27; Chapman, *Gendered Language*, 49–50.

21. For examples, see Chapman, *Gendered Language*, 50–51.

22. Parpola and Watanabe, *Neo-Assyrian Treaties*, 56, lines 616–17. See also Chapman, *Gendered Language*, 48.

23. Rykle Borger, *Die Inschriften Asarhaddons, Königs von Assyrien* (Graz: Weidner, 1956), 99. See also Hillers, *Treaty Curses*, 67.

Whoever shall change the settlement that Abdael made ... may Ishtar deliver him into the hands of those who pursue him; may Ishtar ... impress feminine parts into his male parts.[24]

Again it is Ištar, the goddess of nonprocreative love and battle, who combines male and female attributes within herself, who breaks the soldier's weapons and metaphorically turns him into a female. This text, however, does not describe the male's behavior once he is weaponless and "impressed with feminine parts."

A letter to King Sennacherib concerning the Urartians adds another aspect of what it means to be "like a woman [in general]":

They are very much afraid of the king, my Lord. They tremble and keep silent like women [^{14}[ma-a a-k]i^l MÍ.MEŠ [i^l]-ru^l-ú-[bu^l] i-qúl^l-u ^{15}[ma-a ina$^?$]...].[25]

The fear of the mighty enemy and his military strength is linked directly to trembling and silence or inactivity.

Warriors turning into women were apparently also known in Greek contexts. At the battle of Salamis, Herodotus puts the following words into Xerxes' mouth as Xerxes watches Artemisia sink an enemy ship:

My men have become women, and my women men [οἱ μὲν ἄνδρες γεγόνασί μοι γυναῖκες, αἱ δὲ γυναῖκες ἄνδρες].[26]

Xerxes' sentence is very short and does not go into detail concerning how the warriors-turned-women look or behave. One can only infer that they do not do what was expected of them.

These examples, spanning many centuries and covering a wide geographic area, suggest the conclusion that the idea of warriors turning into women was known all over the ancient Near East. It was apparently so well known that many of the texts are not very elaborate in giving additional information as to what it means to turn from a warrior into a woman. The female characteristics of weakness and inactivity, so defined by male-centered cultures, are always implied. Warriors who have turned into women do what women stereotypically do: they do not bear arms, they wear women's garb, or they passively endure the aggressive or oppressive acts of enemy men. Their masculinity is ridiculed and negated at every level.

---

24. Ephraim A. Speiser, "The Alalakh Tablets," *JAOS* 74 (1954): 18–25; cf. Chapman, *Gendered Language*, 57.

25. Simo Parpola, *The Correspondence of Sargon II: Letters from Assyria and the West* (SAA 1; Helsinki: Helsinki University Press, 1987), 33, lines 13–16; see also Chapman, *Gendered Language*, 48–49.

26. Herodotus 8.88 in Alfred D. Godley, trans., *Herodotus* (Cambridge: Harvard University Press, 1920), 86–87.

Feminized Warriors in the Hebrew Bible

If, as Hoffner described it, the ancient Near Eastern man defined himself through his strength in battle and through his ability to father children, then anyone who would compare such a man with a woman would negate both parts of this definition.[27] In addition, women were seen as victims of war, not as active participants. A man who is no longer an active warrior but is called a passive victim of war would thus have his military abilities ridiculed. Accordingly, a warrior behaving like a woman or becoming a woman is not someone worthy of pity but a laughingstock who no longer needs to be feared or admired. This is the dire destiny of the warriors of Egypt, Babylon, and Nineveh as described in the four Hebrew Bible texts below, and these texts reveal marked differences with the comparison of warriors to women giving birth.

Isaiah 19:16. Isaiah 19 is a pronouncement concerning Egypt. Its first part is poetry and describes Yhwh's actions against the country that cause the Egyptians' hearts to melt within them. Verse 16 then switches to prose:

ביום ההוא יהיה מצרים כנשים וחרד ופחד מפני תנופת יד יהוה צבאות אשר הוא מניף עליו:

In that day the Egyptians will be like women. They [lit., he/it] will shudder and be afraid before the raised hand of Yhwh Sabaoth that he wields against them [lit., him].

This verse is the only text in the Hebrew Bible where male warriors are explicitly compared to women by means of the simile כנשים. The reason why the Egyptians turn into women is the raised hand of Yhwh that wipes away the pharaoh's military might.

How are warriors and women alike, according to Isa 19:16? The second part of the verse uses the two verbs חרד and פחד in describing the feelings of the males who are כנשים, "like women." Both verbs are common and not gender-specific. They appear in texts with the birth metaphor and the simile "like a woman giving birth" (Isa 21:4; Jer 30:5) but are in no way indicative of the birth metaphor. The noun חגא in Isa 19:17, which is often translated as "terror" because of the LXX rendering φόβητρον, is a *hapax legomenon* with uncertain etymology and also not birth metaphor specific. While birth metaphor texts feature a plethora of terms denoting the feeling of terror, none of them is used here, as if to ensure that the comparison is with women in general and not with women in labor. Aside from חרד and פחד, there is a lack of terms and images that describe how these Egyptian warriors-turned-women behave or what they feel. Moreover, there is no report of a change of attire or loss of weapons, as is common in the ancient Near

---

27. Hoffner, "Symbols for Masculinity," 327.

Eastern texts that describe unsuccessful warriors turning into women. One must thus assume that the ancient reader would simply know what a comparison of males with females entails.

Jeremiah 50:37. Jeremiah 50:35–38 is a curse spoken by YHWH upon Babylonia. The group of people who can metaphorically change from male to female is described by the noun ערב, "mixed people," a favorite of the book of Jeremiah:

חרב אל־הבדים ונאלו חרב אל־גבוריה וחתו:
חרב אל־סוסיו ואל־רכבו ואל־כל־הערב אשר בתוכה והיו לנשים חרב אל־אוצרתיה ובזזו:

A sword against her false prophets! They will become fools. A sword against her warriors! They will be filled with terror.
A sword against his horses and his chariots and against all the mixed company in her midst! They turn into women. A sword against her treasures! They will be plundered. (50:36–37)

The reaction of the warriors to the sword directed against them is described with the verb חתת, which denotes feelings of terror and fear and, occasionally, the physical shattering of breaking.[28] This term is common in descriptions of war but never appears in texts with the simile "like a woman giving birth" or in other birth metaphor texts. Like the Isaiah passage above, Jer 50:37 provides no details of what "becoming women" means for the men affected by this change. Yet it implies inactivity on the part of the warriors. They do not succeed in protecting the property that now becomes booty for the enemy. Instead of keeping the doors of the treasuries or storehouses closed and guarded, it is assumed that they are now open, an image that is further explored in Jer 51:30 and Nah 3:13.

Jeremiah 51:30. The oracle in Jer 51:27–33 is part of numerous utterances over Babylon in chapters 50–51. Enveloped in war imagery, Jer 51:29–32 explains the demoralization of Babylon's soldiers:

חדלו גבורי בבל להלחם ישבו במצדות נשתה גבורתם היו לנשים הציתו משכנתיה נשברו בריחיה:

Babylon's warriors have stopped fighting; they remain in their strongholds. Their strength is exhausted; they turn into women. Her dwellings are set on fire; the bars of her gates are broken. (51:30)

Verse 30's short note that Babylon's unsuccessful warriors turn into women is supported by three other images that might explain how the turn from successful warrior to unsuccessful, that is, woman-like, warrior is to be understood here. First, the warriors of Jer 51:30 have stopped their fighting and remain in their strongholds. Their declining strength is described by the verb נשת, "to dry up/be

---

28. *HALOT*, 365.

exhausted," implying that the warriors' valor has been reduced to something like a dried-up spring and at the same time punning with נשים.²⁹ All these images indicate a cessation of activity as well as stillness and silence. Warriors who stop their fighting and remain in their fortresses are quiet and do not move about. So is a spring that is dried up. Thus, Jer 51:30 assumes that warriors who turn into women are quiet, inactive, and weak. This assumption is another indication that the four texts under consideration here deal with women in general and not women giving birth, since the latter are never described as quiet or inactive.

Nahum 3:13. The book of Nahum describes the destruction of Nineveh in much gruesome detail and with much war imagery. Chapter 3 uses imagery of violence on two different occasions based on the idea that cities are female entities and that the destruction of a city can be metaphorically compared to the public shaming of women and the killing of their children. Nahum 3:13 reads,

הנה עמך נשים בקרבך לאיביך פתוח נפתחו שערי ארצך אכלה אש בריחיך:
Look at your troops [or, your people]—they are all women in your midst! The gates of your land are wide open to your enemies; fire has consumed their bars.

This verse states that "your troops" (lit., "your people") are women. The expression here uses neither the comparative כ nor a form of the verb היה combined with the preposition ל, which would indicate that an entity turns into something else. The simile "like a woman giving birth" is likewise not used, again indicating that the comparison is with women in general and not with women in childbirth. As in Jer 51:30, the main characteristic of the people in the city is inactivity. The warriors did not protect their gates from enemies and did not put out the fire that subsequently destroyed their city's protections. Again, this inactivity, although a sign of people in a paralyzing state of shock, is not a characteristic of a woman in labor, who might be terrified but is certainly not inactive.

Some interpreters understand the image of the open gate of the city or the land to be a sexual metaphor alluding to the sexual violence done to the inhabitants of a city that has been overrun by enemies.³⁰ If this is indeed a double entendre, it could also refer to the Assyrian-soldiers-turned-women who are now

---

29. Cf. ibid., 732. One of the few other occurrences of this verb is in Isa 19:5, which stands in close proximity to the comparison of the Egyptians to women in 19:6.

30. F. Rachel Magdalene, "Ancient Near Eastern Treaty-Curses and the Ultimate Texts of Terror: A Study of the Language of Divine Sexual Abuse in the Prophetic Corpus," in *A Feminist Companion to the Latter Prophets* (ed. A. Brenner; FCB 8; Sheffield: Sheffield Academic Press, 1995), 326–52, esp. 333: "'Opening,' פת, typically translated 'secret parts,' is a wordplay on the word for 'gate,' פתח, or the opening of a city. Thus, the metaphor operates to equate both the city with the person of the female and the gate of the city with the vaginal opening of the female body." See also Pamela Gordon and Harold C. Washington, "Rape as Military Metaphor in the Hebrew Bible" in Brenner, *Feminist Companion*, 308–25, and the essay by Brad E. Kelle ("Wartime Rhetoric: The Prophetic Metaphorization of Cities as Female") in this volume.

threatened with sexual violation.[31] As Nineveh has become the battlefield for war and unwanted sexual activity, so the bodies of the female inhabitants of the city (or the bodies of the male warriors turned women) could become a battlefield.

Conclusion: Description of Crisis Versus Ridicule

The data surveyed in this article suggests that readers need to distinguish between texts that compare warriors to women giving birth and texts that compare warriors to women in general. Both metaphors are possible, but they do not convey the same message, just as the terminology used for them is not the same.

The first group of texts, the comparison of warriors in crisis with women giving birth, focuses on the idea of the threshold between life and death common to the experiences of both groups. The metaphor is applied to warriors of Israel and Judah and sometimes to warriors of foreign nations. In Hebrew Bible texts of this type, other terms from the semantic field of the birth metaphor or the simile "like a woman giving birth" appear in order to ensure that the comparison of people in crisis with women giving birth is clarified. This metaphor does not allude to opposites such as strength/weakness or valor/cowardice.[32] Instead, it lifts up the severity of the crisis and the extreme hardship for the person experiencing it. Thus, if a warrior in crisis is compared to a woman giving birth, his pains and his struggle against the crisis are highlighted, as is the severity of the crisis itself. Texts with the simile "like a woman giving birth" or with the birth metaphor aim at invoking the readers' feelings of sympathy and esteem for the one suffering under a crisis like no other. Being in crisis and being (like) a woman giving birth is something to be honored rather than ridiculed.

The second group of texts, the comparison of defeated warriors with women in general, uses stereotypical ideas of differences between the genders. It is based on the dualistic idea that associates men with strength and women with weakness, subjugation, and defeat. Only warriors of foreign nations are described as being like women or as becoming women. In this type of text, no terms from the semantic field of the birth metaphor appear. Instead, the warrior's abilities are ridiculed, and his masculinity and military strength are negated.[33] In fact, these texts suggest that the warrior in question suffers because of his own lack of will or courage. If he only had been more courageous, he would not be in danger now. If he only had been more active, he would not suffer the consequences. But the

---

31. See Julia Myers O'Brien, *Nahum* (Readings; New York: Sheffield Academic Press, 2002), 70.

32. Only one ancient Near Eastern text, Sargon II's royal inscription, describes an enemy as being like a woman giving birth. The enemy's behavior in this text, however, is more like that of a coward (he flees and hides from the enemy) or like that of a sick person (he refuses food and drink).

33. See also Maria Häusl, *Bilder der Not* (Freiburg: Herder, 2003), 109.

defeated enemy does not display the characteristics of a true warrior. From the perspective of the victor or the onlooker, "he" (this enemy) is only a "she."

In summary, the difference between these two metaphors has been underestimated. In the history of interpretation of the texts discussed here, interpreters seem to have assumed either that ancient authors were not precise in their use of metaphor or that they suffered from gender biases. Neither assumption is true without qualification. The ancient authors knew very well that the characteristics and behavior of women in general are different from the characteristics and behavior of women giving birth. As this essay hopefully shows, they clearly distinguished between two metaphors and the accompanying semantic fields. Finally, while ancient authors might have had some culturally determined gender biases regarding women in general, they considered it a badge of honor to compare a warrior to a woman giving birth. In the eyes of ancient authors, a female human being was not automatically a lesser human being.[34] Women struggling to give birth were, in fact, held in the highest regard and compared to warriors who fought and maybe died as heroes of their people.

---

34. Contrary to some modern cultures, where "being (like) a girl" is never something for which one should strive.

Part 3
Writing and Reading the Ethics of War

Conquest Reconfigured: Recasting Warfare in the Redaction of Joshua

L. Daniel Hawk

It is generally held that Josh 2–12 has been rendered to reflect a holy war theology that presents the conquest of Canaan as an act of God executed in strict obedience to divine commandments. Although the origins and content of this holy war theology remain a matter of debate, few have questioned the assumption that the redactors of the corpus affirmed and endorsed the militarism of their source materials. Following Martin Noth, modern scholars generally view the conquest narrative as the product of a redactional process in which local etiological sagas and war narratives were assembled into a sweeping account of conquest and subsequently edited by one or more Deuteronomistic redactors.[1] Compilers and editors embellished, expanded, and perhaps even sacralized the violence that infused early traditions of conquest in order to reinforce Israel's claim to the land. Those traditions that conveyed a different version of Israel's origins in the land (such as those concerning Rahab and the Gibeonites) were made to confirm the party line by placing affirmations of victories by Israel's God in the mouths of Canaanites.[2] From this perspective, then, the militant triumphalism that characterizes Josh 2–12 as a whole differs little from that which infuses its sources.

The theological continuity of the redactional process, however, has been called into question by Lawson Stone, who detected a pattern in six recurring transitions that organize the conquest narrative. The comments, summarized in

---

1. Martin Noth, *Das Buch Josua* (2nd ed.; HAT 7; Tübingen: Mohr Siebeck, 1952). More recently, see Anthony F. Campbell and Mark A. O'Brien, *Unfolding the Deuteronomistic History* (Minneapolis: Fortress, 2000), 101–6. See also A. D. H. Mayes, *The Story of Israel between Settlement and Exile* (London: SCM, 1983), 42–43.

2. E.g., Gene M. Tucker, "The Rahab Saga (Joshua 2): Some Form-Critical and Traditional-Historical Observations," in *The Use of the Old Testament in the New and Other Essays: Studies in Honor of William Franklin Stinespring* (ed. J. M. Efird; Durham, N.C.: Duke University Press, 1972), 66–86; Dennis J. McCarthy, "Some Holy War Vocabulary in Joshua 2," *CBQ* 33 (1971): 228–30; and George W. Coats, "An Exposition for the Conquest Theme," *CBQ* 47 (1985): 47–54.

the chart below, follow a simple report-response formula and occur at strategic junctures in the narrative.³

	Report	Response
2:10–11	"We" (people of Jericho) heard how Yhwh dried up the Red Sea and what you did to Sihon and Og	"Our" hearts melted and everyone lost their "nerve"
5:1	Canaanite kings heard that Yhwh dried up the Jordan	Kings' hearts melted and they lost their nerve
9:1–2	Kings heard what had happened	Kings assembled to fight Joshua and Israel
9:3–5	The Gibeonites heard what Joshua did to Jericho	Gibeonites concocted a ruse
10:1–5	Adoni-zedek of Jerusalem heard that Joshua destroyed Jericho and Ai and made peace with Gibeon	Adoni-zedek was terrified but enlisted four other kings to join him in making war against Gibeon
11:1–5	Jabin of Hazor heard what happened	Jabin assembled the kings of the land to fight against Israel

The first two comments, Rahab's report to the spies (2:10–11) and the narrator's report concerning the kings of the land (5:1), render the actions of the Canaanites as a response to Yhwh's actions. This is accomplished by linking the crossing of the Jordan with the exodus from Egypt (Yhwh's actions) and relating the contrasting responses of Rahab and the kings. Taken together, the comments lead the reader to view the ensuing battles at Jericho and Ai (Josh 6–8) as Yhwh's acts. The last set of transitions (9:1–2, 3–4; 10:1–5; 11:1–5) then frame the rest of the campaigns as responses to the victories, after the pattern established by 2:10–11 and 5:1. The Gibeonites respond by seeking peace (9:3–4); by contrast, the kings of the land become an increasingly aggressive threat to Yhwh (9:1–2; 10:1–5; 11:1–5). By presenting the kings as aggressors, the redactor renders Israel's campaigns in the land as defensive operations, thereby diminishing the militarism within the source materials. Taken together, the transitions construct a theological paradigm that guides "the reader to a nonmilitaristic, nonterritorial actualization of the text" and express a recontextualization of the materials at a time when "the holy war traditions in their earliest form represented an unusable past."⁴

---

3. Lawson G. Stone, "Ethical and Apologetic Tendencies in the Redaction of the Book of Joshua," *CBQ* 53 (1991): 25–35.

4. Stone (ibid., 36) believes this redactional activity occurred after the traditions had been compiled into a unit but before they were taken up by the Deuteronomist.

Stone's study thus challenges the notion that a uniform theological paradigm configured the redaction of Joshua and suggests instead that a later redactor reworked the traditions to conform to a significantly different paradigm. The series of transitional comments that Stone has identified are, I propose, but one element of a comprehensive redactional program that defuses the ethnic antagonism of the conquest traditions by redefining the "enemy" in political rather than ethnic terms and by dissolving the internal boundaries that separate Israelites and Canaanites. A sophisticated reworking of sources materials in Josh 2–12 advances the former agenda by subtly presenting the kings of the land, rather than its peoples, as the enemy that threatens Israel. The latter agenda is accomplished through three vignettes associated with the first three campaigns that, by following a common structure, undermine the sense of ethnic separation between Israel and Canaan. The stories of Rahab and the Gibeonites humanize the peoples of the land by rendering them with attributes associated with Israel, while the story of Achan demonizes a pedigreed Israelite and associates him with Canaan.

1. Redefining the Enemy

The reader who has come to Joshua by way of Deuteronomy is prepared to view the peoples of Canaan as the primary threat to Israelite existence and identity in the land (Deut 7:1–5, 17–26; 9:4–5). When Israelite spies cross over into Jericho, however, one of the inhabitants of the land, Rahab, shows them hospitality and protects them when the king of the city attempts to apprehend them (Josh 2:1–7). The king, by contrast, appears obliquely in the story through his surrogates, the men he has sent to Rahab's house. His introduction into the narrative follows the same report-response pattern that configures the subsequent transitions about the kings of the land:

> The king of Jericho was informed, "Men from the Israelite people have come here by night to scout out the land." So the king of Jericho sent to Rahab and said, "Bring out the men who have come to you, who have come to your house, because they have come to scout out the entire land." (Josh 2:2–3)

The king's aggressive response to the presence of Israelite spies prefigures the actions of the kings of the land reported in 9:1–2, 10:1–5, and 11:1–5 and thereby ties this episode to those reports. Yet it also implicitly sets the king apart from the peoples of the land. Rahab the prostitute, who ostensibly epitomizes the threat represented by the peoples of Canaan, takes the Israelites in; the king of Jericho, however, wants to take them out.

The contrast between king and people becomes more pronounced when Rahab returns to speak to the spies (2:9b–14). Whereas the king has responded aggressively to the presence of the Israelites, she reveals that the *people* are no threat at all; they are terror-stricken and their hearts have melted (2:9). She then adopts the report-response pattern to recall the fate of other kings who had earlier threatened Israel: "We have heard how Yhwh dried up the water of the Red Sea before you when you came out of Egypt, and what you did to the two kings of the Amorites that were beyond the Jordan, to Sihon and Og, whom you devoted to destruction" (2:10). The reference to Sihon and Og, who attacked the Israelites east of the Jordan (Deut 3:32), reinforces the sense that kings are malevolent entities. Rahab, however, aligns herself with Israel by affirming the main tenets of conquest theology: Yhwh has given the land to Israel (Josh 2:9), has defeated the opposing powers (2:10), and is the God of heaven and earth (2:11b; see Deut 4:39).[5] A more direct alignment follows, as Rahab concludes by requesting a reciprocal act of kindness from the spies that will allow her and her family to live with Israel in the land (Josh 2:12–14). The contrast is implicit but direct. Kings are opposing powers who will be devoted to destruction. Canaanites, however, may become friends, allies, and even fellow-Yahwists.

The elements introduced in this episode are subsequently picked up by the first reference to the kings of the land (5:1), which occurs strategically after Joshua has linked the crossing of the Jordan to the exodus (4:39): "When all the kings of the Amorites, who were across the Jordan to the west, and all the kings of the Canaanites who were by the sea, heard that Yhwh dried up the water of the Jordan before the Israelites until they had crossed, their hearts melted and they lost their nerve before the Israelites." The content of the report explicitly transfers an attribute of the peoples of the land—melting hearts and a loss of spirit—to the kings. What was characteristic of the people now characterizes the kings.

The king of Jericho, however, is noticeably absent during the ensuing report of the battle for Jericho, appearing only in the formulaic introduction that opens the account of the battle: "I have handed Jericho over to you, along with its king and warriors" (6:2).[6] In a striking exception to the accounts that follow, the battle of Jericho does not conclude with a report that Joshua put the king to death. Instead, it concludes with a report that Joshua spared the life of certain friendly Canaanites, namely, Rahab and her family. The narrator thus brings the tale to the close by keeping the king off-stage but associating kings with malevolent forces. By contrast, the peoples of the land, represented by Rahab, assume center stage as allies and protectors.

The belligerence of kings is confirmed when the king of Ai enters the narrative. Here, however, the king appears just long enough to launch an attack against

---

5. Rahab even cites a relevant passage from the Song of Moses (2:9; cf. Exod 15:15b–16a).

6. The formulaic introduction to the battle of Jericho follows that which introduces the battles against Sihon and Og in Deut 2:13 and 3:2. The reference to warriors (גבורי החיל) is unique in Joshua and implicitly reinforces the depiction of the king—as opposed to the general population of the city—as the locus of hostile powers. The apparatus of *BHS* identifies this as a gloss but offers no explanation. Its presence, however, is better explained on stylistic grounds; those who attack Joshua are the king and his warriors, as opposed to the people of the city.

the wily Israelites, who have set an ambush (8:14a).⁷ Once the battle is joined, he disappears, reentering the story only after the battle, with the report that he "was taken alive and brought to Joshua" (8:23). In contrast to Jericho, the narrator concludes the battle at Ai by reporting that Joshua hanged the king on a tree until the evening.⁸ At that time, Joshua commanded that his body be thrown down at the city gate and covered by a large heap of stones which, the reader is told, "stands there to this day" (8:29). The note makes a striking visual and symbolic connection with Achan, the Canaanized Israelite whose tale of woe is related in the previous chapter (7:1–26); Achan's story also ends with the elimination of the threat by execution and the raising of a heap of stones that "remains to this day" (7:26).⁹

Taken together, the two stone heaps allude to the punishment Deuteronomy requires of individuals and cities who lead Israel into apostasy (Deut 13:1–18 [MT 13:2–19]). Achan is put to death by stoning, the mode of execution specified for individuals who entice Israel to worship other gods (Josh 7:25; cf. Deut 13:9–10 [MT 13:11–12]). Ai is devoted to destruction and rendered a "permanent ruin" (תל עולם), the specific action prescribed against towns that apostatize [Josh 8:26, 28; cf. Deut 13:15–16]).¹⁰ The heaps of stones raised over Achan and the king cement the association. Achan represents the threat of apostasy from within, just as the king of Ai represents the threat of apostasy from without. By linking the fates of Achan, Ai, and the king together in ways that resemble the elimination of apostates, the narrative subtly reconfigures the symbolism of threat. While Deut 7:1–4 identifies the Canaanites, and particularly Canaanite women such as Rahab, as the threatening and seductive powers that Israel faces in the land, the heaps of stone forge a symbolic association that points to kings as the real danger.

With this symbolic transformation in place, the kings assume center stage as the embodiment of the hostile powers that threaten Israel. The next campaign

---

7. The battle begins with a repetition of the formula that introduces the prior campaign at Jericho: "See I have handed over to you the king of Ai, with his people, his city, and his land. You are to do to Ai and its king what you did to Jericho and its king" (8:2b–3a). Though more expansive, it follows even more closely the language that initiates the campaign against Og in Deut 3:2b–c. It also indirectly confirms the death of the king of Jericho, whose fate has not yet been disclosed. The king of Ai is not mentioned at the outset of the campaign, when a group of overly confident Israelites become aggressors and launch an ill-conceived attack against his town (7:1–5).

8. Hanging signifies an individual's accursed status in Deuteronomy (see 21:22–23).

9. Piles of stones constitute a significant theological motif in Joshua, marking the beginning and end of the conquest (at Gilgal and Makkedah, respectively). They bear testimony to YHWH's power in conquering Israel's enemies and also signal YHWH's preference for obedience over ethnicity and, by implication, YHWH's openness to obedient foreigners (Robert L. Hubbard Jr., "'What Do These Stones Mean?' Biblical Theology and a Motif in Joshua," BBR 11 [2001]: 1–26).

10. The phrase תל עולם occurs in the Hebrew Bible only in these two texts.

involves a pitched battle between Joshua and kings, introduced now by two reports. The first, Josh 9:1–2, reports the formation of a coalition to fight Joshua. The second, 10:1–5, details the plans made by King Adoni-zedek and four other kings to attack Gibeon. The reason for the attack is also specified: Gibeon has made peace with Israel. The third campaign therefore opens with the picture of multiple kings assembling to fight against inhabitants of the land; Israelites and Gibeonites are thus aligned against the kings of the land.

The two reports bracket an account of peacemaking between Israel and Gibeon (9:3–27). Following the pattern of the Rahab's story, the account contrasts the people's response to Israel with that of the kings. When the Gibeonites receive news of Israelite victories, they put on their thinking caps rather than their helmets, don tattered clothing instead of armor, and approach Israel with an offer of friendship (9:4–6). They are no apparent threat, and, more importantly, they have no king. Rather, the Gibeonite emissaries declare that the "elders and all the residents of the city" sent them to seek peace with Israel (9:11). This alternative communal polity renders Gibeon unique among the cities encountered in Joshua. As the story unfolds, it becomes clear that a Canaanite city with no king may be a candidate for inclusion within the land of Israel, even if by subterfuge. Kings make a city a threat, but when there is no king, there is no threat. The surrounding reports of assembled kings (9:1–2; 10:1–5) punctuate the point by way of contrast. Moreover, when the Gibeonites appeal to Joshua, he and his warriors rise to their defense, just as Rahab had defended the Israelite spies (10:6–9). During the ensuing battle, Yhwh therefore fights for Israelites *and* Canaanites against the assembled might of the kings of the land.

The aftermath of the battle at Gibeon features an account of the fate of the defeated kings that is even more elaborate than that devoted to the king of Ai (10:16–27). After rousting the kings from a cave, Joshua orders his officers to put their feet on the necks of the kings, exhorting them with the words, "Do not be afraid or dismayed; be strong and courageous" (10:25b). The exhortation is a virtual quotation of that which Yhwh and the Israelites repeatedly direct to Joshua as he prepares to lead Israel into the occupation of the land (1:6, 7, 9, 18). Its reiteration in this context joins that episode to the present one, thereby aligning the kings with the hostile powers Joshua faced as he looked across the Jordan.[11] The identification is completed by evoking the visual imagery that linked the king of Ai with Achan the apostate. Joshua executes the five kings and orders them to be hanged on trees until the sunset, when their bodies are thrown into the cave

---

11. The structure of the account follows that of the king of Ai, but with considerably more detail. It begins by reporting that the king has been captured (8:23; 10:16–19) and then relates the destruction of the city, the plundering of booty and livestock, and the slaughter of the people (8:24–27; 10:20–21), concluding with the execution of the king (8:27–29; 10:22–27).

and large stones are placed at the site; they too remain there "to this very day" (10:26–27).

Kings thereafter feature prominently in the summaries of Israel's conquests in the south and north. The list of cities captured in the south is symmetrical (10:28–39); victories over kings and cities are placed at the beginning and end of the list (10:28–32, 34–39), with a victory over an aggressive king, but no city, at the center (10:33).

> Joshua took Makkedah and killed its king and people (10:28)
> Joshua took Libnah and killed its king and people (10 29–30)
> Joshua took Lachish and killed its people (10:31–32)
>   Joshua killed Horam king of Gezer and killed his people (10:33)
> Joshua took Eglon and killed its people (10:34–35)
> Joshua took Hebron and killed its king and its people (10:36–37)
> Joshua took Debir and killed its king and people (10:38–39)

The symmetry aligns and realigns the components of city, people, and king. All three appear in the first, second, sixth and seventh reports. Yet the third and fifth reports mention only the cities and their people, while the centerpiece mentions only the deaths of the king and the people.

The editorial preface in 11:1–5 then explicitly renders the conquests in the north as victories over hostile kings: "All these kings assembled, approached, and encamped together at the waters of Merom, in order to join battle with Israel" (11:5). After reporting the defeat of the kings, the text specifically identifies Hazor as "the head of all those kingdoms" and the rest of the cities as "the towns of those kings" (11:12). The ensuing recapitulation of Israel's conquests in the land continues this nomenclature. After a description of the geographical scope of the conquest, the text reports that Joshua "took all their kings, struck them down, and put them to death. Joshua made war a long time with all those kings" (11:17b–18). To cap it off, the narrative includes an aside that informs the reader that "it was YHWH's doing to harden their hearts so that they would come against Israel in battle" (11:20). The comment recalls YHWH's contest with Pharaoh during the exodus from Egypt and, even more directly, Israel's defeat of King Sihon, whom YHWH hardened "in order to hand him over to you" (Deut 2:30b). The kings of Canaan now join Pharaoh and the Amorite kings as the archetypal enemies of Israel.

The transformation of kings into archenemies comes to completion with a summation of Israel's conquests, cast in the form of an impressive list of defeated kings (12:1–24). The accounts of victories east and west of the Jordan are introduced by similar formulae: "these are the kings of the land, whom the Israelites defeated, whose land they occupied beyond the Jordan to the east" (12:1); and "the following are the kings of the land whom Joshua and the Israelites defeated on the west side of the Jordan" (12:7). Thereupon follows an extensive list that meticulously identifies each king defeated by the Israelites ("the king of Jericho, one; the king of Ai, which is next to Bethel, one," etc.) and concludes with a note on the sum of the kings ("a total of thirty-one kings"). The recapitulation leaves no doubt about those who opposed Israel. Having defeated the kings of the land, Israel has overcome its enemies.

To sum up, Josh 2–12, taken as a whole, gradually expands the scope and intensity of the threat represented by the kings of the land and diminishes the threat represented by its peoples. At Jericho, the king appears off-stage but sends a detachment to apprehend a pair of Israelite spies. Then he disappears. At Ai, a king dashes headlong into an Israelite ambuscade, only to be defeated and, in an instance of guilt by allusive association, executed and interred like an apostate. At Gibeon, five kings assemble to assault a kingless city that has recently associated with Israel. Joshua defeats them, and the narrator associates them with their counterparts at Ai. At the waters of Merom, the kings of the whole land converge to fight with Israel but are defeated, finally to appear in a list that meticulously catalogues their demise. The overall scheme reveals a comprehensive and ingenious redactional strategy that has combined various tradition complexes into an account of the conquest of the land but has reworked them in order to redirect Israel's sense of "the enemy" from the peoples of the land to its kings.

2. Humanizing the Canaanites

A second narrative pattern, working in tandem with the first, deconstructs the sense of ethnic difference that demonizes the peoples of the land. As I have elaborated this pattern elsewhere in detail, a summary will suffice here. The stories of Rahab (2:1–24), Achan (7:6–26), and the Gibeonites (9:3–27) immediately precede the paradigmatic battle accounts at Jericho (6:1–27), Ai (8:1–29), and Gibeon (10:6–15), respectively. Although deriving from different contexts, the redactor has rendered each according to a common, complex scheme that centers on identity and hinges on discovering what has been hidden.[12]

	Rahab	Achan	Gibeonites
Concealment	Rahab hides spies (2:4)	Achan the Israelite hides plunder (7:1)	Gibeonites hide identities (9:3–6)
Interrogation	King's men question Rahab (2:2–3)	Joshua questions Yhwh (7:6–9)	Israelite leaders question Gibeonites (9:12–13)
Redirection	Rahab directs the king's men to the hills (2:4b–5)	Yhwh shifts the topic of Joshua's query from defeat to transgression (7:10–12)	Gibeonites direct leaders to sample their provisions (9:12–13)

---

12. See L. Daniel Hawk, *Joshua* (Berit Olam; Collegeville: Liturgical, 2000), 19–33.

Doxology	Rahab spontaneously acclaims YHWH's supremacy and mighty acts (2:8–11)	Joshua commands Achan to give YHWH glory and praise (7:19)	Gibeonites spontaneously acclaim YHWH's supremacy and mighty acts (9:9–11)
Petition	Rahab asks the spies to do חסד and spare her family (2:12–13)	Achan incriminates and thus condemns himself (7:20–21)	Gibeonites asks Joshua to make a peace treaty (9:6)
Response	Spies agree to spare Rahab and her family (2:14)	Achan and his family are condemned and executed (7:24–25)	Joshua and the leaders make a covenant of peace (9:15)
Qualification	Spies qualify the agreement; Rahab agrees (2:17–21)		Joshua consigns the Gibeonites to menial labor; Gibeonites agree (9:16–26)
Etiological Note	Rahab "lives among the Israelites to this day" (6:25)	A heap of stones marks Achan's grave "to this day" (7:26)	Gibeonites "cut wood and carry water to this day" (9:27)
Curse	Joshua curses anyone who rebuilds Jericho (6:26)	Joshua curses Achan (7:24)	Joshua declares the Gibeonites accursed (9:23)

The first and third stories destabilize Israelite identity by depicting peoples of the land who display the initiative, cunning, opportunism, and courage required of Israelites as they endeavor to possess the land. In both cases, Canaanites acclaim the exploits and power of Israel's God (2:8–11; 9:9–10), while Israelites remain mute on matters Yahwistic. Both Rahab and the Gibeonite emissaries actively seek an opportunity to live in the land, and both succeed, remaining among the Israelites "to this day."

The Israelites, however, come off badly in comparison. The spies who take refuge on the roof of Rahab's house display a striking passivity and seem less concerned about obedience to the Mosaic commandments than about their own survival. Although prohibited from sparing any of the land's inhabitants, they agree to spare Rahab and her family in order to save their own lives (Josh 2:14; cf. Deut 7:2–5).[13] In a similar vein, Joshua and the Israelite elders are easily taken in by the Gibeonites' ruse and readily agree to a peace treaty without bothering to seek YHWH's counsel (9:14–15). The resulting nonaggression pact renders an entire city off-limits for Israelite occupation (9:17–19).

---

13. Covenant language pervades the interchange between Rahab and the spies. See K. M. Campbell, "Rahab's Covenant," *VT* 22 (1972): 243–44.

The middle story appropriates the same narrative pattern but reverses the thematic elements (7:1–26). The main character in this case is Achan, a pedigreed Israelite who is Canaanized by taking the plunder of the land and hiding it under his tent. The act constitutes a sacrilege that transforms the entire nation from objects of Yhwh's blessing to objects of Yhwh's wrath (7:1–2). Like the people of Canaan, the Israelites becomes a people "devoted to destruction" (היו לחרם, 7:12) and therefore indistinguishable from those they have come to conquer. The situation requires a remedy through ritual. Yhwh identifies Achan as the offender and then, as noted above, stipulates that he and his family be executed in a manner reminiscent of the execution of apostates (7:22–26; cf. Deut 13:8–10, 16–17 [MT 13:9–11, 17–18]). Achan therefore becomes the antitype of Rahab. She, a condemned Canaanite, confesses Israel's God and secures life in the land for herself and her descendants. Achan is one of Yhwh's people but contaminates himself with Canaan. He and his family share the fate of the peoples; their portion in the land is a grave. The stone pile raised over them links Achan and his family to the kings of the land (8:29; 10:27) as metaphors of primal threats to the destruction of the nation.[14] The stone piles stand in stark and permanent contrast to the surviving peoples of the land. All "remain to this day" (6:25; 7:26; 8:29; 9:27; 10:27).

The common theme of discovering what is hidden manifests an impulse to work out issues of identity and suggests that things may not always be what they appear to be. The face-to-face encounters with the people of Canaan reveal the humanity of the indigenous inhabitants and directly counter the faceless anonymity of the battle reports. In those reports, the peoples of the land are little more than figures in a list. In the personalized accounts, however, Israel sees its face reflected in the indigenous Other.[15]

The narrative reinforces the connection between the personal and corporate by reversing a common structural pattern in the battle reports in the same fashion as the three anecdotes. The accounts of battles at Jericho, Ai, and Gibeon employ a common narrative scheme but, as with the anecdotes, the middle account unfolds in the opposite direction.[16]

---

14. It is likely that the name "Achan" is a cipher for Canaan. The name עכן derives from no known Semitic root. The transposition of the consonants, however, yields כנע, the root from which the name "Canaan" is derived.

15. L. Daniel Hawk, "The Problem with Pagans," in *Reading Bibles, Writing Bodies* (ed. T. K. Beal and D. M. Gunn; London: Routledge, 1997), 53–63. See also John Goldingay, *Israel's Gospel* (vol. 1 of *Old Testament Theology*; Downers Grove: InterVarsity, 2003), 497–503.

16. The chart is adapted from Hawk, *Joshua*, 25, 29–30.

	Assurance of Victory	Means of Victory	Outcome
Jericho (6:1–21)	Yhwh assures Joshua of victory (6:2)	Miracle: Yhwh causes the walls to fall (6:20)	Israel devotes the population to destruction (6:21)
Ai (7:2–5)	Israelite spies give the assurance of victory (7:3)		Israelites are routed (7:4–5)
Ai (8:1–23)	Yhwh assures Joshua of victory (8:1–2a, 18)	Strategy: Yhwh directs the Israelites to set an ambush (8:2, 19–20)	Israelites annihilate the army and devote the population to destruction (8:21–28)
Gibeon (10:6–14)	Yhwh assures Joshua of victory (10:8)	Miracle: Yhwh stops the sun and pelts the enemies with stones (10:11–14)	Israel annihilates the armies of the kings (10:20)

Whereas the story of Rahab envelopes the account of the battle at Jericho, the accounts of battles at Ai envelope the story of Achan. Yhwh wins the victories at Jericho and Gibeon by means of spectacular cosmic phenomena, leaving the Israelites to conduct a mopping-up operation. Yet Yhwh is conspicuously uninvolved during the conflicts at Ai, the site of Achan's sin. In the first of these, Yhwh intentionally withdraws from the Israelites, who subsequently suffer a humiliating defeat (7:2–5, 12). In the second instance, Yhwh does not participate directly but rather divulges a stratagem that leads to a victory on more conventional terms (8:2). In an ironic twist, the strategy that Yhwh dictates plays off the story of Achan. Israelites now become a hidden peril to the Canaanites and, when disclosed, destroy the people and reduce the town to a pile of rubble. Furthermore, the battle combines elements of those at Jericho and Gibeon. As at Gibeon, the Israelites defeat an army on the field (8:18–23), and, as at Jericho, the Israelites assault and destroy a city (8:24–28).

The parallel structures and interconnections between the various stories and accounts display the marks of an intentional combination and reworking of source materials. Three paradigmatic conflicts are presented, with only brief summaries or lists of conquests following. All report the action with a broad scope and no interaction between human characters. Three anecdotes precede each of these paradigmatic accounts and counter the macroscopic contest between peoples with stories that relate encounters with Canaan on the individual level. The stories and battle reports, in each case, are closely intertwined. The encounter with Rahab confirms that Yhwh has given the city into Israel's hands, Achan's sin and punishment are replicated in the battle at Ai and its aftermath, and the Gibeonite treaty precipitates the attack of the five kings that, in turn, leads to the most spectacular of Israel's victories.

Symmetrical structural devices unite the narrative units. The three anecdotes appropriate a common narrative scheme configured by discovery of the hidden, with the middle reversing aspects of the first and third. The second anecdote and battle (Achan at Ai) are rendered as the antithesis of the first (Rahab at Jericho) and forge symbolic connections with the third (the Gibeonites and the five kings). As a whole, these interconnections and parallels point to the organizing hand of a redactor, who has rendered a sophisticated unity among his source materials through organizing schemes and metaphors.

3. The Deuteronomistic Redaction of the Conquest Narrative

Allusions to Deuteronomy have been woven into the fabric of many of the texts that comprise the conquest narrative. Occurring with particular density in Josh 7–11, they associate the redactor with the Deuteronomistic school.[17] Christopher Begg has catalogued a number of parallels in form, motif, and terminology that link the Achan-Ai complex (Josh 7:1–8:29) with Deuteronomy's summary of Israel's wilderness experience (Deut 1:19–3:11; 9:7–10:11). These include, for example, the dispatch and report of spies, an Israelite attack that ends in a rout and a lament, references to Yhwh's anger at the people's obedience and Yhwh's refusal to be with them, a confession of sin, the elimination of the guilty, and a second advance that results in victory.[18] To these we may add the aforementioned allusion to the laws against apostates in Deut 13.

The Gibeonite covenant (Josh 9:3–27) incorporates elements of Israel's covenant- renewal ceremony on the plains of Moab (Deut 29:1–29 [MT 28:68–29:28]). The ruse picks up the reference to worn-out clothing and exhausted provisions in Deut 29:5–6 (MT 29:4–5). The Deuteronomic text expresses Yhwh's blessing and care for Israel during its wilderness sojourn: "I made you walk through the desert for forty years. Your clothes did not fall apart on you and your sandals did not fall to pieces on your feet" (29:5). The Gibeonites, however, appear before

---

17. I find plausible the concept of a Deuteronomistic scribal school, which posits a long editorial process that spanned the exilic and early postexilic periods. For recent discussions and bibliographies, see Raymond F. Person Jr. *The Deuteronomic School: History, Social Setting, and Literature* (SBLSBL 2; Atlanta: Society of Biblical Literature, 2002); and Thomas Römer, *The So-Called Deuteronomistic History: A Sociological, Historical, and Literary Introduction* (London: T&T Clark, 2006). Most interpreters see little evidence of Deuteronomistic editing in Josh 7–11 and, indeed, within the entire conquest narrative. Richard Nelson summarizes the view succinctly: "Chapters 2–11 are linked together in a way that is completely independent of any deuteronomistic interest or language" (*Joshua* [OTL; Philadelphia: Westminster John Knox, 1997], 7). See also Campbell and O'Brien, *Unfolding the Deuteronomistic History*, 101–6; Mayes, *Story of Israel*, 41–57.

18. Christopher T. Begg, "The Function of Josh 7.1–8.29 in the Deuteronomistic History," *Bib* 67 (1986): 321–27.

the Israelites with "clothes falling apart and sandals falling to pieces" (Josh 9:5).[19] Furthermore, they confirm the defeat of Sihon and Og, as does YHWH during the covenant ceremony (Josh 9:20; Deut 29:7 [MT 29:6]). Finally, Joshua's decree that the Gibeonites become water bearers and woodcutters harkens back to the foreign water bearers and woodcutters who stand with Israel to enter the covenant with YHWH (Deut 29:11–12 [MT 29:10–11]).[20] On another note, the Gibeonites' knowledge of the Deuteronomic laws for warfare (20:10–18) constitutes the necessary premise for the implementation and success of their deceit. The laws require Israel to annihilate the towns and peoples of the land but allow for peace treaties with cities outside the land. The Gibeonites' threadbare clothing and crusty provisions are designed to convince the Israelites that they have traveled "from a distant land" and are therefore eligible treaty partners.

An elaborate organizational scheme links the battle reports at Ai (Josh 8:1–29) and the northern coalition (Josh 11:1–15) to the Deuteronomic reports of the victories over Sihon and Og (Deut 2:26–3:7), which themselves harmonize earlier accounts preserved in Numbers 21:21–32 and 21:33–35.[21] The scheme displays a complexity that indicates literary rather than oral shaping and this, along with the strong correspondence in vocabulary, reveals either that the texts were written by the same hand or that the redactor of Joshua has rendered the accounts at Ai and the waters of Merom after the pattern of the Deuteronomic accounts.[22]

	Deut 2:31–36	Deut 3:1b–7	Josh 8:1–29	Josh 11:1–15
Report of the king's attack	Sihon came out (יצא) to meet us for battle (לקרא מלחמה), he and all his people (2:32)	Og came out to meet us for battle, all his people (3:1b)	The king of Ai … came out … to meet us for battle, all his people (8:14)	(The kings) came out, and all their troops with them, a great force (11:4)

---

19. The Gibeonites' ruse may also play off the statement that precedes the Deuteronomic reference to Israel's clothing: "YHWH did not give you a heart to discern, nor eyes to see, nor ears to hear, up to the present time" (Deut 9:4 [MT 9:3]).

20. See Robert Polzin, *Moses and the Deuteronomist* (New York: Seabury, 1980), 117–22.

21. See John R. Bartlett, "The Conquest of Sihon's Kingdom: A Literary Re-examination," *JBL* 97 (1978): 147–51.

22. The chart has been adapted from Hawk, *Joshua*, 161–65. Otto Plöger discerned a simpler oral form, which he termed a *Kampfbericht*. It comprises three elements: (1) declaration that names the adversary and battle site; (2) handing over the enemy; and (3) report of victory and military action (*Literarkritische, formgeschichtliche, und stilkritische Untersuchungen zum Deuteronomium* [BBB; Bonn: Hanstein, 1967], 16–22). It is worth noting, however, that Plöger identifies examples of the form only in Deuteronomy and Joshua.

Divine assurance	I have given (נתן) Sihon and his land to you (2:31a)	Do not fear him (אל תירא אתו). I have given Og, his people and land to you (3:2a)	Do not fear or tremble... I have given the king of Ai, his people, his town, and his land to you (8:1)	Do not fear them, for tomorrow I will give all of them, slain, to Israel (11:6a)
Divine command	Take possession of his land (2:31b)	Do to him (עשית לו) as you did to Sihon (3:2b)	Do to Ai and its king what you did to Jericho and its king (8:2a)	Hamstring their horses and burn their chariots (11:6b)
Confirmation	YHWH gave him to us (2:33a)	YHWH gave Sihon and his people into your hands (3:3a)	YHWH: "I will give it into your hands" (8:14)	YHWH gave them to Israel (11:8a)
Report of victory	We struck him down (נכה) (2:33b)	We struck him down (3:3b)	Israel struck them down (8:22b)	(Israel) struck them down (11:8c, 10a, 11b)
Capture of towns	We captured (לכד) his towns (2:34a)	We captured his towns (3:4a)	They captured the city (8:19b)	Joshua ... captured Hazor (11:10a), all the royal towns (11:12a)
Application of the ban	We devoted them to destruction (חרם) (2:34b)	We devoted to destruction the town, men, women, and children (3:6)	They devoted the inhabitants of Ai to destruction (8:26)	They devoted to destruction (the people of Hazor) (11:11b), all the royal towns (11:12c)
Plundering of towns	We plundered for ourselves (בזזנו לנו) the livestock (בהמה) and booty (שלל) of the towns (2:35)	We plundered for ourselves the livestock and booty of the towns (3:7)	Only the livestock and booty of the towns they plundered for themselves (8:27)	The Israelites plundered for themselves all the livestock and booty of the towns (11:14)
Summary	From the Aroer to the Arnon as far as Gilead, there was no citadel (לא היתה קריה) too high (2:36)	There was no citadel we did not take in the whole region of Argob, the kingdom of Og king of Bashan (3:4b–5)		Joshua took the entire land from the hill country and Negeb ... to the valley of Lebanon (11:16–17)

The Deuteronomistic rendering of the two battle accounts in Joshua has not been recognized by scholars who, in the main, regard the material as pre-Deuteronomistic.[23] The scheme, however, configures no other biblical battle accounts other than the four texts above. They must be regarded, therefore, as the product of Deuteronomistic redaction. Along with the allusions in Josh 7–9, the reworking of the battle reports reveals a comprehensive program that contributes to the literary and theological agenda we have described above. The program extended to the incorporation of Josh 2–6, which displays minimal Deuteronomistic editing (i.e., Rahab's praise of Yhwh in 2:10–11, Yhwh's exaltation of Joshua in 3:7–8 and 4:14, and the transitional note of 5:1) and may have suited the redactor's purpose largely as it stood.[24] Although the extent of editing is difficult to determine, the structural connections made through Rahab's story reveal that the Deuteronomist has been at work in Josh 2–6 as well. The redaction resulted in a reconfiguration of the violent elements of the conquest traditions and the identity of Israel's enemies in the land.

The program as a whole reveals a profound ambivalence about Israel's traditions of conquest. The traditions constituted an integral part of Israel's national narrative and corporate self-consciousness and provided the theological warrant for Israel's claim to the land. They could not, therefore, be discard or diminished. Yet the manner of their reworking reveals that the ethnic violence that infused them had become problematic. The recontextualization of the traditions in the light of Israel's experience of and reflection on life with Yhwh necessitated the construction of a different theological framework in which to understand them.

This recontextualization most likely occurred during the postexilic era, during which claims to the land and ethnic separatism worked in tandem to shape communal identity. Ezra's reform, in particular, defined Israel's identity in starkly ethnic terms, enforced a program of ethnic separation, and laid the blame for the exile squarely at the feet of the deleterious influence of foreign women (Ezra 6:21; 9:1–10:44). Against this agenda, the redactor of Joshua represented an opposing perspective that asserted a broader vision of the people of God based on devotion to Yhwh rather than genetic or ancestral relationships (see Isa 56:1–

---

23. Campbell and O'Brien, e.g., see 11:1–15 as a combination of source material and pre-Deuteronomistic expansions (*Unfolding the Deuteronomistic History*, 133–35).

24. Josh 2–6, in the main, displays a high degree of internal integrity. The liturgical character of the unit and the prominence of Gilgal suggest that it may have its origins in festival liturgies associated with the Israelite shrine at Gilgal. For a discussion of these issues, see Hans-Joachim Kraus, "Gilgal: A Contribution to the History of Worship in Israel" (trans. P. T. Daniels), in *Reconsidering Israel and Judah: Recent Studies on the Deuteronomistic History* (ed. G. N. Knoppers and J. G. McConville; Sources for Biblical and Theological Study 8; Winona Lake, Ind.: Eisenbrauns, 2000), 163–78; and Jan A. Wilcoxen, "Narrative Structure and Cult Legend: A Study of Joshua 1–6," in *Transitions in Biblical Scholarship* (ed. J. C. Rylaarsdam; Chicago: University of Chicago Press, 1968), 43–70.

8; Ruth). The nationalist triumphalism was muted and the peoples of the land receded as threatening figures, while the kings of the land assumed increasingly hostile and malevolent associations. The strategy expresses the fruit of theological reflection on Israel's traditions of origin and an attempt to come to terms with the violence that characterized them. In so doing, the Deuteronomist has offered a theological resource for other nations and peoples who care to rethink and reflect on traditions of violent origins and the ethnic residue of such traditions in their corporate consciousness.

"Go Back by the Way You Came": An Internal Textual Critique of Elijah's Violence in 1 Kings 18–19

Frances Flannery

The famous contest on Mount Carmel in 1 Kgs 18:1–46 between Elijah and the prophets of Baal and Asherah ends with Elijah slaying or ordering the deaths of the 450 prophets of Baal (18:40). The majority of readers understand the brutal scene as exhibiting Elijah's conformity with the command in Deuteronomy to kill prophets who urge apostasy (Deut 13:6). Although several recent interpreters have characterized Elijah negatively, with Bernard P. Robinson even calling him "a tetchy and arrogant prima donna,"[1] few have suggested that he acts on his own initiative in this bloody spectacle of reprisal. Yet 1 Kgs 18–19 contains carefully crafted linguistic structures that illuminate an editorial layer severely critiquing Elijah, who commits acts never mandated by God and who fails to perceive a nonviolent alternative offered by God. As a redacted whole, 1 Kgs 18–19 portrays God as willing to acquiesce to the prophet's level of understanding, inadequate as it is.

Some Interpretations of 1 Kgs 18:40

Many commentators sidestep questions of morality raised by the incident of the slaying of the prophets of Baal in 1 Kgs 18:40, deeming Elijah to be the hero who "saved the Israelite faith."[2] Others, such as Donald J. Wiseman, have sought theological justification by saying the killings were "not an act of wanton cruelty but

---

1. Bernard P. Robinson, "Elijah at Horeb, 1 Kings 19:1–18: A Coherent Narrative?," *RB* 98 (1991): 535. Gregory calls him "disingenuous" and "a prophet plagued by his own ego and exaggerated importance" (Russell I. Gregory, "Irony and the Unmasking of Elijah," in *From Carmel to Horeb: Elijah in Crisis* [ed. A. J. Hauser and R. I. Gregory; JSOTSup 85; Sheffield: Almond, 1990], 94–102).

2. H. H. Rowley, "Elijah on Mount Carmel," *BJRL* 43 (1960): 191. Another strategy for ignoring the violence is to deem this scene to be a late addition; thus Gray thinks it derives from

the necessary retribution, ordered by Elijah as the 'new Moses' on behalf of God, against false prophets as decreed in Deuteronomy (13:5, 13–18; 17:2–5)."[3] Most commentators assume that in the text God sanctions Elijah's violence, although they do find the scene ethically problematic. Typical is Walter Brueggemann's conclusion: "It is not for us to criticize the narrative, but to notice how the same juices of death operate even now."[4] Meanwhile, Mordecai Cogan finds all such positions guilty of "introducing contemporary moral sensitivity into the text" and pronounces the slaughter no different from other slayings, such as those by Moses (Exod 32:26–28), Phinehas (Num 25:78), or Samuel (1 Sam 15:32–33).[5]

However, a few commentators have questioned whether the text in fact portrays Elijah favorably. Paul J. Kissling suggests that Elijah is not the "reliable character" that a first-time reader might assume him to be, lacking as he does in 1 Kgs 17–18 both a prophetic call and the title "prophet"; Kissling wonders if the contest, which is solely "Elijah's idea," is indeed a good idea.[6] In an important article, Olley also questions the validity of the contest, saying, "Elijah believes he is acting by God's orders, but does the narrator?"[7] John Olley considers Elijah's emendation of the customary phrase "As [Adonai] lives" to be suspect, since Elijah adds the phrase "whom *I* serve" (emphasis added; 17:1, 18:15; cf. 17:12; 18:10), signifying an egocentric posture that holds throughout 1 and 2 Kings.[8] That Olley is correct is evident in the obvious etymology of Eli-yahu's name:

Jehu's massacre, illustrating that "[t]he success of the Yahwists was only temporary" (John Gray, *I and II Kings* [OTL; Philadelphia: Westminster, 1963], 359 n. 40).

3. Donald J. Wiseman, *1 and 2 Kings* (TOTC; Leicester: Inter-Varsity Press, 1993), 170.

4. Walter Brueggemann, *1 and 2 Kings* (Smyth & Helwys Bible Commentary; Macon, Ga.: Smyth & Helwys, 2000), 226. Similarly, Montgomery and Gehman state, "For the ugly sequel ... the history of religion and politics down to our own day is sad apology" (J. A. Montgomery and H. S. Gehman, *The Book of Kings* [ICC; Edinburgh: T&T Clark, 1951], 306). Childs clearly views the slaughter as divinely mandated, saying "The ancient Mosaic law of death was once again enforced," but he considers this "convex" or public side of faith to be offset by the "concave" or individual side suggested in the theophany of the quiet voice. I view this as a projection onto the text (Brevard S. Childs, "On Reading the Elijah Narratives," *Int* 34 [1980]: 128). An old-style theological evolution is often posited; thus DeVries states: "Moderns may ask, Is one to demand fire from heaven as a resolution to doubting? The answer is no, because this age has outgrown the conception of that spectacular kind of irruptive supernaturalism.... The ancient Hebrews expected God to answer them by fire because to them he was a God of fire" (S. J. DeVries, *1 Kings* [WBC 12; Nashville: Nelson, 2003], 231).

5. Mordecai Cogan, *1 Kings: A New Translation with Introduction and Commentary* (AB 10; New York: Doubleday, 2001), 444 n. 40.

6. Paul J. Kissling, *Reliable Characters in the Primary History: Profiles of Moses, Joshua, Elijah and Elisha* (JSOTSup 224; Sheffield: Sheffield Academic Press, 1996), 99.

7. John Olley, "YHWH and His Zealous Prophet," *JSOT* 80 (1998): 25–51, esp. 29–30, 35. I thank Stuart Lasine for pointing out this article to me.

8. Ibid., 30. He also adds that Elijah "calls out" (קרא) repeatedly in a way that is uncommon outside of the Elijah stories, except in situations of "urgency, some sense of desperation"

"*my* God is YH," with an emphasis on the *my*. This name stands in marked contrast with the real hero of the story, Obed-yahu, who is genuinely "the servant of YH."[9]

ETYMOLOGICAL AND STRUCTURAL EVIDENCE

There is little agreement on questions of literary unity in 1 Kgs 17–19. Some scholars perceive a unified composition in 17–19 (e.g., Robinson, Sanda), 16:9–19 (Olley), or 18 alone (Wiseman, Gray, Eissfeldt),[10] while others argue that the present narrative lacks cohesion altogether, being built from loosely amalgamated composite traditions (Long).[11] The structure that I derive from etymological clues leads me to conclude that at least chapters 18–19 form an editorial unity that thoroughly redacts earlier materials, save for one discordant section that I will note. In these chapters two carefully constructed chiasms with mutually reinforcing centers structure a tightly woven narrative. The first chiasm begins and ends with the phrase "The word of the LORD came to Elijah"[12] and turns mainly on the verbs "go" (הלך) and "see" (ראה), as well as on certain repetitive catchwords: "alone" (לבד), "road" (דרך), "one" (אחד), "two" (שתי), "cave" (מערה), and "bread and water" (לחם ומים).

CHIASM 1: 1 KINGS 18:1–19:9[13]

A. 18:1: "The word of the LORD came to Eliahu" (היה אל אליהו ודבר יהוה): "*Go, appear to Ahab*" (לך הראה אל אחאב), "and I will send rain upon the earth."

   B. 18:3–4: Obedyahu hid a hundred prophets, fifty to a *cave* (במערה) and gave them *bread and water* (לחם ומים).

      C. 18:5: Ahab said to Obedyahu: "*Go* through the land to the watering places" (לך בארץ אל כל מעיני המים).

(31–32); cf. 1 Kgs 18:25–28. His comparison with Elisha, who is calm and compassionate, is especially striking (32).

9. Olley (ibid., 26) notes that the narrator reserves his best praise for Obadiah: "he feared YHWH greatly" (1 Kgs 18:3).

10. See Albert Sanda, *Die Bücher der Könige* (2 vols.; EHAT 9; Münster: Aschendorf, 1911–12), 1:45–49; Burke O. Long, *1 Kings* (FOTL 9; Grand Rapids: Eerdmans, 1984), 190. See also Wiseman, *1 and 2 Kings*, 167; Gray, *I and II Kings*, 343, 384; Otto Eissfeldt, *Der Gott Karmel* (Berlin: Akademie, 1954), 32–33.

11. Long argues, "No matter how much one seeks a smooth narrative in the present text, loose ends, somewhat contradictory trajectories, and lost motifs remain" (*1 Kings*, 190).

12. Walsh locates a chiasm in 17:17–24 (Jerome T. Walsh, *1 Kings* [Berit Olam; Collegeville, Minn.: Liturgical Press, 1996], 23–31).

13. Catchwords are italicized in the chiastic outline.

D. 18:6: Ahab "*went* on *one road alone*" (הלך בדרך אחד לבדו), and Obedyahu "*went* on *one road alone*" (הלך בדרך אחד לבדו).

E. 18:7: Obedyahu was "on the *road*" (בדרך), "and here was Eliahu to meet him" (והנה אליהו לקראתו).

F. 18:8: Eliahu says to Obedyahu: "*Go* tell your lord, here is Eliahu!" (לך אמר לאדניך הנה אליהו).

G[1]. 18:11: Obedyahu repeats, "*Go* tell your lord, here is Eliahu!" (לך אמר לאדניך הנה אליהו).

G[2]. 18:13: Obedyahu explains that Eliahu is unreliable, that Ahab will kill him on that account. Obedyahu further explains that "I hid a hundred prophets of YHWH, fifty men to a *cave* (במערה) and provided them with *bread and water*" (לחם ומים).

G[1]. 18:14: "And now you say, '*Go* tell your lord, here is Eliahu?!'" (לך אמר לאדניך הנה אליהו).

F[1]. 18:15: Eliahu replies, "Today I will *appear* to him" (היום אראה אליו).

E[1]. 18:16–17: "Obedyahu *went* to meet Ahab" (וילך עבדיהו לקראת אחאב), and "Ahab *went* to meet Eliahu" (וילך אחאב לקראת אליהו). Ahab "*saw*" (כראות) Eliahu.

D[1]. 18:21–24: Contest between the prophets of Baal and Eliahu in which he asks, "How long will you keep hopping between *two choices*?" (על שתי הסעפים) Elijah states, "I am *alone*" (לבדו). "Let them choose *one* bull.... I will prepare *one* bull" (הפר האחד).

C[1]. 19:3: Eliahu "was scared" or "*saw*" (וירא), and "*he went*" (וילך אל נפשו; lit., "he went to his soul"). He dismissed his servant and "*went* on the wilderness *road*" (והוא הלך במדבר דרך).

B[1]. 19:4–9: Elijah wishes to die, lies down and sleeps. Then an angel feeds him "*cake*" (עגת) and "*water*" (מים) twice; he goes forty days and nights until he comes to Mount Horeb and a *cave* (המערה).

A[1]. 19:9: "Then the word of YHWH to him (והנה דבר יהוה אליו): 'Why are you here, Eliahu?'" (מה לך פה אליהו).

The main structure of this chiasm turns on the verbs "to go, to walk" (הלך) and "to see" (ראה), both of which appear in the "word of YHWH" appearing in 18:1: "*Go* (לך), appear (הראה) to Ahab." God's command is expressed in simple terms of cause and effect: when Eliahu goes (הלך) and appears (ראה) to Ahab, God will send rain. Nothing is said of a contest. Nothing is said of assembling some 850 pagan prophets as well as the people of Israel. Nothing is said of a final showdown by means of a miraculous show of power and the bloody slaughter of the losing side. God commands none of this in the passage but says simply: "Go, appear to Ahab, and I will send rain upon that land" (18:1).

Carefully attending to the two verbs from the word of Yhwh in 18:1, הלך and ראה, shows that Eliahu does *not* in fact directly carry out the divine command. Instead of "going" and "appearing" to Ahab as he was instructed to do, Eliahu appears to Ahab's servant Obedyahu, whose name means "the servant of Yhwh."[14] While it could be objected that the servant simply represents Ahab, such that Eliahu does fulfill the divine command, the difference in Eliahu's action and God's command is vital when viewed in light of the hierarchical structuring of power. Eliahu orchestrates a situation in which Ahab will have *to come to Eliahu* to seek an end to the drought, making it clear who retains the upper hand. Eliahu's command to Obedyahu even retains the same imperative that Yhwh originally used in speaking to Eliahu: "*Go*, speak to your lord, 'Here is Eliahu'" (לך אמר לאדניך הנה אליהו, 18:8).[15] Obedyahu will repeat Eliahu's command incredulously, not once but twice (18:11, 14), thus firmly underscoring its importance and drawing our attention to its careful formulation. As Stuart Lasine points out, Obadiah, far from being a person with split loyalties, as some commentators characterize him,[16] is in fact entirely loyal to Yhwh. His hesitation to report to Ahab on Elijah's behalf, as Lasine rightly notes, is due to a legitimate fear that Ahab will execute him, since "Elijah might be disloyal to *him*," that is, to Obadiah, by disappearing before the king arrives.[17]

Thus, the multiple instances of the verb "go" (הלך) structure the plot and chiasm. God instructs Eliahu to "*Go*, appear to Ahab," but Eliahu meets Obedyahu (18:7), who *went* (וילך) to meet Ahab (18:16), who then *went* (וילך) to meet Eliahu (18:16). Consequently, rather than Elijah "appearing" (הראה in the hiphil) to Ahab, Ahab came to Eliahu and "saw" him (כראות in a qal inf. const.), thereby inverting the subject and indirect object of God's initial command in 18:1. The grammatical structure of the sentences stipulating God's command to Eliahu and the actions of Obedyahu and Ahab are illuminating.

18:1: "Go, appear to Ahab" (לך הראה אל אחאב)
18:16: "Obedyahu went to meet Ahab" (וילך עבדיהו לקראת אחאב)
18:16: "Ahab went to meet Eliahu" (וילך אחאב לקראת אליהו)

---

14. Stuart Lasine, *Knowing Kings: Knowledge, Power, and Narcissism in the Hebrew Bible* (SemeiaSt 40; Atlanta: Society of Biblical Literature, 2001), 85.

15. Contrast the view of Wiseman, who takes 18:8–9 as "a challenge to side publicly with Elijah rather than be a secret supporter" (*1 and 2 Kings*, 168). The assumption that Elijah is laudable seems a priori.

16. E.g. Walsh, *1 Kings*, 239, 242, 260.

17. Lasine, *Knowing Kings*, 87.

In terms of action, Eliahu has forced *Ahab to go* and *to see*. Moreover, it is Obedyahu who has carried out God's command.

The narrative clearly distinguishes a path of paganism from a path of fidelity to YHWH. This is most obvious in the contest tale, in which Eliahu presents two bulls, two altars, and two choices to the people: "Let them choose *one bull*.... I will prepare *one bull*" (הפר האחד, 18:23). Eliahu's challenge to Israel is to stop hopping "between two clefts/branches" (על שתי הסעפים, 18:21), by which he means to contrast his own path with that of the pagan prophets. But the story also presents other sets of "two ways."

Metaphorically and literally, Ahab and Obedyahu travel two paths, as Obedyahu "went on one road alone" (הלך בדרך אחד לבדו, 18:6–7) and Ahab "went on one road alone" (הלך בדרך אחד לבדו, 18:6–7). That is, while Eliahu and the pagan prophets form one oppositional pair, Obedyahu and Ahab form another. The pairs structurally mirror one another as a set (D and D¹) in the chiastic structure. Obedyahu's "way" (דרך) of being faithful to YHWH forms a marked contrast to that of Eliahu. Obedyahu works publicly with Ahab's administration, while secretly rescuing one hundred prophets of the Lord, hiding them in two caves. Significantly, he is the provider of bread *and water* for them, even in the midst of this severe drought. Eliahu will, by contrast, publicly defy Ahab and the pagan prophets, pouring copious amounts of water (twelve *seahs*) on his bull as a way of further impressing the crowd with his act of calling down fire from heaven (18:34–35).

At the start of this contest of the bulls, which Kissling rightly notes is Eliahu's own idea entirely,[18] Eliahu defiantly states, "I am the only (לבדי) prophet of the LORD" (18:22). This self-characterization completely negates the existence of the one hundred prophets of YHWH whom Obedyahu has hidden and rescued, despite the fact that Obedyahu has recently reminded Eliahu of these prophets in 18:13. After the contest, which fails to win Israel over genuinely to the Lord (see 19:10), Eliahu will, like Ahab and Obedyahu, subsequently "go" (וילך and הלך) alone[19] on a "road" (דרך) in the wilderness, with Jezebel breathing threats of revenge against him (19:3–4). Eliahu's "way" is a path of constant conflict, Obedyahu's of pacifistic resistance.

Several commentators see Obedyahu's description of his actions in 18:13 as a loose addition in the Eliahu story, being only "secondary to the matter at hand."[20] Rather, this is the heart of the chiasm, presenting Obedyahu's "way" (דרך) literally as a cave (מערה) of refuge in which he risks his own life to rescue the prophets of YHWH and give them bread and water (לחם ומים, 18:13). As the

---

18. Kissling, *Reliable Characters*, 99.

19. Eliahu dismisses his servant in 1 Kgs 19:3, another element in the narrative that some scholars regard as irrelevant (e.g., Long, *1 Kings*, 197).

20. Cogan, *1 Kings*, 44–56.

chiasm concludes, this image is closely paralleled as an angel gives a downcast and petulant Eliahu cake (עגת) and water (מים, 19:6), before he hides *himself* in a cave (במערה, 19:9). Finally, the carefully constructed chiastic structure ends with the formula with which it began, "the word of the LORD came to him" (19:9; cf. 18:1).

Significantly, a large block of material stands as an intrusion into the otherwise perfect chiasm. Thematically and linguistically, the section we may call the "results of the contest" (18:36–19:4), has little linguistic parallel in this chiasm. Fire burns up the altar of YHWH; the people acclaim YHWH as their God; Elijah instructs the people to take the Baal prophets to the river, where he slaughters them; Elijah instructs Ahab, and the rain comes; Elijah runs to Jezreel ahead of Ahab's chariot; Ahab tells Jezebel that Elijah "had put all the prophets to the sword" (19:1); and Jezebel threatens to do the same to Elijah. I suggest that the lack of a parallel with this section (or at least with 18:36–46) highlights an older contest tale that stands theologically against the thrust of the larger passage in 1 Kgs 18–19, whose hero is Obedyahu.

Some assume that a prophet such as Eliahu always acts for God, although it is clear from various episodes in the Hebrew Bible that even true prophets may occasionally act out of their own feelings and actions. Jeremiah wished death on his enemies, earning God's reproach (Jer 15:15). Abraham Heschel coined the term "hypertrophy of sympathy" to help explain and somewhat justify Jeremiah's anger.[21] Yet there are other cases in which the prophet's motive is not even worthy of such legitimization, such as when Moses superstitiously strikes the rock at Meribath-Kadesh (Deut 32:5) or when Elisha lashes out at forty-two boys with two she-bears (2 Kgs 2:23–24).

Since our passage lies in the Deuteronomistic History, Deuteronomy's view of the prophet should play a key role in any interpretation. Prophets could certainly work signs that come to pass, but this is not the sign of a true prophet: "even if the sign or portent that he named to you comes true, do not heed the words of that prophet " (Deut 13:3). What, then, remains of the very logic of Eliahu's contest? Had the Baal prophets succeeded in bringing fire from heaven and Eliahu failed, the Baal prophets would still not be true prophets, nor would Elijah be a false one on that criterion. Rather, according to Deuteronomy, the qualities of a genuine prophet of YHWH are whether a prophet urges fidelity to YHWH, which Eliahu strenuously but ineffectually does, *and whether or not the prophet speaks the commands of God*: "But any prophet who presumes to speak in My name an oracle that I did not command him to utter … shall be put to death" (Deut 18:20). The next chiasm forces us to ask whether and to what extent Eliahu has spoken for God and whether he is deserving of death.

---

21. Abraham Joshua Heschel, *The Prophets* (New York: Harper & Row, 1962; repr., HarperCollins, 2001), 160–62.

Chiasm 2: 1 Kings 19:9–15

A. 19:9b: The word of the Lord came to him, "Why are you here, Eliahu?" (מה־לך פה אליהו).

    B. 19:10: Eliahu answers: "I am indeed zealous for Yhwh, the God of Hosts, because the sons of Israel have forsaken your covenant, torn down your altars, and killed your prophets by the sword, and I *alone* (לבדי) remain, and they are seeking to take my life (נפשי)."

        C. 19:11: God commands Eliahu, "*Come out* and *stand* on the mountain before Yhwh" (צא ועמדת בהר לפני יהוה).

            D. 19:11b–12: The theophany: "Behold, Yhwh passed by" (והנה יהוה עבר).

            D^1. "There was a great and strong wind (רוח) splitting mountains and shattering rocks before Yhwh, but Yhwh was not in the wind (רוח)."

            D^2. "After the wind (רוח)—an earthquake; but Yhwh was not in the earthquake."

            D^3. "After the earthquake—fire; but Yhwh was not in the fire."

            D^4. "And after the fire—a *voice* of *sheer silence*" (קול דממה דקה).

        C^1. 19:13: Elijah hears, hides his face in his mantle, and "*came out* and *stood*" (ויצא ויעמד) in the mouth of the cave.

A^1. 19:13: "Behold, a *voice* addressed him" (והנה אליו קול): "Why are you here, Eliahu?" (מה לך פה אליהו).

    B^1. 19:14: Eliahu gives the same answer: "I am indeed zealous for Yhwh, the God of Hosts, because the sons of Israel have forsaken your covenant, torn down your altars, and killed your prophets by the sword, and I *alone* (לבדי) remain, and they are seeking to take my life (נפשי)."

A^2. 19:15: "Yhwh said to him, '*Go*, return to your *way*'" (לך שוב לדרכך).

The repetition of important catchwords and phrases in 19:9b–15 interlocks the chiasm with that of 1 Kgs 18:1–19:9a through the keywords "alone" (לבדי), "go" (לך), and "way" (דרך). This second chiasm also turns on newly introduced catchwords, especially the two verbs of God's command, "come out" (צא) and "you stand" (ועמדת), as well as "voice" (קל).

The beginning words of the first chiasm, "the word of Yhwh came to Eliahu" (18:1), interlock with the beginning words of the second chiasm, "the word of Yhwh came to him" (19:9). Yet whereas the first "word of Yhwh" consists of a command, the second consists of a question: "Why are you here?" (19:9). Both Cohn and Robinson maintain that the emphasis should rest on "here," since

God never requests Elijah's presence at Mount Horeb.²² Robinson understands the repetition of the question as, "giv[ing] Elijah a last chance to align himself with Yhwh's will. Sadly, he fails to do so."²³ Yet if the imperative "go" (לך) so significantly structures the first chiasm and concludes the second (לך שוב לדרכך, 19:15), there may be a clue in the phrase מה לך, which unpointed and in written form contains the same two letters (לך) that have structured the plot throughout the earlier chiasm (18:1, 8, 11, 14), although this inseparable prefix plus pronominal suffix is clearly a different spoken word than the imperative "go" (לך). I suggest that this hints at the importance of the question word, מה, however one chooses to translate it. Eliahu did not go (לך) to Ahab as God instructed but instead has *gone* (הלך) to Obedyahu, to Mount Carmel, to a broom tree, along a wilderness road, and finally to a cave in the mountain of God, prompting God to ask, "Why are you here, Eliahu?" (מה לך פה אליהו).

The response that Eliahu gives to God's question is possibly correct on the surface. Yet careful attention to etymology again points to a deeper level of interpretation. Eliahu's accusation that the Israelites have "put prophets to the sword" (18:40) is precisely the language that Ahab uses in describing to Jezebel Eliahu's actions against the prophets of Baal (19:1). Also, Eliahu's complaint that "they are seeking to take *my life*" (ויבקשו את נפשי לקחתה, 19:10, 14) is ironic at best and obtuse at worst, in that he has recently asked God to do exactly that: "take my life" (קח נפשי, 19:4).

When God then gives Eliahu a simple command, we rightly expect that Eliahu will only half obey: "*Come out* (צא) and *stand* (ועמדת) on the mountain before Yhwh" (19:11). God's simple command suggests that Eliahu would come out of the cave entirely so that a theophany would ensue. Indeed, this expectation is so strong that interpreters such as Cogan have concluded that the actual theophany is missing but presumed.²⁴ Actually, a series of events noting God's absence occurs first (19:11–12). Although events such as a mighty wind or רוח, earthquake, and even fire pass by Eliahu, God is absent: "Yhwh was not in the fire" (19:12). Just as Deuteronomy had maintained that the test of true prophethood does *not* lie in the prophet's ability to work signs and portents (Deut 13:3), great signs of Yhwh's power do *not* necessarily indicate the presence of God. The assertion that Yhwh was "not in the fire" (19:12) is the most surprising, as it points us directly to the contest on Mount Carmel, so fresh in the flow of the narrative. Eliahu may have successfully called down fire from heaven to illustrate the power of God, but Deut 13:3 and 1 Kgs 19:12 both suggest that great signs are not proof that God is present. Instead, the "sound" or "voice" (קול) of silence in

---

22. Robert L. Cohn, "The Literary Logic of 1 Kings 17–19," *JBL* 101 (1982): 343; Robinson, "Elijah at Horeb," 522.
23. Robinson, "Elijah at Horeb," 522.
24. Cogan, *1 Kings*, 450 nn. 11–12.

this unique theophany stands in contrast to mighty displays of power such as the bloody, noisy, violent spectacle on Mount Carmel.²⁵

Only after Eliahu "hears" the silent voice does he exit the cave, slightly contorting God's instructions once more. Even then Eliahu comes out only partway, hiding his face (cf. Judg 6:22; 13:20–22; Exod 33:22–23) and standing "in the mouth of the cave" (19:13). As in 18:1–19:9, the first chiasm, Eliahu only partly follows God's command. The divine "voice of sheer silence" then proceeds to ask the initial question again in exactly the same words, מה לך פה אליהו but in a new theophanic form. The force of this repetition suggests that Eliahu's first answer is unsatisfactory and that a new understanding and a better response is possible in light of the remarkable phenomenon of the voice of silence.²⁶

Yet Eliahu answers in *exactly* the same way, demonstrating that he is unmoved by the unexpected theophany in 19:11–12. Eliahu has not understood the point, has not allowed himself to conceive of a different way in which God is not necessarily apparent in mighty רוח, earthquakes, and fire, but instead as "a voice of sheer silence." Just as Eliahu ignored Obedyahu's rescue of the one hundred prophets of Yhwh, and indeed their very existence, so too does he ignore the meaning of this quiet theophany. Heschel once insightfully suggested that the divine pathos acts in accordance with human action and pathos, in fact depending on the understanding of humans: "Whatever man does affects not only his own life, but also the life of God insofar as it is directed to man…. He is a consort, a partner, a factor in the life of God."²⁷ Sadly, God answers Eliahu according to the place where he is: "Yhwh said to him, '*Go*, return to your *way*'" (לך שוב לדרכך). The chiasm concludes again with the imperative לך, as God acquiesces to Eliahu's way of combating the Baalism of Ahab's reign: conflict, revenge, and war.

At the conclusion of the chiasm, God gives Eliahu instructions for anointing Elisha, Hazael, and Jehu, thereby inaugurating a war in Israel that will result in the massive bloodshed of all those following Baal (19:15b–18). Perhaps not incidentally, Eliahu fulfills these commands only to some extent by anointing Elisha, who carries out the rest of God's instructions (19:16–18). This reading solves another longstanding puzzle in the larger narrative, namely, Eliahu's failure to carry out two of the three tasks given to him by God.²⁸ Actually, in so doing, he acts in characteristic fashion.

---

25. The translation of קול דממה דקה as "sound/voice of sheer silence" points to another deep contrast, since Baal's response in the contest is likewise silent, it being stated repeatedly that there was "no voice," "no answer" (18:26), "no voice," "no answer," and "no response" (18:29). In the logic of the story, however, the silence of one god is not the same as the silence of the other.

26. Every parent knows that asking a question in the same exact words twice indicates that the first answer is unsatisfactory and a different answer is desired: "Who broke this lamp?" "A monster did it." "*Who* broke this lamp?"

27. Heschel, *The Prophets*, 285–98.

28. Montgomery and Gehman, *Book of Kings*, 314.

Since Eliahu is unmoved by the theophany outside the cave in Mount Horeb, readers sense that a chance has been missed, but they may understand more than does the character Eliahu. The centerpiece of the second chiasm (19:11b–12), Eliahu hiding himself in a cave, points directly to the centerpiece of the first chiasm (18:13), Obedyahu hiding prophets in a cave in pacifistic resistance to Jezebel's attacks.[29] The contrast with Eliahu's way and the ensuing war is startling.[30]

What if Eliahu had simply obeyed God's command in 18:1: "Go, appear to Ahab, then I will send rain"? One can only speculate what the editor/author intends to convey might have happened, but the simplicity of the command suggests something likewise simple. Upon close inspection, Ahab is not the arch-foe of Eliahu in 1 Kgs 18–19 (cf. 21:27–29).[31] Rather, he comes when called by Eliahu via Obedyahu (18:16), assembles all of Israel and 850 prophets when instructed (18:19), listens when Eliahu tells him to ascend and eat and drink (18:41), and obeys when Eliahu tells him to take his chariot to Jezreel (18:44–45). Jezebel is a different story altogether, but Ahab seems to be wholly obedient to Eliahu, if not also simultaneously perturbed with him (18:17). Together with the force of the overall critique of Eliahu, Ahab's characterization suggests that, had Eliahu gone to Ahab as God had instructed it was time to do, things would have worked out another way.

Instead, Eliahu's imprecise obedience of God's commands throughout 1 Kgs 18–19 demonstrates a desire to assert his own authority even within the framework of obeying God, a situation into which Eliahu himself may have had some insight. If we ask why he fled and became so despondent, the narrative provides for multiple possible readings. On the surface, Jezebel threatens to kill him, inspiring fear such that he fled for his life: וירא ויקם וילך אל נפשו (19:3). Yet this fear seems discordant with his ability to call down fire from heaven, as he has just done, with the resulting acclamation of all of Israel. Moreover, the phrase sometimes translated, "and he was afraid [וירא = *wayyira*], and he fled" (LXX), can also be read, "and he saw [וירא = *wayyar*'], arose, and went to his *nephesh*" (וילך אל נפשו).[32] In my view, the latter accords better with the repeated stress on the verb "to see" (ראה) in the first chiasm. Whereas Eliahu was instructed to *appear* (hiphil of ראה) but forced Ahab to come and *see* him, Eliahu is finally the active subject who "*sees*," causing him to have deep insight about himself. This in turn

---

29. Olley also suggested the "sound of sheer silence" represents "an implied criticism of the attitude that YHWH is most present in spectacular events," which leads him to ask: "Does YHWH in fact prefer the silence of Obadiah to the noise of Elijah?" ("YHWH and His Zealous Prophet," 47). My structural analysis supports Olley's conclusion.

30. Olley also points out several contrasts between tempestuous Elijah and calm Elisha (ibid., 32–33).

31. Cogan, *1 Kings*, 447.

32. So in most manuscripts and the MT; see JPS 19:3 n. c.

causes him to dismiss his servant, a seriously misunderstood act that is necessary for his journey "alone on a road" on the way to the cave at Horeb.[33]

What Eliahu "sees"[34] about himself causes him despondency and results in his exclamation: "Now, Yʜᴡʜ, take my life (נפשי), because *I am no better than my fathers* (כי־לא־טוב אנכי מאבתי)" (19:4).[35] Repetition of the *maqqeph* in the ᴍᴛ draws attention to the linguistic package of "because-not-good am I" in a remarkably forceful way, suggesting that Eliahu knew that he had not chosen what is good (1 Kgs 3:9). Perhaps Eliahu requests the death penalty precisely because he had substituted his own will for God's, requesting the punishment that Deuteronomy stipulates is fitting for this crime: "But any prophet who presumes to speak in my name an oracle that I did not command him to utter ... that prophet shall die" (Deut 18:20). If this reading is correct, the passage also attests to outlandish mercy from God, both because in the immediate story an angel tenderly feeds Eliahu cake and water, as Obedyahu fed the rescued prophets bread and water, and because Eliahu *never* dies. Still, as a character Eliahu may represent a prophet who never fully grasps the idea of a mercy that outweighs justice.

Concluding Remarks on Structure

The pervasive structural similarities between the two chiasms indicate a tightly integrated narrative in 1 Kgs 18–19 that heavily reworks earlier strata. There may be an early Ephraimite kernel that is pre-Deuteronomistic, consisting of parts of the contest on Mount Carmel (a noncentralized Yʜᴡʜ sanctuary), with the majority of the contest scene stemming from the hand of the Deuteronomistic Historian at the time of the reforms of Josiah, when Yahwism was battling polytheism. Structurally, this would include the ill-fitting "results of the contest," which is theologically consistent with the Deuteronomistic History as a whole, comfortable as it as with ritualized, wholesale slaughter of polytheists. Around this core Deuteronomistic story with older Ephraimite elements, however, I suggest that a postexilic Deuteronomistic author or redactor (Cross's Dtr²) has crafted a tightly woven critique of Eliahu's warlike behavior. This emphasis is consonant with much literary activity in the postexilic era,[36] with many having

---

33. Robinson muses, "like Miss Garbo, [he] prefers his own company" ("Elijah at Horeb," 517).

34. This crucial verb also looks ahead to 2 Kgs 2:10 and the test of Elisha's prophetic capacity.

35. Walsh, who maintains that Eliahu challenges God by saying, "I am no better than my ancestors," states, "If Elijah has failed, it is because Yahweh demanded too much of him. Elijah is not superhuman, yet Yahweh expects him to convert the king and the whole people singlehandedly" (*1 Kings*, 268).

36. Frank Moore Cross, *Canaanite Myth and Hebrew Epic: Essays in the History of the Religion of Israel* (Cambridge: Harvard University Press, 1973), 285–89.

concluded that the violent reforms of Josiah and Jehu had not saved Judah from defeat.

Whether or not my specific dating of these layers may be refuted, the two carefully constructed chiasms stand as a vibrant, internal critique of one of the bloodiest episodes in prophetic sacred history. Obedyahu's nonretributive, pacifistic defense of Yahwism poses an alternate vision for triumphing over an unjust regime, seriously calling into question the displays of power, might, and conflict favored by Eliahu. Eliahu never acknowledges the validity of this path, but the theophany of the voice of silence may still be heard by the reader.

Shifts in Israelite War Ethics and Early Jewish Historiography of Plundering*

Brian Kvasnica

In reinterpreting Israel's violent tradition, Jewish exegetical interpretations of the Second Temple period demonstrate heightened sensitivities to ethical questions regarding war and plunder. Such sensitivities were part of larger ideological shifts in Jewish piety and identity,[1] which were at times related to the values and outlooks of Jews of Diasporan identity.[2] Three historiographical themes exemplify these sensitivities: (1) Judas Maccabeus's "pious plundering" (2 Macc 8),[3] that is, his unique distribution of war booty to disadvantaged people; (2) the apparent need of Jubilees, Philo, and Ezekiel the Tragedian to justify Israelite "plundering of Egypt"; and (3) the allegation by Josephus that plundering an enemy is against the Torah. Ethical shifts created more pious interpretative traditions, encour-

---

* An earlier version of this article was presented at the 2006 SBL Annual Meeting in Washington, D.C. I wish to thank Brad Kelle, chair of the session, for his encouragement. I also wish to thank my wife, Shoshanna Kvasnica, as well as Daniel Schwartz and Michael Stone for their comments on previous versions. The work, of course, is my responsibility, and any deficiency is my own.

1. Piety here will be defined as a devout deed or statement made in reverence to God and in devotion to the Torah. See George W. E. Nickelsburg and Michael E. Stone, *Faith and Piety in Early Judaism: Texts and Documents* (rev. ed.; Harrisburg, Pa.: Trinity Press International, 1994), 89–115.

2. See especially Daniel R. Schwartz, "From the Maccabees to Masada: On Diasporan Historiography of the Second Temple Period," in *Jüdische Geschichte in hellenistisch-römischer Zeit: Wege der Forschung: vom alten zum neuen Schurer* (ed. A. Oppenheimer; Munich: Oldenbourg Wissenschaftsverlag, 1999), 29–40; and now Noah Hacham, "Exile and Self-Identity in the Qumran Sect and in Hellenistic Judaism," in the *Tenth Orion DSS Conference Volume* (Leiden: Brill, forthcoming).

3. Maccabean narratives related to plunder have not received sufficient attention in important works such as Angelos Chaniotis, *War in the Hellenistic World: A Social and Cultural History* (Oxford: Blackwell, 2005); and William K. Pritchett's monumental work, which noted that "no full-scale study of booty has ever been published" (*The Greek State at War* [5 vols.; Berkeley and Los Angeles: University of California Press, 1971–91], 1:53).

aging readers to act accordingly, and established socioreligious boundaries for identity formation.

Israelite warfare has typically been studied conceptually, with less attention given to the pragmatics of warring.[4] This paper will focus on one aspect of the practicalities of war, that of plunder.[5] I will be examining the Second Temple period historiography of plunder within the larger context of biblical and Hellenistic war.

Some Biblical Descriptions of Plundering

Several instances of plundering in the Hebrew Bible may provide the backdrop for the Second Temple period historiography of plundering. It is commonplace to find mention of war booty in extant ancient literature. Similarly, within the Hebrew Bible, the act of spoiling an enemy, even by biblical heroes, was assumed. Several biblical examples of plundering, however, contain an element atypical to this arguably greedy and vengeful practice: a pious element.

The first biblical instance of a distribution of war booty is Gen 14:17–24, which occurs after Abraham's warring and subsequent covenant ceremony with Melchizedek.[6] Yochanan Muffs notes that Abraham showed his noble character when he went beyond convention in not taking any of the booty for himself, "neither string nor sandal lace" (14:23). Abraham magnanimously distributed the booty to his three fellow-warriors, to the young men, and to the priest Melchizedek.[7] Abraham did not question the morality of transactions of war booty, which

---

4. See the foundational treatments by Gerhard von Rad, *Holy War in Ancient Israel* (trans. and ed. Marva J. Dawn; Grand Rapids: Eerdmans, 1991); and Susan Niditch, *War in the Hebrew Bible: A Study in the Ethics of Violence* (Oxford: Oxford University Press, 1993).

5. Using a socioeconomic emphasis, I am following the lead of Yvon Garlan, William K. Pritchett, and now Angelos Chaniotis. This work adds to the few studies about plunder in the late Hellenistic period such as Elias J. Bickerman, "Remarques sur le droit des gens dans la Grèce classique," *RIDA* (1950): 99–127, repr. as "Bemerkungen über das Völkerrecht im klassischen Griechenland," in *Zur griechishen Staatskunde* (ed. F. Gschnitzer; Wege der Forschung 96; Darmstadt: Wissenschaftliche Buchgesellschaft, 1969); Pierre Ducrey, *Warfare in Ancient Greece* (trans. J. Lloyd; New York: Schocken, 1985); idem, *Le traitement des prisonniers de guerre dans la Grèce antique des origines à la conquête romaine* (2nd ed.; Paris: Boccard, 1999); Yvon Garlan, "Le partage entre alliés des dépenses et des profits de guerre," in *Armées et fiscalité dans le monde antique: Paris, 14–16 Octobre 1976* (Colloques nationaux du Centre national de la recherche scientifique 936. Paris: Éditions du Centre national de la recherche scientifique, 1977), 149–64; and Pritchett, *Greek State at War*.

6. David Elgavish, "The Encounter of Abram and Melchizedek King of Salem: A Covenant Establishing Ceremony," in *Studies in the Book of Genesis: Literature, Redaction and History* (ed. A. Wénin; Leuven: Peeters, 2001), 495–508.

7. Yochanan Muffs, "Abraham the Noble Warrior: Patriarchal Politics and Laws of War in Ancient Israel," *JJS* 33 (1982): 81–107. Muffs compares Gen 14:20 with the *Statue of Idrimi*,

already seem to have incorporated protocol and limitations, but rather explained his actions as reliance upon God. David Elgavish similarly concludes, "Abraham preserves the right of his allies to take booty, even if he himself forgoes the spoils he captured. This example is unique among the instances of the division of the plunder among allies."[8] Abraham's relinquishing of his right to the plunder provides a rare example of "righteous" plundering that may have served as a prototype for the Maccabean portrayals of Judas.[9]

Several biblical passages recount that a portion of the spoils of war were dedicated to the Israelite God. Numbers 31 clarifies who received what after the Israelite war with Midian, and the legal nature of booty-distribution is felt throughout the passage. The account mentions a variety of *recipients* of booty-division: initially the leaders (31:12); then the warriors who had already snatched up plunder (31:27, 53); the Levites (31:52); the Lord, who received the tribute via the clergy (31:28); and, finally, the congregation (31:12, 27).[10] Baruch Levine has commented that, while this passage seems to parallel ancient Near East practices of dedicating spoils of war to the sacred (i.e., gods, temples, priests), "it is curious that relatively little is said about the sacred devotion of spoils elsewhere in the Hebrew Bible."[11] Numbers 31 thus stands out as a unique example within the biblical corpus of an explicit dividing up of war booty between warriors and

---

which seems to have been concerned with showing the king's fairness, exemplified in his distribution of booty to friends and allies: "I took captives from them and took their property valuables and possessions, and distributed them to my auxiliaries, kinsmen, and friends. Together with them I took booty' (ibid., 88 quoting D. Marcus and E. Greenstein, "The Akkadian Inscription of *Idrimi*," *JANES* 8 [1976]: 59).

8. David Elgavish, "The Division of the Spoils of War in the Bible and in the Ancient Near East," *ZABR* 8 (2002): 257.

9. Hugo Grotius, who is known as the "father of international law," observed that Abraham was the first of "all noble conquerors" from Abraham to Marcus Cato who declined spoils for themselves (*De iure praedae commentarius. Commentary on the Law of Prize and Booty* [trans. G. L. Williams and W. H. Zeydel; Classics of International Law 22; Oxford: Clarendon, 1950], 50–51). Muffs pointed out Grotius and a noteworthy study not accessible to me: Alois Musil, *The Manners and Customs of the Rwala Bedouins* (Oriental Explorations and Studies 6; New York: American Geographical Society, 1928), which Muffs described as "a mine of illuminating parallels to biblical patterns of warfare and booty distribution" ("Abraham the Noble Warrior," 88, 93 n. 39).

10. Baruch A. Levine, *Numbers 21–36: A New Translation with Introduction and Commentary* (AB 4A; New York: Doubleday, 2000) 472, 474; Jacob Milgrom, *Numbers: The Traditional Hebrew Text with the New JPS Translation* (JPS Torah Commentary; Philadelphia: Jewish Publication Society, 1994), 262–65. See also the Temple Scroll (11Q19) LVIII 11–15; L. H. Schiffman, "The Laws of War in the Temple Scroll," *RQ* 16 (1988): 299–311; and Bilhah Nitzan, "Benedictions and Instructions for the Eschatological Community (11QBer; 4Q285)," *RQ* 16 (1993): 77–90.

11. Levine, *Numbers 21–36*, 471.

the Lord's servants, and it also seems to have influenced the rendering of Judas's pious distribution in 2 Macc 8.[12]

In 2 Sam 8:9-12, David consecrated to God spoils from King Hadadezar of Aram (cf. 1 Chr 29:1-9), and 1 Chr 26:26-28 reports that David designated a certain Shelomoth to oversee all the spoils dedicated to the temple, implicitly informing the reader that the consecration of booty to God's temple was both common and complex enough to require a person to organize it.

Three other biblical passages of distribution of plunder stand out. In 1 Sam 30 we read that David divided the plunder *equally* between the warriors and the baggage-men after their raid in retaliation of the destruction of Ziklag. In what may be one of the more significant passages for piety in plunder in light of the late redaction of Chronicles, 2 Chr 28 reports that leaders of Israel followed the prophet Oded's command to return the captives of Judah after their civil war with Ahaz and that the victorious northern kingdom not only returned the captives of Judah but used the plunder to care for the captives,

> and with the booty they clothed all that were naked among them; they clothed them, gave them sandals, provided them with food and drink, and anointed them; and carrying all the feeble among them on donkeys, they brought them to their kindred at Jericho, the city of palm trees. Then they returned to Samaria. (2 Chr 28:15 NRSV)

Third, a process of group differentiation based upon piety vis-à-vis plunder can already be seen in the late biblical book of Esther. Esther 3:13 has Haman giving a decree "to destroy, to kill, and to annihilate all Jews ... and to plunder their goods," whereas 9:13 reports that, when the Jews proved victorious, "they laid no hands on the plunder" of their enemies. Josephus and the Maccabean stories may have been influenced by Esther's stark contrast between who did and did not plunder.

These passages may provide bridges between Israel's early and typically violent tradition regarding war booty and Israel's later sensitivity to pious acts in war, as well as a shift in the provenance of the narratives concerning the relevance of warfare in the Israelite community. In either case, these passages help us to understand better the late Second Temple period's reworking of the scriptural tradition and to perceive ethical shifts related to plundering.

---

12. Jonathan A. Goldstein, *2 Maccabees: A New Translation with Introduction and Commentary* (AB 41A; Garden City, N.Y.: Doubleday, 1983), 338–39. Goldstein notes elements of Num 31 that appear in 2 Macc 8:30–31: slaughter of the enemy (31:7–8); towering fortresses (31:10); spoils brought to the camp (31:12) and divided between warriors, noncombatants, and the sanctuary (31:25–54).

PERCEPTIONS OF PLUNDER IN THE ANCIENT WORLD

Daily life in the ancient Greek world was greatly affected by piracy and frequent wars between competing powers.[13] War underwrote armies, state treasuries, and building projects.[14] Conquest through war and division of plunder were two of the driving forces of ancient social history: "[I]f the Macedonian invasion of Asia was possibly the largest plundering and conquering expedition of its kind in ancient history, then the Age of Successors can also be seen as another record, as the most bitter and prolonged dispute over sharing out the spoils of victory between the conquerors."[15] From Austin's comments, Pritchett's work, as well as the insightful work of Finley,[16] it is clear that war booty was big business in the Greek and Hellenistic world. Plundering one's enemies or strangers "whenever it is possible, was an acceptable way of maintaining oneself in antiquity."[17] According to Aristotle, even piracy was considered an accepted occupation.[18]

Questions concerning the morality of war in general and plundering in particular were fairly uncommon, as is suggested by the dearth of extant material on this subject.[19] Considering how common wars were, it is surprising that the ancients did not dwell on the ethical problems of war. Garlan notes, "One would have expected war to have forced them to think about its causes and its effects, to have been the principal subject for historical reflection. But this was far from the

---

13. The Athenians went to war two out of three years for at least a century and a half, and both Greeks and Romans fought wars with "unrelenting regularity" (Moses I. Finley, "War and Empire," in idem, *Ancient History: Evidence and Models* [New York: Viking, 1986], 67). See more recently Angelos Chaniotis, "The Ubiquitous War," in idem, *War in the Hellenistic World: A Social and Cultural History* (Oxford: Blackwell, 2005), 1–17. Pritchett writes, "It seems clear that plunder/booty formed at times a virtual line-item in the ancient economy; but it is also true that classical writers had a disinclination to say so, and further study is needed to establish an overall picture, if indeed it becomes possible" (Pritchett, *The Greek State at War*, 5:ix).

14. Hendrik Bolkestein and Michael I. Rostovetzeff both noted the foundational importance of war and plunder in ancient society. Bolkestein writes that booty was the "principal object" of war, which was the other form of subsistence next to labor (*Economic Life in Greece's Golden Age* [Leiden: Brill, 1958], 141), and Rostovetzeff states that the purpose of war was often not to settle political questions but to enrich the victors (*The Social and Economic History of the Hellenistic World* [3 vols.; Oxford: Clarendon, 1941], 1:195). See the important chapter by Chaniotis, "The Cost and Profit of War: Economic Aspects of Hellenistic Warfare," in *War in the Hellenistic World*, 115–42.

15. M. M. Austin, "Hellenistic Kings, War, and the Economy," *CQ* NS 36 (1986): 455.

16. Finley, "War and Empire," 67–87, 119–22.

17. Jens A. Krasilnikoff, "Aegean Mercenaries in the Fourth to Second Centuries BC. A Study in Payment, Plunder and Logistics of Ancient Greek Armies," *Classica et mediaevalia* 43 (1992): 27.

18. Aristotle, *Pol.* 1256 a–b.

19. Yvon Garlan, *War in the Ancient World: A Social History* (trans. J. Lloyd; London: Chatto & Windus, 1975), 15ff.

case."[20] They do not seem to have dug deeply into the morality of war and plundering, sought to draw parameters for the practice, or questioned its legitimacy. Paradoxically, war preoccupied their everyday lives but not their philosophical energies. This paradox might have been made possible because war and thus plundering were believed to be inevitable—from the gods. Yet we do find reflexes of such moral questions by early Jewish and Roman authors.[21] One of the more outstanding of such reflexes may be the pious plundering and distribution of plunder by Judas Maccabeus, which is discussed below.

It seems that the single extant expression of piety in Greek and Hellenistic plundering was the *dekate*-tithe,[22] a portion of the plunder dedicated to a temple or a god, such as Athena, the goddess of plunder (Homer, *Il.* 10.460). Such *dekate* or firstfruits are known from the earliest Greek sources,[23] and they were even a mandatory practice in the treaties for the Athenian league after its victory in the Persian War. Pritchett observes that "the piety of the Greeks is shown by their consistent gift of a *dekate* from the booty. It was from this *dekate* of booty that most of the shrines and temples at Olympia and Delphi were built to the gods."[24] The irony of this piety is depicted by Plutarch in his juxtaposition of the divine Delphi monuments and war booty: "[Y]ou see the god completely surrounded by choice offerings and tithes from murders, wars, and plunderings, and his temple

---

20. According to Garlan (ibid., 16), we do not have a single Greek philosophical treatise devoted to the subject of war.

21. Other Jewish examples will be discussed below. One additional example is Philo's *Flaccus* §56, which describes a pogrom at Alexandria in 38 C.E. where Alexandrians "ran to the houses left empty and plundered them; they divided the booty among themselves as if it were war." For Philo, plunder was acceptable during war but not in ethnic persecution (P. W. van der Horst, *Philo's Flaccus: The First Pogrom: Introduction, Translation and Commentary* [Philo of Alexandria Commentary Series 2; Leiden: Brill, 2003; repr., Atlanta: Society of Biblical Literature, 2005], 64, 159–60).

With regard to Rome, for example, in the first century B.C.E. Cicero mentioned the Fetial Code (*Off.* 1.36; cf. *Verr.* 4.116), a code of Roman priests, in which he described certain laws governing warfare as *mores belli* (K. Gilliver, "The Roman Army and Morality in War," in *Battle in Antiquity* [ed. A. B. Lloyd; London; Duckworth, 1997], 219–38)

22. *Dekate* here is used both as technical term and as categorical term for dedication of a portion of the spoils; thus "firstfruits," e.g., falls under the rubric of *dekate*.

23. W. H. D. Rouse, *Greek Votive Offerings* (Cambridge: Cambridge University Press, 1902), 55; for a listing, see 102. E.g., Herodotus (8.121) wrote that at Salamis, the victors set apart for the gods, among other firstfruits (ἀκροθίνια) "three Phoenician triremes…. After that they divided the spoil [ληίην] and sent the firstfruits of it to Delphi" (A. D. Godley, ed., *Herodotus in Four Volumes* [Cambridge: Harvard University Press, 1981], 4:125).

24. Personal communication via email, 29 February 2004. Pritchett adds, "Indeed, you might ask what structures did not come from booty. The circumstances of the Maccabean revolt are quite different."

crowded with spoils and booty from the Greeks ... upon the beautiful votive offerings you read the most disgraceful inscriptions."[25]

Such profits from war funded the building of victor's temple cults. Pritchett flatly states that, "without wars, few of the temples and other sacred buildings of Greece would have been built."[26] In this case, the Maccabean narrative preserves a similar tradition: war booty is brought to the Holy City, Jerusalem.

The book of 2 Maccabees seems to have to highlighted differences between Jew and Greek in order better to define Jewish identity. The character of Judas's piety hearkens back to Israelite-based piety; this scriptural tradition related a piety that may be more similar to and likely inherited from ancient Egyptian practices than those of the Greek world. F. Charles Fensham argues, "the protection of widow, orphan, and the poor was the common policy of the ancient Near East."[27] But whereas piety from Egyptian and Israelite circles can be best described as *charity*, H. Bolkestein argues that Greek piety is best described as *well-doing*.[28] It was also more self-regarding, and, while all types of piety may very well be self-interested, most Egyptian and Israelite piety seems to have been more of a religious *duty* than self-regarding social mores.[29] Hans van Wees confirms such an understanding of Greek piety: "the persistence and constant repetition of the themes of friendship, reciprocity and generosity shows that many Greek communities did keep a tally of favours done and received."[30] Hence we can see

---

25. Plut. *Pyth. orac.* 401 [= *Mor.* 5.297] (Babbit, LCL).

26. Pritchett, *Greek State at War*, 1:100. Similarly, materials for the building of the tabernacle (Num 25) may have come as plunder from the Egyptians.

27. F. Charles Fensham, "Widow, Orphan and the Poor in Ancient Near Eastern Legal and Wisdom Literature," in *Studies in Ancient Israelite Wisdom* (ed. J. L. Crenshaw; New York: Ktav, 1976), 161; repr. from *JNES* 21 (1962): 129–39. "It was not started by the spirit of Israelite propheticism" (ibid.) but rather was a shared in Mesopotamian, Egyptian, Canaanite and Israelite worlds.

28. Hendrik Bolkestein contrasts ancient Egyptian and Israelite "charity" with classical "well-doing" in his *Wohltätigkeit und Armenpflege in vorchristlichen Altertum* (Utrecht: Oosthoek, 1939). More recently R. Hands has taken up the theme: 'Philanthropy in our sense means that oriental concept which was stressed as a religious duty in Ancient Egypt and Israel and in large measure inherited by [Jewish and] Christian ethics" (*Charities and Social Aid in Greece and Rome* [London: Thames & Hudson, 1968], 11). He adds, "In the vast majority of texts and documents relating to gifts in the classical world, it is quite clear that the giver's action is self-regarding, in the sense that he anticipates from the recipient of his gift some sort of return" (26).

29. Ronald J. Williams has shown that two ideologies of piety and responsibility competed: repentance for forgiveness; or manipulation with powers of magic for forgiveness. The latter, via the mortuary literature, won out, but not before passing on the Egyptian "highly developed moral sense" to the Israelite traditions ("Piety and Ethics in the Ramessid Age," *Journal of the Society for the Study of Egypt Antiquities* 8 [1978]: 131–37).

30. Hans van Wees, *Greek Warfare: Myths and Realities* (London: Duckworth, 2004), 12. Thucydides puts it thus: 'For it is not by receiving kindness, but by conferring it, that we acquire

that Bolkestein's theory holds up in our case, where Maccabean and Hellenistic practices of war are to be contrasted more than compared.[31]

THE DISTRIBUTION OF PLUNDER BY JUDAS MACCABEUS—AN IDEAL FIGURE

While both 1 and 2 Maccabees did not shy away from reference to their own or others' plundering,[32] only 2 Maccabees reports Judas's distribution after the battle of Ammaus in 165 B.C.E., a distribution that included the disadvantaged. The battle of Ammaus (often transliterated Emmaus; located near present-day Latrun), in which Judas despoiled the Seleucid force in September 165 B.C.E., is the core of our study.[33] The three sources for the battle of Ammaus are 1 Macc 3:38–4:25; 2 Macc 8:8–29, 34–36; and Josephus, *Ant.* 12.298–312.[34] Written between 104 and 63 B.C.E., 1 Maccabees is translation Greek, likely from a Hebrew source. The book is staunchly pro-Hasmonean and stems from a priestly milieu that lacks interest in the afterlife and the supernatural.[35] In contrast, 2 Maccabees is a composite work

---

our friends. Now he who confers the favour is a firmer friend, in that he is disposed, by continued goodwill toward the recipient, to keep the feeling of obligation alive in him" (2.40.4 [Smith, LCL]). See also Hans van Wees, "The Law of Gratitude: Reciprocity in Anthropological Theory," in *Reciprocity in Ancient Greece* (ed. C. Gill, N. Postlethwaite, and R. Seaford; Oxford: Oxford University Press, 1998), 13–49.

31. Stopping on the Sabbath in 1-2 Maccabees is comparable to waiting to fight until sacred days ended in Hellenistic piety (see Pritchett, *Greek State at War*, 1:121–26; van Wees, *Greek Warfare*, 119–22), although the practice of foregoing war in sacred places and times may have been "abandoned after the Persian Wars" (van Wees, *Greek Warfare*, 283 n. 5). While both Hellenistic and Maccabean booty-distribution evidenced a tithe/*dekate*-piety, only in the Maccabean accounts is there an explicit concern for tortured, orphans, widows, and aged in the booty distribution, in such a manner that showed camaraderie (ἰσμοίρους) with those who could not likely repay the favor. See especially Daniel R. Schwartz, *2 Maccabees* [Hebrew] (Jerusalem: Yad Itzak Ben Zvi, 2004), 189.

32. See 1 Macc 1:3, 19, 31, 35; 2:10; 3:12, 20; 4:17, 18, 23; 5:3, 22, 28, 35, 51, 68 (2x); 5:68; 6:3, 6; 7:47 (2x); 8:10; 9:40; 10:84, 87; 11:48, 51, 61; 12:31; 13:34; see also 2 Macc 8:27, 30, 31; 9:16.

33. The Seleucid commander Nicanor and his deputy commander Gorgias were pitted against Judas Maccabeus. The Seleucids undertook this battle as retaliation for their defeat by Judas about six months prior, against Apollonius and Seron. For the location of Ammaus (mentioned in 1 Maccabees and followed by Josephus) and the date of the battle, see Bezalel Bar-Kochva, *Judas Maccabaeus: The Jewish Struggle against the Seleucids* (Cambridge: Cambridge University Press, 1989), 219, 472.

34. See Joseph Sievers, *Synopsis of the Greek Sources for the Hasmonean Period: 1-2 Maccabees and Josephus, War 1 and Antiquities 12–14* (SubBi 20; Rome: Pontifical Biblical Institute, 2001), 48–55.

35. See George W. E. Nickelsburg, "1 and 2 Maccabees—Same Story, Different Meaning," *CTM* 42 (1971): 515–26; Bar-Kochva, *Judas Maccabaeus*, 151–93; and Schwartz, *2 Maccabees*, 45–46. Thus it is not surprising that certain priestly details are narrated in 1 Maccabees, such as

in literary Greek, an epitome of Jason of Cyrene's five-volume history (see 2 Macc 2:23), prefaced by two letters. Its provenance is more proto-Hasidic, expressing itself through subjects such as resurrection and Jewish purity laws (5:27; 6:18–19; 7:1). Again, unlike 1 Maccabees, it is rather hostile to the Hasmoneans, except Judas, who by his good deeds is dignified as a religious hero.[36] In line with the tenor of 2 Maccabees, Judas piously distributed plunder to the disenfranchised.

Before the battle and as the underdog, Judas drew the Seleucid forces up into the mountains by fleeing the area of Ammaus to Mizpah, likely via the Beth Horon ascent,[37] where he led his forces in a prewar ceremony.[38] There Judas bolstered the morale of his forces by reminding them of "the times when help had been given their ancestors … and [they] took much booty" (καὶ ὠφέλειαν πολλὴν ἔλαβον, 2 Macc 8:19–20). It is expedient to review one of the accounts, here taken from 2 Macc 8:25–36, with an eye toward piety and plundering:

> They captured the *money of those who had come to buy them as slaves* [a type of booty]. After pursuing them for some distance, they were obliged to return because the hour was late. It was the day before the Sabbath, and *for that reason they did not continue their pursuit*. When they had collected the arms of the enemy and stripped them of their spoils, they *kept the Sabbath*…. *After the Sabbath they gave some of the spoils* [τῶν σκύλων] *to those who had been tortured and to the widows and orphans, and distributed the rest among themselves and their children*…. (In encounters with the forces of Timothy and Bacchides they killed more than twenty thousand of them and got possession of some exceedingly high strongholds, *and they divided a very large amount of plunder* [λάφυρα] *equally among themselves, and giving to those who had been tortured*

---

the Mizpah prewar ceremony: "They also brought the vestments of the priesthood and the firstfruits and the tithes, and they stirred up the nazirites who had completed their days" (3:49).

36. For important overarching historiographical differences based upon "diasporan historiography" in 1 and 2 Maccabees and Josephus, see Schwartz, *From the Maccabees to Masada*, 34–38. For more concrete contrasts between 1 and 2 Maccabees, see Nickelsburg, "1 and 2 Maccabees," 515–29; Harold W. Attridge, "Historiography: 2 Maccabees," in *Jewish Writings of the Second Temple Period: Apocrypha, Pseudepigrapha, Qumran Sectarian Writings, Philo, Josephus* (ed. M. E. Stone; CRINT 2.2. Assen: Van Gorcum; Philadelphia: Fortress, 1984), 171–83. The book of 2 Maccabees is also more cultic (Hanukkah agenda, Nicanor Day, holiness of Jerusalem, with criticism of the Oniad temple in Leontopolis), and its historiography is concerned with Jerusalem temple propaganda and an affirmation of the veracity of Dan 7–12. See Robert Doran, *Temple Propaganda: The Purpose and Character of 2 Maccabees* (CBQMS 12; Washington, D.C.: Catholic Biblical Association, 1981). Also noteworthy is that 2 Maccabees provides better Seleucid army data than 1 Maccabees (cf. 2 Macc 8:8–9; 14:12 with 1 Macc 3:38; 7:26).

37. For discussion and mapping of the historical geography of this passage, see Bar-Kochva, *Judas Maccabaeus*.

38. This prewar ceremony at Mizpah should not be seen as an anachronism but rather as "well anchored in the geographical background" and "with the *halacha* of the time and the particular circumstances" (ibid., 251).

and to the orphans and widows, and also to the aged. They collected the arms of the enemy, and carefully stored all of them in strategic places; the rest of *the spoils* [τῶν σκύλων] *they carried to Jerusalem....*) So [Nicanor], who had undertaken to secure tribute for the Romans by the capture of the people of Jerusalem, proclaimed that the Jews had a Defender and that therefore the Jews were invulnerable, *because they followed the laws ordained by him.*[39]

While Judas plundered, he did so piously. He uniquely plundered by halting his troops from plundering and dividing the plunder on the Sabbath, then subsequently including widows, orphans, children, and the aged in the distribution of war booty (2 Macc 8:27–30).

How did Judas's forces plunder? From 1 Macc 4:17–18 it is clear they sought to plunder early on and were encouraged to "seize plunder boldly" afterward. This would seemingly have been a kind of freebootery, since they were in the midst of battle.[40] In the Ammaus battle we do not have mention of specific organized groups to gather the booty systematically, as found in some ancient, biblical, and Hellenistic traditions.[41] We are, however, told that Judas's forces "captured the money of those who had come to buy them as slaves" (2 Macc 8:25), a detail that provides a counterpoint to these "traders of the region" described in 1 Macc 3:41.[42]

Further, 1 Macc 4:23 specifies that "they returned to plunder the camp" (ἐπὶ τὴν σκυλείαν τῆς παρεμβολῆς) and "seized a great amount of gold and silver, and cloth dyed blue and sea purple." They stripped the Seleucids of their "spoils" and arms but had to halt due to the Sabbath (2 Macc 8:26–27).[43] After pausing for the Sabbath, "they gave a share [μερίσαντες] of the spoils [τῶν σκύλων] to those who had been tortured [τοῖς ἠκισμένοις] and to the widows [ταῖς χήραις] and orphans [ὀρφανοῖς], and distributed [διεμερίσαντο] the rest among themselves and their

---

39. Adapted from the NRSV, emphasis added.
40. The military code of Philip V includes stipulations that limited seizure of booty and prohibited looting (Bar-Kochva, *Judas Maccabaeus*, 272).
41. On ancient Greek and Hellenistic sources, see Pritchett, *Greek State at War*, 5:363–400; Krasilnikoff, "Aegean Mercenaries," 27–28, where peltasts (light-armed troops) and archers (in contrast to hoplites) seemed to be employed for plundering. For biblical material, see, e.g., Exod 15:9 (cf. Philo, *Cher.* 74); Num 31; 1 Sam 30:22–25; and Elgavish, *Division of Spoils*, 252–54.
42. The logistics in the Hellenistic army camps was based on merchants and businessmen operating as "service contractors." The author, however, does not mention the other dealings of these merchants, because their very inclusion was intended to stress the maliciousness of the enemy and their evil intentions (Bar-Kochva, *Judas Maccabaeus*, 245–46). Thus, these "service contractors" had justice dealt to them, according to 2 Macc 8:25, a "measure for measure" irony that allowed the Maccabean spoils to increase.
43. See the noteworthy article concerning Sabbath issues in M. D. Goodman and A. J. Holladay, "Religious Scruples in Ancient Warfare," *CQ* NS 36 (1996): 151–71; van Wees, *Greek Warfare*, 118–29.

children" (2 Macc 8:28), an order that suggests the destitute received their portion first. This Ammaus distribution dovetails with the parenthetical paragraph in which they divided a very large amount of plunder (λάφυρα πλείονα), giving to those who had been tortured and to the orphans and widows, as well as to the aged, shares equal to their own (ἐμερίσαντο ἰσομοίρους αὐτοῖς).[44] The rest of the spoils (τῶν σκύλων) they carried to Jerusalem (2 Macc 8:30, 31). This section (8:30–33) is best understood as a summary of multiple battles, telescoped into three verses due to the similar narrative material of plunder and the destitute.

We have here some rather substantial material regarding plunder: a desire for freebootery, booty-traders, a kind of dedication (*dekate*) of spoils to Jerusalem (i.e., the temple),[45] and the noble warrior acting as a *hegemon*, himself likely determining who the recipients would be.[46] All this suggests a rather sizeable amount of booty that was collected both unofficially and officially.[47] As previously mentioned, 2 Macc 8:30–33 is best understood as a summary of previous battles, thus suggesting that Judas's distribution of plunder to the destitute may have been a common practice for him; within 2 Maccabean historiography, the Ammaus booty-distribution was not a one-time occurrence. Based upon Hellenistic warring practices and the 2 Maccabees description of Judas, we understand Judas functioning as a *hegemon* by distributing the plunder to whomever he desired prior to bringing the rest of the spoils to Jerusalem.

It could be argued that the tortured, widows, and orphans were thus categorized *after* the battle: those wounded in battle and those having a husband or father killed. This interpretation is possible, although the *additional* category of the "aged" (πρεσβυτέροις) in the section concerning the forces of Timothy and Bacchides (8:30) seems potentially problematic for this interpretation. Goldstein

---

44. Schwartz noted that these shares were equally divided between the two *groups* of warriors and destitutes; there may have been many more destitutes than warriors (*2 Maccabees*, 189). By employing ἰσομοίρους ("sharing alike, equally"), the author of 2 Macc 8:30's summary furthered Judas's empathetic distribution from 8:28's μερίσαντες and διεμερίσαντο.

45. Jerusalem was often understood as referring to the temple, following Daniel R. Schwartz, "Temple or City: What Did Hellenistic Jews See in Jerusalem?" in *The Centrality of Jerusalem: Historical Perspectives* (ed. M. Poorthuis and Ch. Safrai; Kampen: Kok Pharos, 1996), 114–27.

46. The *hegemon* was allowed certain flexibility in distributing the spoils and the proceeds from them prior to their return to their city or center. Pritchett reasoned that prior to the return of the war party: "the conclusion seems safe that the Greek *hegemon* in the field could dispose of the proceeds from the sale of booty in various ways, from awarding prizes to providing *misthos* [pay] for the soldiers; but whatever was brought back became the property of the state" (Pritchett, *Greek State at War*, 1:85).

47. Contra Yigael Yadin, *The Scroll of the War of the Sons of Light against the Sons of Darkness* (trans. B. and C. Rabin; Oxford: Oxford University Press, 1962), 154 n. 2. Yadin does not take into account the dedicated spoils given either to Jerusalem or to the destitute, which would have required some type of official spoils collection.

argued that the category of the πρεσβυτέροις was "probably the elderly recipients who were the parents of the slain martyrs and soldiers who had lost their sons who would have maintained them in the old age."[48] The description of the distribution to these disenfranchised likely is not so much about paying back the loss of life—although it is possible—as about providing for the destitute in the pietistic agenda of 2 Maccabees, using language reminiscent of Torah commands.[49] In fact the construction of 8:30b, ἔτι δὲ καὶ πρεσβυτέροις ποιήσαντες, as "and also did for (provided/esteemed) the aged/elders,"[50] may emphasize Judas's inclusive distribution. While the translation of ποιέω can vary widely, it should be accounted for, and the suggestions of "esteemed" and "provided" may not be far from the mark.

Heightened Piety in Identity-Construction and Hermeneutics

Ideals of piety feature more prominently in 2 Maccabees than in 1 Maccabees, so it is not surprising to find Judas's pious plundering in 2 Maccabees, in which he halted plundering due to the Sabbath and distributed spoils first to widows, orphans, and those tortured, then to the warriors. This parallels another difference between the two works: 1 Maccabees never mentions Judas's keeping of the Sabbath; in 2 Maccabees Judas is described as observing the Sabbath (8:27, 28; 12:38; cf. 15:1).

The Maccabean narratives of the Ammaus battle show themselves to have been written within the latter Second Temple period, at a time when Jewish sensitivity to piety increased, due to transitions in authority, peoples, and geography. The shifts from temple cult to additional and at times alternate forms of individual piety and spirituality are complex, having begun already by the second century

---

48. Goldstein, *2 Maccabees*, 338–39.

49. Some of this tradition is summarized here: according to Deut, God gives justice and provision for orphan, widow, and alien (10:18); widow, poor, alien feast on tithes every third year (14:28–29); Levite, widow, orphan, alien participate in Shavuot and Sukkot (16:10–15); portions of the grain were not fully harvested but were left for the alien, orphan, and widow (24:17–22); ones who act unjustly toward the alien, orphan, and widow are cursed (27:19,26; cf. Exod 23:3; Richard D. M. Patterson, "The Widow, the Orphan and the Poor in the Old Testament and the Extra-Biblical Literature," *BSac* 130 [1973]: 223–34). See also the important work of Moshe Weinfeld, *Social Justice in Ancient Israel and in the Ancient Near East* (Minneapolis: Fortress, 1995).

50. Lev 19:32 provides a possible antecedent for Judas's *paying honor* (τιμάω) via shares to the πρεσβυτέροις: ἀπὸ προσώπου πολιοῦ ἐξαναστήσῃ καὶ τιμήσεις πρόσωπον πρεσβυτέρου. While this biblical antecedent is only possible, its plausibility is strengthened by Daniel R. Schwartz's ("On Something Biblical about 2 Maccabees," in *Biblical Perspectives: Early Use and Interpretation of the Bible in Light of the Dead Sea Scrolls* [ed. M. E. Stone and E. Chazon; Leiden: Brill, 1998], 223–32) argument that 2 Maccabees was more biblically oriented than is typically noted.

B.C.E.[51] Such heightened individual piety was early-on emphasized by Adolph Büchler and later by David Flusser.[52] By placing the Maccabean narratives in this larger religious milieu of shifting religious trends, we can better propose the reasons this piety expressed itself through hermeneutics, a hermeneutic of piety, in two significant areas: (1) piety markers and provenance vis-à-vis Jewish sovereignty as part of identity formation; and (2) ideal figures as embedded models and values.

Piety markers increasingly shaped their construction of identity. Prior to the Babylonian exile in the biblical record, one was either an Israelite, a resident alien aligned with the Israelites, or a foreigner. But after religion (and people) could easily travel in the Hellenistic and Roman periods, conversion became possible and identity became tricky business.[53] In this volatile world of Jewish identity-formation, piety (both deed and exegetically oriented types) played an increasingly significant role. For some, piety trumped genealogy, while others saw it the other way around or as a complicated mix of religious matters.

Piety, as expressed in laws, customs, and other ideological and ethical concerns, increased during this period,[54] and this increased pietistic practice fits well with Schwartz's observations regarding land, people (descent), and law (practice or religious culture) as forming the determinative nexus for who was a true Jew.[55] Religion became increasingly democratized, with the authority of religious life transitioning from the priestly class to pious groups such as Hasidim, Pharisees, and sages, creating a certain "pietization" in the Jewish religion. The unique piety of war-booty distribution in 2 Maccabees is part of a larger trend of expressing identity through piety. Thus, pious practices served as markers that helped construct boundaries. The author[56] of 2 Maccabees seems to have highlighted Judas's piety partly to distinguish who was who. Those who embraced a similar height-

---

51. See Michael E. Stone, *Scriptures, Sects and Visions: A Profile of Judaism from Ezra to the Jewish Revolts* (Philadelphia: Fortress, 1980), 57–86, 107–17.

52. Adolf Büchler, *Types of Jewish-Palestinian Piety from 70 B.C.E. to 70 C.E.: The Ancient Pious Men* (Jew's College Publications 8; London: Jew's College, 1922; repr., New York: Ktav, 1968). David Flusser analyzed the religious aspects of such changes in expression and formulation of piety in "A New Sensitivity in Judaism and the Christian Message," *HTR* 61 (1968): 107–27.

53. Representative of the abundant literature on the topic is Shaye J. D. Cohen, *The Beginnings of Jewishness: Boundaries, Varieties, Uncertainties* (Berkeley and Los Angeles: University of California Press, 1999).

54. New traditions couched in ancestral ways and laws are seen in Albert I. Baumgarten, "Invented Traditions of the Maccabean Era," in *Geschichte-Tradition-Reflection: Festschrift für Martin Hengel zum 70. Geburtstag* (ed. P. Schäfer; 3 vols.; Tübingen: Mohr Siebeck, 1996), 1:197–210.

55. Daniel R. Schwartz, *Studies in the Jewish Background of Christianity* (WUNT 60; Tübingen: Mohr Siebeck, 1992), 5–14. Cf. Cohen, "From Ethnos to Ethno-Religion," 109–39.

56. Be it the editor, the epitomizer, or Jason of Cyrene.

ened or extended practice of the Torah were socio-religiously accepted by the community of 2 Maccabees.

Ideal figures such as Judas embedded models and values of the religious communities of early Judaism. Thus, a helpful way of analyzing a religious movement is to examine not only theology, ritual, or liturgy but also ideals: models to pattern one's life after.[57] Such an analysis of Judas leads us to view him as a pious *hasid* or an *ish ma'aseh*.[58] How does an ideal figure like Judas function? This subject has been elucidated broadly by J. Duyndam.[59] First, he found imitation to be a "creative process, including a kind of translation"[60] of the valuable aspects from another's life—the ideal—to one's own. Second, he found imitation to be ambivalent in that it could be an imitation of values that could be moral, nonmoral, or even immoral and that prudence in interpretation (decoding) of an example is necessary for imitation.[61] Third, he determined that imitation involves decoding to action: "imitation can be considered to be a practical form of hermeneutics. Whereas hermeneutics in the usual sense of the word refers to a theoretical or academic activity acquiring meanings out of texts, imitation is hermeneutics-by-doing."[62] Judas seems to function as this type of ideal figure within the Maccabean authorial community, and Josephus seems to preserve types of piety markers to self-distinguish the Jewish community in his piety-producing understanding of the law.

---

57. For an example of the application of this method to pre-Maccabean religious life, see Michael Stone, "Ideal Figures and Social Context: Priest and Sage in the Early Second Temple Age," in *Ancient Israelite Religion: Essays in Honor of Frank Moore Cross* (ed. P. D. Miller Jr., P. D. Hanson, and S. D. McBride; Philadelphia: Fortress, 1987), 575–86.

58. Here we follow in the tradition of G. G. Scholem's "Three Types of Jewish Piety," *Eranos Jahrbuch* 39 (1969): 331–48, repr. in *On the Possibility of Jewish Mysticism and Other Essays* (Philadelphia: Jewish Publication Society, 1997), 176–90; idem, *Ideal Figures in Ancient Judaism* (ed. J. J. Collins and G. W. E. Nickelsburg; SBLSCS 12; Chico, Calif.: Scholars Press, 1980). It is not part of my present goal to delineate rigid boundaries, as Sean Freyne attempted in "The Charismatic" (in Collins and Nickelsburg, *Ideal Figures in Ancient Judaism*, 223–54). I would think that Scholem's division of *hasid* and *ish ma'aseh* is not as far off as Freyne argued; cf. Shmuel Safrai, "Teaching of Pietists in Mishnaic Literature," *JJS* 16 (1965): 15–33; idem, "Hasidim and Men of Deeds" [Hebrew] *Zion* 50 (1985): 133–54; Chana and Zeev Safrai, "Rabbinic Holy Men," in *Saints and Role Models in Judaism and Christianity* (ed. M. Poorthuis and J. Schwartz; Jewish and Christian Perspectives Series 7; Leiden: Brill, 2004), 59–78. Judas seems to be more in line with the *hasid* than that *tsaddik*: following Scholem, differentiation between the latter two are found in the *tsaddik* as a forensic rational ideal of the norm, whereas the *hasid* is exceptional, extreme, radical, and charismatic in his piety.

59. J. Duyndam, "Hermeneutics of Imitation: A Philosophical Approach to Sainthood and Exemplariness," in Poorthuis and Schwartz, *Saints and Role Models*, 7–21.

60. Ibid., 10. And not just a simple "aping, copying, duplicating, mirroring, or counterfeiting" (11).

61. Ibid., 12.

62. Ibid., 15.

Plundering the Egyptians

The *locus classicus* for ancient Jewish exegetical discussion on the morality of plundering was Exod 12:35–36, in which the Israelites "plundered (וַיְנַצְּלוּ;[63] ἐσκύλευσαν) the Egyptians."[64] Various explanations were offered to justify the plundering, since according to Exodus the Israelites walked off with great riches.[65] Ezekiel the Tragedian's *Exagoge* explained, "But when you go I'll grant the people favor; one woman from another shall receive fine vessels, jewels of silver and of gold and clothing, things which one may carry off, so as to compensate them for their deeds."[66] Thus the Israelites were justified since they had been unjustly treated or had been employed without compensation and received moveable property as compensation. In a similar vein Jub. 48:18–19 also described these items as compensation: they requested and received "utensils and clothing from the Egyptians ... in return for the fact that they were made to work when they enslaved them by force."[67] More prolix was Philo, who in his *Life of Moses* justified the plundering carried out by righteous Israelites because they had endured a loss of liberty:

> [F]or they took out with them much spoil (πολλὴν λείαν), which they carried partly on their backs ... not in avarice, or, as their accusers might say, in covetousness of what belonged to others. No, indeed. In the first place, they were but receiving a bare wage for all their time of service; secondly, they were retaliating, not on an equal but on a lesser scale, for their enslavement. For what resemblance is there between forfeiture of money and deprivation of liberty, for which men of sense are wiling to sacrifice not only their substance but their life? In either case, their action was right, whether one regard it as an act of peace, the acceptance of payment long kept back through reluctance to pay what was due, or as an act of war, the claim under the law of the victors to take their enemies' goods.... The Hebrews, when the opportunity came, avenged themselves without warlike preparations, shielded by justice whose arm was extended to defend them. (Philo, *Moses* 1.140–142 [Colson, LCL])

Philo, Ezekiel the Tragedian, and Jubilees justified the Israelites plundering with compensatory language. Their defense of Israelite plundering suggests that they

---

63. נצל in this form also occurs at 2 Chr 20:25; surprisingly is not discussed in Elgavish's "Division of the Spoils of War."

64. See also Exod 3:22; 11:2–3; 12:35–36.

65. See James L. Kugel, *Traditions of the Bible: A Guide to the Bible as It Was at the Start of the Common Era* (Cambridge Harvard University Press, 1999), 553–57. Kugel pointed out another ancient witness to plundering as compensation in Wis 10:16–17, 20.

66. R. G. Robertson, "Ezekiel the Tragedian," *OTP* 2:815. Robertson noted the ambiguity of the phrase "their deeds," which could refer either to the Egyptians' evil or the Israelites' labor.

67. James C. VanderKam, *The Book of Jubilees* (CSCO; Leuven: Peeters, 1989), 314–15.

felt a need to explain the morality of their ancestors' plundering, which was reported in their scriptures.[68] Additional witnesses to this *locus classicus* appear in later rabbinic literature in a humorous manner,[69] as well as in the non-Jewish Augustan historian Pompeius Trogus's *Historiae Philippicae*, which reports that Moses "carried off by stealth the sacred utensils of the Egyptians."[70]

"Do Not Plunder" in the Law

By looking at Josephus, Mark, and Philo's exegetical comments on plunder and defrauding, we will see a hermeneutic that delegitimized plundering as expressed in apologetic and exegesis.[71] Josephus "presents it as a matter of his virtue as a [military] general that he does not normally permit his soldiers to plunder";[72] he also reports: "[Our legislator] forbids the spoiling [σκυλεύειν] even of fallen combatants."[73] Thackeray comments on Josephus's rhetoric in unequivocal terms: "Not in the Law."[74] Schiffman flatly states, "Josephus claims that despoiling the slain was forbidden by the Torah, although no such prohibition can be found."[75]

---

68. Even recently this thorny issue has resurfaced: a recent Egyptian lawsuit against Israel sought to recoup the exodus plunder. Dr. Nabil Hilmi, Dean of the Faculty of Law and the University of Al-Zaqaziq, with a group of Egyptian expatriates now in Switzerland, were preparing such a lawsuit. See the 9 August 2003 edition of the Egyptian weekly *Al-Ahram Al-Arabi* and Judah Gribetz, "Swiss Holocaust Payments in Doubt," *Jerusalem Post*, 9 October 2003, p. 4.

69. See Gen. Rab. 61:7 and the longer version in b. Sanh. 61a: "On another occasion the Egyptians came in a lawsuit against the Jews before Alexander of Macedon." They quoted the Torah (Exod 12:36) as their case to ask for the return of the gold and silver. The Israelites used Exod 12:40 as a reply, stating that 430 years of wages for 600,000 would be worth more than what their ancestors had carried off. The Egyptians could not find an answer (H. Freedman, trans., *The Babylonian Talmud, Seder Nezikin III* [London: Soncino, 1937], 609–10). See a similar tradition found in *Megillat Ta'anit* (MS Oxford), as pointed out and translated by Kugel, *Traditions of the Bible*, 556; Verad Noam, *Megillat Ta'anit: Versions, Interpretation, History* [Hebrew] (Jerusalem: Yad Ben-Zvi, 2003).

70. Marcus Junianus Justinus, *Historiae Philippicae: Epitome of the Philippic History of Pompeius Trogus/Justin* (trans. J. C. Yardley; introduction and explanatory notes by R. Develin; Atlanta: Scholars Press, 1994).

71. I wish to thank Randall Buth, who was a helpful critic for some of the material in this section.

72. Steve Mason, ed., *Flavius Josephus: Translation and Commentary* (9 vols.; Leiden: Brill, 1999–2004), 9:135, §333 n. 1362. For the references in the *Life*, see §§67–8, 80–81, 126–129, 244.

73. Josephus, *Ag. Ap.* 1.379 (Thackeray, LCL).

74. Ibid.

75. L. H. Schiffman, "The Laws of War in the Temple Scroll," *RQ* 16 (1988): 305.

Josephus states in his autobiography, "ἀποστερεῖν [robbing/spoiling] even an enemy is forbidden by our law."⁷⁶ But where is it stated in the Tanak that robbing an enemy is forbidden? In the Greek version of the Tanak, the term ἀποστερεῖν is found only in Exod 21:10 (concerning conjugal rights) and Mal 3:5 (depriving wages).⁷⁷ Various solutions have been offered to harmonize the seeming discrepancy between the Bible and Josephus's statements. Whiston read Josephus's comment as reflecting Josephus's supposed conversion to Christianity as an Ebionite.⁷⁸ More soberly, both Thackeray and Mason suggest Exod 23:4 as the basis for Josephus's statement: "ἀποστερεῖν an enemy is proscribed in our laws."⁷⁹ Exodus 23:4 reads, "If you meet your enemy's ox or his donkey wandering away, you shall surely return it to him." But is this what Josephus meant by "robbing enemies"? In 23:4 the person is required to *return* an enemy's donkey gone *astray*, a command that seems more related to a time of relative peace, as these are animals of agricultural import that have likely wandered away.

It is interesting that Mark used the same word (ἀποστερεῖν) in Jesus' summary of the Decalogue when he was being questioned about what is required for eternal life: "You know the commandments: 'You shall not murder; You shall not commit adultery; You shall not steal; You shall not bear false witness; You shall not defraud [μὴ ἀποστερήσῃς]; Honor your father and mother'" (Mark 10:19 NRSV).⁸⁰ It is noteworthy that Josephus and Mark 10:19 use ἀποστερεῖν similarly

---

76. Josephus, *Life* §128 (Thackeray, LCL): ἀπηγόρευται δ' ἡμῖν ὑπὸ τῶν νόμων μηδὲ τοὺς ἐχθροὺς ἀποστερεῖν. Winston in his translation understood ἀποστερεῖν here as spoiling. This comment was given in the context of an incident involving a raid upon an entourage of the wife of Ptolemy, the procurator of Agrippa II.

77. The word ἀποστερέω occurs in the LXX at Exod 21:10 (conjugal rights); 4 Macc 8:23 (depriving of pleasures); Sir 4:1 (robbing/cheating the poor); 29:6. 7 (borrowing and not repaying); 34:21, 22 (depriving the needy); Mal 3:5 (withholding wages); in the New Testament, in 1 Cor 6:7 (willingness to be defrauded); 7:5 (conjugal rights); 1 Tim 6:5 (bereft of truth); Jas 5:4 (withholding wages).

78. Whiston notes, "I take it that Josephus, having been now for many years an Ebionite Christian, had learned this interpretation of the law of Moses from Christ, whom he owned for the true Messiah" (W. Whiston, *The Works of Josephus: Complete and Unabridged* [Peabody, Mass.: Hendrickson, 1987], 9 n. k). See also Mason, *Flavius Josephus*, 9:135 n. 1362.

79. Mason, *Flavius Josephus*. 9:80 n. 622; Thackeray, *Life*, 51 n. a.

80. Unconvincing is the suggestion by A. H. McNeile (*The Gospel according to St. Matthew* [London: Macmillan, 1915; repr., Grand Rapids: Baker, 1978], 278) and others that Mark's ἀποστερήσῃς may be a scribal addition, since it does not agree with either the MT or the LXX. Still difficult, another text-critical direction is to note the manuscript tradition of A and F of the LXX on Deut 24:14, which contains αποστερησεις in place of απαδικησεις. This variant may explain Mark's reference, although it still proves unsuccessful for Josephus's statements, since Josephus's context is plundering in war or in a raid rather than wages for the poor and needy. Bruce M. Metzger proposes, "Since the command, 'Do not defraud' (a reminiscence of Ex 20.17 or Dt 24.14 [Septuagint MSS A F] or Sir 4.1), may have seemed to be inappropriate in a list of several of the Ten Commandments, many copyists ... omitted it" (*A Textual Commentary on*

as being forbidden in the commandments. Concerning Mark 10:19, Morna D. Hooker comments, "do not defraud has somewhat surprisingly replaced 'do not covet'. No satisfactory explanation of this has ever been given."[81]

Could Josephus and Mark witness to an early tradition that understood the enigmatic tenth commandment, "do not covet," expansively to include the actions that could follow covetous thoughts, such as plundering?[82] Mark's context seems to be the Decalogue. Already within the MT there is a reworking of the Decalogue: in Exod 20:17, the phrase לא תחמד (LXX οὐκ ἐπιθυμήσεις) appears twice, whereas in Deut 5:21 the second phrase in the MT has hw)tt)lw. Alexander Rofé argues for the resultant nature of dmx: desire manifesting itself through actual plans or efforts to seize or take another's property,[83] whereas אוה might well relate to an internal state.[84] If this is the case, ἀποστερεῖν may reflect a pietistic-

---

the Greek New Testament [3rd ed.; London: United Bible Societies, 1971], 105). Vincent Taylor suggests that μὴ ἀποστερήσῃς may be a negative form of the eighth commandment, οὐ κλέψεις (*The Gospel according to St. Mark* [2nd ed.; London: Macmillan, 1966], 428. See also Henry B. Swete, *The Gospel according to St. Mark* (3rd ed.; London: Macmillan, 1913), 224; Robert H. Gundry, *Mark: A Commentary on His Apology for the Cross* (Grand Rapids: Eerdmans, 1993), 553.

81. Morna D. Hooker, *A Commentary on the Gospel according to St. Mark* (BNTC 2; London: Black, 1990), 241. This point is echoed by Francis J. Moloney, *The Gospel of Mark: A Commentary* (Peabody, Mass.: Hendrickson, 2002), 199. Hooker continues, "we expect Jesus to substitute the inner cause for the consequential action, not vice versa."

82. This argument is held by many without turning to a specific Torah text for support. R. T. France (*The Gospel of Mark: A Commentary on the Greek Text* [NIGTC; Grand Rapids: Eerdmans, 2002], 402), states, as do others, that the move from κλέπτω to ἀποστερέω is "better seen simply as an attempt to draw out in more behavioral terms the implications of the tenth commandment: appropriating someone else's possession is likely to be a practical result of coveting." Hooker (*Commentary on the Gospel*, 241) mentions Mal 3:5's use of ἀποστερεῖν in a Decalogue context, but Mal 3 does not provide as many echoes of the Decalogue as Lev 19, a broader possible basis for Josephus and Mark. See below.

83. Alexander Rofé, "The Tenth Commandment in the Light of Four Deuteronomic Laws," in *The Ten Commandments in History and Tradition* (ed. B.-Z. Segal and G. Levi; Jerusalem: Magnes, 1990), 45–65.

84. Translations following the MT carefully differentiate between חמד and אוה, observing that אוה is a state of mind, whereas חמד relates to visual attraction (W. L. Moran, "The Conclusion of the Decalogue [Ex 20,17 = Dt 5,21]," *CBQ* 29 [1967]: 548 n. 18; cf. Rofé, *Tenth Commandment*, 54 n. 31; B. Jacob, "The Decalogue," *JQR* NS 14 [1923–24]: 141–87. The two words in the MT of Deuteronomy are thought to signify either (1) a parallel that further interprets and highlights both verbs as connoting primarily internal aspects; or (2) a descending gradation as exemplified in a paraphrase of the passage, "You shall not covet your neighbor's wife, and you shall not *even* crave (think after longingly)" the property of your neighbor. The first position is held by Etan Levine, who argues that "the exclusive meaning of the Heb root *hmd* is 'to desire,' or 'to take pleasure in.'… It is undeniable and understandable that in some ancient texts of the Near East coveting may often precede an actual appropriation" ("You Shall Not Covet," in *Heaven and Earth, Law and Love: Studies in Biblical Thought* [BZAW 303; Berlin:

hermeneutical shift to extend the commands "do not steal" and "do not covet" to explicitly include "do not plunder." Such a hermeneutical shift may be reflected not only in Josephus but also in Mark, as well as more loosely in Philo, *The Sentences of Pseudo-Phocylides*,[85] and other Hellenistic Jewish literature.[86]

Yet another avenue of clarification comes from within the LXX's use of ἀποστερεῖν and its MT corollary. LXX Mal 3:5 uses ἀποστερεῖν, which is rendered in the MT as עשק. If these words could be in parallel between the MT and the LXX, then we might look for usages of עשק in Torah legislation against extorting or defrauding. Such an association between עשק and defrauding is suggested in the reworked Decalogue section of Lev 19:13,[87] which reads: "You shall not defraud your neighbor. You shall not steal" (NRSV; לא־תעשק את־רעך ולא תגזל; οὐκ ἀδικήσεις τὸν πλησίον καὶ οὐχ ἁρπάσεις).[88] The usage here of עשק and תגזל linked with wronging or defrauding and snatching up in the context of a reworked Decalogue material is noteworthy,[89] since Deut 5 and Lev 19 are pas-

---

de Gruyter, 2000], 155). Moran ("Conclusion of the Decalogue") argues for the similar meaning of the two verbs (i.e., desire) but concentrates on the version of the Decalogue in Exodus.

85. Verses 3–8 of *The Sentences of Pseudo-Phocylides* are a summarizing paraphrase of the Decalogue. Verses 5–6 condemn greed: "Do not become unjustly rich, but live from honourable means. Be content with what you have and abstain from what is another's." These correspond to the commandments of "you shall not steal" and "you shall not covet" (Exod 20:15, 17; Deut 5:19, 21). Most of the precepts in vv. 9–41 allude to Lev 19, which itself is a reworking of Decalogue traditions (Pieter W. van der Horst, *The Sentences of Pseudo-Phocylides* [SVTP 4; Leiden, Brill: 1978], 110–17; idem, "Pseudo-Phocylides: A New Translation and Introduction," OTP 2:565–82). Verses 9–10, for example, find parallels in Lev 19:15 (cf. Exod 23:1–3; Deut 1:17; 16:18–20; Prov 24:23). The linking together of the Decalogue with the commandments in Leviticus can also be found in Philo, *Hypoth.* 7.1–9; Josephus, *C. Ap.* 2.190–219. See P. W. van der Horst, "Pseudo-Phocylides and the New Testament," ZNW 69 (1978): 187–202, esp. 191.

86. See A. Cronbach ("Social Ideals of the Apocrypha and the Pseudepigrapha," HUCA 18 [1944]: 119–56), mentioning T. Ash 2:6 and Sir 4:1 with Box and Oesterley's reading of תג־עש for תלעג. T. Ash 2:5–6 describes the evil double-face person: "Another steals, acts unjustly, plunders [ἁρπάζει], defrauds [πλεονεκτεῖ], and he pities the poor. This too has two faces, but the whole is evil. Defrauding [πλεονεκτῶν] his neighbor he provokes God and swears falsely by the Most High.... this too has two faces, but the whole is evil."

87. See also the MSS A and F of Deut 24:14, as noted above. Jacob Milgrom states, "It stands to reason that the author of Lev 19 knew the Decalogue and made use of it." He also affirms that "most of the Torah's essential laws can be derived from it [Sipra Qedoshim 1:1, on 19:1]" (*Leviticus 17–22* [AB 3A; New York: Doubleday, 2000], 1601–2). See also Lev. Rab. 24:5. Horst similarly states, "Leviticus 19 was probably considered by the Jews in antiquity as a kind of summary of the Torah" ("Pseudo-Phocylides and the New Testament," 191).

88. The words ἀδικήσεις and ἁρπάσεις complement each other, thus providing a meaning similar to תעשק and תגזל.

89. See Lev 5:21 and 23. The general connotation of עשק is "oppress, extort" (Milgrom, *Leviticus 17–22*, 1601). Its usage in Lev 19:13 is more generalizing than in Lev 5:21 and 23; see also Jacob Milgrom, *Cult and Conscience: The 'Asham' and the Priestly Doctrine of Repentance* (SJLA 18; Leiden: Brill, 1976), 101 n. 376.

sages of reworked Decalogue material that may be the most likely antecedent for Josephus and Mark.

A further support for the Decalogue as part of the inspiration for this understanding is Philo's comments in *Decalogue* §135–136:

> The third commandment in the second five forbids stealing [μη κλπέτειν], for he who gapes after what belongs to others is the common enemy of the State, willing to rob all.... his covetousness [πλεονεξίαν] extends indefinitely.... So all thieves who have acquired the strength rob [προσέλαβον; Winston: "plunder"] whole cities, careless of the punishment because their high distinction seems to set them above the laws [τῶν νόμων]. (Philo, *Decalogue* 72–75, Colson, LCL)

While plundering was not apparently considered to be prohibited by the Mosaic law before the Second Temple period, by the late Second Temple period it seems that Josephus and Mark's Jesus understood such a prohibition to be within the law and even the Decalogue. Philo and texts such as *The Sentences of Pseudo-Phocylides* may also place an expanded understanding of "do not plunder" or "do not defraud" back into the law or Decalogue itself. In the context of referencing God's commands or amplifying the Decalogue, certain segments of early Judaism seem to have understood that not only are stealing (גנב; κλέφεις) and coveting (חמד; ἐπιθυμέω) prohibited, but also plundering or defrauding (ἀποστερεῖν) and despoiling (σκυλεύειν).[90] Through a pietistic hermeneutic, the Decalogue was understood expansively[91] in part through engaging Lev 19's own reworked Decalogue. That is, ἀποστερεῖν functions as a hermeneutical extension of the Decalogue via Lev 19 (and Deut 24:14) and may be best understood as one more witness to a broader movement within early Judaism that expanded application of the Torah, either for intrinsic or rhetorical purposes.

Conclusion

It seems that in the late Second Temple period exegetes and narrators alike were envisioning ideal patterns of conduct, which often entered into their writing through exemplary figures,[92] as well as through pious interpretations of scripture. These forces helped form a dialectic of piety.[93] A practice of writing piety into

---

90. This expansion may have been a reaction to earlier Greek understandings of "the right to plunder" even to the point of legitimizing piracy.

91. E. P. Gould ironically provides support for this "expansion of the Torah fence," even though he criticizes the law (*The Gospel according to St. Mark* [ICC; Edinburgh: T&T Clark, 1896], 191).

92. Here, Judas. See Stone, "Ideal Figures and Social Context," 575–86.

93. Dialectic in that pious interpretive traditions acted back upon the community to encourage greater piety in deeds. This dialectic of piety may have been spawned in part by a

and reading piety out of ancient texts was initiated within the scriptural tradition but accelerated in the late Second Temple period,⁹⁴ as can be seen with the examples discussed above such as in 2 Maccabees, Josephus, Philo, and Mark. Genesis 14 with Abraham's magnanimous distribution of booty, 2 Chr 28 with its return of plunder to the kingdom of Judah, and Esth 9 with its differentiated plundering provided general examples of piety vis-à-vis plundering. Judas had no prior example of a warrior distributing plunder to such destitutes. Beyond this, no other extant Hellenistic, Jewish, or Roman literature included such destitutes in booty-distribution.⁹⁵ Josephus's assessment that plundering was unlawful was not so much based upon the ideal figures of the Bible (e.g., Abraham, Moses, and David) but was an outgrowth of a heightened hermeneutic of piety that questioned the ethics of plundering as assumed within the ancient world. Similarly, Mark's inclusion of "no defrauding" by Jesus suggests that Late Second Temple Judaism inherited a piety based more on ancient Near Eastern charity than Greek well-doing.⁹⁶

In light of the ethical hermeneutical shift toward interpreting plunder as unlawful by the late Second Temple period, it may be that Judas was already seeking ways in which "unlawful" plunder could be "pietized."⁹⁷ But such motivations are too tricky to accurately determine. In any case, it seems that a trend of questioning the legitimacy of unlimited plundering of enemies was beginning, perhaps because of broad Hellenistic approval and practice. It would seem also that the Hellenistic culture,⁹⁸ which held the uncontested right to plunder and conquer, lost out to the Maccabean narratives' mores of regard for the weak and altruistic giving to those who could not return the favor.

An ideological shift seems evident in the communities writing and reading in the Second Temple period. Esther, 2 Chr 28, 2 Maccabees, and Josephus evidence

---

sociological need for group identification, which was especially volatile in the Hasmonean and early Roman periods.

94. This trend continued. David Levine writes, "in the development of Talmudic religion, temple and cult recede while individual piety comes to the fore.... the focal point of religious experience resides in the person, not in the institution" ("Holy Men and Rabbis in Talmudic Antiquity," in Poorthuis and Schwartz, *Saints and Role Models*, 48).

95. Many sources have been checked to justify this statement, although the author invites any similar material if found (kvasnica@js.org).

96. See n. 28 and discussion above.

97. One should be increasingly aware of the influence Diaspora or diasporan-type attitudes may have had on the historiography of our authors; 2 Chronicles, Esther, 2 Maccabees, and Josephus's *Antiquities* (as slightly opposed to the *War*) seem to demonstrate some diasporan attitudes. See Schwartz, *From the Maccabees to Masada*, 32–34.

98. See Elias J. Bickerman, "The Historical Foundations of Postbiblical Judaism," in *The Jews: Their History, Culture, and Religion* (ed. L. Finkelstein; New York: Schocken, 1972), 72–118, repr. in *Emerging Judaism: Studies on the Fourth and Third Centuries B.C.E.* (ed. M. E. Stone and D. Satran; Minneapolis: Augsburg Fortress, 1989), 9–48.

a new sensitivity toward ideal patterns of conduct[99] and the desire that even war practices be subject to God's law. The Ammaus battle and Judas's distribution confirm the important historiographical place piety had among the values of the author of 2 Maccabees and his community. If "armies are a reflection of cultures," as Robert Kaplan recently said,[100] then the Maccabean culture as presented in the Maccabean narratives was indeed a culture of heightened piety. Judas's pious distribution confirms the historiographical place piety had within the values of the author of 2 Maccabees and the rise of such hermeneutical piety in the late Second Temple period. During the later Second Temple period, shifts in ideology of Israelite warfare allowed Israel to be interpreted more piously, which in turn encouraged its constituents to act accordingly.

Late Second Temple exegetes and historians, it seems, went beyond the "pietistic plundering" of Judas and expanded their understanding of the Israelite law to include a prohibition against plundering altogether. This expansion may have generated new views on biblical instances of plundering, specifically the plundering of the Egyptians by the Israelites. Those who expressed such views were essentially calling all Jews to a life of more careful adherence to the Israelite Law. More specifically, the prohibition against plundering seems to stem from an amplified understanding of the Decalogue, the application of which had expanded to enemies as well as neighbors, to situations of war as well as peace.

---

99. See Baumgarten, "Invented Traditions of the Maccabean Era," 197–210; Stone, "Ideal Figures and Social Context," 575–86.

100. Robert Kaplan, as interviewed on C-SPAN, 4 October 2005.

Gideon at Thermopylae? On the Militarization of Miracle in Biblical Narrative and "Battle Maps"

Daniel L. Smith-Christopher

On the back cover of a book published in 2002 by Zonderkidz, an imprint of Zondervan Press, we read the following question: "What excites boys more than action, adventure, and cool weapons? In *Bible Wars and Weapons*, boys age 8 to 12 can read all about the action and adventure of battle in Bible Times."[1] You might have missed this monograph, but perhaps you may recall that it appears in the same series as another Zonderkidz title, *Weird and Gross Bible Stuff*. In *Bible Wars and Weapons*, each "Bible Battle" is highlighted in a separate chapter and is accompanied by "Battle Maps" and hand-drawn illustrations of specific battle tactics. Gideon's "Midnight Raid" is also illustrated with maps and drawings (see fig. 1).[2]

In this essay I wish to explore an interesting tendency in the history of interpretation of biblical battles (both popular and academic), especially those that feature clearly miraculous elements in their textual descriptions. The tendency, quite simply, is to reinterpret the miraculous elements in these narratives as solid military strategy and thus praise the military wisdom of the biblical heroes who are presented as quite rational strategists. This tendency is not limited to more conservative interpreters of battle narratives in Joshua and Judges and is thus a clear case of military and strategic presuppositions coloring the interpretation of the Bible. A particularly interesting example of this approach to biblical battle narratives is the construction of battle maps claiming to show actual troop movements with arrows, in different colors to indicate different sides in the conflict. That such maps are standard fare in many Bible atlases points to a further example of subtle, and not so subtle, interpretive strategies of biblical narratives in favor of a militarization and rationalization of biblical literature—especially war narratives that may well be interpreted in entirely different ways that have very little to do with actual military practice. However, the militarization of these nar-

---

1. Rick Osborne, Marnie Wooding, and Ed Strauss, *Bible Wars and Weapons* (Grand Rapids: Zonderkidz, 2002).
2. Ibid., 56.

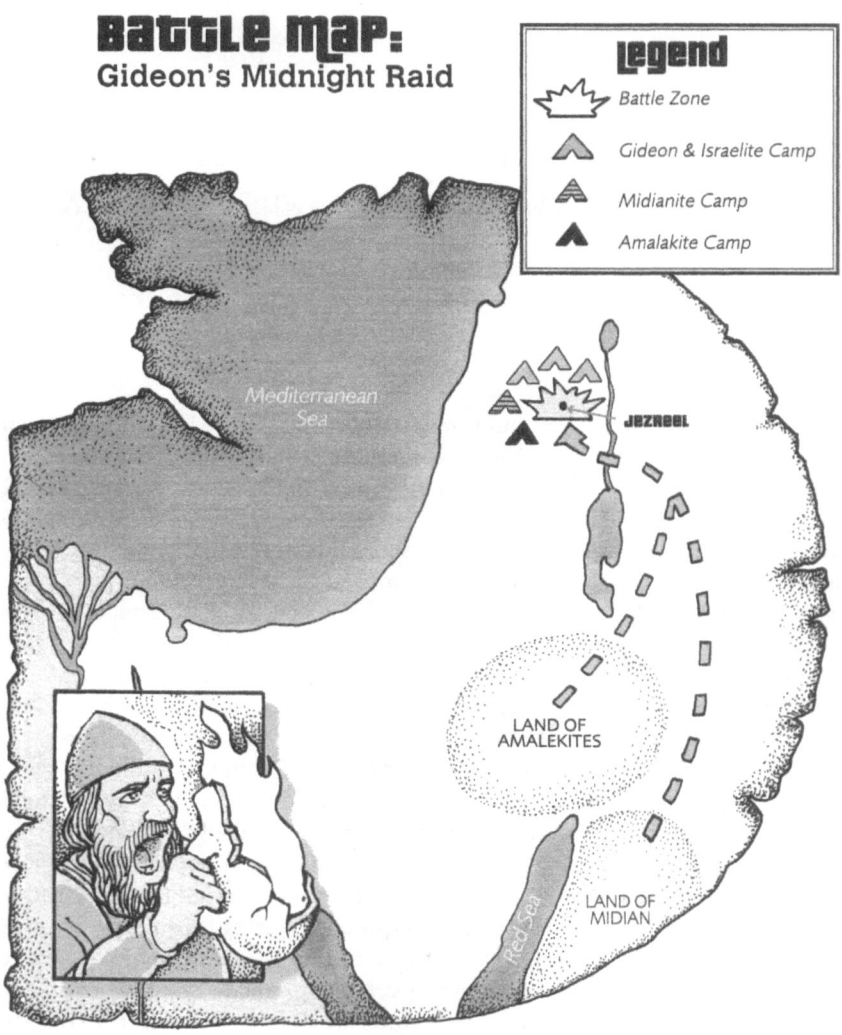

Figure 1. Although this illustration appears, obviously, in a children's work, the genre of "troop movement" Bible maps is common to even many of the most serious academic-based atlas projects for the ancient Near East. Map from Rick Osborne, Marnie Wooding, and Ed Strauss, *Bible Wars and Weapons* (Grand Rapids: Zonderkidz, 2002), 56. Used by permission.

ratives often obscures the ability to interpret this literature in other ways—such as the ritual aspects of the Jericho narrative or the religious polemics of the Gideon narratives in Judges.

I began with a children's book. It comes as no surprise that a children's book from an influential conservative press treats all battles of the Bible as literal historical events—including the battle of Jericho in the book of Joshua and Gideon's battle with the Midianites in Judg 7–8. What is interesting, however, is one particular aspect of a literal reading: not only are these battles treated as literal historical events, but tactical and strategic moves are presented as rational and logical forms of military practice. The biblical text's clear emphasis that human beings had minimal involvement and its message that victory in battle was to be attributed to God's miracle play a strangely muted roll in these descriptions, which seek, rather, to emphasize tactics, warfare, and strategic preparations for warfare. Strategy becomes the rational category of "history." I would like to argue further, however, that this approach is just as clear in graphic representations of these passages in the nearly ubiquitous battle maps featured in many Bible atlases, purporting to demonstrate the military "strategies" of biblical narratives using troop-movement arrows overlaid on maps. Both types of interpretation, narrative and graphic, represent examples of militarizing the academic biblical narrative as a means of doing historical-critical analysis.

It is not surprising that more serious materials intended for pastors and laity also reflect this "strategic" interpretation of biblical battle narratives. Donald Madvig, in the *Expositor's Bible Commentary*, repeats an observation that was a staple of more critical commentary literature earlier in the twentieth century, namely, that the circling of the city of Jericho was a tactic that would have successfully confused the defenders of the city.[3] Why God's miracle requires the enemy also to be confused is not addressed. Similarly, in his commentary on Judges in the same volume, Herbert Wolf repeats an equally common interpretation of Gideon's battle with the Midianites by suggesting that Gideon actually reduced his army to an "elite corps" by focusing on the three hundred and reading their strategies like a "Biblical Thermopylae." Wolf argues that the three hundred who were selected must have stayed on their feet and lapped water with their hands, suggesting that using cupped hands while staying alert is the meaning of drinking water "with their tongues like a dog."[4] In each case, the question why any tactical or strategic considerations have any role to play in what is described as a miraculous defeat at the hand of God virtually alone does not enter into their analysis. Yet the central theme of this passage is surely to be sought in God's phrase: "Israel would only take the credit away from me, saying, 'My own hand has delivered me'" (Judg 7:2). In modern readings, however, miracle is being "militarized" in favor of a rationalized reading of military strategy.

---

3. Donald Madvig, "Joshua," in *Deuteronomy, Joshua, Judges, Ruth, 1 and 2 Samuel* (vol. 3 of *The Expositor's Bible Commentary*; ed. F. E. Gaebelein; Grand Rapids: Zondervan, 1992), 278.

4. Herbert Wolf, "Judges," in Gaebelein, *Deuteronomy, Joshua, Judges, Ruth, 1 and 2 Samuel*, 425.

Turning to earlier critical studies of Joshua and Judges, we find that similar interests in the presumed "strategic" aspects of these stories also tended to focus on military details, and, thus, detailed discussions tried to elicit the tactical information that can be gleaned from stories of early biblical battles. Of course, we are used to claims about the presumed tactical wisdom of circling cities to confuse the enemy—although, to be honest, the strategic value of marching in front of archers every day in broad daylight ("early in the morning") always struck me as a particularly confusing "tactic." To refer to another children's rendition of a Bible tradition, I would only note that the strategic absurdity of this "tactic" is wonderfully captured in the "Veggie Tales" animated version, where the soldiers of Jericho are portrayed as exclaiming that circling in front of their archers is "a wonderful idea!" This children's cartoon arguably reflects much more effectively the textual point than does the *Expositor's Bible Commentary*, namely, the message that military power is not the central concern when God is "on your side." This rationalizing, or militarizing, tendency becomes particularly interesting in the case of a definite theme in the interpretation of Judg 7.

C. F. Burney's 1903 commentary on Judges, for example, contained quite an extended discussion of the details of Gideon's reduction of his thirty-two thousand soldiers to three hundred by going into interesting detail about the test of drinking water. He made note of the various debates about the postures of drinking that are presumed to be described in this famous passage. What is particularly interesting about Burney's summary in this venerable old commentary is that the critical discussions about the original Hebrew form of the passage, especially 7:5– 6, were clearly driven by attempts to derive rational, strategically sound, military tactics from the narrative. For example, the phrase "putting hand to mouth" (7:6) is an apparent further description of the three hundred who are described in the previous verse as "lapping as a dog."[5] (Note that the editors of the NRSV, for example, have determined to move the phrase about "putting hand to mouth" to describe the second, larger group who knelt down, and they noted their proposed change in a footnote.) I am by no means a hardened advocate of leaving the phrase where it appears in the Hebrew texts, but at least part of the reasoning behind moving the phrase seems to be motivated by the notion that kneeling would require bringing water up to drink, while lapping "as a dog" would mean having one's face quite close to the water. What is important to note is how the rationalized strategic military considerations certainly entered into the textual and critical discussion. It is presumed that the more alert would be kneeling, and the crude peasants would be floundering on their stomachs, drinking with their face to the water "like a dog." But if one wants to argue that the three hundred were the more alert, then the "hand to mouth" phrase is interpreted to mean that

---

5. C. F. Burney, *The Book of Judges: Introduction and Notes* (ICC; Edinburgh: T&T Clark, 1918; repr., Eugene, Ore.: Wipf & Stock, 2004).

the three hundred were, in fact, the more militarily prepared, and thus Gideon was engaging in a very clever, indeed sophisticated, militarily sensible technique for determining the bravest and most alert. In short, Gideon was preparing his three hundred "Spartans" for a Thermopylae-like stand against the Midianites.

There was a strong tradition, in the later decades of the twentieth century, particularly for Israeli scholars, academics, and military theorists, to continue this interest in the battle tactics of the Bible, including the narratives of Jericho and Gideon. For example, the famous Israeli military officer and archaeologist Yigael Yadin writes with frankly amusing understatement when he describes the biblical story of Jericho, which in his view "describes another kind of stratagem whose military implications, however, have been obscure."[6] This has not prevented others from trying to make the tactical rationality of such stories clearer. Trent Butler's 1983 commentary on Joshua is a case in point. Butler wants to discern a root tradition, a basic historical report, of an actual battle and approvingly cites Yadin for helpful tactical information in the process.[7]

One of the most notable scholarly attempts to articulate military tactics was Abraham Malamat's famous series of articles, one of which appeared in the *Encyclopedia Judaica Yearbook* of 1975–76.[8] Malamat quite explicitly wants to claim that rational military tactics can be read behind the admittedly theological "overlay" that now appears in the history of the conquest narratives particularly: "Whereas in the relatively raw, early depictions of the Israelite wars the mortal and the divine are intertwined, the later redactors (the so-called Deuteronomist) have accentuated and brought to the fore the role of the Lord of Israel, submerging human feats."[9] Throughout this work Malamat explains early Israelite use of intelligence gathering, logistics, direct and indirect military approaches, and tactics of conquering fortified cities such as neutralization of city defenses, enticement of city defenders, and night operations. Of the last, Malamat writes, "Bolder still and more exacting in planning and execution were actual night attacks. The classical example—throughout military history—is Gideon's assault upon the Midianites.... Despite the theological tendentiousness and several enigmas in the texts, analysis of the story reveals characteristics and maxims of night warfare still valid today."[10] Note Malamat's somewhat startling dismissal of whole sections of the text, motivated entirely by his methodology of seeking literal, rational, mili-

---

6. Yigael Yadin, *The Art of Warfare in Biblical Lands in the Light of Archaeological Discovery* (trans. M. Pearlman; London: Weidenfeld & Nicolson, 1963), 99.

7. Trent Butler, *The Book of Joshua* (WBC 7; Nashville: Nelson, 1983), 67–68.

8. Abraham Malamat, "Israelite Conduct of War in the Conquest of Canaan," in *Symposia Celebrating the Seventy-Fifth Anniversary of the Founding of the American Schools of Oriental Research (1900–1975)* (ed. F. M. Cross; Cambridge: American Schools of Oriental Research, 1979), 35–56.

9. Ibid., 36.

10. Ibid., 54.

tary strategy. He concludes his survey by stating, "By preserving a clear view of the objective and applying means unanticipated by the enemy, a bold and imaginative Israelite leadership was successful in translating what we today would call a specific military doctrine into spontaneous victory. An overriding factor was the Israelite soldier's basic motivation—his deep sense of national purpose."[11]

In their 1978 book, *Battles of the Bible*, Chaim Herzog (at one time Director of Military Intelligence for Israel) and Mordechai Gichon, an Israeli military historian, further attempt to derive rational military "strategies":

> By a spark of inspiration, Gideon chose his small task force by observing the habits and behaviour of his men while we led them in full daylight to the spring of Harod.... the men chosen were those who, in spite of their thirst, remained cautious of the presence of the enemy nearby and did not abandon their weapons even when drinking, which they managed to do by lying down upon their bellies and lapping up the water, which they gathered in one cupped hand, with their tongues.[12]

As we have observed, the notion that Gideon reduced his army to some kind of elite force of three hundred has a long history and is often cited by those who wish to derive realistic strategy from the biblical accounts. Gichon and Herzog, and Malamat as well, cite among their sources the observations of General Sir Archibald P. Wavell, who was for a time Commander in Chief of British Soldiers in the Middle East and was based in Egypt during World War II. In Wavell's 1948 book, *The Good Soldier*, he proposed this reading of Gideon's battle as a master strategy of selecting three hundred soldiers to accomplish what thirty-two thousand could not. I think it is worth listening to Wavell's interpretation carefully, where the influence of classical sources is explicit:

> The only water available for the Israelites lay at the foot of the hills on which they had taken up their position, and thus close to their enemy. This explains the fitness of the test by which Gideon chose his three hundred (the same number, it may be noted, as made history under Leonidas at Thermopylae). The majority of his men, parched by the heat on the bare, rocky hills, flung themselves down full-length by the stream when their opportunity came, and drank heedless and careless. Only the seasoned warrior, with experience of snipers and ambushes, kept his weapon in one hand and his eyes toward his foes, while he dipped the

---

11. Ibid. Note that articles continue to be produced such as the Israel David's, "Lanchester Modeling and the Biblical Account of the Battles of Gibeah" (*Naval Research Logistics* 42 [1995]: 579–84), which seeks through a complex mathematical formula known as "Lanchester modeling" to work out the precise details of the battles as described in selected biblical texts.

12. Chaim Herzog and Mordechai Gichon, *Battles of the Bible* (rev. ed.; London: Greenhill, 1997), 75.

other hand in the water and lapped from it, ready for action at the slightest sign of danger.[13]

My point is citing this quote is not the minor point that Wavell has blatantly misread the passage and reversed the descriptions of the two groups, making the majority drink like dogs, but rather that this misreading clearly served his purpose of revealing the "secret" of Gideon's military and tactical wisdom.

I began with popular literature where such interpretations are hardly matters of surprise but have now moved into more critically significant literature, albeit dated, to show how these interpretive strategies continue. In these cases, historicity is debated on the basis of militarily rational strategies being identified, and these strategies are considered harder historical evidence than the theological obscurantism attributed to later editors of the older stories.

BIBLE ATLASES AND "MAPPING" BATTLE STRATEGY

There is another noteworthy element to the interpretive history that I am here calling "the militarization of miracle," and arguably it remains a significant aspect of the history of interpretation of Joshua and Judges. I refer to mapping biblical battles, especially in Bible atlases.

The influence of images is hardly a debatable point, and I believe that one can question the subtle (and not so subtle) interpretative assumptions that operate behind the drawing of a "Bible map," but especially the construction of a battle map showing proposed troop movements. We are used to the serious questions asked by modern biblical scholars about the legitimacy of television documentaries engaging the dramatic reproductions of proposed historical arguments, knowing that a "reenactment" suggests historical credibility in modern media culture. I would suggest, however, that something similar to historical "reenactment" has largely escaped critical reflection when it comes to the publication of Bible atlases. Although not as powerful as a television image, a map drawn in relation to the Bible has a magical quality, and the magic is even more effective when ancient "troop movements" are indicated by color-coded arrows on a World War II–style map. This is especially evident in the case of narratives such as the battle of Jericho or Gideon's battle with the Midianites. In these cases, I would argue, such "battle maps" have a quality that serves, in an interesting way, as a kind of antidote to magic and theology, but especially as an antidote to miracle.[14]

---

13. Archibald P. Wavell, *The Good Soldier* (London: Macmillan, 1948), 164.

14. E.g., see James Pritchard, ed., *The Harper Atlas of the Bible* (San Francisco: Harper & Row, 1987), 68–69. Many other examples can be cited, of course. Examples are provided in the children's book that I referred to earlier, *Bible Wars and Weapons* (for Gideon, see 56), but more serious volumes also contain such battle maps: *Discovering the Biblical World* (ed. H. T. Frank; Maplewood: Hammond, 1988); Arthur Banks, *Atlas of Ancient and Medieval Warfare* (New

It is interesting to sample Bible atlases, some of which provide battle maps (e.g., Harper, Macmillan, Hammond) and others that do not (Oxford).[15] But even those that will risk mapping a campaign such as Gideon's night raid rarely try to "map" the battle of Jericho. I think I know why. The essence of the Joshua narrative is not military strategy. Imagine what a map would look like! A "troop arrow" circling the city seven times and then heading off toward Ai! It would be so silly as to make obvious that "strategy" is not the point in this text. -To attempt to "map" the circling of a city seven times would render absurd the attempt to illustrate "military strategy" in some pseudo-realistic fashion, because if such a map were to be printed, it would immediately raise questions about the legitimacy of all the other presumed "troop movement" arrows and the related attempts to strategize on Bible maps.

If it is suggested that we have only two options, either believing in a literal miracle or interpreting rational military tactics, to get at the "real history," I would argue that it is a false either/or. There is, of course, the option that suggests that many of these "battle reports" are not, in fact, reports of actual battles at all but rather narrative descriptions influenced by ritual traditions about God leading the people into the land. Furthermore, this is arguably not a recent idea. In my own reading on this matter, I was frankly surprised to discover that having doubts about the "strategic value" of, for example, the Jericho story is a view that has quite ancient roots. Medieval illustrators of the Bible created "Jericho Labyrinths," anticipating by hundreds of years the more recent trends in historical-critical scholarship of the Jericho material as ritual in nature (see fig. 2).

The construction of a labyrinth presumes a ritual, and one may infer that these medieval commentators suggested a ritual means of embodying the interpreting of these texts. Such a view is merely a step away from concluding that the texts themselves are descriptions of a ritual. Indeed, it is now widely agreed that one of the main theological tasks of the Jericho and Gideon battle narratives (among many others, of course) is to illustrate the miraculous power of God over against the mundane military strength of the Israelites themselves. I would like to acknowledge that some of the influence of this interest in miracle can be attributed to work of one of my own teachers, Millard C. Lind, and his arguments about the critical role of miracle in the interpretation of these battle narratives.[16] More recent analysis has moved much further, and ritualized interpretations are

---

York: Hippocrene, 1982), 9; Martin Gilbert, *The Routledge Atlas of Jewish History* (London: Routledge, 1995), 3; John Rogerson, *Atlas of the Bible* (New York: Facts on File, 1985), 30.

15. Herbert G. May, ed., *Oxford Bible Atlas* (3rd ed.; New York: Oxford University Press, 1984). I note that none of the editions of the *Oxford Bible Atlas* featured such battle maps, since 1962, which was one of the older atlases that I consulted.

16. Millard C. Lind, *Yahweh Is a Warrior* (Scottdale, Pa.: Herald, 1980).

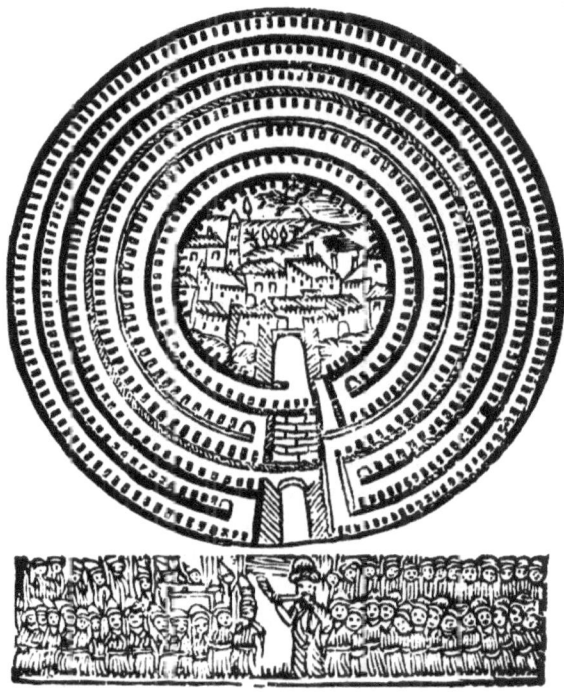

Figure 2. Although the argument that the battle of Jericho story may be derived from ancient ritual practice (marching in circles, blowing trumpets) rather than ancient battle descriptions is considered a recent idea, medieval illustrators of the Bible may well have supposed a similar context by associating the story with labyrinths. In short, do these labyrinths reveal a medieval interpretation of the story as a ritual text?

by no means the only options available for understanding the meaning and/or significance of biblical battle narratives.

Carolyn Pressler argues that the exilic setting of the final edition of the Deuteronomistic History provides a reasonable context for historical narratives that want to emphasize the strength of God for a people who are traumatized and powerless after the catastrophic events of 587 B.C.E.[17] Dating the material a bit earlier, Lori Rowlett, on the other hand, is also interested in the violent rhetoric of Joshua in general (not only in the Jericho narrative) as a rhetorical strategy useful during the reforms of Josiah in galvanizing support for his regime and

---

17. Carolyn Pressler, *Joshua, Judges, Ruth* (Westminster Bible Companion; Louisville: Westminster John Knox, 2002).

its resistance to Assyrian and Egyptian interests in Palestine.[18] L. Daniel Hawk's work on Joshua also focuses on the theological agenda that is seen in the writer's careful outlining of each of God's commands and then in the writer's careful articulation of Israel's compliance to each command as an essential theological aspect of the ritualized reenactment of the conquest of Jericho in early Israelite cultic tradition.[19] I think it is fair to say that ritual reenactment is the generally agreed source of the detailed descriptions of the encirclement of Jericho. As Pressler writes, "The story does not speak of human strategizing or human feats of war."[20] Similar observations are now common about narratives in Judges, and one cannot improve on Manfred Görg's rather curt statement, made in his 1991 commentary on Judges, that "augenfaellig, dass militarische Kraft is dieser Auseinandersetzung nichts zahlt" ("obviously, military strength 'does not count' in these discussions").[21]

Having said this, however, attempts to glean tactical information from the battle descriptions of Joshua and Judges have not entirely ceased in critical examination of Joshua and Judges. Despite the monumental archaeological difficulties with virtually any attempt to bring the narratives of Joshua into any relationship whatsoever to the present archaeological remains of the ruins of Tell es-Sultan/Jericho, there remains the nagging desire to see a real battle somewhere in these texts, although this is far more evident in popular biblical studies than in the most recent academic approaches.

Consider, for example, tendencies in the critical commentary literature dealing with Joshua and Judges. In Wolfgang Richter's famous commentary on Judges from the early 1960s, he mounted one of the first major challenges to some aspects of Noth's influential thesis of the redaction of a Deuteronomistic Historian in the late Judean monarchy and after 587 B.C.E. Richter suggested a *Grundlage* called the "Book of Saviors," a source that he proposed as one of the early layers of three judge stories, including the story of Gideon. He then argued that the parts that emphasized the miracle of God (7:1, 3–11, 22–25) were added by the first redactors.[22] It seems clear that one of the implications of Richter's analysis is the working presumption that actual battles of some kind are being described in the oldest sources.

---

18. Lori Rowlett, *Joshua and the Rhetoric of Violence: A New Historicist Analysis* (JSOTSup 226; Sheffield: Sheffield Academic Press, 1996).

19. L. Daniel Hawk, *Joshua* (Berit Olam; Collegeville, Minn.: Liturgical Press, 2000).

20. Pressler, *Joshua, Judges, Ruth*, 48.

21. Manfred Görg, *Richter* (NEchtB 31; Würzburg: Echter, 1993), 42.

22. Albert de Pury and Thomas Römer, "Deuteronomistic Historiography (DH): History of Research and Debated Issues," in *Israel Constructs Its History: Deuteronomistic Historiography in Recent Research* (ed. A. de Pury, T. Römer, and J.-D. Macchi: JSOTSup 306; Sheffield: Sheffield Academic Press, 2000), 24–143.

Soggin was already expressing serious reservations in his volume on Judges in 1981 but acknowledged that he was raising questions where questions had not normally been raised. Soggin wrote cautiously about the Gideon episode narrated in Judg 6–8 by stating that "among historians and exegetes there is a tendency not to doubt the substantial historicity of the event, and therefore the difficulties in which Israel found itself, without, however, any success in defining the exact nature of the phenomenon."[23] Soggin himself then makes a number of suggestions about what may lie behind the present narrative. Was Judg 7, he wonders, based on an incursion by Midianites seeking to plunder and pillage? Was it a clash between seminomadic peoples in conflict over grazing rights? Was it migrating Midianites looking for land? Notably, Soggin does not seem to entertain the idea that no fighting at all stands behind this story, even though he later concludes: "The problem is not easy to solve, given the difficulties presented by the biblical material. As it stands now, it does not try to give an account of a political or military event, but to proclaim the need for Israel to trust in the God who had also liberated them in the past, rather than in its own might and strength."[24] The situation with the Jericho narratives are even more complicated, of course, as I earlier hinted, by the important work of Kenyon in the 1950s and 1960s, which radically questioned any ability to derive history, much less military tactics, from the Joshua narratives. Changes were not slow in coming

Moving from Maps to Rhetorical Analysis

Already in 1967 John Grey was suggesting that the Jericho narrative is entirely fictional, an etiology built around the occasion when Israelite tribal groups happened onto the already old ruins of Jericho, and this legend was then combined with a ritualized reenactment of the battle as part of later tribal historical reflections and rituals.[25] Recently Görg further suggests that the narrative may have been built around a later conflict between Ahab and Moab (1 Kgs 16:34).[26] Still, in the *HarperCollins Bible Commentary* of 2000, Joshua Rast cautiously writes that the historical aspects of the battle of Jericho "remain debated,"[27] and in the same volume J. Cheryl Exum remains cautious about Gideon's water-drinking test, the point of which, she indicates, is "not clear."[28]

---

23. J. A. Soggin, *Judges: A Commentary* (OTL; Philadelphia: Westminster John Knox, 1981), 105.
24. Ibid., 107.
25. John Grey, *Joshua, Judges, Ruth* (NCB: London: Attic, 1967), 75–76.
26. Görg, *Richter*, 27–28.
27. Joshua Rast, "Joshua," in *The HarperCollins Bible Commentary* (rev. ed.; ed. J. L. Mays; San Francisco: Harper 2000), 217.
28. J. Cheryl Exum, "Judges," in Mays, *HarperCollins Bible Commentary*, 231.

The most recent work on the Jericho story is moving almost entirely toward a ritualized interpretation of the narrative descriptions, while at the same time focusing even more specific interest on the *herem* and its role in many of the biblical battle narratives. Görg's 1991 work makes the important observation that the use of shouting and horns connects the battles of Jericho and Gideon with ritually significant details.[29]

Increased interest in the ritualized aspects of Israelite battle traditions, whether as a literary form or historical practice, is represented in the recent work of Susan Niditch, who renews interest in biblical warfare narratives after a period of time when the work of von Rad, Smend, Miller, and, more recently, Sa-Moon Kang seemed at the time to summarize adequately what we knew of the traditions of miraculous warfare in the Deuteronomistic Historian and even the Pentateuch. Central to the more recent interest has been new attention to unraveling the role and significance of the *herem* in biblical battle accounts and the possible late-historical social or political agendas that may be at work in editing these accounts.[30]

For example, in a fascinating study K. Lawson Younger compares biblical battle reports with reports from the Assyrians, Hittites, and Egyptians with an eye toward the literary forms and rhetoric of such reporting. He discovers many common themes, including gods assisting in the achievement of a glorious victory, enemies killed in huge numbers, and enemies terrified by wondrous powers and armies.[31] One of Younger's most interesting conclusions, however, is that many biblical battle scenes follow a set pattern inspired by highlighting God's leading rather than human involvement. The significance of the miraculous elements of biblical battle reports are now combining with the developing theories about ritualized narratives of battle, such as Jericho and Gideon. Robert H.

---

29. Manfred Görg, *Josua* (NEchtB 30; Würzburg: Echter, 1991), 28.

30. The literature, of course, is extensive on this subject. A survey of important titles in English would begin with one of the classic works that established much of the vocabulary of the study of war in the Hebrew Bible, namely, the extended essay by Gerhard von Rad, *Holy War in Ancient Israel*, with its important forward by Ben C. Ollenberger and expanded bibliography by Judith E. Sanderson (trans. and ed. M. J. Dawn; Grand Rapids: Eerdmans, 1991); see also Sa-Moon Kang, *Divine War in the Old Testament and in the Ancient Near East* (BZAW 177; Berlin: de Gruyter, 1989); T. R. Hobbs, *A Time for War: A Study of Warfare in the Old Testament* (OTS 3; Wilmington, Del.: Glazier, 1989); Rudolf Smend, *Yahweh War and Tribal Confederation* (trans. M. Rogers, Nashville: Abingdon, 1970); John A. Wood, *Perspectives on War in the Bible* (Macon, Ga.: Mercer University Press, 1998); Susan Niditch, *War in the Hebrew Bible: A Study in the Ethics of Violence* (New York: Oxford University Press, 1995); Peter C. Craigie, *The Problem of War in the Old Testament* (Grand Rapids, 1978; repr., Eugene, Ore.: Wipf & Stock, 2002); Patrick D. Miller Jr., *The Divine Warrior in Early Israel* (HSM 5; Cambridge: Harvard University Press, 1973; repr., Atlanta: Society of Biblical Literature, 2006); and Lind, *Yahweh Is a Warrior*.

31. K. Lawson Younger Jr., *Ancient Conquest Accounts: A Study in Ancient Near Eastern and Biblical History Writing* (JSOTSup 98; Sheffield: JSOT Press, 1990).

O'Connell, writing in 1996, further suggests that an intentional contrast is being set up between Gideon, who is viewed positively, and Saul, who is viewed negatively, when the Judges narrative is lined up against 1 Sam 13–14. Gideon blows horns to call troops, O'Connell notes, indicating faith in God's power. Saul blows a horn to rally even more troops, indicating his lack of trust (1 Sam 13:3–4). A major thrust in O'Connell's reading of Judges is to find rhetorical references to the Saul and David narratives.[32]

In the *Eerdmans Commentary on the Bible*, published in 2003, Younger writes that the Jericho narrative really stresses ritual interests over military interests, and more recent fascinations with the miraculous destruction of the walls combined with a reticence to deal with unsavory subjects like the *herem*, has actually caused more confusion than clarification about this and other battle texts. His emphasis on the *herem* suggests that one of the most important ritual concerns of the Jericho narrative is actually total separation from foreign religions and peoples; the emphasis is on ending foreign influence totally with exaggerated rhetoric about total destruction of that foreign influence.[33] In the same volume, P. D. Guest writes that the Gideon narrative may actually intend to portray Gideon in a negative light as a critique of kingship.[34] Finally, while Graeme Auld's interesting 1989 article suggesting a Persian period date for the Gideon narratives has not attracted widespread agreement, it is nonetheless further testimony to the move away from historical details and military tactics and toward the social and rhetorical motivations of the narratives like Jericho and Gideon.[35]

Having said this, I am not so quick to dismiss Auld's instinct to see major connections between the Gideon (and, I would add, Jericho) narratives and the issues and concerns of the postexilic period as noted in clearly later textual material. For example, what I find particularly interesting about some of the Deuteronomistic descriptions that include the ban is the growing tendency to see the violent destruction of the enemy as more recent additions in the older battle descriptions. They may not be "ancient" reports about genocidal violence. In other words, these genocidal reports of killing all living things may actually have been added to these battle reports in the years after the exile!

I acknowledge that a possible problem with assigning many ban reports to the postexilic period is the similar "ban" in the ninth-century Moabite "Mesha

---

32. Robert H. O'Connell, *The Rhetoric of the Book of Judges* (VTSup 63; Leiden: Brill, 1996).

33. K. Lawson Younger, Jr., "Joshua," in *Eerdmans Commentary on the Bible* (ed. J. Dunn and J. Rogerson; Grand Rapids: Eerdmans, 2003), 174–89.

34. P. Deryn Guest, "Judges," in Dunn and Rogerson, *Eerdmans Commentary on the Bible*, 190–207.

35. A. Graeme Auld, "Gideon: Hacking at the Heart of the Old Testament," *VT* 39 (1989): 257–67.

Stela" (dated to ca. 830 B.C.E.?),[36] but consider the fact that violent destruction of enemies most certainly plays an increasingly significant role in postexilic literature and legend and may well relate to the angry circumstances of postexilic feelings of revenge as much as postexilic concerns for purity and separation from foreign influence. When we read these descriptions of destruction of "all living things"—women and children included—we really are not so far from descriptions like the following clearly postexilic sentiment: "O daughter Babylon, you devastator! Happy shall they be who pay you back what you have done to us! Happy shall they be who take your little ones and dash them against the rock!" (Ps 137:8–9 NRSV). Recall that later postexilic stories include punishment of the enemies of the Jews in equally genocidal language. In the telling of these otherwise charming tales, these details are gracefully left unmentioned in the presence of children, but they exist nonetheless. The end of the book of Esther, famously, includes the permission to kill the whole family of any who would threaten Israelites: "By these letters the king allowed the Jews who were in every city to assemble and defend their lives, to destroy, to kill, and to annihilate any armed force of any people or province that might attack them, with their children and women, and to plunder their goods" (Esth 8:11 NRSV). In the next chapter, one finds the even more chilling image: "So the Jews struck down all their enemies with the sword, slaughtering, and destroying them, and did as they pleased to those who hated them" (Esth 9:5 NRSV). In the book of Daniel, when those who plotted against Daniel and had him thrown to the lions are discovered, the punishment they intended for Daniel is handed out to the evil advisors of King Darius: "The king gave a command, and those who had accused Daniel were brought and thrown into the den of lions—they, their children, and their wives. Before they reached the bottom of the den the lions overpowered them and broke all their bones in pieces" (Dan 6:24 NRSV).

The tendency continues into the Hellenistic literature, as noted in the request from the Jews to slaughter those other Jews who betrayed the community in times of trouble, after their miraculous deliverance from Ptolemy, as narrated in the very late work known as 3 Maccabees:

> On receiving this letter the Jews did not immediately hurry to make their departure, but they requested of the king that at their own hands those of the Jewish nation who had willfully transgressed against the holy God and the law of God should receive the punishment they deserved. They declared that those who for the belly's sake had transgressed the divine commandments would never be favorably disposed toward the king's government. The king then, admitting and approving the truth of what they said, granted them a general license so that freely, and without royal authority or supervision, they might destroy those

---

36. On this, see Bruce Routledge, *Moab in the Iron Age: Hegemony, Polity, Archaeology* (Archaeology, Culture, and Society; Philadelphia: University of Pennsylvania Press, 2004).

everywhere in his kingdom who had transgressed the law of God. (3 Macc 7:10–12 NRSV)

Once again, these violent themes and images are deeply troubling, but it is hard to avoid the observation that they are essential aspects of the rhetoric of violence and tales deeply colored by anger and resentment. I believe that we must keep in mind that these expressions of violence come from a time when the Hebrew people were most certainly not actually capable of engaging in anything like this level of destructive violence against resented enemies, so the power of God, rather than their own weapons, becomes a central motif. Like the dreams of Frantz Fanon's colonized peoples, who long to rise up and destroy the colonizer communities, the biblical battle narratives are angry fantasies that can be directed within the community.[37]

My point is this: biblical descriptions of miraculous wars and devastation of enemies and their entire families are not simply calm records of historical events. The language is at least that of anguish and certainly anger, and I quite agree with the recent trends toward analyzing battle reports as rhetorical statements. I would only insist that the issue of reading angry rhetoric be placed on the critical agenda for rhetorical studies.

To summarize what I think is the significance of this experiment. I believe that it was a serious historical-critical mistake to take these descriptions of miraculous wars and accompanying destruction and annihilation and then to proceed to draw literal or figurative maps as if actual "strategies" can be gleaned from angry rhetoric! Violent rhetoric arguably describes suffering, but—and this is historically significant—it does not necessarily describe actual events or serious social, theological, or military policy. We can read such descriptions of war—including the wish for God to intervene and destroy our enemies for us when we cannot—as the psychology of grief and the rhetoric of anger. Descriptions of war need not be interpreted as expressions of mature theological reflection or actual tactics of war. Could it be that the historical-critical focus on military tactical strategies in biblical narratives constituted precisely the kind of biased readings of texts that fogs our understanding of these ancient texts and thus is precisely the kind of "biased reading" of which biblical scholars who are "interested in peace" are frequently accused?

What I find interesting is precisely this: the recent tendencies to read biblical battle narratives as literature and rhetoric has been accompanied by a clear move away from trying to glean actual battle tactics in biblical battle narratives. This is now also combined with a renewed interest in the role of the ban as a ritual category rather than a military tactic. The result is, somewhat paradoxically,

---

37. Of the many works, see Frantz Fanon, *The Wretched of the Earth* (New York: Grove, 2005).

demilitarizing the battle reports of Joshua and Judges, while taking seriously the language of miracle as part of the ritual categories of analysis. The older (and still occasionally noted) attempts to read tactical information from Joshua and Judges in the name of finding actual historical information was often motivated by a notion that rational military information is a reliable test of historicity; tactics and strategy were treated as the real, the historical, and the trustworthy, despite the fact that it consciously must be read against the miraculous, the militarily self-effacing, nature of the actual textual narratives. Even critical discussions of the Hebrew and Greek texts were arguably motivated, on occasion, by presumptions about military rationality and strategic reliability, such as the placement of the "hand to mouth" phrase in Judg 7:5–6.

I was once warned by one of my teachers in the anonymous past, upon discovering that I was a Quaker, that I must take special care so as not to "read your hippie values into the ancient texts you are reading," and I doubt that I will ever forget the wording of this warning. Now, in this postmodern era, when nobody gets away with grandiose claims of objectivity, we can say that we pacifists were not the only ones whose bias on the issues of war and peace deeply colored our academic and critical interests in biblical texts. I believe that I have shown through popular literature and academic literature, and especially in the seemingly objective world of map-drawing, that interests in what was alleged to be the historicity of biblical battle narratives were guided in part by a bias toward military criteria to determine what is "real" and thus "historical." I would suggest that those who are willing to do violence *with* the text clearly also risk doing violence *to* the text.

BIBLIOGRAPHY

Abel, P. F.-M. *Les Livres Des Maccabees*. Paris: Librairie Lecoffre Gabalda, 1949.
Abma, Richtsje. *Bonds of Love: Methodic Studies of Prophetic Texts with Marriage Imagery (Isaiah 50:1-3 and 54:1-10, Hosea 1-3, Jeremiah 2-3)*. SSN 40. Assen: Van Gorcum, 1999.
Adam, Klaus-Peter. *Der königliche Held: Die Entsprechung von kämpfendem Gott und kämpfendem König im Psalm 18*. WMANT 19. Neukirchen-Vluyn: Neukirchener, 2001.
Ahlström, Gösta W. *The History of Ancient Palestine*. Minneapolis: Fortress, 1993.
Albenda, Pauline. "Gravevines in Ashurbanipal's Garden." *BASOR* 215 (1974): 5–17.
———. "Landscape Bas-Reliefs in the *Bīt Ḥilāni* of Ashurbanipal." *BASOR* 224 (1976): 49–72; 225 (1977): 29–48.
Albright, William F. *From the Stone Age to Christianity: Monotheism and the Historical Process*. 2nd ed. Garden City, N.Y.: Doubleday, 1957.
Alt, Albrecht. "Das Königtum in den Reichen Israel und Juda." *VT* 1 (1951): 3–22. Repr. as pages 116–34 in *Kleine Schriften zur Geschichte des Volkes Israel*. 2 vols. Munich: Beck, 1953. Trans. by R. A. Wilson as pages 311–35 in "The Monarchy in the Kingdoms of Israel and Judah" in Alt, *Essays on Old Testament History and Religion*. Garden City, N.Y.: Doubleday, 1968.
Amir, Yehoshua. "The Decalogue according to Philo." Pages 121–60 in *The Ten Commandments in History and Tradition*. Edited by Ben-Zion Segal and Gershon Levi. Jerusalem: Magnes, 1990.
Amit, Yairah. *The Book of Judges: The Art of Editing*. Translated by J. Chipman. BibInt 38. Leiden: Brill, 1998.
Andersen, T. David. "Renaming and Wedding Imagery in Isaiah 62." *Bib* 67 (1986): 75–80.
Attridge, Harold W. "Historiography: 2 Maccabees." Pages 171–83 in *Jewish Writings of the Second Temple Period*. Edited by Michael E. Stone. CRINT 2.2. Assen: Van Gorcum; Philadelphia: Fortress, 1984.
Auld, A. Graeme. "Gideon: Hacking at the Heart of the Old Testament." *VT* 39 (1989): 257–67.
———. *Joshua Retold: Synoptic Perspectives*. Edinburgh: T&T Clark, 1998.
Austin, M. M. "Hellenistic Kings, War, and the Economy." *CQ* NS 36 (1986): 450–66.
Aymard, A. "Le partage des profits de la guerre dans les traités d'alliance antiques." *Revue Historique* 217 (1957): 233–40.
Babbit, Frank Cole, trans. *Plutarch: Moralia*. 15 vols. LCL. Cambridge: Harvard University Press, 1927–69.

Bach, Robert. "Bauen und Pflanzen." Pages 7–32 in *Studien zur Theologie der alttestamentlichen Überlieferungen*. Edited by R. Rendtorff and K. Boch. Neukirchen-Vluyn: Neukirchener, 1962.
Balz-Cochois, Helgard. "Gomer oder die Macht der Astarte: Versuch einer feministischen Interpretation von Hos 1–4." *EvT* 42 (1982): 37–65.
Banks, Arthur. *Atlas of Ancient and Medieval Warfare*. New York: Hippocrene, 1982.
Bar-Kochva, Bezalel. *Judas Maccabaeus: The Jewish Struggle against the Seleucids*. Cambridge: Cambridge University Press, 1989.
―――. *The Seleucid Army: Organization and Tactics in the Great Campaigns*: Cambridge: Cambridge University Press, 1976.
Barker, Rodney. *Legitimating Identities: The Self-Presentation of Rulers and Subjects*. Cambridge: Cambridge University Press, 2001.
Barnett, Richard D. *Sculptures from the North Palace of Ashurbanipal at Nineveh (668–627 B.C.)*. London: British Museum Press, 1976.
Barnett, Richard D., Erika Bleibtreu, and Geoffrey Turner, *Sculptures from the Southwest Palace of Sennacherib at Nineveh*. 2 vols. London: British Museum Press, 1998.
Barnett, Richard D., and Margarete Falkner. *The Sculptures of Aššur-nasir-pali II (883–859 B.C.) Tiglath-Pileser III (745–727 B.C.) Esarhaddon (681–669 B.C.) from the Central and South-West Palaces at Nimrud*. London: British Museum Press, 1962.
Barnett, Richard D., and Werner Forman. *Assyrian Palace Reliefs and Their Influence on the Sculptures of Babylonia and Assyria*. London: Batchworth, 1960.
Bartlett, John R. "The Conquest of Sihon's Kingdom: A Literary Re-examination." *JBL* 97 (1978): 347–51.
Barton, John. "History and Rhetoric in the Prophets." Pages 51–64 in *The Bible as Rhetoric: Studies in Biblical Persuasion and Credibility*. Edited by Martin Warner. Warwick Studies in Philosophy and Literature. London: Routledge, 1990.
Bassford, Christopher. "Interpreting the Legacy of Clausewitz." *Joint Force Quarterly* 35 (2004): 18–19.
Batsch, Christoph. *La Guerre et les ries de guerre des le judaisme du deuxième Temple*. Leiden: Brill, 2005.
Baumann, Gerlinde. *Love and Violence: Marriage as Metaphor for the Relationship between YHWH and Israel in the Prophetic Books*. Translated by L. Maloney. Collegeville, Minn.: Liturgical Press, 2003.
Baumgarten, Albert I. *The Flourishing of Jewish Sects in the Maccabean Era: An Interpretation*. Leiden: Brill, 1997.
―――. "Invented Traditions of the Maccabean Era." Pages 197–210 in vol. 1 of *Geschichte-Tradition-Reflection: Festschrift für Martin Hengel zum 70. Geburtstag*. Edited by Peter Schäfer. 3 vols. Tübingen: Mohr Siebeck, 1996.
Beal, Richard H. "Hittite Military Rituals." Pages 63–76 in *Ancient Magic and Ritual Power*. Edited by Marvin W. Meyer and Paul A. Mirecki. Leiden: Brill, 1995.
Becker, Uwe. *Richterzeit und Königtum: Redaktionsgeschichtliche Studien zum Richterbuch*. BZAW 192. Berlin: de Gruyter, 1990.
Becking, Bob. "'Wie Töpfe sollst du Sie Zerschmeissen': Mesopotamische Parallelen zu Psalm 2,9b." *ZAW* 102 (1990): 56–79.
Begg, Christopher T. "The Function of Josh 7.1–8.29 in the Deuteronomistic History." *Bib* 67 (1986): 320–34.

Ben Zvi, Ehud. "Observations on the Marital Metaphor of *YHWH* and Israel in Its Ancient Israelite Context: General Considerations and Particular Images in Hosea 1.2." *JSOT* 28 (2004): 363–84.
Berman, Joshua. *Narrative Analogy in the Hebrew Bible: Battle Stories and Their Equivalent Non-battle Narratives.* VTSup 103. Leiden: Brill, 2004.
Bickerman, Elias J. "The Historical Foundations of Postbiblical Judaism." Pages 72–118 in *The Jews: Their History, Culture, and Religion.* Edited by L. Finkelstein. New York: Schocken, 1972. Repr. as pages 9–48 in *Emerging Judaism: Studies on the Fourth and Third Centuries B.C.E.* Edited by M. E. Stone and D. Satran. Minneapolis: Augsburg Fortress, 1989.
———. "Remarques sur le droit des gens dans la Grèce classique." *RIDA* (1950): 99–127. Repr. as "Bemerkungen über das Völkerrecht im klassischen Griechenland." Pages 474–502 in *Zur griechisher Staatskunde.* Edited by Fritz Gschnitzer. Wege der Forschung 96. Darmstadt: Wissenschaftliche Buchgesellschaft, 1969.
Biddle, Mark E. "The Figure of Lady Jerusalem: Identification, Deification, and Personification of Cities in the Ancient Near East." Pages 173–94 in *The Biblical Canon in Comparative Perspective.* Edited by K. Lawson Younger Jr., William W. Hallo, and Bernard F. Batto. Scripture in Context 4. Ancient Near Eastern Texts and Studies 11. Lewiston, N.Y.: Mellen, 1991.
Binford, Lewis R. "Archaeological Perspectives." Pages 5–32 in *New Perspectives in Archaeology.* Edited by Sally R. Binford and Lewis R. Binford. Chicago: Aldine, 1968.
Bird, Phyllis. "'To Play the Harlot': An Enquiry into an Old Testament Metaphor." Pages 75–94 in *Gender and Difference in Ancient Israel.* Edited by Peggy L. Day. Minneapolis: Fortress, 1989.
Bitzer, Lloyd F. "The Rhetorical Situation." Pages 247–60 in *Rhetoric: A Tradition in Transition.* Edited by Walter R. Fisher. Ann Arbor: University of Michigan Press, 1974.
Bleibtreu, Erika. "Grisly Assyrian Record of Torture and Death." *BAR* 17/1 (1991): 52–61, 75.
———. "Zerstörung der Umwelt durch Bäumefällen und Dezimierung des Löwenbestandes in Mesopotamien." Pages 219–33 in *Der orientalische Mensch und seine Beziehungen zur Umwelt, Beiträge zum 2. Grazer morgenländischen Symposion (2.–5. März 1989).* Edited by B. Scholz. Grazer morgenländische Studien 2. Graz: GrazKult, 1989.
Blum, Erhard. "Der kompositionelle Knoten am Übergang von Josua zu Richter: Ein Entflechtungsvorschlag." Pages 181–212 in *Deuteronomy and Deuteronomic Literature: Festschrift C. H. W. Brekelmans.* Edited by M. Vervenne and J. Lust. BETL 133. Leuven: Leuven University Press, 1997.
———. *Studien zur Komposition des Pentateuch.* BZAW 189. Berlin: de Gruyter, 1990.
Boadt, Lawrence. "The Poetry of Prophetic Persuasion: Preserving the Prophet's Persona." *CBQ* 59 (1997): 1–21.
Bolkestein, Hendrik. *Economic Life in Greece's Golden Age.* Leiden: Brill, 1958.
———. *Wohltatigkeit und Armenpflege in vorchristlichen Altertum.* Utrecht: Oosthoek, 1939.
Borger, Rykle. "Assyrische Staatsverträge: Der Vertrag Assurniraris mit Mati'ilu von Arpad." Pages 155–58 in vol. 1 of *Texte aus der Umwelt des Alten Testament.* Edited by Otto Kaiser. Gütersloh: Gütersloher Verlagshaus, 1984–.
———. *Die Inschriften Asarhaddons, Königs von Assyrien.* Graz Weidner, 1956.

Borowski, Oded. *Daily Life in Biblical Times*. SBLABS 5. Atlanta: Society of Biblical Literature, 2003.
Braulik, Georg. *The Theology of Deuteronomy: Collected Essays of Georg Braulik*. BIBAL Collected Essays 2. Richland Hills, Tex: BIBAL, 1994.
Brechtel, Lyn. "What If Dinah Is Not Raped?" *JSOT* 62 (1994): 19–36.
Breemer, Jan S. "Statistics, Real Estate, and the Principles of War: Why There Is No Unified Theory of War." *Military Review* 86 (2006): 84–89.
Brenner, Athalya. *Colour Terms in the Old Testament*. JSOTSup 21. Sheffield: Sheffield Academic Press, 1982.
———. "The Hebrew God and His Female Complements." Pages 56–71 in *Reading Bibles, Writing Bodies: Identity and the Book*. Edited by Timothy K. Beal and David M. Gunn. Biblical Limits. London: Routledge, 1997.
Brueggemann, Walter. *1 and 2 Kings*. Smyth & Helwys Bible Commentary. Macon, Ga.: Smyth & Helwys, 2000.
Brunner, Hellmut. *Die Geburt des Gottkönigs: Studien zur Überlieferung eines altägyptischen Mythos*. Wiesbaden: Harrossowitz, 1986.
Büchler, Adolf. *Types of Jewish-Palestinian Piety from 70 B.C.E. to 70 C.E.: The Ancient Pious Men*. Publications 8. London: Jew's College, 1922. Repr., New York: Ktav, 1968.
Burke, Peter. "Overture: The New History: Its Past and Its Future." Pages 1–23 in *New Perspectives on Historical Writing*. Edited by Peter Burke. University Park: Pennsylvania State University Press, 1992.
Burney, C. F. *The Book of Judges: Introduction and Notes*. ICC. Edinburgh: T&T Clark, 1918. Repr., Eugene, Ore.: Wipf & Stock, 2004.
Butler, Trent. *The Book of Joshua*. WBC 7. Nashville: Nelson, 1983.
Camp, Claudia. *Wisdom and the Feminine in the Book of Proverbs*. Bible and Literature 11. Sheffield: Almond, 1985.
Campbell, Anthony F., and Mark A. O'Brien. *Unfolding the Deuteronomistic History*. Minneapolis: Fortress, 2000.
Campbell, Edward F., Jr. "A Land Divided: Judah and Israel from the Death of Solomon to the Fall of Samaria." Pages 206–41 in *The Oxford History of the Biblical World*. Edited by Michael D. Coogan. Oxford: Oxford University Press, 2001.
Campbell, K. M. "Rahab's Covenant." *VT* 22 (1972): 243–44.
Carneiro, Robert L. Foreword to *The Evolution of War*. Edited by Keith F. Otterbein. Cambridge, Mass.: HRAF Press, 1970.
Carr, David M. *Reading the Fractures of Genesis: Historical and Literary Approaches*. Louisville: Westminster John Knox, 1996.
Carroll, Robert P. "Desire under the Terebinths: On Pornographic Representation in the Prophets—A Response." Pages 275–307 in *A Feminist Companion to the Latter Prophets*. Edited by Athalya Brenner. FCB 8. Sheffield: Sheffield Academic Press, 1995.
———. "Whorusalamin: A Tale of Three Cities as Three Sisters." Pages 67–82 in *On Reading Prophetic Texts: Gender-Specific and Related Studies in Memory of Fokkelien van Dijk-Hemmes*. Edited by Bob Becking and Meindert Dijkstra. BibInt 18. Leiden: Brill, 1996.
———. "War in the Hebrew Bible." Pages 25–44 in *War and Society in the Greek World*. Edited by J. Rich and G. Shipley. Leicester-Nottingham Studies in Ancient Society 4. London: Routledge, 1993.

Chagnon, Napoleon A. "*Yanomamö* Social Organization and Warfare." Pages 109-159 in *War: The Anthropology of Armed Conflict and Aggression*. Edited by Morton Fried, Marvin Harris, and Robert Murphy. New York: Natural History Press, 1968.

Chaney, Marvin L. "Accusing Whom of What? Hosea's Rhetoric of Promiscuity." Pages 97-115 in *Distant Voices Drawing Near*. Edited by Holly E. Hearon, Marvin L. Chaney, and Antoinette Clark Wire. Collegeville, Minn.: Liturgical Press, 2004.

———. "Bitter Bounty: The Dynamics of Political Economy Critiqued by the Eighth-Century Prophets." Pages 15-30 in *Reformed Faith and Economics*. Edited by Robert L. Stivers. Lanham, Md.: University Press of America, 1989.

Chaniotis, Angelos. *War in the Hellenistic World: A Social and Cultural History*. Oxford: Blackwell, 2005.

Chapman, Cynthia R. *The Gendered Language of Warfare in the Israelite-Assyrian Encounter*. HSM 62. Winona Lake, Ind.: Eisenbrauns, 2004.

Childs, Brevard S. *Isaiah and the Assyrian Crisis*. SBT 2/3. London: SCM, 1967.

———. "On Reading the Elijah Narratives." *Int* 34 (1980): 128-37.

Christensen, Duane L. *Transformations of the War Oracle in Old Testament Prophecy: Studies in the Oracles against the Nations*. HDR 3. Missoula, Mont.: Scholars Press, 1975.

Clausewitz, Carl von. *On War*. Edited and translated by Michael Howard and Peter Paret. Princeton: Princeton University Press, 1976.

Clements, Ronald E. "The Deuteronomic Law of Centralization and the Catastrophe of 587 BC." Pages 5-25 in *After the Exile: Essays in Honour of Rex Mason*. Edited by John Barton and David J. Reimer. Macon, Ga.: Mercer University Press, 1996.

Coats, George W. "An Exposition for the Conquest Theme." *CBQ* 47 (1985): 47-54.

Cogan, Mordechai. *1 Kings: A New Translation with Introduction and Commentary*. AB 10. New York: Doubleday, 2001.

———. "Sennacherib's Siege of Jerusalem." *BAR* 27/1 (2001): 40-45, 69.

Cohen, Chayim. "Neo-Assyrian Elements in the First Speech of the Biblical Rab-Shaqe." *IOS* 9 (1979): 32-48.

———. "The 'Widowed' City." *JANES* 5 (1973): 75-81.

Cohen, Shaye J. D. *The Beginnings of Jewishness: Boundaries, Varieties, Uncertainties*. Berkeley and Los Angeles: University of California Press, 1999.

Cohn, Robert L. "The Literary Logic of 1 Kings 17-19." *JBL* 101 (1982): 333-50.

Cole, Steven W. "The Destruction of Orchards in Assyrian Warfare." Pages 29-40 in *Assyria 1995: Proceedings of the 10th Anniversary Symposium of the Neo-Assyrian Text Corpus Project. Helsinki, September 7-11, 1995*. Edited by Simo Parpola and Robert M. Whiting. Helsinki: Neo-Assyrian Text Corpus Project, 1997.

Collier, Paul, and Anke Hoeffler "Greed and Grievance in Civil War." *Oxford Economic Papers* 56 (2004): 563-95.

Collins, John J., and George W. E. Nickelsburg, eds. *Ideal Figures in Ancient Judaism. Profiles and Paradigms*. SBLSCS 12. Chico, Calif.: Scholars Press, 1980.

Colson, F. H., et al., trans. *Philo*. 10 vols. LCL. Cambridge: Harvard University Press, 1929-62.

Conrad, Edgar W. *Fear Not Warrior: A Study of 'al tira' Pericopes in the Hebrew Scriptures*. BJS 75. Chico, Calif.: Scholars Press, 1985.

Coogan, Michael David. "Canaanite Origins and Lineage: Reflections on the Religion of Ancient Israel." Pages 115-24 in *Ancient Israelite Religion: Essays in Honor of Frank*

Moore Cross. Edited by Patrick D. Miller Jr., Paul D. Hanson, and S. Dean McBride. Philadelphia: Fortress, 1987.

Coote, Robert B., and Mary P. Coote. *Power, Politics, and the Marking of the Bible: An Introduction.* Minneapolis: Fortress, 1990.

Craigie, Peter C. *The Book of Deuteronomy.* NICOT. Grand Rapids: Eerdmans, 1976.

———. *The Problem of War in the Old Testament.* Grand Rapids: Eerdmans, 1978. Repr., Eugene, Ore.: Wipf & Stock, 2002.

Cronbach, A. "Social Ideals of the Apocrypha and the Pseudepigrapha." *HUCA* 18 (1944): 119–56.

Cross, Frank Moore. *Canaanite Myths and Hebrew Epic: Essays in the History of the Religion of Israel.* Cambridge: Harvard University Press, 1973.

Crüsemann, Frank. *The Torah: Theology and Social History of Old Testament Law.* Minneapolis: Fortress, 1996.

Dahood, Mitchell. *Psalms 101–150: Introduction, Translation, and Notes.* AB 17A. Garden City, N.Y.: Doubleday, 1965.

Dalley, Stephanie. "Ancient Mesopotamian Military Organization." Pages 413–22 in vol. 1 of *Civilizations of the Ancient Near East.* Edited by Jack M. Sasson. 4 vols. Peabody, Mass.: Hendrickson, 1995.

Dancy, J. C. *A Commentary on I Maccabees.* Blackwell's Theological Texts. Oxford: Blackwell, 1954.

Darley, William M. "Clausewitz's Theory of War and Information Operations." *Joint Force Quarterly* 40 (2006): 73–79.

David, Israel. "Lanchester Modeling and the Biblical Account of the Battles of Gibeah." *Naval Research Logistics* 42 (1995): 579–84.

Davies, Philip R. "Defining the Boundaries of Israel in the Second Temple Period: 2 Chronicles 20 and the 'Salvation Army.'" Pages 43–54 in *Priests, Prophets, and Scribes: Essays on the Formation and Heritage of Second Temple Judaism in Honour of Joseph Blenkinsopp.* Edited by E. Ulrich et al. JSOTSup 149. Sheffield: JSOT Press, 1992.

———. *In Search of "Ancient Israel."* JSOTSup 148. Sheffield: JSOT Press, 1992.

Davies, Philip R., and John Rogerson. *The Old Testament World.* 2nd ed. Louisville: Westminster John Knox, 2005.

Davis, Julie Hirschfeld. "If This Means War, What Does 'War' Mean?" *CQ Weekly* 59/35 (2001): 2110.

Day, Linda. "Rhetoric and Domestic Violence in Ezekiel 16." *BibInt* 8 (2000): 205–30.

Day, Peggy L. "Adulterous Jerusalem's Imagined Demise: Death of a Metaphor in Ezekiel XVI." *VT* 50 (2000): 285–309.

———. "The Bitch Had It Coming to Her: Rhetoric and Interpretation in Ezekiel 16." *BibInt* 8 (2000): 231–54.

———. "Metaphor and Social Reality: Isaiah 23.17–18, Ezekiel 16.35–37 and Hosea 2.4–5." Pages 63–71 in *Inspired Speech: Prophecy in the Ancient Near East: Essays in Honor of Herbert B. Huffmon.* Edited by John Kaltner and Louis Stulman. JSOTSup 378. New York: T&T Clark, 2004.

———. "The Personification of Cities as Females in the Hebrew Bible: The Thesis of Aloysius Fitzgerald, F.S.C." Pages 283–302 in *Social Location and Biblical Interpretation in Global Perspective.* Vol. 2 of *Reading from This Place.* Edited by Fernando F. Segovia and Mary Ann Tolbert. Minneapolis: Fortress, 1995.

———. "A Prostitute Unlike Women: Whoring as a Metaphoric Vehicle for Foreign Alliances." Pages 167–73 in *Israel's Prophets and Israel's Past: Essays on the Relationship of Prophetic Texts and Israelite History in Honor of John H. Hayes*. Edited by Brad E. Kelle and Megan Bishop Moore. LHB/OTS 446. New York: T&T Clark, 2006.

———. "Why Is Anat a Warrior and Hunter?" Pages 141–46 in *The Bible and the Politics of Exegesis: Essays in Honor of Norman K. Gottwald on His Sixty-Fifth Birthday*. Edited by Peggy L. Day, David Jobling, and Gerald T. Sheppard. Cleveland: Pilgrim, 1991.

———. "Yahweh's Broken Marriages as Metaphoric Vehicle in the Hebrew Prophets." In *Sacred Marriages in the Biblical World*. Edited by Martti Nissinen and Risto Uro. Winona Lake, Ind.: Eisenbrauns, forthcoming.

Dearman, John Andrew. *Property Rights in the Eighth-Century Prophets: The Conflict and Its Background*. SBLDS 106. Atlanta: Scholars Press, 1988.

Dempsey, Carol J. "The 'Whore' of Ezekiel 16: The Impact and Ramifications of Gender-Specific Metaphors in Light of Biblical Law and Divine Judgment." Pages 57–78 in *Gender and Law in the Hebrew Bible and the Ancient Near East*. Edited by Victor H. Matthews, Bernard M. Levinson, and Tikva Frymer-Kensky. JSOTSup 262. Sheffield: Sheffield Academic Press, 1998.

Dentan, Robert Knox. "Hawks, Doves, and Birds in the Bush: A Response to Keith Otterbein, Neil Whitehead, and Leslie Sponsel." *American Anthropologist* 104 (2002): 278–80.

———. "Spotted Doves at War: The *Praak Sangkill*." *Asian Folklore Studies* 58 (1999): 397–436.

DeVries, Simon J. *1 Kings*. WBC 12. Nashville: Nelson, 2003.

Dijk-Hemmes, Fokkelien van. "The Imagination of Power and the Power of Imagination: An Intertextual Analysis of Two Biblical Love Songs: The Song of Songs and Hosea 2." *JSOT* 44 (1989): 75–88.

———. "The Metaphorization of Woman in Prophetic Speech: An Analysis of Ezekiel XXIII." *VT* 43 (1993): 162–70.

Dillmann, August. *Die Bücher Numeri, Deuteronomium und Josua*. Leipzig: Hinrichs, 1886.

Dion, Paul. *Les Araméens à l'âge du fer: Histoire politique et structures sociales*. EBib NS 34. Paris: Gabalda, 1997.

Dobbs-Allsopp, Frederick W. "The Syntagma of *bat* Followed by a Geographical Name in the Hebrew Bible: A Reconsideration of Its Meaning and Grammar." *CBQ* 57 (1995): 451–70.

———. *Weep, O Daughter of Zion: A Study of the City-Lament Genre in the Hebrew Bible*. BibOr 44. Rome: Pontifical Biblical Institute, 1993.

Doran, Robert. *Temple Propaganda: The Purpose and Character of 2 Maccabees*. CBQMS 12. Washington, D.C.: Catholic Biblical Association, 1981.

Dozeman, Thomas B., and Konrad Schmid, eds. *A Farewell to the Yahwist? The Composition of the Pentateuch in Recent European Interpretation*. SBLSymS 34. Atlanta: Society of Biblical Literature, 2006.

Dressler, Harold. "Is the Bow of Aqhat a Symbol of Virility?" *UF* 7 (1975): 217–25.

Driver, S. R. *A Critical and Exegetical Commentary on Deuteronomy*. ICC 5. New York: Scribner's, 1916.

Ducrey, Pierre. *Le traitement des prisonniers de guerre dans la Grèce antique des origines à la conquête romaine*. 2nd ed. Paris: Boccard, 1999.

———. *Warfare in Ancient Greece*. Translated by Janet Lloyd. New York: Schocken, 1985.

Duyndam, Joachim. "Hermeneutics of Imitation: A Philosophical Approach to Sainthood and Exemplariness." Pages 7–21 in *Saints and Role Models in Judaism and Christianity*. Edited by Marcel Poorthuis and Joshua Schwartz. Jewish and Christian Perspectives Series 7. Leiden: Brill, 2004.

Edelman, Diana Vikander. "Doing History in Biblical Studies." Pages 13–25 in *The Fabric of History: Text, Artifact and Israel's Past*. Edited by Diana Edelman. JSOTSup 127. Sheffield: JSOT Press, 1991.

———. *King Saul in the Historiography of Judah*. JSOTSup 121. Sheffield: Sheffield Academic Press, 1991.

Eilberg-Schwarz, Howard. *God's Phallus and Other Problems for Men and Monotheism*. Boston: Beacon, 1994.

———. *The Savage in Judaism: An Anthropology of Israelite Religion and Ancient Judaism*. Bloomington: Indiana University Press, 1990.

Eissfeldt, Otto. *Der Gott Karmel*. Berlin: Akademie, 1954.

Elat, Moshe. "The Campaigns of Shalmaneser III against Aram and Israel." *IEJ* 25 (1975): 25–35.

Elgavish, David. "The Division of the Spoils of War in the Bible and in the Ancient Near East." *ZABR* 8 (2002): 242–73.

———. "The Encounter of Abram and Melchizedek King of Salem: A Covenant Establishing Ceremony." Pages 495–508 in *Studies in the Book of Genesis: Literature, Redaction and History*. Edited by A. Wénin. Leuven: Peeters, 2001.

Emerton, John A. "The Value of the Moabite Stone as an Historical Source." *VT* 52 (2002): 483–92.

Eph'al, Israel. "On Warfare and Military Control in the Ancient Near Eastern Empires: A Research Outline." Pages 88–106 in *History, Historiography and Interpretation: Studies in Biblical and Cuneiform Literatures*. Edited by H. Tadmor and M. Weinfeld. Jerusalem: Magnes, 1983.

———. *Siege Warfare and Its Ancient Near Eastern Manifestations* [Hebrew]. Jerusalem: Magnes, 1996.

Exum, J. Cheryl. *Fragmented Women: Feminist (Sub)versions of Biblical Narratives*. Valley Forge, Pa.: Trinity Press International, 1993.

———. "Judges." Pages 223–39 in *The HarperCollins Bible Commentary*. Edited by James Luther Mays. Rev. ed. San Francisco: Harper, 2000.

———. *Plotted, Shot and Painted: Cultural Representations of Biblical Women*. JSOTSup 215. GCT 3. Sheffield: Sheffield Academic Press, 1996.

Eynikel, Erik. *The Reform of King Josiah and the Composition of the Deuteronomistic Historian*. OtSt 33. Leiden: Brill, 1996.

Fanon, Frantz. *The Wretched of the Earth*. New York: Grove, 2005.

Fensham, F. Charles. "Widow, Orphan and the Poor in Ancient Near Eastern Legal and Wisdom Literature." *JNES* 21 (1962): 129–39. Repr. as pages 161–74 in *Studies in Ancient Israelite Wisdom*. Edited by J. L. Crenshaw. New York: Ktav, 1976.

Finkelstein, Israel, et al., eds. *Megiddo IV: The 1998–2002 Seasons*. The Emery and Claire Yass Publications in Archaeology. Monograph Series of the Institute of Archaeology 24. Tel Aviv: Tel Aviv University, 2006.

Finley, Moses I. *The Ancient Economy*. Berkley and Los Angeles: University of California Press, 1999.

———. "War and Empire." Pages 67–87, 119–22 in idem, *Ancient History: Evidence and Models*. New York: Viking, 1986.
Fitzgerald, Aloysius. "*BTWLT* and *BT* as Titles for Capital Cities." *CBQ* 37 (1975): 167–83.
———. "The Mythological Background for the Presentation of Jerusalem as a Queen and False Worship as Adultery in the Old Testament." *CBQ* 34 (1972): 406–13.
Flusser, David. "A New Sensitivity in Judaism and the Christian Message." *HTR* (1968): 107–27.
Follis, Elaine R. "The Holy City as Daughter." Pages 173–84 in *Directions in Biblical Hebrew Poetry*. Edited by Elaine R. Follis. JSOTSup 40. Sheffield: JSOT Press, 1987.
Foucault, Michel. *The Archaeology of Knowledge*. World of Man. New York: Pantheon, 1972.
Fox, Michael. "The Rhetoric of Ezekiel's Vision of the Valley of the Bones." *HUCA* 51 (1980): 1–15. Repr. as pages 176–90 in *The Place Is Too Small for Us: The Israelite Prophets in Recent Scholarship*. Edited by R. Gordon. SBTS 5. Winona Lake, Ind.: Eisenbrauns, 1995.
Fox, William T. R. "World Politics as Conflict Resolution." Pages 7–14 in *International Conflict and Conflict Management*. Edited by Robert O. Matthews. Scarborough: Prentice-Hall, 1984.
Frame, Grant. *Rulers of Babylonia: From the Second Dynasty of Isin to the End of Assyrian Domination (1157–612 BC)*. RIMB 2. Toronto: University of Toronto Press, 1995.
———. *Siege and Its Ancient Near Eastern Manifestations*. Jerusalem: Magnes, 1996.
———. "Ways and Means to Conquer a City, Based on Assyrian Queries to the Sungod." Pages 49–54 in *Assyria 1995: Proceedings of the 10th Anniversary Symposium of the Neo-Assyrian Text Corpus Project, Helsinki, September 7–11, 1995*. Edited by S. Parpola and R. M. Whiting. Helsinki: Neo-Assyrian Text Corpus Project, 1997.
France, R. T. *The Gospel of Mark. A Commentary on the Greek Text*. NIGTC. Grand Rapids: Eerdmans, 2002.
Frank, Harry Thomas, ed. *Discovering the Biblical World*. Maplewood: Hammond, 1988.
Frankena, R. "Vassal-Treaties of Essarhaddon and the Dating of Deuteronomy." Pages 122–44 in *Oudtestamentlich Werkgezelschap in Nederland*. Edited by Pieter Arie Hendrik de Boer. OtSt 14. Leiden: Brill, 1965.
Fredriksson, Henning. *Jahwe als Krieger: Studien zum alttestamentlichen Gottesbild*. Lund: Gleerup, 1945.
Freedman, David Noel. *The Nine Commandments: Uncovering the Hidden Pattern of Crime and Punishment in the Hebrew Bible*. New York: Doubleday, 2000.
Fretz, Mark J. "Weapons and Implements of Warfare." *ABD* 6:893–95.
Frick, Frank S. *The City in Ancient Israel*. SBLDS 36. Missoula, Mont.: Scholars Press, 1977.
Friedrich, Johannes. "Aus dem hethitischen Schrifttum: II. Gebet und die Istar von Ninive, aus fremden Ländern herbeizukommen," *AO* 25 (1925): 20–22.
———. "Der hethitische Soldateneid," *ZA* NS 1 (1924): 161–92.
Frishman, Judith. "Why Would a Man Want to Be Anyone's Wife? A Response to Satlow." Pages 43–48 in *Families and Family Relations as Represented in Early Judaisms and Early Christianities: Texts and Fictions—Papers Read at a NOSTER Colloquium in Amsterdam, June 9–11, 1998*. Edited by J. W. van Henten and A. Brenner. Studies in Theology and Religion 2. Leiden: Deo, 2000.

Fritz, Volkmar. *The City in Ancient Israel*. Biblical Seminar 29. Sheffield: Sheffield Academic Press, 1995.
Fuchs, Andreas. *Die Inschriften Sargons II aus Khorsabad*. Göttingen: Cuvillier, 1994.
Fuchs, Esther. *Sexual Politics in the Biblical Narrative: Reading the Hebrew Bible as a Woman*. JSOTSup 310. Sheffield: Sheffield Academic Press, 2000.
Gabriel, Ingeborg. *Friede über Israel: Eine Untersuchung zur Friedenstheologie im Chronik I 10–II 36*. ÖBS 10. Klosternueberg: Österreichisches Katholisches Bibelwerk, 1990.
Gadd, C. J. *The Stones of Assyria*. London: Chatto & Windus, 1936.
Galambush, Julie. *Jerusalem in the Book of Ezekiel: The City as Yahweh's Wife*. SBLDS 130. Atlanta: Scholars Press, 1992.
Galil, Gershon. "War, Peace, Stones and Memory." *PEQ* 139 (2007): 79–84.
Garlan, Yvon. "Le partage entre alliés des dépenses et des profits de guerre." Pages 149–64 in *Armées et fiscalité dans le monde antique. Paris, 14–16 Octobre 1976*. Colloques nationaux du Centre national de la recherche scientifique 936. Paris: Éditions du Centre national de la recherche scientifique, 1977.
———. *War in the Ancient World: A Social History*. Translated by J. Lloyd. London: Chatto & Windus, 1975.
Geertz, Clifford. *The Interpretation of Cultures*. New York: Basic Books, 1973.
Gertz, Jan Christian, Konrad Schmid, and Markus Witte, eds. *Abschied vom Jahwisten: Die Komposition des Hexeteuch in der jüngsten Diskussion*. BZAW 315. Berlin: de Gruyter, 2002.
Gilbert, Martin. *The Routledge Atlas of Jewish History*. London: Routledge, 1995
Gilliver, K. "The Roman Army and Morality in War." Pages 219–38 in *Battle in Antiquity*. Edited by Alan B. Lloyd. London: Duckworth, 1997.
Gitay, Yehoshua. *Prophecy as Persuasion: A Study of Isaiah 40–48*. Forum theologiae linguisticae 14. Bonn: Linguistica Biblica, 1981.
Gitay, Yehoshua. "Prophetic Criticism—'What Are They Doing?': The Case of Isaiah—A Methodological Assessment." *JSOT* 96 (2001): 101–27.
———. "Rhetorical Criticism and Prophetic Discourse." Pages 13–24 in *Persuasive Artistry*. Edited by Duane F. Watson. Sheffield: Sheffield Academic Press, 1991.
Glock, Albert E. *Warfare in Mari and Early Israel*. Missoula, Mont.: Scholars Press, 1973.
Gluckman, Max. *Custom and Conflict in Africa*. Oxford: Blackwell, 1963.
Godley, Alfred D., trans. *Herodotus*. 3 vols. LCL. Cambridge: Harvard University Press, 1920–22.
Goelet, Ogden, Jr., and Baruch A. Levine. "Making Peace in Heaven and On Earth: Religious and Legal Aspects of the Treaty Between Ramesses II and Hattusili III." Pages 252–99 in *Boundaries of the Ancient Near Eastern World: A Tribute to Cyrus H. Gordon*. Edited by Meir Lubetski, Claire Gottlieb, and Sharon Keller. JSOTSup 273. Sheffield: Sheffield Academic Press, 1998.
Goffman, Erving. *The Presentation of Self in Everyday Life*. New York: Doubleday, 1959.
Goldingay, John. *Israel's Gospel*. Vol. 1 of *Old Testament Theology*. Downers Grove, Ill.: InterVarsity Press, 2003.
Goldstein, Jonathan A. *1 and 2 Maccabees: A New Translation with Introduction and Commentary*. 2 vols. AB 41–41A. Garden City, N.Y.: Doubleday, 1976–83.
Goodman, M. D., and A. J. Holladay. "Religious Scruples in Ancient Warfare." *CQ* NS 36 (1996): 151–71.

Gordon, Pamela, and Harold C. Washington. "Rape as a Military Metaphor in the Hebrew Bible." Pages 308–25 in *A Feminist Companion to the Latter Prophets*. Edited by Athalya Brenner. FCB 8. Sheffield: Sheffield Academic Press, 1995.

Görg, Manfred. *Josua*. NEchtB 30 Würzburg: Echter, 1991.

———. *Richter*. NEchtB 31. Würzburg: Echter, 1993.

Gould, Ezra P. *The Gospel according to St. Mark*. ICC. Edinburgh: T&T Clark, 1896.

Grabbe Lester L., and Robert D. Haak, eds. *"Every City Shall Be Forsaken": Urbanism and Prophecy in Ancient Israel and the Near East*. JSOTSup 330. Sheffield: Sheffield Academic Press, 2001.

Gray, John. *I and II Kings: A Commentary*. OTL. Philadelphia: Westminster, 1963.

Green, Barbara. "Pregnant Passion: Gender, Sex, and Violence in the Bible—A Response to Part 3: Types, Stereotypes, and Archetypes." Pages 221–33 in *Pregnant Passion: Gender, Sex, and Violence in the Bible*. Edited by Cheryl A. Kirk-Duggan. SemeiaSt 44. Atlanta: Society of Biblical Literature, 2003.

Greengus, Samuel. "A Textbook Case of Adultery in Ancient Mesopotamia." *HUCA* 40–41 (1969–70): 33–44.

Gregory, Russell I. "Irony and the Unmasking of Elijah." Pages 94–102 in *From Carmel to Horeb: Elijah in Crisis*. Edited by Alan J. Hauser and Russell I. Gregory. JSOTSup 85. Sheffield: Almond, 1990.

Grey, John. *Joshua, Judges, Ruth*. NCB. London: Attic, 1967.

Grimm, Carl Ludwig Wilibald. *Das erste Buch der Maccabaer, Kurzgefasstes exegetisches Handbuch zu den Apokryphen des Alten Testamentes*. Leipzig: Hirzel, 1853.

———. *Das zweite, dritte, und vierte Buch der Maccabaer, Kurzgefasstes exegetisches Handbuch zu den Apokryphen des Alten Testamentes*. Leipzig: Hirzel, 1857.

Grotius, Hugo. *De iure praedae commentarius. Commentary on the Law of Prize and Booty*. Translated by Gwladys L. Williams and Walter H. Zeydel. Classics of International Law 22. Oxford: Clarendon, 1950.

Guest, P. Deryn. "Judges." Pages 190–207 in *Eerdmans Commentary on the Bible*. Edited by James D. G. Dunn and John Rogerson. Grand Rapids: Eerdmans, 2003.

Gundry, Robert H. *A Commentary on His Apology for the Cross*. Grand Rapids: Eerdmans, 1993.

Haas, Jonathan. "Warfare and the Evolution of Tribal Polities in the Prehistoric Southwest." Pages 171–89 in *The Anthropology of War*. Edited by Jonathan Haas. Cambridge: Cambridge University Press, 1990.

Hacham, Noah. "Exile and Self-Identity in the Qumran Sect and in Hellenistic Judaism." In the *Tenth Orion DSS Conference Volume*. Leiden: Brill, forthcoming.

Hackett, Jo Ann. "Can a Sexist Model Liberate Us? Ancient Near Eastern Fertility Goddesses." *JFSR* 5 (1989): 65–76.

Haddox, Susan E. "(E)Masculinity in Hosea's Political Rhetoric." Pages 175–200 in *Israel's Prophets and Israel's Past: Essays on the Relationship of Prophetic Texts and Israelite History in Honor of John H. Hayes*. Edited by Brad E. Kelle and Megan Bishop Moore. LHB/OTS 446. New York: T&T Clark, 2006.

Hallett, Brien. *The Lost Art of Declaring War*. Champaign: University of Illinois Press, 1998.

Halligan, John M. *A Critique of the City in the Yahwist Corpus*. Notre Dame, Ind.: University of Notre Dame Press, 1975.

Hallpike, Christopher R. "Functionalist Interpretations of Primitive Warfare." *Man* 8 (1973): 451–70.
Halpern, Baruch. *The Constitution of the Monarchy in Israel*. HSM 25. Chico, Calif.: Scholars Press, 1981.
Hamblin, William J. *Warfare in the Ancient Near East to 1600 BC: Holy Warriors at the Dawn of History*. Warfare and History. London: Routledge, 2006.
Hamilton, Victor P. *The Book of Genesis Chapters 1–17*. NICOT. Grand Rapids: Eerdmans, 1990.
Hands, R. *Charities and Social Aid in Greece and Rome*. London: Thames & Hudson, 1968.
Hanson, Victor D. *Warfare and Agriculture in Classical Greece*. Berkeley and Los Angeles: University of California Press, 1998.
Hardy, Thomas. *The Dynasts*. London: Macmillan, 1904–8.
Harrelson, Walter J. "Law in the OT." *IDB* 4:77–89.
Harrington, Daniel J. *The Maccabean Revolt: Anatomy of a Biblical Revolution*. Wilmington, Del.: Glazier, 1998.
Hasel, Michael G. "The Destruction of Trees in the Moabite Campaign of 2 Kgs 3:4–27: A Study in the Laws of Warfare." *AUSS* 40 (2002): 197–206.
———. *Military Practice and Polemic: Israel's Laws of Warfare in Near Eastern Perspective*. Berrien Springs, Mich.: Andrews University Press, 2005.
Hassig, Ross. *War and Society in Ancient Mesoamerica*. Berkeley and Los Angeles: University of California Press, 1992.
Hauer, Christian E. "Foreign Intelligence and Internal Security in Davidic Israel." *Concordia Journal* 7 (1981): 96–99.
Hauser, Alan Jon. "Two Songs of Victory: A Comparison of Exodus 15 and Judges 5." Pages 265–84 in *Directions in Biblical Hebrew Poetry*. Edited by Elaine R. Follis. JSOTSup 40. Sheffield: JSOT Press, 1987.
Häusl, Maria. *Bilder der Not*. Freiburg: Herder, 2003.
Havice, Harriet K. "The Concern for the Widow and the Fatherless in the Ancient Near East: A Case Study in Old Testament Ethics." Ph.D. diss. Yale University, 1978.
Hawk, L. Daniel. *Joshua*. Berit Olam. Collegeville, Minn.: Liturgical Press, 2000.
———. "The Problem with Pagans." Pages 153–63 in *Reading Bibles, Writing Bodies*. Edited by Timothy K. Beal and David M. Gunn. London: Routledge, 1997.
Hayden, Robert M. "Schindler's Fate: Genocide, Ethnic Cleansing, and Population Transfers." *Slavic Review* 55 (1996): 727–48.
Hayes, John H. "The Usage of Oracles against Foreign Nations in Ancient Israel." *JBL* 87 (1968): 81–92.
Hedges, Chris. *War Is a Force That Gives Us Meaning*. New York: Anchor Books, 2003.
Hendrickson, Ryan C. Review of Brien Hallett, *The Lost Art of Declaring War*. *The American Political Science Review* 93 (1999): 754–55.
Henten, Jan Willem van. *The Maccabean Martyrs as Saviours of the Jewish People: A Study of 2 and 4 Maccabees*. Leiden: Brill, 1997.
Herold, Anja. *Streitwagentechnologie in der Ramses-Stadt: Bronze an Pferd und Wagen*. Forschungen in der Ramses-Stadt. Die Grabungen des Pelizaeus-Museums Hildesheim in Qantir—Pi-Ramesse 2. Maniz: von Zabern, 1999.
Herrmann, Siegfried. *A History of Israel in Old Testament Times*. Rev ed. Philadelphia: Fortress, 1981.

Herzog, Chaim, and Mordechai Gichon. *Battles of the Bible*. Rev. ed. London: Greenhill, 1997.
Herzog, Ze'ev. "Settlement and Fortification Planning in the Iron Age." Pages 231–74 in *The Architecture of Ancient Israel*. Edited by Aharon Kempinski and Ronny Reich. Jerusalem: Israel Exploration Society, 1992.
Heschel, Abraham Joshua. *The Prophets*. New York: Harper & Row, 1962. Repr., New York: HarperCollins, 2001.
Hillers, Delbert R. "A Convention in Hebrew Literature: The Reaction to Bad News." *ZAW* 77 (1965): 86–90.
———. *Treaty Curses and the Old Testament Prophets*. BibOr 16. Rome: Pontifical Biblical Institute, 1964.
Hippler, Thomas. "Uwe Steinhoff: What is War?" The Oxford Leverhulme Programme on the Changing Character of War Lunchtime Discussion Series, Week 4, 2 November 2004. Online: http://ccw.politics.ox.ac.uk/events/archives/mt04_steinhoff.pdf.
Hobbs, T. R. *A Time for War: A Study of Warfare in the Old Testament*. OTS 3 Wilmington, Del.: Glazier, 1989.
Hoffman, Yair. "The Deuteronomistic Concept of the *Herem*." *ZAW* 111 (1999): 196–210.
Hoffmeier, James K. *Israel in Egypt*. New York: Oxford University Press, 1997.
———. "The Structure of Joshua 1–11 and the Annals of Thutmose III." Pages 165–79 in *Faith, Tradition, and History: Old Testament Historiography in Its Near Eastern Context*. Edited by Alan R. Millard, James K. Hoffmeier, and David W. Baker. Winona Lake, Ind.: Eisenbrauns, 1994.
Hoffner, Harry A. "Symbols for Masculinity and Feminity: Their Use in Ancient Near Eastern Sympathetic Magic Rituals." *JBL* 85 (1966): 326–34.
Holladay, William L. *Jeremiah 2*. Hermeneia. Minneapolis: Fortress, 1989.
Hollander, Harm W. *Joseph as an Ethical Model in the Testaments of the Twelve Patriarchs*. SVTP 6. Leiden: Brill, 1981.
Hooker, Morna D. *A Commentary on the Gospel according to St. Mark*. BNTC 2. London: Black, 1990.
Hopkins, David. "The Dynamics of Agriculture in Monarchical Israel." Pages 177–202 in *Society of Biblical Literature 1983 Seminar Papers*. SBLSP 22. Chico, Calif.: Scholars Press, 1983.
Horn, Siegfried H. "Did Sennacherib Campaign Once or Twice Against Hezekiah?" *AUSS* 4 (1966): 1–28.
Horst, Pieter W. van der. *Philo's Flaccus: The First Pogrom: Introduction, Translation and Commentary*. Philo of Alexandria Commentary Series 2. Leiden: Brill, 2003. Repr., Atlanta: Society of Biblical Literature, 2005.
———. "Pseudo-Phocylides: A New Translation and Introduction." *OTP* 2:565–82.
———. "Pseudo-Phocylides and the New Testament." *ZNW* 69 (1978): 187–202.
———. *The Sentences of Pseudo-Phocylides*. SVTP 4. Leiden, Brill: 1978.
Hubbard, Robert L., Jr. "'What Do These Stones Mean?' Biblical Theology and a Motif in Joshua." *BBR* 11 (2001): 1–26.
Hurowitz, Victor, and Joan Goodnick Westenholz. "LKA 63: A Heroic Poem in Celebration of Tiglath-pileser I's Musru and Qumana Campaign." *JCS* 42 (1990): 14–18.
Isserlin, Benedikt S. J. *The Israelites*. Minneapolis: Fortress, 2001.
Jackson, A. H. "Plundering in War and other Depredations in Greek History from 800 B.C. to 146 B.C." Ph.D. diss. Cambridge University, 1969.

Jacoby, Ruth. "The Representations and Identification of Cities on Assyrian Reliefs." *IEJ* 41 (1991): 112–31.
Jobert, Bruno, and Pierre Müller. *L'État en action: Politiques publiques et corporatismes.* Paris: Presses Universitaires de France, 1987.
Johnson, Hubert C. "Warfare, Strategies and Tactics of." Pages 759–62 in vol. 3 of *Encyclopedia of Violence, Peace, and Conflict.* Edited by Lester Kurtz. 3 vols. New York: Academic, 1999.
Jones, Gwilym H. *1 and 2 Kings.* 2 vols. NCB. Grand Rapids: Eerdmans, 1984.
Kang, Sa-Moon. *Divine War in the Old Testament and in the Ancient Near East.* BZAW 177. Berlin: de Gruyter, 1989.
Kantorowicz, Ernst. *The King's Two Bodies: A Study in Mediaeval Political Theology.* 2nd ed. Princeton: Princeton University Press, 1966.
Kataja, Laura, and Robert Whiting, eds. *Grants, Decrees and Gifts of the Neo-Assyrian Period.* SAA 12. Helsinki: Helsinki University Press, 1995.
Keefe, Alice A. *Woman's Body and the Social Body in Hosea.* JSOTSup 338. GCT 10. Sheffield: Sheffield Academic Press, 2001.
Keegan, John. *The Face of Battle.* New York: Penguin, 1974.
———. *War and Our World: The Keith Lectures.* New York: Vintage, 1998.
Keen, Sam. *Faces of the Enemy: Reflections on the Hostile Imagination.* Enlarged edition. New York: Harper & Row, 2004.
Kelle, Brad E. *Ancient Israel at War 853–586 BC.* Essential Histories 67. Oxford: Osprey, 2007.
———. "Ancient Israelite Prophets and Greek Political Orators: Analogies for the Prophets and Their Implications for Historical Reconstruction." Pages 57–82 in *Israel's Prophets and Israel's Past: Essays on the Relationship of Prophetic Texts and Israelite History in Honor of John H. Hayes.* Edited by Brad E. Kelle and Megan Bishop Moore. LHB/OTS 446. New York: T&T Clark, 2006.
———. *Hosea 2: Metaphor and Rhetoric in Historical Perspective.* SBLAcBib 20. Atlanta: Society of Biblical Literature, 2005.
———. "Warfare (Imagery)." In *Dictionary of the Old Testament: Wisdom, Poetry, and Writings.* Edited by Tremper Longman III and Peter Enns. Downers Grove, Ill.: Intervarsity Press, forthcoming.
Kelly, Raymond C. *Warless Societies and the Origin of War.* Ann Arbor: University of Michigan Press, 2000.
Kern, Paul Bentley. *Ancient Siege Warfare.* Bloomington: Indiana University Press, 1999.
King, Leonard W., and E. A. Wallis Budge. *Bronze Reliefs from the Gates of Shalmaneser, King of Assyria, B.C. 860–825.* London: British Museum Press, 1915.
King, Philip J., and Lawrence E. Stager. *Life in Biblical Israel.* Library of Ancient Israel. Louisville: Westminster John Knox, 2001.
Kissling, Paul J. *Reliable Characters in the Primary History: Profiles of Moses, Joshua, Elijah and Elisha.* JSOTSup 224. Sheffield: Sheffield Academic Press, 1996.
Kiyofuku, Chuma. "The Choice Is Clear: Diplomacy over Force." *Japan Quaterly* 38/2 (1991): 142–47.
Klassen, William. "War in the NT." *ABD* 6:867–75.
Knauf, Ernst Axel. "Does the 'Deuteronomistic Historiography' (DtrH) Exist?" Pages 388–98 in *Israel Constructs Its History: Deuteronomistic History in Recent Research.* Edited

by Albert de Pury, Thomas C. Römer, and Jean-Daniel Macchi. JSOTSup 306. Sheffield: JSOT Press, 2000.

Knoppers, Gary N. "'Battling against Yahweh': Israel's War against Judah in 2 Chr. 13:2–20." *RB* 100 (1993): 511–32.

———. "Jerusalem at War in Chronicles." Pages 55–76 in *Zion, City of Our God*. Edited by Richard S. Hess and Gordon J. Wenham. Grand Rapids: Eerdmans, 1999.

Krasilnikoff, Jens A. "Aegean Mercenaries in the Fourth to Second Centuries BC. A Study in Payment, Plunder and Logistics of Ancient Greek Armies." *Classica et mediaevalia* 43 (1992): 23–36.

Kratz, Reinhard G. *Die Komposition der erzählenden Bücher des Alten Testaments*. Göttingen: Vandenhoeck & Ruprecht, 2000.

Kraus, Hans-Joachim. "Gilgal: A Contribution to the History of Worship in Israel." Translated by Peter T. Daniels. Pages 163–78 in *Reconsidering Israel and Judah: Recent Studies on the Deuteronomistic History*. Edited by Gary N. Knoppers and J. Gordon McConville. Sources for Biblical and Theological Study 8. Winona Lake, Ind.: Eisenbrauns, 2000.

Kraus, Hans-Joachim. *Psalms 60–150*. Translated by Hilton C Oswald. CC. Minneapolis: Augsburg, 1989.

Kugel, James L. *Traditions of the Bible: A Guide to the Bible as It Was at the Start of the Common Era*. Cambridge: Harvard University Press, 1999.

Kugler, Jacek. "War." Pages 894–96 in *The Oxford Companion to the Politics of the World*. Edited by Joel Krieger. 2nd ed. New York: Oxford University Press, 2001.

Laato, Antti. "Assyrian Propaganda and the Falsification of History in the Royal Inscriptions of Sennacherib." *VT* 45 (1995): 198–226.

Laffey, Alice. *An Introduction to the Old Testament: A Feminist Perspective*. Philadelphia: Fortress, 1988.

Lakoff, George, and Mark Turner. *More Than Cool Reason*. Chicago: University of Chicago Press, 1989.

Lambert, Wilfred G. "A Middle Assyrian Medical Text," *Iraq* 31 (1969): 28–39.

Lasine, Stuart. *Knowing Kings: Knowledge, Power, and Narcissism in the Hebrew Bible*. SemeiaSt 40. Atlanta: Society of Biblical Literature, 2001.

Leith, Mary J. Winn. "Verse and Reverse: The Transformation of the Woman Israel in Hosea 1–3." Pages 95–108 in *Gender and Difference in Ancient Israel*. Edited by Peggy L. Day. Minneapolis: Fortress, 1989.

Lekson, Stephen H. "War in the Southwest, War in the World." *American Antiquity* 67 (2002): 607–24.

Lemaire, Andre. "'Avec un Sceptre de Fer': Ps. II, 9 et l'archéologie." *BN* 32 (1986): 25–30.

Lemche, Niels Peter. *Ancient Israel: A New History of Israelite Society*. Sheffield: JSOT Press, 1988.

———. "The Old Testament—A Hellenistic Book?" *SJOT* 7 (1993): 163–93.

Lemos, Tracy. "Shame and Mutilation of Enemies in the Hebrew Bible." *JBL* 125 (2006): 225–41.

Lepper, Steven J. "On (the Law of) War: What Clausewitz Meant to Say." *Airpower Journal* 13/2 (1999): 103–8.

Levine, Baruch A. *Numbers 21–36: A New Translation with Introduction and Commentary*. AB 4A. New York: Doubleday, 2000.

Levine, David. "Holy Men and Rabbis in Talmudic Antiquity. Pages 45–58 in *Saints and Role Models in Judaism and Christianity*. Edited by Marcel Poorthuis and Joshua Schwartz. Jewish and Christian Perspectives Series 7. Leiden: Brill, 2004.

Levine, Etan. "You Shall Not Covet." Page 141–59 in *Heaven and Earth, Law and Love: Studies in Biblical Thought*. BZAW 303. Berlin: de Gruyter, 2000.

Lewy, Julius. "The Old West Semitic Sun-God Hammu." *HUCA* 18 (1944): 436–43.

Lincoln, Bruce. "War and Warriors: An Overview." *ER* 15:339–44.

Lind, Millard C. *Yahweh Is a Warrior*. Scottdale, Pa.: Herald, 1980.

Linville, James Richard. *Israel in the Book of Kings: The Past as a Project of Social Identity*. JSOTSup 272. Sheffield: JSOT Press, 1998.

Liverani, Mario. *Israel's History and the History of Israel*. London: Equinox, 2005.

———. *Prestige and Interest: International Relations in the Near East ca. 1600–1100 B.C.* History of the Ancient Near East 1. Padova: Sargon, 1990.

Lohfink, Norbert. *Theology of the Pentateuch: Themes of the Priestly Narrative and Deuteronomy*. Minneapolis: Fortress, 1994.

Long, Burke O. *1 Kings*. FOTL 9. Grand Rapids: Eerdmans, 1984.

Long, V. Philips. "How Reliable are Biblical Reports? Repeating Lester Grabbe's Comparative Experiment." *VT* 52 (2002): 367–84.

Longman, Tremper III, and Daniel G. Reid. *God Is a Warrior*. Grand Rapids: Zondervan, 1995.

Luckenbill, Daniel David. *The Annals of Sennacherib*. OIP 2. Chicago: University of Chicago Press, 1924.

Machinist, Peter. "Assyria and Its Image in First Isaiah." *JAOS* 103 (1983): 719–37.

Madvig, Donald. "Joshua." Pages 239–374 in *Deuteronomy, Joshua, Judges, Ruth, 1 and 2 Samuel*. Vol. 3 of *The Expositor's Bible Commentary*. Edited by Frank E. Gaebelein. Grand Rapids: Zondervan, 1992.

Magdalene, F. Rachel. "Ancient Near Eastern Treaty-Curses and the Ultimate Texts of Terror: A Study of the Language of Divine Sexual Abuse in the Prophetic Corpus." Pages 326–52 in *A Feminist Companion to the Latter Prophets*. Edited by Athalya Brenner. FCB 8. Sheffield: Sheffield Academic Press, 1995.

Magen, Ursula. *Assyrische Königsdarstellungen: Aspekte der Herrschaft*. Baghdader Forschungen 9. Mainz: von Zabern, 1986.

Maier, Christl. "Jerusalem als Ehebrecherin in Ezechiel 16: Zur Verwendung und Funktion einer biblische Metapher." Pages 85–105 in *Feministische Hermeneutik und Erstes Testament: Analysen und Interpretationen*. Edited by H. Jahnow. Stuttgart: Kohlhammer, 1994.

———. "Die Klage der Tochter Zion: Ein Beitrag zur Weiblichkeitsmetaphorik im Jeremiabuch." *BThZ* 15 (1998): 176–89.

Malamat, Abraham. "Israelite Conduct of War in the Conquest of Canaan." Pages 35–56 in *Symposia Celebrating the Seventy-Fifth Anniversiay of the Founding of the American Schools of Oriental Research (1900–1975)*. Edited by Frank Moore Cross. Cambridge: American Schools of Oriental Research, 1979.

Malinowski, Bronislaw. "An Anthropological Analysis of War." Pages 245–68 in *War: Studies from Psychology, Sociology, Anthropology*. Edited by Leon Bramson and George W. Goethals. Rev. ed. New York: Basic Books, 1968.

Marcus, David, and Edward L. Greenstein. "The Akkadian Inscription of *Idrimi*." *JANES* 8 (1976): 59–96.

Mason, Steve, ed. *Flavius Josephus: Translation and Commentary*. 9 vols. Leiden: Brill, 1999–2005.
Matthews, Victor H. *A Brief History of Ancient Israel*. Louisville: Westminster John Knox, 2002.
———. "Legal Aspects of Military Service in Ancient Mesopotamia." *Military Law Review* 94 (1981): 135–51.
———. "Messengers and the Transmission of Information in the Mari Kingdom." Pages 267–74 in *Go to the Land I Will Show You: Studies in Honor of Dwight W. Young*. Edited by Victor H. Matthews and Joseph Coleson. Winona Lake, Ind.: Eisenbrauns, 1996.
———. *Studying the Ancient Israelites: A Guide to Sources and Methods*. Grand Rapids: Baker, 2007.
Matthews, Victor H., and Don C Benjamin, *Social World of Ancient Israel: 1250–587 BCE*. Peabody, Mass.: Hendrickson, 1993.
May, Herbert G., ed. *Oxford Bible Atlas*. 3rd ed. New York: Oxford University Press, 1984.
Mayer, Walter. "Sargons Feldzug gegen Urartu—714 v. Chr. Text und Übersetzung." *MDOG* 115 (1983): 65–132.
Mayer, Walter. "Sennacherib's Campaign of 701 BCE: The Assyrian View." Translated by Julia Assante. Pages 168–200 in *'Like a Bird in a Cage': The Invasion of Sennacherib in 701 BCE*. Edited by Lester L. Grabbe. JSOTSup 363. London: Sheffield Academic Press, 2003.
Mayes, A. D. H. *Deuteronomy*. NCB. Grand Rapids: Eerdmans.
———. "Deuteronomy 4 and the Literary Criticism of Deuteronomy." *JBL* 100 (1981): 23–51.
———. *The Story of Israel between Settlement and Exile*. London: SCM, 1983.
Mazar, Ahimai. *Archaeology of the Land of the Bible 10,000–586 B.C.E.* New York: Doubleday, 1990.
———. "Ritual Dancing in the Iron Age." *NEA* 66 (2003): 126–32.
McAllister, Ian. Review of John Keegan, *War and Our World: The Keith Lectures. Peacekeeping & International Relations* 29/3–4 (2000): 23–24.
McCarthy, Dennis J. "Some Holy War Vocabulary in Joshua 2." *CBQ* 33 (1971): 228–30.
Mendenhall, George. "The Suzerainty Treaty Structure: Thirty Years Later." Pages 85–100 in *Religion and Law: Biblical-Judaic and Islamic Perspectives*. Edited by Edwin B. Firmage, Bernard G. Weiss, and John W. Welch. Winona Lake, Ind.: Eisenbrauns, 1990.
Metzger, Bruce M. *A Textual Commentary on the Greek New Testament*. 3rd ed. London: United Bible Societies, 1971.
Meyers, Carol. "Of Drums and Damsels: Women's Performance in Ancient Israel," *BA* 54 (1991): 16–27.
Mierzejewski, Alfred C. "La technique de siège assyrienne aux IX–VII siècle savant notre ère." *Etudes et Travaux* 7 (Varsovie): 11–20.
Milgrom, Jacob. *Cult and Conscience: The 'Asham' and the Priestly Doctrine of Repentance*. SJLA 18. Leiden: Brill, 1976.
———. *Leviticus 17–22*. AB 3A. New York: Doubleday, 2000.
———. *Numbers: The Traditional Hebrew Text with the New JPS Translation*. JPS Torah Commentary. Philadelphia: Jewish Publication Society, 1994.
Miller, J. Maxwell. "Is It Possible to Write a History of Israel without Relying on the Hebrew Bible?" Pages 93–102 in *The Fabric of History: Text, Artifact and Israel's Past*. Edited by Diana Edelman. JSOTSup 127. Sheffield: JSOT Press, 1991.

Miller, J. Maxwell, and John H. Hayes. *A History of Ancient Israel and Judah.* 2nd ed. Louisville: Westminster John Knox, 2006.
Miller, Patrick D., Jr. *The Divine Warrior in Early Israel.* HSM 5. Cambridge: Harvard University Press, 1973. Repr., Atlanta: Society of Biblical Literature, 2006.
Moloney, Francis J. *The Gospel of Mark: A Commentary.* Peabody, Mass.: Hendrickson, 2002.
Montgomery, James A., and Henry S. Gehman. *The Book of Kings.* ICC. Edinburgh: T&T Clark, 1951.
Moore, Megan Bishop. *Philosophy and Practice in Writing a History of Ancient Israel.* LHB/OTS 435. New York: T&T Clark, 2006.
Moran, William L. "The Ancient Near Eastern Background of the Love of God in Deuteronomy." *CBQ* 25 (1963): 77–87.
———. "The Conclusion of the Decalogue (Ex 20,17 = Dt 5,21)." *CBQ* 29 (1967): 543–54.
Morgan, T. Clifton. "The Concept of War: Its Impact on Research and Policy." *Peace & Change* 15/4 (1990): 413–41.
Muffs, Yochanan. "Abraham the Noble Warrior: Patriarchal Politics and Laws of War in Ancient Israel." *JJS* 33 (1982): 81–107.
Müller, Reinhard. *Königtum und Gottesherrschaft: Untersuchungen zur alttestamentlichen Monarchiekritik.* FAT 2/3. Tübingen: Mohr Siebeck, 2004.
Muscarella, Oscar White. "The Location of Ulhu and Urse in Sargon II's Eighth Campaign, 714 B.C." *JFA* 13 (1986): 466–75.
Musil, Alois. *The Manners and Customs of the Rwala Bedouins.* Oriental Explorations and Studies 6. New York: American Geographical Society, 1928.
Nelson, Richard. *Joshua.* OTL. Philadelphia: Westminster John Knox, 1997.
Newcomb, William W. "A Re-examination of the Causes of Plains Warfare." *American Anthropologist* 63 (1950): 317–30.
Nickelsburg, George W. E. "1 and 2 Maccabee—Same Story, Different Meaning." *CTM* 42 (1971): 515–26.
Nickelsburg, George W. E., and Michael E. Stone. *Faith and Piety in Early Judaism: Texts and Documents.* Rev. ed. Harrisburg, Pa.: Trinity Press International, 1994.
Niditch, Susan. "The 'Sodomite' Theme in Judges 19–20: Family, Community, and Social Disintegration." *CBQ* 44 (1982): 365–78.
———. "War, Women, and Defilement in Numbers 31." *Semeia* 61 (1993): 39–57.
———. *War in the Hebrew Bible: A Study in the Ethics of Violence.* New York: Oxford University Press, 1993.
Nissinen, Martti. *Homoeroticism in the Biblical World: A Historical Perspective.* Minneapolis: Fortress, 1998.
Nitzan, Bilhah. "Benedictions and Instructions for the Eschatological Community (11QBer; 4Q285)." *RQ* 16:1 (1993): 77–90.
Noll, Kurt L. *Canaan and Israel in Antiquity: An Introduction.* London: Sheffield Academic Press, 2001.
Noort, Edward. "Das Kapitulationsangebot im Kriegsgesetz Dtn 20:10ff. und in den Kriegserzählungen." Pages 199–207 in *Studies in Deuteronomy in Honour of C. J. Labuschagne on the Occasion of His 65th Birthday.* Edited by Florentino García Martínez, A. Hilhorst, J. T. A. M. G. van Ruiten, and Adam S. van der Woude. VTSup 53. Leiden: Brill, 1994.

Nora, Pierre. "From *lieux de mémoire* to Realms of Memory." Pages xv–xxiv in vol. 1 of *Realms of Memory: Rethinking the French Past: Conflicts and Divisions*. Edited by Pierre Nora and Lawrence D. Kritzman. New York: Columbia University Press, 1996.
Noth, Martin. *Das Buch Josua*. 2nd ed. HAT 7. Tübingen: Mohr Siebeck, 1952.
———. *The History of Israel*. 2nd ed. New York: Harper & Row, 1960.
O'Brien, Julia Myers. *Nahum*. Readings. New York: Sheffield Academic Press, 2002.
O'Connell, Robert H. *The Rhetoric of the Book of Judges*. VTSup 63. Leiden: Brill, 1996.
Oded, Bustenay. "'The Command of the God' as a Reason for Going to War in the Assyrian Royal Inscriptions." Pages 223–30 in *Ah, Assyria…: Studies in Assyrian History and Ancient Near Eastern Historiography Presented to Hayim Tadmor*. Edited by Mordecai Cogan. Jerusalem: Magnes, 1991.
Oded, Bustenay. "Cutting Down the Gardens in the Descriptions of the Assyrian Kings—A Chapter in Assyrian Historiography." Pages 27–36 in *Michael: Historical, Epigraphical and Biblical Studies in Honor of Prof. Michael Heltzer*. Edited by Y. Avishur and R. Deutsch. Tel Aviv: Archaeological Center Publications, 1999.
———. "The Inscriptions of Tiglath-pileser III: Review Article." *IEJ* 47 (1997): 104–10.
———. *War, Peace and Empire: Justifications for War in Assyrian Royal Inscriptions*. Wiesbaden: Reichert, 1992.
Oden, Robert. *The Bible without Theology: The Theological Tradition and Alternatives To It*. San Francisco: Harper & Row, 1987.
Ollenburger, Ben C. "Gerhard von Rad's Theory of Holy War." Pages 1–33 in Gerhard von Rad, *Holy War in Ancient Israel*. Translated and edited by Marva J. Dawn. Bibliography by Judith E. Sanderson. Grand Rapids: Eerdmans, 1991.
Olley, John. "*YHWH* and His Zealous Prophet." *JSOT* 80 (1998): 25–51.
Olmstead, A. T. *History of Assyria*. New York: Scribner's, 1923.
Olyan, Saul M. "'In the Sight of Her Lovers': On the Interpretation of *nablūt* in Hosea 2,12." *BZ* 36 (1992): 255–61.
Oppenheim, A. Leo. 'Siege-documents from Nippur." *Iraq* 17 (1955): 69–89.
Osborne, Rick, Marnie Wooding, and Ed Strauss. *Bible Wars and Weapons*. Grand Rapids: Zonderkidz, 2002.
Otterbein, Keith F. "A History of Research on Warfare in Anthropology." *American Anthropologist* 101 (1999): 794–805.
Otto, Eckart. *Krieg und Frieden in der hebräischen Bibel und im alten Orient: Aspekte für eine Friedensordnung in der Moderne*. Theologie und Frieden 18. Stuttgart: Kohlhammer, 1999.
———. "Ps 2 in neuassyrischer Zeit: Assyrische Motive in der judäischen Königsideologie." Pages 335–49 in *Textarbeit: Studien zu Texten und ihrer Rezeption aus dem Alten Testament und der Umwelt Israels: Festschrift für Peter Weimar*. Edited by K. Kiesow and T. Meurer. AOAT 294. Münster: Ugarit-Verlag, 2003.
———. "Tora und Charisma: Legitimation und Delegitimation des Königtums in 1 Samuel 8–2 Samuel 1 im Spiegel neuerer Literatur." *ZABR* 12 (2006): 225–44.
Parpola, Simo. *The Correspondence of Sargon II: Letters from Assyria and the West*. SAA 1. Helsinki: Helsinki University Press, 1987.
Parpola, Simo, and Kazuko Watanabe, eds. *Neo-Assyrian Treaties and Loyalty Oaths*. SAA 2. Helsinki: Helsinki University Press, 1988.
Patterson, Richard D. M. "The Widow, the Orphan and the Poor in the Old Testament and the Extra-biblical Literature." *BSac* 130 (1973): 223–34.

Patton, Corrine L. "'Should Our Sister Be Treated Like a Whore?' A Response to Feminist Critiques of Ezekiel 23." Pages 221–39 in *The Book of Ezekiel: Theological and Anthropological Perspectives*. Edited by Margaret S. Odell and John T. Strong. SBLSymS 9. Atlanta: Society of Biblical Literature, 2000.

Paul, Shalom M. "Literary and Ideological Echoes of Jeremiah in Deutero-Isaiah." Pages 102–20 in *World Congress of Jewish Studies 5*. Jerusalem: Magnes, 1971.

———. "Sargon's Administrative Diction in II Kings 17:27." *JBL* 88 (1969): 73–74.

Person, Raymond F., Jr. *The Deuteronomic School: History, Social Setting, and Literature*. SBLSBL 2. Atlanta: Society of Biblical Literature, 2002.

Petersen, David L. "Genesis and Family Values," *JBL* 124 (2005): 5–23.

Plöger, Otto. *Literarkritische, formgeschichtliche, und stilkritische Untersuchungen zum Deuteronomium*. BBB. Bonn: Hanstein, 1967.

Polzin, Robert. *Moses and the Deuteronomist*. New York: Seabury, 1980.

Poorthuis, Marcel, and Joshua Schwartz, eds. *Saints and Role Models in Judaism and Christianity*. Jewish and Christian Perspectives Series 7. Leiden: Brill, 2004.

Pressler, Carolyn. *Joshua, Judges, Ruth*. Westminster Bible Companion. Louisville: Westminster John Knox, 2002.

Preuß, Horst D. *Deuteronomium*. EdF 164. Darmstadt: Wissenschaftliche Buchgesellschaft, 1982.

Pritchard, James, ed. *The Harper Atlas of the Bible*. San Francisco: Harper & Row, 1987.

Pritchett, William K. *The Greek State at War*. 5 vols. Berkeley and Los Angeles: University of California Press, 1971–91.

Proença, Domício, Jr., and E. E. Duarte. "The Concept of Logistics Derived from Clausewitz: All That Is Required So That the Fighting Force Can Be Taken as a Given." *The Journal of Strategic Studies* 28 (2005): 645–77.

Provan, Iain, V. Philips Long, and Tremper Longman III. *A Biblical History of Israel*. Louisville: Westminster John Knox, 2003.

Pury, Albert de, and Thomas Römer. "Deuteronomistic Historiography (DH): History of Research and Debated Issues." Pages 24–143 in *Israel Constructs Its History: Deuteronomistic Historiography in Recent Research*. Edited by Albert de Pury, Thomas Römer, and Jean-Daniel Macchi. JSOTSup 306. Sheffield: Sheffield Academic Press, 2000.

Rad, Gerhard von. *Deuteronomy: A Commentary*. Philadelphia: Westminster, 1966.

———. *Holy War in Ancient Israel*. Translated and edited by Marva J. Dawn. Introduction by Ben C. Ollenburger. Bibliography by Judith E. Sanderson. Grand Rapids: Eerdmans, 1991.

———. *Der Heilige Krieg im Alten Israel*. 4th ed. Göttingen: Vandenhoeck & Ruprecht, 1965.

———. "Das judäische Königsritual," *TLZ* 72 (1947): 211-15.

Rahlfs, Alfred, ed. *Septuaginta*. Stuttgart: Deutsche Bibelgesellschaft, 1979.

Raitasalo, Jyri and Joonas Siplila. "Reconstructing War after the Cold War." *Comparative Strategy* 23 (2004): 239–61.

Rappaport, Uriel. "1 Maccabees." Pages 710–34 in *The Oxford Bible Commentary*. Edited by J. Barton and J. Muddiman. Oxford: Oxford University Press, 2001.

Rappaport, Uriel. *1 Maccabees*. Jerusalem: Yad Itzak Ben Zvi, 2005 [Hebrew].

Rast, Joshua. "Joshua." Pages 214–222 in *The Harper Collins Bible Commentary*. Rev. ed. Edited by James Luther Mays. San Francisco: Harper, 2000.

Rendtorff, Rolf. "Between Historical Criticism and Holistic Interpretation: New Trends in Old Testament Exegesis." Pages 298–303 in *Congress Volume: Jerusalem, 1986*. Edited by John A. Emerton. VTSup 40. Leiden: Brill, 1988.

———. "The Paradigm Is Changing: Hopes and Fears." *BibInt* 1 (1993): 34–53.

———. *The Problem of the Process of Transmission in the Pentateuch*. JSOTSup 89. Sheffield: JSOT Press, 1990.

Rengstorf, Karl H., ed. *A Complete Concordance to Flavius Josephus: Unabridged Study Edition*. 2 vols. Leiden: Brill, 2002.

Restovetzeff, Michael I. *The Social and Economic History of the Hellenistic World*. 3 vols. Oxford: Clarendon, 1941.

Robarchek, Clayton, and Robert Knox Dentan. "Blood Drunkenness and the Bloodthirsty Semai: Unmaking Another Anthropological Myth." *American Anthropologist* 89 (1987): 356–65.

Roberts, Jim J. M. "Bearers of the Polity: Isaiah of Jerusalem's View of Eighth-Century Judean Society." Pages 145–52 in *Constituting the Community: Studies on the Polity of Ancient Israel in Honor of S. Dean McBride Jr.* Edited by John T. Strong and Steven Shawn Tuell. Winona Lake: Eisenbrauns, 2005.

Robertson, R. G. "Ezekiel the Tragedian." Pages 162–6 in *The Old Testament Pseudepigrapha*. Edited by J. H. Charlesworth. Garden City: Doubleday, 1985.

Robinson, Bernard P. "Elijah at Horeb, 1 Kings 19:1–18: A Coherent Narrative?" *RB* 98 (1991): 513–36.

Rofé, Alexander. "The Tenth Commandment in the Light of Four Deuteronomic Laws." Pages 45–65 in *The Ten Commandments in History and Tradition*. Edited by B.-Z. Segal and G. Levi. Jerusalem: Magnes, 1990.

Rogerson, John. *Atlas of the Bible*. New York: Facts on File, 1985.

Römer, Thomas C. "The Book of Deuteronomy." Pages 178–212 in *The History of Israel's Traditions: The Heritage of Martin Noth*. Edited by Steven L. McKenzie and M. Patrick Graham. JSOTSup 182. Sheffield: JSOT Press, 1994.

———. *The So-Called Deuteronomistic History: A Sociological, Historical, and Literary Introduction*. London: T&T Clark, 2006.

Römer, Thomas C., and Marc Z. Brettler. "Deuteronomy and the Case for a Persian Hexateuch." *JBL* 119 (2000): 401–19.

Römer, Thomas C., and Albert de Pury. "Deuteronomistic Historiography (DH): History of Research and Debated Issues." Pages 24–141 in *Israel Constructs Its History: Deuteronomistic History in Recent Research*. Edited by Albert de Pury, Thomas C. Römer, and Jean-Daniel Macchi. JSOTSup 306. Sheffield: JSOT Press, 2000.

Rossing, Barbara R. *The Choice between Two Cities: Whore, Bride, and Empire in the Apocalypse*. HTS 48. Harrisburg, Pa.: Trinity Press International, 1999.

Routledge, Bruce. *Moab in the Iron Age: Hegemony, Polity, Archaeology*. Archaeology, Culture, and Society. Philadelphia: University of Pennsylvania Press, 2004.

Rowlett, Lori. *Joshua and the Rhetoric of Violence: A New Historicist Analysis*. JSOTSup 226. Sheffield: Sheffield Academic Press, 1996.

Rowley, H. H. "Elijah on Mount Carmel." *BJRL* 43 (1960): 190–219.

Ruffing, Andreas. *Jahwekrieg als Weltmetapher: Studien zu Jahwekriegstexten des chronistischen Sondergutes*. SBB 24. Stuttgart: Verlag Katholisches Bibelwerk, 1993.

Russell, John Malcolm. "The Program of the Palace of Assurnasirpal II at Nimrud: Issues in the Research and Presentation of Assyrian Art." *AJA* 102 (1998): 655–715.

———. *Sennacherib's Palace without Rival at Nineveh*. Chicago: University of Chicago Press, 1991.
Safrai, Chana, and Zeev Safrai. "Rabbinic Holy Men." Pages 59–78 in *Saints and Role Models in Judaism and Christianity*. Edited by Marcel Poorthuis and Joshua Schwartz. Jewish and Christian Perspectives Series 7. Leiden: Brill, 2004.
Safrai, Shmuel. "Hasidim and Men of Deeds" [Hebrew]. *Zion* 50 (1985): 133–54.
Safrai, Shmuel. "Teaching of Pietists in Mishnaic Literature." *JJS* 16 (1965): 15–33.
Saggs, H. W. F. *The Might That Was Assyria*. London: Sidgwick & Jackson, 1984.
———. "The Nimrud Letters." *Iraq* 17 (1955): 21–56, 126–60.
Sallaberger, Walter and Aage Westenholz. *Mesopotamien: Akkade-Zeit und Ur III-Zeit*. Edited by P. Attinger and M. Wäfler. OBO 160. Göttingen: Vandenhoeck & Ruprecht, 1999.
Sanda, Albert. *Die Bücher der Könige*. 2 vols. EHAT 9. Münster: Aschendorf, 1911–12.
Sanders, E. P., A. I. Baumgarten, and A. Mendelson, eds. *Aspects of Judaism in the Graeco-Roman Period*. Vol. 2 of *Jewish and Christian Self-Definition*. Philadelphia: Fortress, 1981.
Saur, Markus. *Die Königspsalmen: Studien zur Entstehung und Theologie*. BZAW 340. Berlin: de Gruyter, 2004.
Schiffman, L. H. "The Laws of War in the Temple Scroll." *RQ* 16 (1988): 299–311.
Schmitt, Götz. *Du sollst keinen Frieden schließen mit den Bewohnern des Landes: Die Weisungen gegen die Kanaanäer in Israels Geschichte und Geschichtsschreibung*. BWANT 91. Stuttgart: Kohlhammer, 1970.
Schmitt, John J. "The Gender of Ancient Israel." *JSOT* 26 (1983): 115–25.
———. "The Motherhood of God and Zion as Mother." *RB* 92 (1985): 557–69.
———. "The Virgin of Israel: Referent and the Use of the Phrase in Amos and Jeremiah." *CBQ* 53 (1991): 365–87.
———. "The Wife of God in Hosea 2." *BR* 34 (1989): 7–11.
———. "Yahweh's Divorce in Hosea 2—Who Is That Woman?" *SJOT* 9 (1995): 119–32.
Schmitt, Rüdiger. *Bildhafte Herrschaftsrepräsentation im eisenzeitlichen Israel*. AOAT 283. Münster: Ugarit-Verlag, 2001.
Schofer, Jonathan Wyn. *The Making of a Sage: A Study in Rabbinic Ethics*. Madison: University of Wisconsin Press, 2005.
Scholem, G. G. "Three Types of Jewish Piety." *Eranos Jahrbuch* 39 (1969): 331–48. Repr. as pages 176–90 in idem, *On the Possibility of Jewish Mysticism and Other Essays*. Philadelphia: Jewish Publication Society, 1997.
Schoske, Sylvia. "Das Erschlagen der Feinde: Ikonographie und Stilistik der Feindvernichtung im alten Ägypten." Ph.D. diss. University of Heidelberg, 1982.
Schwally, Friedrich. *Der heilige Krieg im alten Israel*. Leipzig: Dietrich, 1901.
Schwartz, Daniel R. *2 Maccabees* [Hebrew]. Jerusalem: Yad Itzak Ben Zvi, 2004.
———. "From the Maccabees to Masada: On Diasporan Historiography of the Second Temple Period." Pages 29–40 in *Jüdische Geschichte in hellenistisch-römischer Zeit: Wege der Forschung: Vom alten zum neuen Schurer*. Edited by A. Oppenheimer. Schriften des Historischen Kollegs Kolloquien 44. Munich: Oldenbourg Wissenschaftsverlag, 1999.
———. "On Something Biblical about 2 Maccabees." Pages 223–32 in *Biblical Perspectives: Early Use and Interpretation of the Bible in Light of the Dead Sea Scrolls. Proceedings of the First International Symposium of the Orion Center for the Study of the Dead Sea*

Scrolls and Associated Literature, 12–14 May 1996. Edited by Michael E. Stone and Esther Chazon. Leiden: Brill, 1998.
———. *Studies in the Jewish Background of Christianity*. WUNT 60. Tübingen: Mohr Siebeck, 1992.
———. "Temple or City: What Did Hellenistic Jews See in Jerusalem?" Pages 114–27 in *The Centrality of Jerusalem. Historical Perspectives*. Edited by Marcel Poorthuis and Chana Safrai. Kampen: Kok Pharos, 1996.
Schwartz, Regina. "Adultery in the House of David: The Metanarrative of Biblical Scholarship and the Narratives of the Bible." *Semeia* 54 (1991): 35–55.
Selvidge, Marla J. "Reflections on Violence and Pornography: Misogyny in the Apocalypse and Ancient Hebrew Prophecy." Pages 274–86 in *A Feminist Companion to the Hebrew Bible in the New Testament*. Edited by Athalya Brenner. FCB 10. Sheffield: Sheffield Academic Press, 1996.
Selz, Gebhard J. "Über Mesopotamische Herrschaftskonzepte: Zu den Ursprüngen Mesopotamischer Herrscherideologie im 3. Jahrtausend." Pages 281–344 in *Dubsar anta-men: Studien zur Altorientalistik: Festschrift für Willem H. Ph. Römer*. Edited by M. Dietrich and O. Loretz. AOAT 253. Münster: Ugarit-Verlag, 1998.
Setel, T. Drorah. "Prophets and Pornography: Female Sexual Imagery in Hosea." Pages 86–95 in *Feminist Interpretation of the Bible*. Edited by Letty M. Russell. Philadelphia: Westminster, 1985.
Shanks, Hershel. *Ancient Israel: From Abraham to the Roman Destruction of the Temple*. Rev. ed. Washington, D.C.: Biblical Archaeological Society, 1999.
Sharpe, Jim. "History from Below." Pages 24–41 in *New Perspectives on Historical Writing*. Edited by Peter Burke. University Park: Pennsylvania State University Press, 1992.
Shay, Jonathan. *Achilles in Vietnam: Combat Trauma and the Undoing of Character*. New York: Atheneum, 1994.
———. *Odysseus in America: Combat Trauma and the Trials of Homecoming*. New York: Scribner, 2002.
Shea, William H. "Jerusalem under Siege: Did Sennacherib Attack Twice?" *BAR* 25/6 (1999): 36–44, 64.
———. "The New Tirhakah Text and Sennacherib's Second Palestinian Campaign." *AUSS* 35 (1997): 181–87.
———. "Sennacherib's Second Palestinian Campaign." *JBL* 104 (1985): 401–18.
Shields, Mary E. "An Abusive God? Identity and Power/Gender and Violence in Ezekiel 23." Pages 129–51 in *Postmodern Interpretations of the Bible: A Reader*. Edited by A. K. M. Adam. St. Louis: Chalice, 2001.
———. *Circumscribing the Prostitute: The Rhetorics of Intertextuality, Metaphor, and Gender in Jeremiah 3:1–4:4*. JSOTSup 387. London: T&T Clark, 2004.
Sievers, Joseph. *Synopsis of the Greek Sources for the Hasmonean Period: 1–2 Maccabees and Josephus, War 1 and Antiquities 12–14*. SubBi 20. Rome: Pontifical Biblical Institute, 2001.
Skjelsbaek, Inger. "Sexual Violence and War: Mapping Out a Complex Relationship." *European Journal of International Relations* 7 (2001): 211–38.
Smend, Rudolf. *Yahweh War and Tribal Confederation: Reflections upon Israel's Earliest History*. Translated by M. G. Rogers. 2nd ed. Nashville: Abingdon, 1970.
Smith, C. F., trans. *Thucydides: History of the Peloponnesian War*. 4 vols. LCL. Cambridge: Harvard University Press, 1919–23.

Smith, Daniel L. *The Religion of the Landless: The Social Context of the Babylonian Exile.* Bloomington, Ind.: Meyer Stone, 1989.
Smith, Gary V. *The Prophets as Preachers: An Introduction to the Hebrew Prophets.* Nashville: Broadman & Holman, 1994.
Smith, George Adam. *The Book of Deuteronomy in the Revised Version: With Introduction and Notes.* Cambridge Bible for Schools and Colleges. Cambridge: Cambridge University Press, 1918.
Smith, Hugh. *On Clausewitz: A Study of Military and Political Ideas.* New York: Palgrave Macmillan, 2005
Smith, Jonathan Z. *Imagining Religion: From Babylon to Jonestown.* CSJH. Chicago: University of Chicago Press, 1982.
———. *Map Is Not Territory: Studies in the History of Religions.* Chicago: University of Chicago Press, 1993.
Smith, Sydney. *The First Campaign of Sennacherib, King of Assyria, B.C. 705–681.* London: Luzac, 1921.
Smith-Christopher, Daniel L. "Ezekiel in Abu Ghraib: Rereading Ezekiel 16:37–39 in the Context of Imperial Conquest." Pages 141–57 in *Ezekiel's Hierarchical World: Wrestling with a Tiered Reality.* Edited by Stephen L. Cook and Corrine L. Patton. SBLSymS 31. Atlanta: Society of Biblical Literature, 2004.
Soggin, J. Alberto. *An Introduction to the History of Israel and Judah.* 3rd ed. London: SCM, 1999.
———. *Judges: A Commentary.* OTL. Philadelphia: Westminster John Knox, 1981.
Solis, Gary D. "Are We Really at War?" *United States Naval Institute. Proceedings* 127/12 (2001): 34–39.
Sommer, Ferdinand. "Ein hethitisches Gebet." *ZA* 33 (1921): 85–102.
Speiser, Ephraim A. "The Alalakh Tablets." *JAOS* 74 (1954): 18–25.
Steck, Odil H. "Zion als Gelande und Gestalt." *ZTK* 86 (1989): 261–81.
Steible, Horst. *Die altsumerischen Bau- und Weihinschriften.* 2 vols. Freiburger Altorientalische Studien 5/2. Wiesbaden: Steiner, 1982.
Stoessinger, John E. *Why Nations Go to War.* 7th ed. New York: St. Martin's, 1998.
Stolz, Fritz. *Jahwes und Israels Krieg: Kriegstheorien und Kriegserfahrungen im Glaube des alten Israels.* ATANT 69. Zurich: Theologischer Verlag, 1972.
Stone, Lawson G. "Ethical and Apologetic Tendencies in the Redaction of the Book of Joshua." *CBQ* 53 (1991): 25–35.
Stone, Michael E. "Ideal Figures and Social Context: Priest and Sage in the Early Second Temple Age." Pages 575–86 in *Ancient Israelite Religion: Essays in Honor of Frank Moore Cross.* Edited by Patrick D. Miller Jr., Paul D. Hanson, and S. Dean McBride. Philadelphia: Fortress, 1987.
———. *Scriptures, Sects and Visions: A Profile of Judaism from Ezra to the Jewish Revolts.* Philadelphia: Fortress, 1980.
———. "Three Transformations in Judaism." *Numen* 32/2 (1985): 218–35.
Streck, Maximilian. *Assurbanipal und die letzten assyrischen Könige bis zum Untergange Ninivehs.* Leipzig: Hinrichs, 1916.
Swete, Henry B. *The Gospel according to St. Mark.* 3rd ed. London: Macmillan, 1913.
Tadmor, Hayim. *The Inscriptions of Tiglath-pileser III, King of Assyria: Critical Edition with Introductions, Translations, and Commentary.* Jerusalem: Israel Academy of Sciences and Humanities, 1994.

Tadmor, Hayim, and Mordechai Cogan. "Ahaz and Tiglath-pileser in the Book of Kings: Historiographic Considerations." *Bib* 60 (1979): 491–508.
Talmon, Shemaryahu. "Polemics and Apology in Biblical Historiography: 2 Kings 17:24–41." Pages 57–75 in *The Creation of Sacred Literature*. Edited by R. E. Friedman. Berkeley and Los Angeles: University of California Press, 1981.
Tarlin, Jan W. "Utopia and Pornography in Ezekiel: Violence, Hope, and the Shattered Male Subject." Pages 175–83 in *Reading Bibles, Writing Bodies: Identity and the Book*. Edited by Timothy K. Beal and David M. Gunn. Biblical Limits. London: Routledge, 1997.
Thackeray, H. St. J., et al., trans. *Josephus*. 9 vols. LCL. London: Heineman, 1926–81.
Thompson, J. A. *Deuteronomy: An Introduction and Commentary*. TOTC. Downers Grove, Ill.: InterVarsity Press, 1974.
Tigay, Jeffrey H. *Deuteronomy*. JPS Torah Commentary. Philadelphia: Jewish Publication Society, 1996.
Törnkvist, Rut. *The Use and Abuse of Female Sexual Imagery in the Book of Hosea: A Feminist Critical Approach to Hos 1–3*. Women in Religion 7. Uppsala: Acta Universitatis Upsaliensis, 1998.
Tucker, Gene M. "The Rahab Saga (Joshua 2): Some Form-Critical and Traditional-Historical Observations." Pages 66–86 in *The Use of the Old Testament in the New and Other Essays: Studies in Honor of William Franklin Stinespring*. Edited by James M. Efird. Durham, N.C.: Duke University Press, 1972.
Tuman, Joseph S. *Communicating Terror: The Rhetorical Dimensions of Terrorism*. London: Sage, 2003.
Turner, Mary Donovan. "Daughter Zion: Giving Birth to Redemption." Pages 193–204 in *Pregnant Passion: Gender, Sex, and Violence in the Bible*. Edited by Cheryl A. Kirk-Duggan. SemeiaSt 44. Atlanta: Society of Biblical Literature, 2003.
Underhill, Anne P. "Warfare and the Development of States in China." Pages 253–85 in *The Archaeology of Warfare: Prehistories of Raiding and Conquest*. Edited by Elizabeth N. Arkush and Mark W. Allen. Gainesville: University Press of Florida, 2006.
Ussishkin, David. *The Conquest of Lachish by Sennacherib*. Tel Aviv: Tel Aviv University, Institute of Archaeology, 1982.
———. "Excavations at Tel Lachish 1978–1983: Second Preliminary Report." *TA* 10 (1983): 97–175.
———. "Lachish." *NEAEHL* 3:897–911.
———. "Lachish: Renewed Archaeological Excavations." *Expedition* 20/4 (1978): 18–28.
———. "The 'Lachish Reliefs' and the City of Lachish." *IEJ* 30 (1980): 174–95.
Van Seters, John. "Joshua's Campaign and Near Eastern Historiography." *SJOT* 2 (1990): 1–12.
VanderKam, James C. *The Book of Jubilees*. CISC. Leuven: Peeters, 1989.
Vaux, Roland de. *Ancient Israel: Its Life and Institutions*. Translated by John McHugh. Biblical Resource Series. London: Darton, Longman & Todd, 1961. Repr., Grand Rapids: Eerdmans, 1997.
Vayda, Andrew P. Foreword to Roy A. Rappaport, *Pigs for the Ancestors*. New Haven: Yale University Press, 1968.
Vedder, Ursula. "Frauentod: Kriegertod im Spiegel der attischen Grabkunst des 4. Jhs. v. Chr." *MDAI* 103 (1988): 161–91.

Veijola, Timo. *Die ewige Dynastie: David und die Entstehung seiner Dynastie nach der deuteronomistischen Darstellung.* Suomalainen Tiedeakatemia Toimituksia 193. Helsinki: Suomalainen Tiedeakatemia, 1975.

———. *Das Königtum in der Beurteilung der deuteronomistischen Historiographie: Eine redaktionsgeschichtliche Untersuchung.* Suomalainen Tiedeakatemia Toimituksia 198. Helsinki: Suomalainen Tiedeakatemia, 1977.

Vermeylen, Jacques "Os 1–3 et son histoire littéraire." *ETL* 79 (2003): 23–52.

Vidal-Naquet, Pierre. *The Black Hunter: Forms of Thought and Forms of Society in the Ancient World.* Translated by A. Szegedy-Maszak. Baltimore: Johns Hopkins University Press, 1986.

Wacker, Marie-Theres. "Frau-Sexus-Macht: Eine feministisch-theologische Relecture des Hoseabuches." Pages 101–25 in *Der Gott der Männer und die Frauen.* Edited by Marie-Theres Wacker. Düsseldorf: Patmos, 1987.

Walsh, Carey Ellen. *The Fruit of the Vine: Viticulture in Ancient Israel.* Harvard Semitic Museum Publications. Winona Lake, Ind.: Eisenbrauns, 2000.

Walsh, Jerome T. *1 Kings.* Berit Olam. Collegeville, Minn.: Liturgical Press, 1996.

Washington, Harold C. "'Lest He Die in the Battle and Another Man Take Her': Violence and the Construction of Gender in the Laws of Deuteronomy 20–22." Pages 185–213 in *Gender and Law in the Hebrew Bible and the Ancient Near East.* Edited by Victor H. Matthews, Bernard M. Levinson, and Tikva Frymer-Kensky. JSOTSup 262. Sheffield: Sheffield Academic Press, 1998.

Waters, John W. "The Political Development and Significance of the Shepherd-King Symbol in the Ancient Near East and in the Old Testament." Ph.D. diss. Boston University, 1970.

Watson, Duane F. "The Contributions and Limitations of Greco-Roman Rhetorical Theory for Constructing the Rhetorical and Historical Situations of a Pauline Epistle." Pages 125–51 in *The Rhetorical Interpretation of Scripture: Essays from the 1996 Malibu Conference.* Edited by Stanley E. Porter and Dennis L. Stamps. JSOTSup 180. Sheffield: Sheffield Academic Press, 1999.

Wavell, Archibald. *The Good Soldier.* London: Macmillan, 1948.

Weber, Max. *Ancient Judaism.* Translated and edited by H. H. Gerth and D. Martindale. Glencoe, Ill.: Free Press, 1952.

Weems, Renita J. *Battered Love: Marriage, Sex, and Violence in the Hebrew Prophets.* Minneapolis: Fortress, 1995.

Wees, Hans van. *Greek Warfare: Myths and Realities.* London: Duckworth, 2004.

———. "The Law of Gratitude: Reciprocity in Anthropological Theory." Pages 13–49 in *Reciprocity in Ancient Greece.* Edited by Christopher Gill, Norman Postlethwaite, and Richard Seaford. Oxford: Oxford University Press, 1998.

Weidner, Ernst F. "Der Staatsvertrag Assurniraris VI von Assyrien mit Mati'ilu von Bit-Agusi." *AfO* 8 (1932–33): 2–27.

Weinfeld, Moshe. "Deuteronomy, Book of." *ABD* 2:168–83.

———. "Deuteronomy: The Present State of Inquiry." *JBL* 87 (1967): 49–62.

———. "Divine Intervention in War in Ancient Israel and in the Ancient Near East." Pages 121–47 in *History, Historiography and Interpretation: Studies in Biblical and Cuneiform Literatures.* Edited by H. Tadmor and M. Weinfeld. Jerusalem: Magnes, 1983.

———. "The Loyalty Oath in the Ancient Near East." *UF* 8 (1977): 379–414.

———. *Social Justice in Ancient Israel and in the Ancient Near East*. Minneapolis: Fortress, 1995.

———. "Traces of Assyrian Treaty Formulae in Deuteronomy." *Bib* 46 (1965): 417–27.

Weippert, Manfred. "'Heiliger Krieg' in Israel und Assyrien: Kritische Anmerkungen zu Gerhard von Rads Konzept des 'Heiligen Krieges im alten Israel.'" *ZAW* 84 (1972): 460–93.

Wellhausen, Julius. *Die Composition des Hexateuchs und der historischen Bücher des Alten Testaments*. 3rd ed. Berlin: Reimer, 1899.

Westenholz, Joan Goodnick. *Legends of the Kings of Akkade*. Mesopotamian Civilizations 7. Winona Lake, Ind.: Eisenbrauns, 1997.

———. "Tamar, *Qedeša*, *Qadištu*, and Sacred Prostitution in Mesopotamia." *HTR* 82 (1989): 245–65.

Westermann, Claus. *Die Geschichtsbücher des Alten Testaments: Gab es ein deuteronomistisches Geschichtswerk?* TBAT 87. Gütersloh: Mohn, 1994.

Wette, W. M. L. de. "Dissertatio critico-exegetica qua Deuteronomium a propribus pentateuchi libris diversum, alius cuiusdam recentioris auctoris opus esse monstratur." Doctoral diss. Jena, 1805.

Wilcoxen, Jan A. "Narrative Structure and Cult Legend: A Study of Joshua 1–6." Pages 43–70 in *Transitions in Biblical Scholarship*. Edited by J. C. Rylaarsdam. Chicago: University of Chicago Press, 1968.

Wildung, Dietrich. "Erschlagen der Feinde." *LdÄ* 2:14–17.

Winter, Irene. "Royal Rhetoric and the Development of Historical Narrative in Neo-Assyrian Reliefs." *Studies in Visual Communication* 7 (1981): 2–38.

———. "Sex, Rhetoric, and the Public Monument: The Alluring Body of Naram-Sîn of Agade." Pages 11–26 in *Sexuality in Ancient Art: Near East, Egypt, Greece, and Italy*. Edited by N. B. Kampen. Cambridge: Cambridge University Press, 1996.

———. "Tree(s) on the Mountain: Landscape and Territory on the Victory Stele of Naram-Sin of Agade." Pages 66–72 in *Landscapes: Territories, Frontiers and Horizons in the Ancient Near East: Papers Presented to the XLIV Recontre Assyriologique Internationale Venezia, 7–11 July 1997*. Edited by L. Milano et al. Padova: Sargon, 1999.

Wiseman, Donald J. *1 and 2 Kings*. TOTC. Leicester: Inter-Varsity Press, 1993.

Wolf, Herbert. "Judges." Pages 375–508 in *Deuteronomy, Joshua, Judges, Ruth, 1 and 2 Samuel*. Vol. 3 of *The Expositor's Bible Commentary*. Edited by Frank E. Gaebelein. Grand Rapids: Zondervan, 1992.

Wong, Gregory T. K. *Compositional Strategy of the Book of Judges: An Inductive, Rhetorical Study*. VTSup 111. Boston: Brill, 2006.

Wood, John A. *Perspectives on War in the Bible*. Macon, Ga.: Mercer University Press, 1998.

Wright, Jacob L. *War and the Formation of Society in Ancient Israel*. New York: Oxford University Press, forthcoming.

Würthwein, Ernst. "Erwägungen zum sog: deuteronomistischen Geschichtswerk: Eine Skizze." Pages 1–11 in *Studien zum Deuteronomistischen Geschichtswerk*. Edited by Ernst Würthwein. BZAW 227. Berlin: de Gruyter, 1994.

Xinbo, Wu. "The End of the Silver Lining: A Chinese View of the U.S.–Japanese Alliance." *The Washington Quarterly* 29/1. (2005/2006): 119–30.

Yadin, Yigael. *The Art of Warfare in Biblical Lands in the Light of Archaeological Discovery*. Translated by M. Pearlman. London: Weidenfeld & Nicolson, 1963.

———. *The Scroll of the War of the Sons of Light against the Sons of Darkness*. Translated by B. and C. Rabin. Oxford: Oxford University Press, 1962.

Yee, Gale A. *Poor Banished Children of Eve: Woman as Evil in the Hebrew Bible*. Minneapolis: Fortress, 2003.

———. "'She Is Not My Wife and I Am Not Her Husband': A Materialist Analysis of Hosea 1–2." *BibInt* 9 (2001): 345–83.

Younger, K. Lawson, Jr. *Ancient Conquest Accounts: A Study in Ancient Near Eastern and Biblical History Writing*. JSOTSup 98. Sheffield: JSOT Press, 1990.

———. "Joshua." Pages 174–89 in *Eerdmans Commentary on the Bible*. Edited by James D. G. Dunn and John Rogerson. Grand Rapids: Eerdmans, 2003.

CONTRIBUTORS

Frank Ritchel Ames is Professor and Director of Library Services at Colorado's new medical college, Rocky Vista University. He has served as Director of Programs and Initiatives for the SBL and as Editor of *SBL Forum*. He has contributed articles to the *Encyclopedia of Protestantism* (Routledge, 2003) and the *New International Dictionary of Old Testament Theology and Exegesis* (Zondervan, 1997), and reviews books in the field of biblical studies for the American Library Association's *Choice: Current Reviews for Academic Libraries*.

Claudia D. Bergmann is an Assistant Professor at Kirchlicher Fernunterricht in Germany and an Adjunct Instructor at the Lutheran Theological Seminary at Gettysburg. She just published her book *Childbirth as a Metaphor for Crisis: Evidence from the Ancient Near East, the Hebrew Bible, and 1QH XI, 1–18* (de Gruyter, 2008) and is currently writing on the use of metaphors in Isa 42.

Frances Flannery is Associate Professor of Religion at James Madison University. She is the author of *Dreamers, Scribes, and Priests: Jewish Dreams in the Hellenistic and Roman Eras* (Brill, 2004) and is a contributor to *Paradise Now: Essays on Early Jewish and Christian Mysticism* (Society of Biblical Literature, 2006). She is co-chair of the SBL program unit Religious Experience in Early Judaism and Early Christianity, is founding editor of *GOLEM: Journal of Religion and Monsters*, and serves on the editorial board of the *Journal of Religion and Film*.

Michael G. Hasel is Professor of Near Eastern Studies and Archaeology at Southern Adventist University and Curator of the Lynn H. Wood Archaeological Museum. His publications on ancient warfare include *Domination and Resistance: Egyptian Military Activity in the Southern Levant, 1300–1185 BC* (Brill, 1998) and *Military Practice and Polemic: Israel's Laws of Warfare in Near Eastern Perspective* (Andrews University Press, 2005).

L. Daniel Hawk is Professor of Old Testament and Hebrew at Ashland Theological Seminary. His publications on Joshua include two books, *Every Promise Fulfilled: Contesting Plots in Joshua* (Westminster John Knox, 1991) and *Joshua* (Berit Olam; Liturgical Press, 2000).

Alice A. Keefe is Professor of Religious Studies at the University of Wisconsin–Stevens Point. Her publications include *Woman's Body and the Social Body in Hosea* (Sheffield Academic Press, 2001) and several articles focusing on issues of gender and sexuality in the Hebrew Bible. She also serves as book review editor for the *Journal of Buddhist-Christian Studies*.

Brad E. Kelle is Associate Professor of Old Testament at Point Loma Nazarene University. He is currently writing on the prophetic literature and developments within the modern study of Israelite and Judean history. His publications include *Hosea 2: Metaphor and Rhetoric in Historical Perspective* (Society of Biblical Literature), *Ancient Israel at War 853–586 BC* (Osprey), and the co-editor of *Israel's Prophets and Israel's Past: Essays on the Relationship of Prophetic Texts and Israelite History in Honor of John H. Hayes* (T&T Clark).

Brian Kvasnica, a Ph.D. student at Hebrew University, teaches at the Biblical Language Center and is a member of the faculty at the Jerusalem Institute for Biblical Exploration. His essay, "Temple Authorities and Tithe-Evasion: The Linguistic Background and Impact of the Parable of the Vineyard Tenants and the Son," appeared in *Jesus' Last Week* (Jerusalem Studies in the Synoptic Gospels; Brill, 2006).

Victor H. Matthews is Associate Dean of the College of Humanities and Public Affairs and Professor of Religious Studies at Missouri State University. His most recent publications include *Studying the Ancient Israelites* (Baker, 2007), *Judges and Ruth* (Cambridge University Press, 2004), and he has a forthcoming volume, *More Than Meets the Ear: Understanding the Hidden Contexts of Old Testament Conversations* (Eerdmans, 2008).

Megan Bishop Moore is Visiting Assistant Professor at Wake Forest University. Her publications include *Philosophy and Practice in Writing a History of Ancient Israel* (T&T Clark, 2006) and *Israel's Prophets and Israel's Past: Essays on the Relationship of Prophetic Texts and Israelite History in Honor of John H. Hayes* (co-editor with Brad E. Kelle; T&T Clark, 2006). She is currently writing *Biblical History and Israel's Past* with Brad E. Kelle.

Susan Niditch is Samuel Green Professor of Religion at Amherst College. Her most recent books are *Judges: A Commentary* and *"My Brother Esau Is a Hairy Man": Hair and Identity in Ancient Israel*. Her interests in war and the Hebrew Bible are long-standing. Her new project deals with personal religion in the Second Temple period.

Daniel L. Smith-Christopher is Professor of Theological Studies at Loyola Marymount University. In addition to commentaries on *Daniel* (*NIB*; Abingdon, 1996) and *Ezra and Nehemiah* (Oxford Bible Commentary, 2001), his publications include *The Religion of the Landless* (1989), *Subverting Hatred: The Challenge of Nonviolence in Religious Traditions* (Orbis, 2007), *A Biblical Theology of Exile* (Augsburg Fortress, 2002), and *Jonah, Jesus, and Other Good Coyotes: Speaking Peace to Power in the Bible* (Abingdon, 2007).

Jeremy D. Smoak is currently a Lecturer in the Department of Near Eastern Languages and Cultures at UCLA. He is currently writing on the history of the Priestly Blessing in the biblical literature and the Dead Sea Scrolls. His article entitled "Building Houses and Planting Vineyards: The Early Inner-biblical Discourse on an Ancient Israelite Wartime Curse" was published recently in *Journal of Biblical Literature*.

Jacob L. Wright is Assistant Professor of Hebrew Bible at Emory University in the Candler School of Theology and the Tam Institute for Jewish Studies. He is the author of *Rebuilding Identity: The Nehemiah Memoir and Its Earliest Readers* (de Gruyter, 2004), winner of a 2008 John Templeton Award. Wright is currently finishing a book on *War and the Formation of Society in Ancient Israel* (Oxford University Press).

Index of Ancient Sources

Hebrew Bible/Old Testament

Genesis	35, 35 nn.7–8, 46, 47, 51, 52, 125	15:15b–16a	148 n. 5
13:1–18	35	15:18	48
14	35, 195	15:21	41 n. 25
14:17–24	176	17	35
14:20	176 n. 7	17:8–16	10 n. 31, 12
14:23	176	17:14–16	10 n. 31
21:22–34	35	20:15	193 n. 85
26:20–34	35	20:17	191 n. 80, 192, 193 n. 85
26:26–33	35	21:10	191, 191 n. 77
31:43–54	35	23:1–3	193 n. 85
34	119	23:3	186 n. 49
34:1–35:5	35	23:4	191
37	22	23:23–33	36
		23:27–28	34 n. 5
Exodus	35, 35 n. 8, 36, 189, 193 n. 84	23:27	34 n. 5
1:8	51 n. 51	23:32	35
3:22	189 n. 64	32	46, 46 n. 39
10:29	26 n. 33	32:2	46
11:2–3	189 n. 64	32:26–28	162
12:35–36	189, 189 n. 64	33:22–23	170
12:36	190 n. 69		
12:40	190 n. 69	**Exodus–Joshua**	51, 52
14	40		
14–15	35, 50	**Leviticus**	193 n. 85
14:4	34 n. 5	5:21	193 n. 89
14:13	34 n. 5, 48	5:23	193 n. 89
14:14	34 n. 5	19	192 n. 82, 193, 193 nn. 85 and 87, 194
14:18	34 n. 5		
14:24	52	19:1	193 n. 87
14:30	48	19:13	193, 193 n. 89
15:1–18	3, 10 n. 31	19:15	193 n. 85
15:2	48	19:32	186 n. 50
15:9	184 n. 41	26:36	34 n. 5
15:14–16	34 n. 5		

Numbers
11:12	110 n. 57
21:2	34 n. 5
21:21–32	157
21:33–35	157
25	181 n. 26
25:78	162
31	20 n. 4, 177, 178 n. 12, 184 n. 41
31:7–8	178 n. 12
31:10	178 n. 12
31:12	177, 178 n. 12
31:25–54	178 n. 12
31:27	177
31:28	177
31:52	177
31:53	177

Deuteronomy 13, 47, 67, 68, 69, 147, 149, 149 n. 8, 156, 157 n. 22, 161, 162, 167, 172, 186 n. 49, 192 n. 84

1:17	193 n. 85
1:19–3:11	156
1:30	34 n. 5
2:13	148 n. 6
2:25	34 n. 5
2:26–3:7	157
2:30b	151
2:31–36	157
2:31a	158
2:31b	158
2:32	157
2:33a	158
2:33b	158
2:34a	158
2:34b	158
2:35	158
2:36	158
3:1b	157
3:1b–7	157
3:2	148 n. 6
3:2a	158
3:2b	158
3:2b–c	149 n. 7
3:3a	158
3:3b	158
3:4a	158
3:4b–5	158
3:6	158
3:7	158
3:32	148
4:39	148
5	193
5:19	193 n. 85
5:21	192, 193 n. 85
7:1–4	149
7:1–5	147
7:2–5	153
7:17–26	147
7:23	34 n. 5
9:4	157 n. 19
9:4–5	147
9:7–10:11	156
10:18	186 n. 49
11:25	34 n. 5
13	156
13:1–18	149
13:3	167, 169
13:5	162
13:6	161
13:8–10	154
13:9–10	149
13:13–18	162
13:15–16	149
13:16–17	154
14:28–29	186 n. 49
16:10–15	186 n. 49
16:18–20	193 n. 85
17	40
17:2–5	162
17:14–20	47
17:15	42 n. 28
18:20	167, 172
20	19, 47, 68, 70 n. 19
20:1	47, 48
20:2–3	47
20:3	34 n. 5
20:4	34 n. 5, 47
20:9	47
20:10–18	157
20:19	68 n. 9
20:19–20	70
21:22–23	149 n. 8
23:10–15	34 n. 5
24:14	191 n. 80, 193 n. 87, 194

24:17–22	186 n. 49	5:1	34 n. 5, 146, 148, 159
27:19	186 n. 49	6–8	146
27:26	186 n. 49	6:1–21	155
28:30	84	6:1–25	12
29:1–29	156	6:1–27	152
29:5	156	6:2	34 n. 5, 148, 155
29:5–6	156	6:5	34 n. 5
29:7	157	6:16	34 n. 5
29:11–12	157	6:18–19	28
32:5	167	6:20	155
		6:21	155
Deuteronomy–Judges	69	6:25	153, 154
		6:26	153
Joshua xi, 20, 35 n. 6, 47, 52 n. 55, 58, 147,		7–9	159
149 n. 9, 157, 157 n. 22, 159, 197, 199,		7–11	156, 156 n. 17
200, 201, 203, 204, 205, 206, 207, 212		7:1	152
1:6	150	7:1–2	154
1:7	150	7:1–5	149 n. 7
1:9	150	7:1–26	149, 154
1:18	150	7:1–8:29	156
2	12	7:2–5	155
2–6	159, 159 n. 24	7:3	155
2–11	156 n. 17	7:4–5	155
2–12	12, 145, 147, 152	7:5	34 n. 5
2:1	2	7:6–9	152
2:1–7	147	7:6–26	152
2:1–24	152	7:10–12	152
2:2–3	147, 152	7:12	154, 155
2:4	152	7:19	153
2:4b–5	152	7:20–21	153
2:8–11	153	7:22–26	154
2:9	34 n. 5, 147, 148, 148 n. 5	7:24	153
2:9b–14	147	7:24–25	153
2:10	148	7:25	149
2:10–11	146, 159	7:26	149, 153, 154
2:11b	148	8:1	34 n. 5, 158
2:12–13	153	8:1–2a	155
2:12–14	148	8:1–23	155
2:14	153	8:1–29	152, 157
2:17–21	153	8:2	155
2:24	34 n. 5	8:2a	158
3:5	34 n. 5	8:2b–3a	149 n. 7
3:7–8	159	8:14	157, 158
3:10	58	8:14a	149
3:11	34 n. 5	8:18	34 n. 5, 155
4:14	159	8:18–23	155
4:39	148	8:19–20	155

Joshua (cont.)		10:25	34 n. 5
8:19b	158	10:25b	150
8:21–28	155	10:26–27	151
8:22b	158	10:27	154
8:23	149, 150 n. 11	10:28	151
8:24–27	150 n. 11	10:28–32	151
8:24–28	155	10:28–39	151
8:26	149, 158	10:29–30	151
8:27–29	150 n. 11	10:31–32	151
8:28	149	10:33	151
8:29	149, 154	10:34–35	151
9–11	12	10:34–39	151
9:1–2	146, 147, 150	10:36–37	151
9:3–4	146	10:38–39	151
9:3–5	146	10:42	34 n. 5
9:3–6	152	11	40
9:3–27	150, 152, 156	11:1–5	146, 147, 151
9:4–6	150	11:1–15	157, 159 n. 23
9:5	157	11:4	157
9:6	153	11:5	151
9:9–10	153	11:6	34 n. 5
9:9–11	153	11:6a	158
9:11	150	11:6b	158
9:12–13	152	11:8a	158
9:14–15	153	11:8c	158
9:15	153	11:10a	158
9:16–26	153	11:11b	158
9:17–19	153	11:12	151
9:20	157	11:12a	158
9:23	153	11:12c	158
9:27	153, 154	11:16–17	158
10:1–5	146, 147, 150	11:17b–18	151
10:2	34 n. 5	11:20	34 n. 5, 151
10:6–9	150	12:1	151
10:6–14	155	12:1–24	151
10:6–15	152	12:7	151
10:8	34 n. 5, 155	23:10	34 n. 5
10:10	34 n. 5, 52	24:7	34 n. 5
10:11	34 n. 5	24:12	34 n. 5
10:11–14	155		
10:14	34 n. 5	**Judges** 7, 35 n. 6, 36, 41, 44, 47, 48, 48 n.	
10:16–19	150 n. 11	44, 49, 50, 50 n. 48, 51, 52, 53, 53 n. 57,	
10:16–27	150	55, 56, 58, 197, 198, 199, 200, 203, 206,	
10:19	34 n. 5	207, 209, 212	
10:20	155	1:1–2:5	50 n. 49
10:20–21	150 n. 11	1:6–7	3
10:22–27	150 n. 11	1:12	44 n. 36

2:6–9	50 n. 49	8:22–23	51
2:10	51	8:22–27	48
2:11–23	3, 49	8:24	46
2:14	50 n. 49	8:28	50
3	1	9	51
3:2	9	9:2	45
3:10	53 n. 57	9:16	44 n. 34
3:11	50	10:1	44 n. 34
3:12–13	49	10:7	49
3:27	34 n. 5	10:10–16	44, 45
3:28	34 n. 5	10:17	44
3:30	50	10:18	44
4–5	40, 50	10:18–11:3	44
4:5	50 n. 48	11:4	44
4:7	34 n. 5	11:5–10	44
4:9	48	11:6	44
4:14	34 n. 5	11:9	44 n. 34
4:15	34 n. 5, 52	11:29	53 n. 57
5:11	34 n. 5	11:29–12:6	51
5:13	34 n. 5	11:30–40	45
5:31	50	11:34	41 n. 25
6–8	207	11:36	34 n. 5
6:1–6	45	12:1–6	45
6:12	45 n. 38	13:5	44 n. 36
6:14	45 n. 38	13:20–22	170
6:15	45 n. 38	13:25	53 n. 57
6:16	45 n. 38	14:6	53 n. 57
6:22	170	14:9	53 n. 57
6:34–35	34 n. 5	15:14	53 n. 57
6:36–37	45 n. 38	17:6	49 n. 45, 52
7	200, 207	18:1	49 n. 45, 52
7–8	199	18:10	34 n. 5
7:1	206	19	119
7:2	199	19–21	19, 20
7:3	34 n. 5	19:1	49 n. 45, 52
7:3–11	206	20:2	34 n. 5
7:5–6	200, 212	20:23	34 n. 5
7:6	200	20:26	34 n. 5
7:8	47 n. 40	20:27	34 n. 5
7:9	34 n. 5	20:28	34 n. 5
7:15	34 n. 5	20:35	34 n. 5
7:20	34 n. 5	21:25	49 n. 45, 52
7:22	34 n. 5		
7:22–25	206	**Ruth**	160
8	46		
8:21	45	**1 Samuel**	
8:22	45, 47 n. 40	1:1	45 n. 37

1 Samuel (cont.)

2:1–6	45 n. 37
4:1	49
4:7–8;	34 n. 5
5	58
7	50 n. 49
7:8	52
7:9	34 n. 5
7:10	34 n. 5, 52
7:12	52
7:14	50 n. 49
8	40, 42 n. 26, 48
8:1–5	49 n. 45, 52
8:7	53
8:11–18	49, 53
8:18	54 n. 59
8:20	42 n. 26, 49, 53, 58
9–10	43, 53, 54 n. 61
9–11	43
9:1–2	54 n. 61
9:2	53. 58
10	42
10–11	43, 43 n. 33
10:1–26	42
10:24	43, 54 n. 59
10:26	43 n. 33
10:27	43, 43 n. 34
11	42, 43 n. 33, 44 n. 35, 45 n. 38, 46 n. 40, 53, 54, 54 n. 61
11:1	49
11:1–11	43
11:1ff.	54 n. 61
11:3	42 n. 29
11:4	34 n. 5
11:6–8	42 n. 29
11:6a	53 n. 57
11:7	42 n. 29
11:9	42 n. 29, 53
11:11	42 n. 29
11:11–12	47 n. 40
11:12–13	43
11:13	42 n. 29
11:13b	43
11:14	43
11:14–15	43, 43 n. 32
11:15	42, 42 n. 29, 43, 47 n. 40
11:15–16	43
12	48, 53
12:9–11	49
12:10	53
12:12	53
12:13	54 n. 59
13–14	209
13:3	34 n. 5
13:3–4	209
13:5	49 n. 46
13:9–10	34 n. 5
13:12	34 n. 5
14:8–9	34 n. 5
14:12	34 n. 5
14:15	34 n. 5
14:20	34 n. 5
14:23	34 n. 5
14:24	34 n. 5
15:32–33	162
16	53
16:7	54 n. 58
16:8–13	54 n. 59
16:12	53 n. 58
17	54
17:11	34 n. 5
17:12–15	54 n. 61
17:20	34 n. 5
17:42	53 n. 58
17:46	34 n. 5
17:52	34 n. 5
18:6–9	41
21:6	34 n. 5
21:11	41 n. 25
23:4	34 n. 5
23:16	34 n. 5
24:5	34 n. 5
26:8	34 n. 5
28:5	34 n. 5
29:1–11	49 n. 46
29:5	41 n. 25
30	178
30:4	34 n. 5
30:6	34 n. 5
30:22–25	184 n. 41
31:1	49 n. 46

INDEX OF ANCIENT SOURCES 249

1–2 Samuel 7, 36, 39, 41, 47, 48, 48 n. 43, 49, 50, 50 n. 48, 51, 52, 53, 54, 54 nn. 59 and 61, 55, 56		12:16	35 n. 5
		15:25–32	39
		16:8	40
		16:8–14	39
2 Samuel		16:9–19	163
1:21	34 n. 5	16:15–20	39
3:18	53	16:16–17	47 n. 40
5	41	16:21–22	40
5:1	42	16:34	207
5:1–3	46, 46 n. 40	17–18	162
5:1–3	50	17–19	163
5:2	42, 42 n. 26	17:1	162
5:2a	42	17:12	162
5:2b	42	17:17–24	163 n. 11
5:6	3	18	163
5:17–18	49 n. 46	18–19	9, 161, 163, 167, 171, 172
5:19	34 n. 5	18:1	163, 164, 165, 167, 168, 169, 171
5:22	49 n. 46	18:1–19:9a	168
5:23	34 n. 5	18:1–19:9	170
5:24	34 n. 5	18:1–46	161
6:11	45 n. 37	18:3	163 n. 9
6:21	54 n. 59	18:3–4	163
7:14	38 n. 15	18:5	163
8:1–3	45 n. 37	18:6	164
8:2	3	18:6–7	166
8:4	3	18:7	164, 165
8:9–12	178	18:8	164, 165, 169
10:3–4	3	18:8–9	165 n. 15
10:12	34 n. 5	18:10	162
11	58, 119	18:11	164, 165, 169
11:1	1	18:13	164, 166, 171
11:11–12	34 n. 5	18:14	164, 165, 169
15–19	39	18:15	162, 164
15:1	40	18:16	165, 171
15:1–6	42 n. 27	18:16–17	164
16:18	54 n. 59	18:17	171
20	39	18:19	171
20:1	3, 35 n. 5	18:21	166
23:8–39	3	18:21–24	164
		18:22	166
Samuel–Kings	51, 52	18:23	166
		18:25–28	163 n. 8
1 Kings	61 n. 18	18:26	170 n. 25
1–2	39	18:29	170 n. 25
1:5	40	18:34–35	166
3	42 n. 27	18:36–19:4	167
3:9	172	18:36–46	167

1 Kings (cont.)		24:13–25:21	58
18:40	161, 169	25:12	63
18:41	171		
18:44–45	171	**1 Chronicles**	
19:1	167, 169	26:26–28	178
19:3	164, 166 n. 19, 171	29:1–9	178
19:3–4	166		
19:4	169, 172	**1–2 Chronicles**	35 n. 6, 178
19:4–9	164		
19:6	167	**2 Chronicles**	195 n. 97
19:9	164, 167, 168	20:25	189 n. 63
19:9b	168	27–28	22
19:9b–15	168	28	178, 195
19:10	166, 168, 169	28:15	178
19:11	168, 169	32	59
19:11–12	169, 170		
19:11b–12	168, 171	**Ezra**	
19:12	169	6:21	159
19:13	168, 170	9:1–10:44	159
19:14	168, 169		
19:15	168, 169	**Esther**	178, 195, 195 n. 97, 210
19:15b–18	170	3:13	178
19:16–18	170	8:11	210
20:28	34 n. 5	9	195
21	118, 121	9:5	210
21:27–29	171	9:13	178
22:36	35 n. 5		
		Psalms	47 n. 41
1–2 Kings	39, 51, 56, 162	2	38
		2:7–9	38
2 Kings		12	3
2:10	172	18	38
2:23–24	167	18:4	47 n. 41
8:12	3	20	3
9:1–10:17	40	21:2	47 n. 41
13	119	48	134
15:8–13	40	48:7	133
15:14–16	40	48:12	100
15:23–29	40	89:27	38 n. 15
15:30–31	40	120	26
15–16	22	120:1–4a	26
16:3	62	120:2–3	26 n. 33
17	58	120:3	26 n. 33
18	59	120:4b–7	26
18:19–35	3	120:7	26 n. 33
18:28–35	62	123:2	110 n. 57
19	58	137	3

INDEX OF ANCIENT SOURCES

137:8–9	210	50:1–3	96 n. 2, 100 n. 17
		51:3	96 n. 2, 100 n. 17
Proverbs		51:17–23	96 n. 2, 100 n. 17
24:23	193 n. 85	52:1–2	96 n. 2, 98, 100 n. 17, 104 n. 31
		52:7–8	96 n. 2
Song of Songs	62	54:1	100
		54:1–7	96 n. 2
Isaiah	100 n. 17, 122	54:1–17	100 n. 17
1:8	96 n. 2	54:6	96 n. 4
1:21–31	96 n. 2	56:1–8	159–60
2:4	1	60:1–22	96 n. 2, 100 n. 17
5:8	118	62:1–5	96 n. 4
5:8–17	14, 83	62:1–12	96 n. 2, 100 n. 17
7	22	62:4	100
9:6	38 n. 15	65:17–25	3
10:30	96 n. 5, 104 n. 30	65:21–22	14, 91
11:6	95	66:7–12	96 n. 2, 100 n. 17
13:7	134 n. 14		
13:7–8	134	**Jeremiah**	139
13:8	133, 133 n. 13	2:2	96 nn. 2 and 4
13:8a	134	2:16–28a	96 n. 2
16:1	96 n. 2, 100	2:32–37	96 n. 2
16:2	97 n. 5	3	99
19	138	3:1	96 n. 4
19:5	140	3:1–13	96 n. 2, 99
19:6	140	3:8	96 n. 4
19:16	105, 138	4:31	133
19:17	138	5:7–11	96 n. 2
21:3	133	6:2–8	96 n. 2
21:4	138	6:23	134
23:1–18	96 n. 2	6:24	105, 133
23:4	96 n. 5	13:21	133
23:10	96 n. 5, 104 n. 30	13:22–27	96 n. 2, 98
23:12	96 n. 5, 104 n. 30	15:15	167
23:15	97 n. 5	18:13	96 n. 2, 97 n. 5
26:17	133	21:3–6	58
36	8	22:23	133
40:1–2	96 n. 2, 100 n. 17, 104 n. 31	30:5	138
42:13–14	110 n. 57	30:5–7	133
42:14	133	30:6	133
47:1	97 n. 5	31:4–6	14, 91
47:1–3	100	34:7	59
47:1–5	98	39:10	63
47:1–15	96 n. 2	46:11	96 n. 2, 97 n. 5
49:14–26	96 nn. 2 and 4	48:41	133
49:14–27	100 n. 17, 104 n. 31	49:3	96 n. 5
50:1	96 n. 4	49:3–6	96 n. 2

Jeremiah (cont.)

49:22	133
49:23–27	96 n. 2, 100
49:24	100, 133, 134 n. 14
50–51	139
50:24	105
50:35–38	139
50:37	105, 139
50:42	96 n. 2, 97 n. 5
50:43	133, 134 nn. 14–15
51:27–33	139
51:29–32	139
51:30	105, 139, 140

Lamentations

1–2	96 n. 4

Ezekiel

16	96 n. 4, 104 n. 31, 106
16:1–63	98
16:4	97 n. 5
16:27	97 n. 5
16:37–41	98
16:39–41	99
16:48–49	97 n. 5
16:53	97 n. 5
16:55	97 n. 5
16:57	97 n. 5
19	24
23	95, 96 n. 4, 104 n. 31, 106, 108
23:1–49	96, 98
23:25–26	95, 98
26:1–21	96 n. 2
26:6	97 n. 5
26:8	97 n. 5
28:26	14, 91
32:18	97 n. 5

Daniel

	210
6:24	210
7–12	183 n. 36

Hosea

14, 113, 114, 120, 122, 123, 125, 126, 127

1	120
1–2	116, 120, 124
1–3	14, 103 n. 27, 113, 114, 115, 116, 118
1:2	126
1:4	121
2	99, 99 n. 15, 106, 114, 120, 121, 123
2:4b–25	96 n. 2, 99
2:5	126
2:7–9	123
2:7b	121
2:10b	121
2:15	123
2:19	123
4–14	116
5:7	14, 113, 122
5:8–9a	122
6:10	122
7:4	122
7:8	123
7:9	123
7:16	124
8:9	123
8:13	124
9	126
9:3	124
9:6	124
9:11–12	126
9:11–14	14, 113
9:14	126
10:14b	14, 113
10:14b–15a	125
11:1	124
11:1–5	110 n. 57
11:5	124
13:12	125
13:13	125
13:16	14, 113
14:1	14, 113, 125

Joel

1:4	10
2:6	133 n. 13

Amos

	122
1:7	96 n. 5
1:14	96 n. 5
3:9	96 n. 5
5:2	96 n. 2, 97 n. 5

INDEX OF ANCIENT SOURCES

5:5	89	4:10	133
5:9	89	5:1–2	96 n. 2
5:10–12	118	5:2	97 n. 5
5:11	14, 83	6:8	95
5:11–13	89		
5:17	89	**Nahum**	140
		2:10	133 n. 13
Jonah		3	95, 96 n. 4, 104 n. 31, 140
3:7–9	24	3:1–7	96 n. 2, 98
		3:5	95, 98
Micah	122	3:8–17	96 n. 2
1:1–9	100	3:13	105, 139, 140
1:6–7	100	6:1–9	42 n. 27
1:6–9	96 n. 2		
1:13	96 n. 2	**Zephaniah**	
2:2	118	1:12–16	89
4:3	1	1:13	84
4:8	96 n. 5		
4:8–13	96 n. 2	**Malachi**	
4:9	133	3:5	191, 191 n. 77, 192 n. 82, 193

APOCRYPHAL AND PSEUDEPIGRAPHAL LITERATURE

Ezekiel the Tragedian	175, 189	5:28	182 n. 32
		5:35	182 n. 32
Jubilees	175, 189	5:51	182 n. 32
48:18–19	189	5:68	182 n. 32
		6:3	182 n. 32
1 Maccabees	182, 182 nn. 33 and 35,	6:6	182 n. 32
183, 183 n. 36, 186		7:26	183 n. 36
1:3	182 n. 32	7:47	182 n. 32
1:19	182 n. 32	8:10	182 n. 32
1:31	182 n. 32	9:40	182 n. 32
1:35	182 n. 32	10:84	182 n. 32
2:10	182 n. 32	10:87	182 n. 32
3:12	182 n. 32	11:48	182 n. 32
3:20	182 n. 32	11:51	182 n. 32
3:38	183 n. 36	11:61	182 n. 32
3:38–4:25	182	12:31	182 n. 32
3:41	184	13:34	182 n. 32
3:49	183 n. 35		
4:17	182 n. 32	**1–2 Maccabees**	182 n. 31
4:17–18	184		
4:18	182 n. 32	**2 Maccabees**	181, 182, 183, 183 n. 36,
4:23	182 n. 32, 184	185, 186, 186 n. 50, 187, 188, 195, 195 n.	
5:3	182 n. 32	97, 196	
5:22	182 n. 32	2:23	183

2 Maccabees (cont.)

5:27	183
6:18–19	183
7:1	183
8	175, 178
8:8–9	183 n. 36
8:8–29	182
8:19–20	183
8:25	184, 184 n. 42
8:25–36	183
8:26–27	184
8:27	182 n. 32, 186
8:27–30	184
8:28	185, 185 n. 44, 186
8:30	182 n. 32, 185, 185 n. 44
8:30b	186
8:30–31	178 n. 12
8:30–33	185
8:31	182 n. 32, 185
8:34–36	182
9:16	182 n. 32
12:38	186
14:12	183 n. 36
15:1	186

3 Maccabees

7:10–12	210
	211

4 Maccabees

8:23	191 n. 77

Sirach

4:1	191 nn. 77 and 80, 193 n. 86
29:6	191 n. 77
29:7	191 n. 77
34:21	191 n. 77
34:22	191 n. 77

Testament of Asher

2:5–6	193 n. 86
2:6	193 n. 86

Wisdom of Solomon

10:16–17	189 n. 65
10:20	189 n. 65

NEW TESTAMENT

Mark 190, 191, 191 n. 80, 192, 192 n. 82, 193, 194, 195
10:19   191, 192

1 Corinthians
6:7   191 n. 77
7:5   191 n. 77

1 Timothy
6:5   191 n. 77

James
5:4   191 n. 77

Revelation
18–21   58

CLASSICAL SOURCES

Aristotle, *Politica* 129
1256 a–b   179, 179 n. 18

Cicero, *De officiis*
1.36   180 n. 21

Cicero, *In Verrem*
4.116   180 n. 21

Euripides, *Medea*
5.248–251   132, 132 n. 10

Herodotus
8.121   180 n. 23
8.88   137, 137 n. 26

Homer, *Ilias*   xi
10.460   180

Josephus   175, 178, 182 n. 33, 183 n. 36, 188, 190, 191, 191 n. 80, 192, 192 n. 82, 193, 194, 195

INDEX OF ANCIENT SOURCES 255

Josephus, *Against Apion*
1.379 — 190 n. 73
2.190–219 — 193 n. 85

Josephus, *Jewish Antiquities* — 182, 195 n. 97

Josephus, *Life*
51 — 191 n. 79
67–8 — 190 n. 72
80–81 — 190 n. 72
126–129 — 190 n. 72
244 — 190 n. 72
128 — 191 n. 76

Josephus, *Jewish War* — 195 n. 97

Marcus Junianus Justinus, *Historiae Philippicae* — 190 n. 70

Philo — 175, 190, 194, 195

Philo, *Against Flaccus*
§56 — 180 n. 21

Philo, *Cherubim*
74 — 184 n. 41

Philo, *Decalogue*
§§135–136 — 194

Philo, *Hypothetica*
7.1–9 — 193 n. 85

Philo, *Life of Moses*
1.140–142 — 189

Sentences of Pseudo-Phocylides — 193, 194
3–8 — 193 n. 85
5–6 — 193 n. 85
9–10 — 193 n. 85
9–41 — 193 n. 85

Pompeius Trogus, *Historiae Philippicae* — 190

Plutarch, *De Pythiae oraculis*
401 — 181 n. 25

Plutarch, *Moralia*
5.297 — 181 n. 25

Plutarch, *Lycurgus*
27.3 — 132 n. 11

Thucydides
2.40.4 — 182 n. 30

MISHNAH, TALMUD, AND RELATED LITERATURE

b. Sanhedrin
61a — 190 n. 69

Genesis Rabbah
61:7 — 190 n. 69

Leviticus Rabbah
24:5 — 193 n. 87

Megillat Ta'anit — 190 n. 69

Sipra Qedoshim
1:1 — 193 n. 87

OTHER EXTRABIBLICAL TEXTS

Alalakh Tablets — 136
18–25 — 137 n. 24

Annals of Ashurbanipal — 90

Annals of Sennacherib — 10 n. 33, 88

Annals of Sargon II — 59 n. 10

Annals of Tiglath-pileser III — 59 n. 10, 86

Arad Ostraca   59 n. 11

Assyrian Annals   10, 11 n. 37, 12, 12 n. 38, 13 n. 40

Babylonian Chronicle   59 n. 10

Code of Hammurabi   71 n. 20

Esarhaddon's Succession Treaty   90, 136

Inscription of Lugal-zagesi of Uruk   37 n. 11

Kurkh Monolith Inscription of Shalmaneser III   40

Lachish Ostraca   59 n. 11

Lamentation over the Destruction of Ur   131, 131 n. 8, 132

LKA 63 r. 14–18   71 n. 22

Merneptah Stela   59 n. 9

Mesha Stela   47 n. 41, 58 n. 7

Middle Assyrian Medical Text   131 n. 6

Narmer Palette   37

Samaria Ostraca   59 n. 11

Sargon Legend   131

Sargon II Royal Inscription   131–32, 141 n. 32

Sennacherib's Palace Inscription   59 n. 13

Sennacherib's Siege of Jerusalem   59 n. 10

Shalmaneser III's Black Obelisk   58 n. 8, 72, 72 n. 33

Shalmaneser III's Monolith Inscription   58 n. 6, 60 n. 16

Siloam Water Tunnel Inscription   59 n. 11

Stela of the Vultures   38 n. 14

Suḫu Annals   72, 72 n. 32, 85

Victory Stela of Naram-Sîn   37, 37 n. 14

Index of Modern Authors

Abma, Richtsje 98 n. 9
Adam, A. K. M. 108 n. 50
Adam, Klaus-Peter 38 n. 16
Ahlström, Gösta W. 60 n. 18, 61 nn. 20 and 22–24, 62, 62 n. 26
Albenda, Pauline 75 n. 61, 78 n. 76
Albright, William F. 47 n. 41, 63, 64, 64 n. 35
Allen, Mark W. 6 n. 25
Alt, Albrecht 54 n. 60
Ames, Frank Ritchel 4
Amit, Yairah 48 n. 44
Andersen, T. David 96 n. 4
Arkush, Elizabeth N. 6 n. 25
Attinger, P. 38 n. 14
Attridge, Harold W. 183 n. 36
Auld, A. Graeme 68 n. 5, 209, 209 n. 35
Austin, M. M. 179, 179 n. 15
Avishur, Y. 85 n. 5
Bach, Robert 84 n. 3
Baker, D. W. 70 n. 16
Balz-Cochois, Helgard 116, 116 n. 8
Banks, Arthur 203 n. 14
Barker, Rodney 36 n. 9
Bar-Kochva, Bezalel 182 nn. 33 and 35, 183 n. 37, 184 nn. 40 and 42
Barnett, Richard D. 76 nn. 62–66 and 68, 78 nn. 72 and 77–79, 80 nn. 84–85
Bartlett, John R. 157 n. 21
Barton, John 69 n.12, 101, 101 n. 20
Bassford, Christopher 27 n. 39
Batto, B. 96 n. 1
Baumann, Gerlinde 103 nn. 26 and 29, 109, 109 n. 55
Baumgarten, Albert L. 187 n. 54, 196 n. 99
Beal, Richard H. 3 n. 7
Beal, T. K. 107 n. 45, 110 n. 57, 154 n. 15

Becker, Uwe 46 n. 39, 48 n. 44
Becking, Bob 38 n. 15, 110 n. 58
Begg, Christopher T. 156, 156 n. 18
Ben Zvi, Ehud 96 n. 1, 103, 103 n. 28, 104 n. 31, 106, 106 n. 45
Benjamin, Don C. 6 n. 25, 22, 22 n. 13, 23, 23 n. 16
Bergmann, Claudia D. 7, 8, 105 n. 35
Berman, Joshua 42 n. 30
Bickerman, Elias J. 176 n. 5, 195 n. 98
Biddle, Mark E. 96 n. 1, 97 n. 7, 98 n. 9
Binford, Lewis R. 57 n. 3
Binford, S. R. 57 n. 3
Bird, Phyllis 104 n. 32, 120 n. 17
Bitzer, Lloyd F. 102 n. 22
Bleibtreu, Erika 3 n. 6, 70 n. 17, 71 n. 20, 75 n. 61, 78 n. 79, 79 n. 81, 80 nn. 84–85, 85 n. 5
Blenkinsopp, Joseph 35 n. 6
Blum, Erhard 50 n. 49, 68 n. 4
Boadt, Lawrence 101 n. 20
Boer, P. A. H. de 69 n. 14
Bolkestein, Hendrik 179 n. 14, 181, 181 n. 28, 182
Borger, Rykle 135 n. 20, 136 n. 23
Borowski, Oded 22, 22 n. 13
Box, George H. 193 n. 86
Braulik, Georg 69 n. 12
Brechtel, Lyn 119 n. 13
Breemer, Jan 10, 10 n. 30
Brekelmans, C. H. W. 50 n. 49
Brenner, Athalya 98 n. 11, 102 n. 25, 103 n. 26, 104 n. 32, 110 nn. 57 and 59, 133 n. 13, 140 n. 30
Brettler, Marc Z. 68, 68 n. 7
Brueggemann, Walter 162, 162 n. 4
Brunner, Hellmut 38 n. 15

-257-

Büchler, Adolph 187, 187 n. 52
Budge, E. A. Wallis 79 n. 80, 86 n. 14
Burke, Peter 64 n. 37
Burney, C. F. 200, 200 n. 5
Buth, Randall 190 n. 71
Butler, Trent 201, 201 n. 7
Camp, Claudia 119, 120 n. 15
Campbell, Anthony F. 145 n. 1, 156 n. 17, 158 n. 23
Campbell, Edward F., Jr. 60 n. 18, 61 n. 20, 61 n. 22
Campbell, K. M. 153 n. 13
Cantrell, Deborah O. 40 n. 18
Carneiro, Robert L. 5 n. 19
Carr, David M. 68 n. 4
Carroll, Robert 102, 102 n. 25, 103 n. 29, 104 n. 32, 106, 106 n. 40, 110 n. 58
Chagnon, Napoleon A. 5 n. 16
Chaney, Marvin L. 114 n. 1, 118 n. 10, 123 n. 20
Chaniotis, Angelos 175 n. 3, 176 n. 5, 179 nn. 13–14
Chapman, Cynthia R. 83 n. 1, 91, 91 nn. 28–29, 105 n. 35, 109 n. 53, 129, 129 n. 3, 135 nn. 18–19, 136 nn. 20–22, 137 nn. 24–25
Chazon, E. 186 n. 50
Childs, Brevard S. 77 n. 69, 162 n. 4
Chipman, J. 48 n. 44
Christensen, Duane L. 33 n. 4
Cifola, Barbara 71 n. 27
Clausewitz, Carl von 2 n. 3, 10 n. 32, 27, 27 nn. 38–40, 28, 28 n. 41
Clements, Ronald E. 69 n. 12
Coats, George W. 145 n. 2
Cogan, Mordecai 77 n. 69, 83 n. 1, 162, 162 n. 5, 166 n. 20, 169, 169 n. 24, 171 n. 31
Cohen, Chayim 83 n. 1, 95 n. 1
Cohen, Shaye J. D. 187 n. 53 and 55
Cohn, Robert L. 168, 169 n. 22
Cole, Steven 71 n. 20, 72 n. 39, 75 n. 61, 85, 85 nn. 5 and 8
Coleson, J. 2 n. 3
Collier, Paul 23, 23 n. 17
Collins, J. J. 188 n. 58
Colson, F. H. 189, 194

Conrad, Edgar W. 34 n. 4
Coogan, Michael D. 61 n. 18, 115 n. 6
Cook, S. L. 105 n. 37
Coote, Mary P. 123, 123 n. 19
Coote, Robert B. 123, 123 n. 19
Craigie, Peter C. 34 n. 4, 69, 69 n. 13, 208 n. 30
Crenshaw, J. L. 181 n. 27
Cronbach, A. 193 n. 86
Cross, Frank Moore 9, 115 n. 6, 172 n. 36, 188 n. 57, 201 n. 7
Crüsemann, Frank 69 n. 12
Dahood, Mitchell 26 n. 33
Dalley, Stephanie 2 n. 2
Daniels, P. T. 158 n. 24
Darley, William M. 2 n. 3
Davies, James Chowning 27 n. 37
Davies, Philip R. 35 n. 6, 62 n. 27, 68 n. 6
Davis, Julie Hirschfeld 19
Dawn, Marva J. 28 n. 44, 33 n. 3, 176 n. 4, 208 n. 30
Day, Linda 103 n. 26
Day, Peggy L. 95 n. 1, 97, 98, 98 n. 8, 102, 102 nn. 24–25, 103 n. 26, 104 n. 32, 105 nn. 36–37, 120 n. 17, 134, 134 n. 16
Dearman, John Andrew 118 n. 10
Dempsey, Carol J. 103 n. 27
Dentan, Robert Knox 25 nn. 28–30
Deutsch, R. 85 n. 5
Develin, R. 190 n. 70
DeVries, S. J. 162 n. 4
Dietrich, M. 36 n. 10
Dijk-Hemmes, Fokkelien van 96 n. 1, 101 n. 18, 116 n. 8
Dijkstra, M. 110 n. 58
Dillmann, August 69, 69 n. 10
Dion, Paul 41 n. 22
Dobbs-Allsopp, Frederick W. 97 n. 5, 104 n. 30, 107 n. 47
Doran, Robert 183 n. 36
Dozeman, Thomas B. 35 n. 8
Dressler, Harold 135 n. 19
Driver, S. R. 69 n. 11
Duarte, E. E. 2 n. 1
Ducrey, Pierre 176 n. 5
Dunn, J. 209 nn. 33–34
Duyndam, J. 188, 188 n. 59

INDEX OF MODERN AUTHORS

Edelman, Diana Vikander 43 n. 31, 54 n. 60, 57 nn. 2–3
Efird, J. M. 145 n. 2
Eilberg-Schwartz, Howard 111 n. 61, 127 n. 22
Eissfeldt, Otto 163, 163 n. 10
Elat, M. 62 n. 24
Elgavish, David 176 n. 6, 177, 177 n. 8, 184 n. 41, 189 n. 63
Emerton, John A. 3 n. 11, 67 n. 4
Enns, P. 58 n. 5
Eph'al, Israel 2 n 4, 84 n. 4
Exum, J. Cheryl 103 n. 26, 105 n. 37, 127 n. 22, 207, 207 n. 28
Eynikel, Erik 67 n. 3
Falkner, Margarete 76 n. 68, 78 n. 79
Fanon, Frantz 211 n. 37
Fensham, F. Charles 181, 181 n. 27
Finkelstein, I. 40 n. 18, 195 n. 98
Finley, Moses I. 179, 179 n 13 and 16
Firmage, E. B. 4 n. 13
Fisher, W. R. 102 n. 22
Fitzgerald, Aloysius 95 n. 1, 97, 97 nn. 5–7, 99 n. 14, 100 n. 16
Flannery, Frances 9
Flusser, David 187, 187 n. 52
Follis, Elaine R. 50 n. 50, 96 n. 1
Forman, Werner 76 nn. 62–66, 78 nn. 72 and 77
Foucault, Michel 64 n. 37
Fox, Michael 101, 101 n. 20
Fox, William T.R. 28, 28 n. 43
Frame, Grant 85 n. 6
France, R. T. 192 n. 82
Frank, H. T. 203 n. 14
Frankena, R. 69, 69 n. 14
Fredriksson, Henning 33 n. 2
Freedman, H. 190 n. 69
Fretz, Mark J. 29, 29 n. 49
Freud, Sigmund xi
Freyne, Sean 188 n. 58
Frick, Frank S. 108 n. 49
Fried, M. 5 n. 16
Friedman, R. E. 83 n. 1
Friedrich, Johannes 135 nn. 17–18
Frishman, Judith 104 n. 32
Fritz, Volkmar 108 n. 49

Frymer-Kensky, T. 98 n. 11, 103 n. 27
Fuchs, Andreas 87 n. 15
Fuchs, Esther 110 n. 58
Gabriel, Ingeborg 35 n. 6
Gadd, C. J. 76 nn. 65–66 and 68, 77 fig. 1, 78 nn. 74–75 and 77–78, 79 fig. 2
Gaebelein, F. E. 199 nn. 3–4
Galambush, Julie 96 n. 1, 98 n. 9, 99 n. 14, 100 n. 16
Galil, Gershon 6 n. 24
García Martínez, F. 70 n. 16
Garlan, Yvon 176 n. 5, 179, 179 n. 19, 180 n. 20
Geertz, Clifford 22, 22 n. 11, 23 n. 15
Gehman, H. S. 162 n. 4, 170 n. 28
Gerth, H. H. 33 n. 2
Gertz, Jan Christian 68 n. 4
Gichon, Mordechai 202, 202 n. 12
Gilbert, Martin 204 n. 14
Gill, C. 180 n. 30
Gilliver, K. 180 n. 21
Gitay, Yehoshua 101, 101 n. 20
Glock, Albert E. 33 n. 4
Gluckman, Max 6 n. 21
Godley, Alfred D. 137 n. 26, 180 n. 23
Goelet, Ogden, Jr. 4 n. 13
Goffman, Erving 26 n. 9
Goldingay, John 154 n. 15
Goldstein, Jonathan A. 178 n. 12, 186 n. 48
Goodman, M. D 184 n. 43
Gordon, Cyrus H. 4 n. 13
Gordon, Pamela L. 98 n. 11, 100 n. 16, 102 n. 23, 105 n. 32, 111 n. 60, 140 n. 30
Görg, Manfred 206, 206 n. 21, 207, 207 n. 26, 208, 208 n. 29
Gottlieb, C. 4 n. 13
Gottwald, Norman K. 134 n. 16
Gould, E. P. 194 n. 91
Grabbe, Lester L. 3 n. 11, 108 n. 49
Graham, M. P. 67 n. 3
Gray, John 161–62 n. 2, 163
Green, Barbara 111, 111 n. 62
Greengus, Samuel 102 n. 23
Greenstein, E. 177 n. 7
Gregory, Russell I. 161 n. 1
Grey, John 207, 207 n. 25

Gribetz, Judah	190 n. 68	Herzog, Ze'ev	2 n. 4
Grotius, Hugo	177 n. 9	Heschel, Abraham Joshua	167, 167 n. 21, 170, 170 n. 27
Gschnitzer, F.	176 n. 5		
Guest, P. Deryn	209, 209 n. 34	Hess, Richard S.	34 n. 4
Gundry, Robert H.	192 n. 80	Hilhorst, A.	70 n. 16
Gunn, D. M.	107 n. 46, 110 n. 57, 154 n. 15	Hillers, Delbert R.	129, 129 n. 2, 135 nn. 17–18, 136 n. 23
Haak, Robert D.	108 n. 49	Hilmi, Nabil	190 n. 68
Haas, Jonathan	5 n. 15	Hippler, Thomas	25 n. 26
Hacham, Noah	175 n. 2	Hobbs, T. Raymond	34 n. 4, 208 n. 30
Hackett, Jo Ann	116 n. 9	Hoeffler, Anke	23, 23 n. 17
Haddox, Susan E.	105 n. 35, 108 n. 52, 109 n. 56	Hoffman, Yair	3 n. 10
		Hoffmeier, James K.	69, 69 n. 13 and 16
Hallett, Brien	30, 30–31 n. 54	Hoffner, Harry A.	104 n. 32, 135 n. 19, 138, 138 n. 27
Halligan, John M.	108 n. 49		
Hallo, W. W.	96 n. 1	Holladay, A. J.	184 n. 43
Hallpike, Christopher R.	5 nn. 15 and 20, 7 n. 27	Holladay, William L.	129, 129 n. 2
		Hooker, Morna D.	192, 192 nn. 81–82
Halpern Baruch	54 n. 60	Hopkins, David	122 n. 18
Hamblin,	29 n. 48	Horn, Siegfried H.	77 n. 69
Hamilton, Victor P.	108 n. 49	Horst, Pieter W. van der	180 n. 21, 193 n. 85 and 87
Hands, R.	181 n. 28		
Hanson, P. D.	115 n. 6, 188 n. 57	Howard, M.	10 n. 32, 27 n. 38
Hardy, Thomas	33 n. 1	Hubbard, Robert L., Jr.	149 n. 9
Harrelson, Walter J.	69 n. 11	Huffmon, Herbert B.	102 n. 25
Harris, M.	5 n. 16	Hurowitz, Victor	71 n. 22
Hasel, Michael G.	13, 70 nn. 18–19, 81 n. 86, 85 nn. 5 and 9–10, 87 n. 18, 89, 89 n. 24	Isserlin, Benedikt S. J.	63, 63 n. 29, 64
		Jacob, B.	192 n. 84
		Jahnow, H.	103 n. 26
Hassig, Ross	7 n. 26	Jobert, Bruno	37 n. 12
Hauer, Christian E.	2 n. 3	Jobling, D.	134 n. 16
Hauser, Alan Jon	50 n. 50, 161 n. 1	Johnson, Hubert C.	27, 27 n. 34
Häusl, Maria	141 n. 33	Kaltner, J.	102 n. 25
Hawk, L. Daniel	12, 152 n. 12, 154 nn. 15–16, 157 nn. 21–22, 206, 206 n. 19	Kampen, N. B.	37 n. 14, 91 n. 28
		Kang, Sa-Moon	34 n. 4, 208, 208 n. 30
Hayden, Robert M.	6 n. 22	Kantorowicz, Ernst	37 n. 14
Hayes, John H.	58 n. 4, 60 n. 18, 61 n. 22, 63, 63 n. 33, 64, 101 n. 20	Kaplan, Robert	196, 196 n. 100
		Kataja, Laura	89 n. 27
Hearon, H. E.	114 n. 1	Keefe, Alice A.	14, 101 n. 19, 103 n. 27, 106, 106 nn. 41–42, 107, 114 n. 2, 116 nn. 7 and 9, 119 n. 11, 123 n. 20, 126 n. 21
Hedges, Chris	23, 23 n. 19, 24		
Heltzer, Michael	85 n. 5		
Hendrickson, Ryan C.	31 n. 54		
Hengel, Martin	187 n. 54	Keegan, John	23 n. 18, 30, 30 n. 52
Henten, J. W. van	104 n. 32	Keen, Sam	24 n. 24
Herold, Anja	40 n. 19	Kelle, Brad E.	8, 22, 22 n. 14, 58 n. 5, 60 n. 15, 61 n. 19, 63, 63 n. 31, 95 n. 1, 99 n. 15, 101 nn. 20–21, 103 n. 26, 104
Herrmann, Siegfried	62 n. 27		
Herzog, Chaim	202, 202 n. 12		

INDEX OF MODERN AUTHORS 261

n. 31, 105 n. 35, 114 n. 1, 120 n. 16, 140 n. 30, 175
Keller, S.   4 n. 13
Kelly, Raymond C.   8 n. 29
Kempinski, A.   2 n. 4
Kenyon, Kathleen   207
Kern, Paul Bentley   23 n. 18
Kiesow, K.   38 n. 15
King, Leonard W.   79 n. 80, 86 n. 14
King, Philip J.   2 n. 4, 22, 22 n. 13, 63, 63 n. 28
Kirk-Duggan, C. A.   100 n. 17, 111 n. 62
Kissling, Paul J.   162, 162 n. 6, 166, 166 n. 18
Kiyofuku, Chuma   25 n. 30
Klassen, William   22, 22 n. 10
Knauf, Ernst Axel   68 n. 5
Knoppers, Gary N.   34 n. 4, 35 n. 6, 158 n. 24
Koch, K.   84 n. 3
Krasilnikoff, Jens A.   179 n. 17, 184 n. 41
Kratz, Reinhard G.   42 n. 29, 51 nn. 52 and 54
Kraus, Hans-Joachim   26 n. 33, 158 n. 24
Kritzman, L. D.   52 n. 56
Kugel, James L.   189 n. 65, 190 n. 69
Kugler, Jacek   21, 21 n. 9
Kurtz, L.   27 n. 34 and 37
Kvasnica, Brian   9
Labuschagne, C. J.   70 n. 16
Laffey, Alice   96 n. 5, 97 n. 5
Lakoff, George   130, 130 n. 4
Lambert, Wilfred G.   131 n. 6
Lasine, Stuart   165, 165 n. 14 and 17
Leith, Mary J. Winn   104 n. 32, 105 n. 33
Lekson, Stephen H.   6 n. 23
Lemaire, Andre   38 n. 15
Lemche, Niels-Peter   68 n. 6, 115 n. 6
Lemos, Tracy   3 n. 8
Lepper, Steven J.   28 n. 41
Levi, G.   192 n. 83
Levine, Baruch A.   4 n. 13, 177, 177 nn. 10-11
Levine, David   195 n. 94
Levine, Etan   192 n. 84
Levinson, B. M.   98 n. 11, 103 n. 27
Lewy, Julius   97 n. 6

Lincoln, Bruce   21, 21 n. 7, 24, 24 n. 25
Lind, Millard C.   34 n. 4, 204, 204 n. 16, 208 n. 30
Linville, James Richard   68 n. 5
Liverani, Mario   38 n. 17, 62 n. 27
Lloyd, A. B.   180 n. 21
Lloyd, J.   176 n. 5, 179 n. 19
Lohfink, Norbert   69 n. 12
Long, Burke O.   163, 163 nn. 10-11, 166 n. 19
Long, V. Philips   3 n. 11, 60 nn. 17 and 18, 61 n. 20 and 23
Longman, Tremper, III   34 n. 4, 58 n. 5, 60 nn. 17 and 18, 61 n. 20 and 23
Loretz, O.   36 n. 10
Lubetski, M.   4 n. 13
Luckenbill, Daniel David   71 nn. 21, 23-24, 26-27 and 29, 72 nn. 30-31 and 34-38, 73, 73 nn. 40 and 45-46, 74, 74 nn. 47-55, 75, 75 nn. 57-59, 77 n. 69, 79 n. 82, 80 nn. 83-84, 85 n. 7, 87 nn. 15-17, 88 nn. 19-23
Lust, J.   50 n. 49
Macchi, J.-D.   67 n. 3, 68 nn. 5 and 7, 206 n. 22
Machinist, Peter   83 n. 1
Madvig, Donald   199, 199 n. 3
Magdalene F. Rachel   140 n. 30
Magen, Ursula   36 n. 10
Maier, Christl   103 n. 26
Malamat, Abraham   201, 201 n. 8, 202
Malinowski, Bronislaw   21, 21 n. 8
Maloney, L.   103 n. 26
Marcus, D.   177 n. 7
Martindale, D.   33 n. 2
Mason, Rex   59 n. 12
Mason, Steve   190 n. 72, 191, 191 nn. 78-79
Matthews, R. O.   28 n. 43
Matthews, Victor H.   2 n. 3, 3 n. 5, 4 n. 12, 6 n. 25, 22, 22 n. 13, 23, 23 n. 16, 30, 30 n. 51, 61 nn. 20 and 22 and 24, 98 n. 11, 103 n. 27
May, Herbert G.   204 n. 15
Mayer, Walter   10 n. 33, 132 n. 9
Mayes, A. D. H.   68, 68 n. 9, 69 n. 12, 145 n. 1, 156 n. 17

Mays, J. L. 207 nn. 27–28
Mazar, Amihai 3 n. 7, 61 n. 21
McAllister, Ian 30 n. 52
McBride, S. Dean, Jr. 107 n. 47, 115 n. 6, 188 n. 57
McCarthy, Dennis J. 145 n. 2
McConville, J. G. 158 n. 24
McHugh, J. 22 n. 12
McKenzie, S. L. 67 n. 3
McNeile, A. H. 191 n. 80
Meek, Theophile J. 71 n. 20
Mendenhall, George 4 n. 13
Metzger, Bruce M. 191 n. 80
Meurer, T. 38 n. 15
Meyers, Carol 41 n. 25
Mierzejewski, Alfred C. 84 n. 4
Milano, L. 91 n. 28
Milgrom, Jacob 177 n. 10, 193 nn. 87 and 89
Millard, A. R. 70 n. 16
Miller, J. Maxwell 57 n. 2, 60 n. 18, 61 n. 22, 63, 63 n. 33, 64
Miller, Patrick D., Jr. 33 n. 4, 115 n. 6, 188 n. 57, 208, 208 n. 30
Mirecki, P. A. 3 n. 7
Moloney, Francis J. 192 n. 81
Montgomery, J. A. 162 n. 4, 170 n. 28
Moore, Megan Bishop 1, 57 n. 1, 101 n. 20, 103 n. 26, 105 n. 35
Moran, William 83 n. 1, 193 n. 84
Morgan, T. Clifton 27, 27 n. 35, 28, 28 n. 42
Muffs, Yochanan 176, 176 n. 7, 177 n. 9
Müller, Pierre 37 n. 12
Müller, Reinhard 44 n. 36, 48 n. 43, 51 n. 52
Murphy, R. 5 n. 16
Muscarella, Oscar White 74 n. 53
Musil, Alois 177 n. 9
Nelson, Richard 156 n. 17
Newcomb, William W. 5 n. 17
Nickelsburg, George W. E. 175 n. 1, 182 n. 35, 183 n. 36, 188 n. 58
Niditch, Susan xii n. 1, 3 n. 9, 19, 24 n. 23, 34, 35, 54, 119, 119 nn. 11–12, 176 n. 4, 208, 208 n. 30
Nissinen, Martti 95 n. 1, 105 n. 38
Nitzan, Bilhah 177 n. 10
Noam, Verad 190 n. 69
Noll, Kurt L. 62 n. 25
Noort, Edward 70 n. 16
Nora, Pierre 52, 52 n. 56
Noth, Martin 63, 63 n. 32, 67 n. 3, 145, 145 n. 1, 206
O'Brien, Julia Myers 141 n. 31
O'Brien, Mark A. 145 n. 1, 156 n. 17, 158 n. 23
O'Connell, Robert H. 209, 209 n. 32
Oded, Bustenay 5 n. 18, 73 n. 44, 85 n. 5
Odell, M. S. 104 n. 32
Oden, Robert 115 n. 5
Oesterley, W. O. E. 193 n. 86
Ollenburger, Ben C. 28 n. 46, 30 n. 50, 33 n. 3, 208 n. 30
Olley, John 162, 162 n. 7, 163, 163 n. 9, 171 nn. 29–30
Olmstead, A. T. 79 n. 82, 80 n. 83
Olyan, Saul M. 126 n. 21
Oppenheim, A. Leo 84 n. 4, 175 n. 2
Osborne, Rick 197 n. 1, 198 figure 1
Oswald, H. C. 26 n. 33
Otterbein, Keith F. 5 n. 19, 8 n. 28, 25 n. 30, 27 n. 37
Otto, Eckart 34 n. 4, 38 n. 15, 53 n. 57
Pardee, Dennis 59 n. 11
Paret, P. 27 n. 38
Parpola, Simo 71 n. 20, 84 n. 4, 85 n. 5, 89 n. 26, 105 n. 36, 135 n. 20, 136 n. 22, 137 n. 25
Patterson, Richard D. M. 186 n. 49
Patton, Corrine L. 104 n. 32, 105 n. 37, 107 n. 46, 109 n. 56
Paul, Shalom M. 83 n. 1, 91 n. 30
Pearlman, M. 201 n. 6
Person, Raymond F., Jr. 68 n. 7, 156 n. 17
Petersen, David L. 35 n. 7
Plöger, Otto 157 n. 22
Polzin, Robert 157 n. 20
Poorthuis, M. 185 n. 45, 188 nn. 58–59, 195 n. 94
Porter, S. 102 n. 22
Postlethwaite, N. 180 n. 30
Pressler, Carolyn 205, 205 n. 17, 206, 206 n. 20

INDEX OF MODERN AUTHORS 263

Preuß, Horst D. 67 n. 3
Pritchard, James 203 n. 14
Pritchett, William K. 175 n 3, 176 n. 5, 179, 179 n. 13, 180, 180 n. 24, 181 n. 26, 182 n. 31, 184 n. 41, 185 n. 46
Proença, Domício, Jr. 2 n. 1
Provan, Iain 60 n.n. 17 and 18, 61 n. 20 and 23
Pury, Albert de 67 n. 3, 68 n. 5 and 7, 206 n. 22
Rabin, Batya 185 n. 47
Rabin, Chaim 185 n. 47
Rad, Gerhard von 28, 28 n. 44 and 46, 29, 30 n. 50, 33, 34, 34 n. 4, 35 n. 5, 38 n. 15, 68, 68 n. 8, 69 n. 15, 176 n. 4, 208, 208 n. 30
Raitasalo, Jyri 30 n. 53
Rappaport, Roy A. 4 n. 14
Rast, Joshua 207, 207 n. 27
Reich, R. 2 n. 4
Reid, Daniel G. 34 n. 4
Reimer, D. J. 69 n. 12
Rendtorff, Rolf 67, 67 n. 4, 84 n. 3
Richter, Wolfgang 206, 206 n. 21
Robarchek, Clayton 25 n. 28
Roberts, J. J. M. 107 nn. 47–48
Robertson, R. G. 189 n. 66
Robinson, Bernard P. 161, 161 n. 1, 163, 168, 169, 169 nn. 22–23, 172 n. 33
Rofé, Alexander 192, 192 nn. 83–84
Rogers, M. G. 33 n. 4, 208 n. 30
Rogerson, J. 62 n. 27, 209 nn. 33–34
Römer, Thomas C. 67 n. 3, 68, 68 nn. 5 and 7, 156 n. 17, 206 n. 22
Römer, Willem H. Ph. 36 n. 10
Rossing, Barbara R. 102 n. 25, 110 n. 59
Rostovetzeff, Michael I. 179 n. 14
Rouse, W. H. D. 180 n. 23
Routledge, Bruce 210 n. 36
Rowlett, Lori 205, 206 n. 18
Rowley, H. H. 161 n. 2
Ruffing, Andreas 34 n. 4, 35 n. 6
Russell, John Malcolm 76 nn. 62–64, 79 n. 82, 80 n. 85, 86 nn. 12–13
Russell, L. M. 116 n. 8
Rylaarsdam, J. C. 158 n. 24
Safrai, Chana 185 n. 45, 188 n. 58
Safrai, Shmuel 188 n. 58
Safrai, Zeev 188 n. 58
Saggs, Henry W. F. 70 n. 17, 86 n. 11
Sallaberger, Walther 38 n. 14
Sanda, Albert 163, 163 n. 10
Sanderson, Judith E. 33 n. 3, 208 n. 30
Sasson, Jack M. 2 n. 2
Satlow, 104 n. 32
Satran, D. 195 n. 98
Saur, Markus 38 n. 15
Schäfer, P. 187 n. 54
Schiffman, L. H. 177 n. 10, 190, 190 n. 75
Schmid, Konrad 35 n. 8, 68 n. 4
Schmitt, Götz 69 n. 11
Schmitt, John J 95 n. 1, 97 n. 5, 98 n. 10, 99 nn. 13 and 15, 100 n. 16, 120 n. 16
Schmitt, Rüdiger 41 nn. 20 and 23
Scholem, G. G. 188 n. 58
Scholz, B. 71 n. 20, 85 n. 5
Schoske, Sylvia 37 n. 13
Schwally, Friedrich 28, 30, 33 n. 2
Schwartz, Daniel R. 175, 175 n. 2, 182 nn. 31 and 35, 183 n. 36, 185 nn 44–45, 186 n. 50, 187, 187 n. 55, 195 n. 97
Schwartz, J. 188 nn. 58–59, 195 n. 94
Schwartz, Regina 119 n. 14
Seaford, R. 182 n. 30
Segal, B.-Z. 192 n. 83
Segovia, F. 95 n. 1
Selvidge, Marla J. 110 n. 59
Selz, Gebhard J. 36 n. 10
Setel, T. Drorah 116 n. 8
Shanks, Hershel 61 n. 18
Sharpe, Jim 64 n. 37
Shay, Jonathan xii, xii n. 2
Shea, William H. 77 n. 69
Sheppard, G. T. 134 n. 16
Shields, Mary E. 95 n. 1, 99 n. 15, 103 n. 27, 105, 105 n. 34, 106 n. 40, 108, 108 n. 50, 111 n. 61
Sievers, Joseph 182 n. 34
Siplilä, Joonas 30 n. 53
Skjelsbaek, Inger 109, 109 n. 54
Smend, Rudolf 33 n. 4, 208, 208 n. 30
Smith, Daniel L. 84 n. 3
Smith, Gary V. 101 n. 20

Smith, George Adam	69 n. 11	Turner, Geoffrey	80 nn. 84–85
Smith, Hugh	27 n. 39	Turner, Mark	130, 130 n. 4
Smith, Jonathan Z.	20, 31, 31 n. 55	Turner, Mary Donovan	100 n. 17, 104 n. 30
Smith, S.	74 n. 56		
Smith-Christopher, Daniel L.	11, 84 n. 3, 105 n. 37, 107 n. 46, 109 n. 54	Ulrich, E.	35 n. 6
		Underhill, Anne P.	6 n. 25
Smoak, Jeremy D.	14	Uro, R.	95 n. 1
Soggin, J. Alberto	62 n. 27, 64 n. 36, 207, 207 n. 23	Ussishkin, David	59 n. 14, 77 nn. 70–71, 78 nn. 72–73
Sommer, Ferdinand	135 n. 17	Van Ruiten, J. T. A. M. G.	70 n. 16
Speiser, Ephraim A.	137 n. 24	Van Seters, John	69, 69 nn. 15–16, 70 n. 16
Sponsel, Leslie	25 n. 30		
Stager, Lawrence E.	2 n. 4, 22, 22 n. 13, 63, 63 n. 28	VanderKam, James C.	189 n. 67
		Vaux, Roland de	22, 22 n. 12, 33 n. 2, 63, 63 n. 30, 64
Stamps, D.	102 n. 22		
Steck, Odil H.	96 n. 1	Vayda, Andrew P.	4 n. 14
Steible, Horst	37 n. 11, 38 n. 14	Vedder, Ursula	132 nn. 10–11
Steinhoff, Uwe	25 n. 26	Veijola, Timo	48 n. 43
Stinespring, William Franklin	145 n. 2	Vermeylen, Jacques	99 n. 15
Stivers, R. L.	118 n. 10	Vervenne, M.	50 n. 49
Stoessinger, John	12	Vidal-Naquet, Pierre	46 n. 40
Stolz, Fritz	33 n. 4	Wacker, Marie-Theres	105 n. 32
Stone, Lawson G.	145, 146 nn. 3–4, 147	Wäfler, M.	38 n. 14
Stone, Michael E.	175, 175 n. 1, 183 n. 36, 186 n. 50, 187 n. 51, 188 n. 57, 194 n. 92, 195 n. 98, 196 n. 99	Walsh, Carey Ellen	84 n. 3
		Walsh, Jerome T.	163 n. 12, 165 n. 16, 172 n. 33
Strauss, Ed	197 n. 1, 198 figure 1	Warner, M.	101 n. 20
Strawn, Brent A.	111 n. 63	Washington, Harold C.	98 n. 11, 100 n. 16, 102 n. 23, 105 n. 32, 111 n. 60, 140 n. 30
Streck, Maximilian	89 n. 25		
Strong, J. T.	104 n. 32, 107 n. 47		
Stulman, L.	102 n. 25	Watanabe, Kazuko	89 n. 26, 105 n. 36, 135 n. 20, 136 n. 22
Swete, Henry B.	192 n. 80		
Szegedy-Maszak, A.	46 n. 40	Waters, John W.	37 n. 11
Tadmor, Hayim	34 n. 4, 73, 73 n. 41, 83 n. 1, 84 n. 4, 85 n. 9, 86 n. 11	Watson, Duane F.	101 n. 20, 102 n. 22
		Wavell, Archibald P.	202, 203, 203 n. 13
Talmon, Shemaryahu	83 n. 1	Weber, Max	35 n. 5
Tarlin, Jan W.	107 n. 46	Weber, Otto	33 n. 2
Taylor, Vincent	192 n. 80	Weems, Renita J.	103 n. 26
Thackeray, H. St. J.	191, 191 n. 79, 190 n. 73	Weidner, Ernst F.	136 n. 20
		Weimar, Peter	38 n. 15
Thompson, J. A.	69 n. 13, 71 n. 20	Weinfeld, Moshe	34 n. 4, 67, 67 n. 1, 69, 69 nn. 11 and 14–16, 83 n. 1, 84 n. 4, 186 n. 49
Tigay, Jeffrey H.	69, 69 n. 13		
Tolbert, M.	95 n. 1		
Törnkvist, Rut	103 n. 26	Weippert, Manfred	34 n. 4
Tucker, Gene M.	145 n. 2	Weiss, B. G.	4 n. 13
Tuell, S. S.	107 n. 47	Welch, J. W.	4 n. 13
Tuman, Joseph S.	25 n. 27	Wellhausen, Julius	28, 43 n. 33, 54 n. 61

INDEX OF MODERN AUTHORS 265

Wenham, Gordon J. 34 n. 4
Wénin, A. 176 n. 6
Wees, Hans van 131, 181 n. 30, 182 nn. 30–31, 184 n. 43
Westenholz, Aage 38 n. 14
Westenholz, Joan Goodnick 71 n. 22, 115 n. 5, 131 n. 7
Westermann, Claus 68 n. 5
Wette, W. M. L. de 67, 67 n. 2
Whiston, W. 191, 191 n. 78
Whitehead, Neil 25 n. 30
Whiting, Robert M. 71 n. 20, 84 n. 4, 85 n. 5, 89 n. 27
Wilcoxen, Jan A. 158 n. 24
Wildung, Dietrich 37 n. 13
Williams, G. L. 177 n. 9
Williams, Ronald J. 181 n. 29
Wilson, R. A. 54 n. 60
Winston, William 191 n. 76
Winter, Irene 37 n. 14, 83 n. 2, 91, 91 n. 28
Wire, A. C. 114 n. 1
Wiseman, Donald J. 161, 162 n. 3, 163, 165 n. 15
Witte, Markus 58 n. 4
Wolf, Herbert 199, 199 n. 4
Wood, John A. 203 n. 30
Wooding, Marnie 197 n. 1, 198 figure 1
Woude, A. S. van der 70 n. 16
Wright, Jacob L. 6
Würthwein, Ernst 51, 51 n. 53, 68 n. 5
Xinbo, Wu 26 n. 32
Yadin, Yigael 2 n. 4, 185 n. 47, 201, 201 n. 5
Yardley, J. C. 190 n. 70
Yass, Claire 40 n. 18
Yass, Emery 40 n. 18
Yee, Gale A. 95 n. 1, 96 n. 3, 99 n. 12, 101 n. 19, 104 n. 32, 106, 106 nn. 39 and 41 and 43, 107, 107 n. 46, 108 n. 51, 110, 110 n. 59, 113 n. 1, 115 n. 4, 123 n. 20
Young, Dwight W. 2 n. 3
Younger, K. Lawson, Jr. 72 n. 32, 96 n. 1, 208, 208 n. 31, 209, 209 n. 33
Zeydel, W. H. 177 n. 9

---

* Indices prepared by Noah Marsh.

www.ingramcontent.com/pod-product-compliance
Lightning Source LLC
Chambersburg PA
CBHW031708230426
43668CB00006B/152